D1228365

Judge Frank Johnson and
Human Rights in Alabama

To the memory of

my father

my father-in-law Wesley S. Thompson

and my teacher Robert J. Frye

Tinsley E. Yarbrough

Judge Frank Johnson and Human Rights in Alabama

THE UNIVERSITY OF ALABAMA PRESS / UNIVERSITY, ALABAMA

GARDNER WEBB COLLEGE LIBRARY

Copyright ©1981 by
The University of Alabama Press
All rights reserved
Manufactured in the United States of America

Library of Congress Cataloging in Publication Data

Yarbrough, Tinsley E. 1941–
    Judge Frank Johnson and human rights in Alabama.

    Bibliography: p.
    Includes index.
    1. Johnson, Frank Minis, 1918– 2. Judges—
Alabama—Biography. 3. Civil rights—Alabama.
I. Title.
KF373.J55Y37   347.73′2234 [B]   80–17433
ISBN 0–8173–0056–2

KF
373
.J55
y37

Contents

Preface

In the struggle for racial justice, Dwight D. Eisenhower could hardly have been ranked as a stalwart. During the Little Rock school desegregation crisis, Ike for a time appeared no match for Arkansas's brand of massive resistance. Even as originally introduced, moreover, the Eisenhower administration proposal, which would become the Civil Rights Act of 1957, was more loophole than law. Thurgood Marshall exaggerated only slightly when he said of Eisenhower's second piece of racial reform legislation, "The Civil Rights Act of 1960 isn't worth the paper it's written on." As Daniel M. Berman aptly observed, "Mr. Eisenhower . . . chose equivocation and inaction rather than resolute leadership on civil rights."[1]

In one respect, however, President Eisenhower had a profound impact on modern human rights reform in the South. Unencumbered by the dictates of senatorial courtesy under which his Democratic counterparts were expected to rubber stamp the choices of Democratic (and racially conservative) southern senators, Eisenhower had a relatively free hand in the selection of southern federal judges. And while their unreconstructed peers engaged in outright defiance or more subtle obstructionist tactics, many of the Eisenhower appointees to lower federal courts in the South withstood community pressure and vigorously enforced congressional policy and developing Supreme Court precedent in the civil rights field, gradually changing the complexion of human rights in the southern states.

In terms at least of his impact on human rights, Judge Frank M. Johnson, Jr., chief judge of the United States District Court for the Middle District of Alabama until his elevation to the Court of Appeals for the Fifth Circuit in 1979, was perhaps Eisenhower's most significant lower court appointment. Judge Johnson's selection to the bench in 1955 followed by only a few months the Supreme Court's second historic decision in *Brown v. Board of Education*. During his tenure, his court invalidated segregation and other forms of racial discrimination in Alabama's transportation facilities, voter registration processes, schools and colleges, administrative agencies, system of jury selection, prisons, mental institutions, museums, recreational centers, political parties, and government grant programs, among other institutions. In fact, most of the state's major racial crises—from the Montgomery bus

boycott, which launched the modern civil rights movement, to early
battles over school desegregation and voter registration, to the Selma-
Montgomery voting rights march—were resolved in his courtroom. His
impact on Alabama human rights policy was by no means confined to
racial contexts, however. Among other significant developments, the
Middle District court ordered reapportionment of the state's governing
bodies and invalidated its grossly inequitable property tax system. In
his most controversial and innovative decisions, he found conditions
in Alabama's mental institutions and prisons constitutionally deficient
and ordered implementation of massive reforms or release of the
prisoners and those mental patients subject to involuntary confinement. With considerable justification, he was praised—and condemned—as Alabama's de facto governor.

Judge Johnson's decisions made him one of the most widely respected and controversial trial judges in the country. He has been
regularly mentioned for a seat on the United States Supreme Court.
President Jimmy Carter offered him several posts with his administration; and he was Carter's nominee as FBI director until medical problems forced his withdrawal. Until recently, however, his name was
anathema to many white Alabamians; and he and his family were
subjected to ostracism, threats, violence, and vitriolic editorial and
verbal abuse, the latter flowing most notably from George Wallace—a
law school classmate, former friend, and not infrequent defendant in
Judge Johnson's court. Moreover, although the sentiments of white
Alabamians have mellowed considerably over the past decade, critics
of judicial activism now score certain of his more recent rulings as
affronts to legislative authority and basic principles of majoritarian
democracy.

In 1978, Governor Wallace announced his retirement from elected
office, bringing to a conclusion almost two decades of confrontation
politics with Judge Johnson's court. This book examines Judge Johnson's life through the end of the Wallace era and the judge's appointment to the Fifth Circuit, two not entirely coincidental events.[2] More
broadly, however, it is a history of modern human rights reform in
Alabama, cast in the biographical idiom. For, in a very real sense, the
history of that reform and of Judge Johnson's judicial career have been
synonymous.

Although reflecting my deep concern about excesses of judicial
power, the book's tone is largely sympathetic to its subject. I am a
native Alabamian who grew to manhood during the troubled post-
Brown years, ever loyal to a great state and to my unreconstructed
relatives and friends, yet painfully aware of the enormous gaps separating Alabama's racial politics and the Constitution's commitment to

equality. During that turbulent period, Alabama produced few heroic figures. Judge Frank Johnson was one.

Professor Robert J. Frye first stimulated my interest in Judge Johnson. This book is respectfully dedicated to his memory. The East Carolina University Research Council provided partial financial support for my research; and librarians at East Carolina University, the Library of Congress, the University of North Carolina, the Alabama State Department of Archives and History, the University of Virginia, The University of Alabama, and the Birmingham Public Library furnished valuable assistance, as did personnel at the Army Court of Military Review in Washington, D.C.

My research was drawn in part from interviews with Judge Johnson, his devoted and perceptive wife Ruth, law clerks, judges, politicians, attorneys, bureaucrats, and others connected with the judge's career. I appreciate greatly their time, candor, and the willingness of most of them to submit to tape-recorded interviews. My graduate assistant Mark L. Clark typed transcripts for a number of the interviews. I am also deeply indebted to Jane P. Gordon, clerk of Alabama's Middle District court, and her considerate staff; to Judge Johnson's former court reporter Glynn Henderson; and to the judge's office staff, especially his secretary Dorothy Perry, a truly gracious lady. I camped in Judge Johnson's law library through much of one summer, subjected him to many hours of interviews, made numerous follow-up visits, and wrote or telephoned Mrs. Perry and the judge repeatedly with pleas for "one last bit" of assistance. They endured it all with remarkable good humor. For encouragement and editorial care, I also owe much to Malcolm M. MacDonald of The University of Alabama Press.

Finally, my wife Mary Alice and our truly beautiful children, Sarah and Cole, deserve my gratitude. I have often remarked, only half-jokingly, that if I completed this book, it would be in spite of their conspiracies to lure me away from my work toward more leisurely pursuits. In truth, of course, their affection and support sustained me through the entire project.

Greenville, North Carolina   T.E.Y.
1981

The Early Years

Frank Johnson's judicial reputation was forged in the racial politics of the Black Belt, but his roots run deep in the hills of northwestern Alabama. A montage of beautiful rolling countryside and rough mountain terrain, the region boasts no cities of any appreciable size. Much of the land is unsuited for farming, and for many years rich coal deposits furnished the backbone of the region's economy—a pattern now re-emerging in the wake of the nation's growing energy crisis. Ugly gashes in the earth offer mute testimony of the extent to which strip-mining once dominated the area. Today, however, the region's economy turns not only on the shifting fortunes of the mines but on those of mobile-home factories, textile plants, and similar enterprises attracted there by the promise of cheap labor and power. By and large, its people are hardworking, simple folk who have known hard times. As with their lives in general, they prefer their religion simple; fundamentalist churches of every variety dot the landscape.

In political heritage, the counties of northwestern Alabama stand in marked contrast to the rest of the state, and that contrast is most evident in Winston County, where Frank Johnson was born and reared. When a majority of Alabamians began clamoring for secession in 1860, Winston's citizens and, to a lesser extent, those of neighboring counties, balked. They had few slaves and opposed what they believed would be a futile struggle to protect the interests of a slave economy. Shortly after the state seceded, delegates from the northwestern counties, joined by like-minded groups from neighboring states, met in convention in Winston and adopted resolutions reflecting their desire for neutrality, support for the Union, opposition to secession, and hope that they would be left alone to work out their own political and financial destinies. As the war progressed and the Confederacy attempted to conscript troops in the region, the hill counties' desire for neutrality was soon transformed into open hostility against the rebels, with Winston—by then called "The Free State"—the center of opposition. An increasing number of northern Alabama Unionists, or "tories" as they came to be called, left their homes and hid beneath mountain bluffs to avoid conscription, while many of those inducted into the Confederacy's service later deserted and several thousand actually enlisted in the Union army. Others left the state or organized into "prowling brigades" that preyed on people in counties to the south and on northern Alabama Confederate sympathizers. Homes were burned, and secessionists were hanged, shot, whipped, and butchered at the hands of tory vigilantes. In retaliation, Confederate troops imprisoned Unionist leaders and committed numerous atrocities against the tories.[1]

With the defeat of the South, the hill country's aversion to the war reflected itself in an enduring attachment to the Republican party. To the tories of northwestern Alabama, the Democratic party was the planter's party and the war party; their only alternative was to embrace the party of Lincoln, and this they did in substantial numbers. In Winston, a pocket of Republican strength developed that would persist for over a century. While much of the rest of the state placed its support solidly behind the Democracy, in a politics based largely on race, the citizens of Winston County, the vast majority of whom were white, consistently returned Republican majorities in both presidential elections and local races.[2]

Whatever the ultimate impact on his judicial philosophy, many of Frank Johnson's ancestors figured in the development of northwestern Alabama's pro-Union, pro-Republican political heritage. During the Civil War, his father's people lived in Fayette County, like Winston a stronghold of tory sentiment. Although some of their number fought for the Confederacy, six or more joined the 101st Cavalry, U.S.A. After the war, Johnson's great-grandfather Johnson—a blunt, direct, honest man nicknamed "Straight-Edge," an appellation the press would one day confer on his great-grandson—was elected sheriff of Fayette County on the Republican ticket. Other family members were also active in Fayette politics, and in time Frank's father became a major force in the Republican politics of Winston County and the state.[3]

Frank Minis Johnson, Sr., was born in 1895, reared in Fayette County, and trained as a teacher in the only adequate school in the area at the time, a normal school operated by the Baptists at Eldridge, a tiny community in neighboring Walker County. After a year of study, Frank, Sr., was awarded a teaching certificate and began teaching at Dog Town, a village near the academy. While there, he married another teacher, Alabama Long. Alabama's parents were Pennsylvania natives who had first moved to the state before her birth. Unable to make a living, they soon returned north. But they did not forget Alabama, and when their daughter was born, they named her after their adopted state. Later, her family returned to Alabama and settled at Delmar, a Winston community located five miles from Haleyville, the county's largest town. Her father and other family members operated small mines in the Delmar area.[4]

In the waning months of World War I, Frank, Sr., joined the army and took Alabama to Delmar to live with her family. While in Officers

Candidate School at Camp Pike, Arkansas, he got a wire informing him that a son had been born October 30, 1918. The army granted him a ten-day leave to visit his wife and young Frank. By the end of his leave, the newspapers were filled with stories of the war's end, but the army denied him a request for an extension. On November 11, 1918, the day Armistice was declared, he returned to Camp Pike—and soon after received his discharge papers.[5]

After the war, Frank, Sr., moved his little family to Haleyville and got a job in a general store. Later, he and a man named McNutt became partners briefly in a meat market. In 1921, however, the GOP returned to the White House, and Alabama's Republicans began dividing the spoils of victory. For Frank, Sr., faithful devotion to the party meant Haleyville's postmastership, an office he would hold through the administrations of Harding, Coolidge, and Hoover.[6]

The postmaster's position meant a steady income and relatively comfortable life for the Johnsons, and young Frank acquired brothers and sisters at the rate of about one every two and a half years: first Wallace, then Bill, Jean, Jimmy, Mary Ann, and, finally, when Frank was about seventeen, Ellen Ruth. When his parents were away, his brother Jimmy recalled, Frank "was put in command. And he could fulfill that job well. He could keep us all under control." "I helped get the other children started," Frank remembers, "changed their diapers, took care of them. In a large family like that, . . . your Mama has to have some help."[7]

In part, perhaps, because of his role in helping to raise the younger children, Frank's relationship with his parents was extremely close. Frank, Sr., was a natural politician, a hale fellow well met with a winning personality. Those who know the private Judge Johnson see in him many of his father's qualities. But most of his personality traits seem to have been drawn from Alabama Johnson. "Frank's mother," a longtime family friend has remarked, "is a lovely lady, less socially and politically inclined than his father, a woman of strong character, strong morals, strong convictions, the courage of her convictions—a strong, strong woman. And Frank inherited an awful lot of that. He has always shown the courage of his convictions—sometimes to a fault."[8]

Frank's youth was not unlike that of most boys growing up in a small-town southern environment during the 1920s and 1930s. The family's home rested in the shadow of the First Baptist Church, where his father served as a deacon, and church every Sunday morning and evening, as well as Wednesday night prayer meeting, were expected routine for the Johnson children. In school, Frank was an indifferent student who generally sat in the rear of the classroom and rarely responded to the teacher's questions though he generally knew the answers, partly because he was painfully shy, partly because he did not want his peers to consider him a sissy. He enjoyed history, geography, civics—"anything that didn't take too much application," he would later say—but did poorly in math and the sciences. On the athletic field, he excelled at football for the Haleyville High Lions. As a teenager, he took a strong interest in agriculture and seemed bent on a career in farming. With his mother's help, he raised corn and other crops as a 4-H Club project. Other details of his youth sound equally familiar: swimming in creeks, stomach aches from too many green apples, a love for fishing and frequent trips north with his father for all-night fishing on the Tennessee River, hunting for squirrel and birds in the woods and fields around Haleyville, stealing watermelons, Saturday westerns at the Princess Theater whenever he could scrape up the dime needed for admission, and sitting with his brothers and sisters in his father's car on Main Street Saturday nights while Frank, Sr., got a haircut and talked politics with his cronies.[9]

In his youth, Frank was called "F. M.," but he also acquired a nickname, and under particularly ironic circumstances given his later decisions in behalf of Alabama's mentally handicapped. Plez McCuller, a large, slightly retarded town character, worked for the railroad in Haleyville, separating cars. As a joke, Frank rigged the cars so they could not be separated, then watched gleefully as the hapless Plez attempted, with growing frustration, to break them apart. Enraged when he learned what had happened, he chased his tormentor through Haleyville's streets, prompting Frank's companions quickly to dub their friend "Plez." At the time, the incident seemed hilariously amusing. Later, however, it would gnaw at Frank's conscience.[10]

By the ninth grade, Frank had become attracted to the thin, pretty, raven-haired girl he would eventually marry. Ruth Jenkins was born in Walker County near the Galloway Coal Company, one of the region's principal coal-mining operations. If Frank's early life was economically secure, Ruth's was precarious at best. Her father had worked a small mine with his brother, but in the late 1920s had lost everything. Unable to cope with his plight, he walked away from his family one Sunday afternoon and never returned.[11]

Faced with supporting Ruth and six older brothers and sisters, Ruth's mother begged her relatives for help without success. Finally, friends in Winfield, a neighboring Marion County community, agreed to take them in, and Ruth's mother obtained a job as a cook in a Winfield cafe. A year later, their Winfield friends moved to Haleyville and took Ruth and her family along. In Haleyville, the two families lived together in a large old house, and Ruth's mother took in boarders. The income was meager, but at least Ruth's family was now eating well.[12]

Ruth first noticed Frank shortly after the move to Haleyville, watching enviously as he rode a family pony through the streets of town. Within a few years, the dark-eyed brunette and gangly youth were sweethearts; and when Frank's parents allowed him to name his youngest sister, he named her after Ruth. A premature baby plagued by illness as a young child, Ruth had begun school late. In marked contrast to Frank, however, at Haleyville she became an honor student; and if anything, their relationship merely aggravated Frank's increasingly undistinguished academic record.[13]

Given his parents' political leanings, it was natural that Frank would readily embrace the tenets of mountain Republicanism—a politics considerably more moderate in tone than the rabidly conservative Goldwater movement that would sweep Alabama in 1964, but one that nevertheless stressed self-reliance, free enterprise, and limited government. When Franklin D. Roosevelt was inaugurated in 1933, Frank was not yet fifteen; but already he knew the enemy. He and his family admired the Civilian Conservation Corps and other FDR public employment and public works projects. They viewed with alarm, however, certain of his welfare measures and, most of all, his attempt to pack the courts and centralize federal power in the presidency. "We thought," he would later remark, "that Roosevelt had usurped all of the authority and prerogatives of the Congress. I watched the court-packing episode very, very intently, and I cheered with all of the other people in the country when it failed. We thought Roosevelt was a real tyrant, just too liberal."[14]

Initially, of course, Roosevelt's ascension to power had a more mundane effect on the Johnsons: Frank, Sr., lost his patronage position as Haleyville's postmaster. But while the GOP was experiencing hard times elsewhere, in Winston County there was still considerable life in the party. In 1934, Frank, Sr., was elected Winston's probate judge, winning handily in every voting beat.[15]

Although Haleyville was Winston's largest town, Double Springs had long been the county seat. When Frank, Sr., moved into his new office at the courthouse in Double Springs, he moved his family to the town. Initially, Frank stayed behind to finish the school year and continue his courtship of Ruth. But in the summer, he, too, joined the family.[16]

It was to be an eventful period for Frank—and an exasperating one for his father. On arriving in Double Springs, he quickly formed new friendships and renewed old ones. His closest friend would be Lee Pershing (Pert) Dodd. Pert's uncle had worked in Haleyville's post office, and Pert and Frank had known each other for several years before Frank's move to Double Springs. Now, they, a young man named

Frank Wilson who later would enter the ministry, and several other Double Springs teenagers became virtually inseparable companions, and subjected their parents to a variety of headaches, including a short-lived attempt to run away from home (for no particular reason, Pert Dodd later said) and several automobile accidents.[17]

The auto accidents, coupled with Frank's indifference to schoolwork and his parents' concern that his relationship with Ruth was getting too serious, convinced the judge that his eldest son needed a change of scenery. In the fall of his senior year, Frank was packed off to Gulfport, Mississippi, and a stint at Gulf Coast Military Academy. When he graduated the following May, his study habits—and grades—had improved noticeably. He also seemed to have gained maturity and self-confidence.[18]

He was not yet ready, however, to break entirely with the past. The summer after graduation, he worked for the state highway department, then enrolled at the Double Springs high school, ostensibly to make up course deficiencies needed for admission to college, but actually to play football with Pert Dodd and his other chums on the Double Springs team. After a brief tenure there—roughly the length of the football season—he applied for admission to Birmingham-Southern College, a small Methodist school with, by Alabama standards, an excellent reputation. Frank was admitted on a football scholarship, but did poorly academically, and for that and other reasons now obscure, found the experience totally unsatisfying. At the end of his first term, Southern dropped its small football program, and Frank withdrew.[19]

Next he enrolled at Birmingham's Massey Business College, the state's leading training ground for future secretaries and bookkeepers. At Massey, he learned the rudiments of accounting and became a fast and accurate typist, and soon he got a job as an accountant with a Birmingham firm. Now gainfully employed, he asked Ruth to marry him. Ruth was only seventeen, and though her mother approved, her sisters strongly opposed the marriage.

Johnson's parents remained concerned that the couple were not ready for marriage, but gave their blessing. "Frank went in to see the judge," Pert Dodd recalls, "and told him they were going to get married. . . . During the conversation, . . . Frank says, 'Daddy, I just don't believe I can do any better.' The judge agreed. He loved Ruth." On January 14, 1938, they were married. Soon after, they moved into a tiny Birmingham apartment.[20]

Johnson's employers seemed pleased with his work, and, with the added responsibilities of marriage, he decided to ask for a raise. Instead of receiving a pay increase, he was fired as a security risk. The pay of junior employees was so poor, his supervisor explained, that a family man might be tempted to steal from the company.[21]

One of Ruth's sisters sent the couple fifty dollars to keep them in groceries until Johnson could find other employment. In those days, fifty dollars was a handsome sum. But when the money finally ran out, Johnson remained jobless. With their last twenty cents, he and Ruth bought two bags of peanuts and two R.C. colas, then called his father collect. The judge sent a friend in a pickup truck to gather up their few belongings and take them to Johnson's grandparents, who invited them to live at their Carbon Hill home until Johnson found a job.[22]

Johnson's grandparents enjoyed having the young couple with them. But after a few weeks, Johnson landed a position, compliments of the hated Democrats, with the Works Projects Administration. In comparatively rapid succession, his work with the WPA took them to a series of northwestern Alabama villages and towns. He had begun his work with the WPA as a timekeeper, but eventually received a change in status. As part of its effort to civilize rural Alabama, the government had undertaken an elaborate campaign to construct high-quality outhouses, complete with screening, finished woodwork, and marble slabs, behind every home in the region. And the man who one day would oversee the quality and quantity of toilet facilities in Alabama's prisons and mental hospitals was made supervisor over their construction in Walker and Fayette counties. Despite ribbing from his friends, he took considerable pride in his work and turned out an excellent product.[23]

Johnson might well have spent the remainder of his life in the hills of northwestern Alabama, farming or marking time in some routine task, perhaps dabbling in Republican politics. He had long had an interest in law, however, and the chance to watch lawyers practicing before his father had whetted his appetite for a legal career. When he had first spoken of his ambition to Ruth, she had been skeptical at best, thinking to herself that he might become the worst attorney ever. But after watching the shy youth become a confident, aggressive advocate in high school debate classes, she had come to share his enthusiasm. After a year and a half with the WPA, Frank decided to pursue his goal. The state's only law school at the time was part of The University of Alabama's Tuscaloosa campus. In the fall of 1939, he and Ruth moved to Tuscaloosa and enrolled as undergraduates at the university.[24]

In early 1941, Frank, Sr.'s six-year term as probate judge ended, and he moved his family back to their home in Haleyville. For a time, he turned his attention almost exclusively to a sizable farming operation and to a brief and unprofitable stint at running the Cleere Hotel, an aging Haleyville landmark that had seen better days. But in 1942, he was back in politics, elected as Winston's delegate to the Alabama House of Representatives. As the legislature's only Republican, he was something of an oddity, but extremely popular with his colleagues. "Ask anyone [at the capitol] what sort of fellow is Frank Johnson?" a

Birmingham Post columnist wrote in a profile of the Winston solon. "The answer is always enthusiastic and emphatic. One hell of a good one. Never met a better. He has only one bad fault. He's a damned Republican." After serving half his term, however, Frank, Sr., resigned his position for financial reasons and took a job with the Veterans Administration, commuting each day to his work in Tuscaloosa from Haleyville while Mrs. Johnson taught at Pebble, Alabama, in a rural Winston County school. In 1946, he moved to the Veterans Administration's Montgomery office; and he and Mrs. Johnson settled in Alabama's capital.[25]

Frank, Sr.'s decision to leave the rough and tumble of elective office came too late, however, to spare his eldest son his only scrape with the law. "Some fellow named Timmons," Johnson recalls, "set up a public speaker system, one of those electronic outfits, one Saturday afternoon. I was in a dentist chair up on the second floor of a building across the street, and he made some very slanderous statements about my Daddy. . . . Timmons was running for county commissioner or something. He carried a Star Route, carried the mail . . . from Haleyville to Double Springs. And I sat and waited until he came that afternoon." After their confrontation, a justice of the peace fined Frank five dollars. "I was guilty of a breach of the peace," he now readily concedes. "I don't remember what he said. It was just something that set me on fire."[26]

On arriving in Tuscaloosa, the Johnsons rented a small apartment on Hackberry Lane, near the outskirts of town. They had a car and some furniture, but no money, and Frank quickly found a job with the university as a carpenter, building dormitory furniture, tacking down roofs, mending windows, and making other repairs. Ruth also enrolled at the university and soon began working as a grader for a professor in the History Department. Later, Frank earned additional income running real estate title searches for a Tuscaloosa firm.[27]

Frank's prelaw curriculum provided heavy doses of political science, history, and economics—subjects he enjoyed and found easy to comprehend—and enabled him largely to avoid the math and science courses that had been the bane of his high school career. As a prelaw student, he was exempt from the demanding foreign language courses required of Ruth and other liberal arts students. Moreover, his year's exile at Gulf Coast Military Academy had improved his study habits. Even so, he found, to his consternation, that he had to study much harder than Ruth to maintain a high grade average—a consequence, no doubt, of his indifference to school work at Haleyville. English grammar, in particular, caused considerable anguish.[28]

Despite such hurdles, Johnson consistently earned As and Bs in his undergraduate courses, compiling such a respectable average that the brothers of Pi Kappa Alpha invited him to pledge their fraternity and exempted him from its dues requirement, apparently in the hope that his grades might offset those of the chapter's more fun-loving members. After three years of prelaw, he entered law school. He enjoyed all the subjects in the school's limited curriculum and received an A in almost every course.[29]

At that time, Alabama's law school was small, most of the students knew each other, and the Johnsons made many friends. Among them were Eric Embry, a future justice of the Alabama Supreme Court; Forrest Adams, later to become a prominent state circuit judge; and a pugnacious little fellow from Barbour County named George Corley Wallace.

Johnson and Wallace now tend to discredit stories of their closeness at the university, but they clearly enjoyed more than a passing acquaintance. And when Jimmy Johnson and Wallace's brother Gerald attended the university in later years, they formed a close friendship that would endure long after their older brothers had parted company. The Johnsons and Wallace first met while they were undergraduates. The first time Ruth saw Wallace, he was perched on a soap box in front of the student union, making a speech in a now long-forgotten campus campaign. Later, she and other Independents supported his unsuccessful effort to wrest control of the campus Cotillion Club from the fraternities. Johnson and Wallace took debate together, once arguing the merits of the TVA, with Wallace applauding public power and Johnson espousing the anti-New Deal, free enterprise philosophy he had learned at his father's knee.[30]

In law school, the Johnsons often socialized with Wallace and Glen Curlee, a boy from Wetumpka, an Elmore County town north of Montgomery, who later would serve intermittently, as a circuit solicitor (prosecutor) and become one of Wallace's closer political cronies. On Saturday nights, their friends often gathered at the apartment on Hackberry Lane to dance to tunes provided by an old, hand-cranked record player, then took in a midnight movie at a local theater. Wallace and Curlee were generally in the group. On a number of occasions, they also attended school dances together, Johnson and Curlee nattily attired in somewhat ill-fitting tuxedoes, the "average citizen's" future defender in a business suit.[31]

At times, too, they speculated about the future. "We chided Frank because he was a Republican," Curlee recalls. "Roosevelt was in his heyday, and we were talking one night. I asked him, 'Why in hell do you want to be a Republican? . . . They'll never come back. They're dead. The party's dead.' He says, 'Well, there's so few of us that one day I might be a federal judge.' George says, 'Well, that'll be the day. I'll be governor by then.' "[32]

The Tuscaloosa campus was not entirely untouched by the war then raging in Europe and the Pacific. Johnson completed the university's

ROTC program and was slated for active duty after law school. By taking a heavy course load, Mrs. Johnson graduated in three years with a double major in political science and history. The History Department offered her a graduate fellowship, but the family's sparse finances dictated that she find a job. While Johnson finished law school, she taught at Tuscaloosa County High School. She enjoyed teaching; but as her husband's graduation and enlistment neared, Leigh Harrison, a university law professor who later would serve as dean of the law school, urged her also to consider enlisting. She was making only $85 a month and teaching subjects outside her major fields, so one day she went to a recruiting office in Birmingham to inquire about joining the WAVES. Before the day was over, she had completed an examination and taken the oath. Three months before her husband finished law school, she left Tuscaloosa for basic training, followed by tours in Miami and Washington and an assignment as administrative assistant to the chief of naval operations.[33]

Johnson graduated in the spring of 1943 and returned to Haleyville. On August 19, he enlisted in the army and prepared to leave for boot camp. After basic training, he went to Officers Candidate School at Fort Benning, Georgia. The program's physical regimen posed no difficulties, but math remained a problem. With the help of a university classmate, however, he overcame that perennial deficiency. When his Fort Benning tour ended, he was named the outstanding cadet in his unit. After additional training in Oregon, he shipped out for Europe and a stint with the Third Army in France.[34]

The infantry unit Johnson commanded moved into combat shortly after D-Day. A good soldier whose efficiency ratings would range from excellent to superior, he ultimately rose to the rank of captain and received a Bronze Star, Combat Infantryman Award, and Meritorious Action Medal. After twice being wounded, he was also awarded the Purple Heart. The first wound, received near Paris, was relatively minor, requiring only a few weeks of hospitalization. The second was serious, leading to kidney complications; and on October 30, 1944, he was placed on limited duty.[35]

After his release from an army hospital, he was assigned to the Tenth Reinforcement Depot at Lichfield, England, in the Midlands near Birmingham. The Lichfield depot housed a military police unit and served as a stockade for the army in the London area. Frank served as the installation's chief investigating officer, prosecuting a number of cases before general courts-martial and preparing others for prosecution. At this point in the war, the army and other branches of the service had begun shipping American prison inmates to the war front for combat. Naturally, many of these reluctant warriors deserted at the first opportunity. Such deserters, AWOL soldiers, and a wide assortment of other servicemen-prisoners were confined at Lichfield, providing Johnson

with an extremely busy caseload. In time, the army transferred him to
the Second Reinforcement Depot in Belgium for a final assignment and
discharge. His association with the Lichfield barracks, however, was far
from over.[36]

Like the Alabama prison conditions Frank Johnson would confront
some thirty years later, conditions at the Lichfield stockade were grim
at best. Its ugly red brick buildings, begrimed with industrial smoke, sat
on a treeless limestone hogback. Many of its barracks windows were
broken, its few toilets filthy, and its grounds barren of lawns. The
installation included three guardhouses. Guardhouse No. 1 served as
headquarters for the military police detachment and booking center for
new inmates. Guardhouse No. 2 housed men charged or convicted on
all but the most serious offenses. Those inmates confined for rape,
murder, or other serious offenses were held under heavy guard in the
No. 3 Guardhouse. The guardhouses were often grossly overcrowded.
The sleeping capacity in Guardhouse No. 2, for example, was only 250,
yet at times it held as many as 700 prisoners. There had also been ugly
rumors about the treatment accorded Lichfield's inmates—horror
stories of beatings at the hands of prison guards, grossly inadequate
heating and poor health care, six-hour calisthenic sessions, inmates
forced to eat cigarettes found in their possession, black prisoners forced
to crawl on the floor and bark like dogs before being fed, and a slogan
reportedly circulating among the barracks guards, "Shoot a prisoner
and be made a sergeant." At a time when Nazi concentration camp
conditions were first being exposed to the world, Lichfield posed an
army public relations problem of significant proportions.[37]

The military's immediate solution was to charge nine enlisted men
and two lieutenants with brutality against the Lichfield inmates. Under
the army court-martial manual, the defendants were allowed to select
any serviceman attorney reasonably available to defend them. They
chose Frank Johnson, and he returned to England to prepare for trial.[38]

Initially, the defendants were to be tried jointly, but Johnson moved
successfully for separate proceedings. The first of his clients to be tried
was Sergeant Judson Smith of Harlan County, Kentucky, a slightly built
former coal miner with an eighth-grade education and, to that point, an
unblemished military record who had served as a provost sergeant at
Lichfield. Smith's trial began in London on December 3, 1945, in a
dirty-windowed Grosvenor Square department store salesroom recently converted into a courtroom. It would last thirty trial days and
consume almost four thousand pages of transcript.[39]

As Smith, dressed neatly in an Eisenhower jacket bearing three hash
marks and six overseas stripes, sat listening, a parade of prosecution
witnesses made damaging allegations about his mistreatment of inmates and conditions at Lichfield. Staff Sergeant James Gallandry, a
combat infantryman and holder of the Bronze Star and Purple Heart

who was confined at Lichfield after being several hours late returning from leave, testified that Smith had once beaten him on the back with a billy club. Another witness said that, on one occasion, he had been forced to double-time with his nose and toes against a wall, as guards beat him on the back and legs with a club. Yet another claimed that he had once been forced to spend thirty-three days in solitary confinement, emerging with four front teeth missing, hollow cheeks, smashed eyeglasses, and thirty pounds underweight. Other witnesses made similar allegations. At one point, the prosecution presented evidence suggesting that a recent Lichfield inmate death had resulted from a severe beating, rather than from the brain tumor originally diagnosed as the cause of death.[40]

When asked why they had failed to report their mistreatment, the witnesses invariably responded that inmate abuse was common knowledge at Lichfield and that they feared retribution if they talked. "I'd get beat up," said one private. "It was healthier to keep my mouth shut." Other witnesses were more specific. A black soldier testified, for example, that Smith had threatened him; then a few weeks later two guards had grabbed him in a London pub, hauled him outside, and beaten him. Gallandry testified that Lichfield's executive officer had offered to remit his sentence and restore his staff sergeant's rating if he would "forget about" his mistreatment. A week later, he said, he was returned to his unit with his rating restored, sentence suspended, and full back pay.[41]

Johnson and an assistant pursued several lines of defense. In often lengthy cross-examination, they attempted to discredit the prosecution's testimony and drive a wedge between their client and the allegations of prosecution witnesses. At one point, for example, Johnson reminded a witness who claimed that a beating administered by Smith had left severe bruises of his earlier, contradictory statements indicating that no bruising had occurred.

The defense also elicited testimony designed to improve upon the image given their client and Lichfield's conditions by the prosecution witnesses. Lieutenant Granville Cubage, one of the two junior officers charged along with Smith and the other enlisted men, swore that he had seen Smith strike a prisoner only once, and then in self-defense. And a former Lichfield provost marshal applauded Smith's character and effectiveness, testifying that he had "handled the prisoners in an excellent manner at all times." Colonel James A. Kilian, Lichfield's former commanding officer and himself a subject of investigation in the case, praised the defendant and testified that during his Lichfield tenure, he had interviewed as many as fifteen to twenty inmates daily, yet not one had ever complained of mistreatment. Kilian further testified that the army had conducted frequent inspections of his facility, that in one month, in fact, eight generals had conducted inspections. Each inspection, he claimed, had produced uniformly favorable comments. Several chaplains testified that they, too, had noticed nothing improper about Lichfield's treatment of its inmates.[42]

The army produced rebuttal witnesses who effectively challenged much of this testimony. And when Smith took the stand in his own defense, prosecution attorneys subjected the perspiring defendant to almost four hours of intense questioning. Nevertheless, the defense testimony had raised doubt, at least, whether conditions at Lichfield were as critical—or Smith's guilt as obvious—as the prosecution had alleged.

The crux of Johnson's defense, however, was a legal argument then in vogue among defendants at the Nazi war crimes trials—the claim that Smith and company had simply been following the orders of their superiors. "It was our theory," he would later say, "that these men had received instructions, to some extent explicit, but mostly of the implicit type, to make it so hard on [Lichfield's inmates] that they'd rather be in combat than in the stockade. And [the guards] being combat men and [some of the inmates] being deserters, they welcomed the opportunity. . . . And they approached their job with some enthusiasm— there's no question about that."[43]

The testimony clearly established that the defendants had been encouraged by superior officers to make life miserable for Lichfield's clientele. Central to such a defense, however, was the proposition that a soldier is expected to obey even illegal orders. Under military law, a soldier was to resist compliance with palpably illegal policies; and the prosecution contended that Smith and the other defendants surely had been aware that any order to mistreat prisoners was clearly improper. In his closing argument in the case, Johnson did not directly challenge this assertion. Instead, he cited a variety of army regulations and court decisions underscoring the predicament of any soldier confronted with a potentially illegal order. One rule stipulated "That an inferior 'should act upon the reasonable presumption that his superior *was* authorised to issue an order which he *might* be authorised to issue. If he acts otherwise, he does so at his peril, and subjects himself to the risk of being punished for disobedience to orders.' " Another read: "For the inferior to assume to determine the question of the lawfulness of an order given him by a superior would, of itself, as a general rule, amount to insubordination, and such an assumption carried into practice would subvert military discipline."

But Johnson would rely solely on neither such regulations nor weaknesses in the prosecution's testimony. Appealing to more human elements, he cited Smith's humble origins and exemplary military record, the "terrible mental and physical strain" to which his client had already been subjected, the inordinate publicity given the case, and the obvious contrasts between Smith's treatment and that accorded Colonel Kilian and one of the officer defendants in the case (both of whom had been given an extended leave in the states, while the sergeant was placed on restriction). Then, Frank concluded his defense. "If there are not three members of this court who will enter a finding of not guilty in respect of these charges," he told the court, "I . . . will lose my faith in human nature."

Repeated delays, including a lengthy one caused by the disappearance of a former Lichfield officer subpoenaed as a defense witness, had extended the trial well into February. On February 13 it ended. Two days later, Sergeant Smith was convicted on several charges, found not guilty on the rest, and sentenced to three years at hard labor, a dishonorable discharge, and forfeiture of all pay and allowances. It could have been worse. Smith had been charged with numerous counts of assault and cruel and inhuman disciplinary treatment involving nine named Lichfield inmates and others unknown. If convicted on all counts, he had faced a possible thirty-seven years in prison.

Smith's trial had served simply to aggravate the image problem Lichfield posed for the army. The *Stars and Stripes* had continued to give the case extensive and largely unfavorable coverage, and reports in the American press had been equally negative. Such publicity apparently convinced the army high command that the Lichfield matter had gotten entirely out of hand. The judge advocate for the European theater at the time was Brigadier General Edward C. Betts of Huntsville, Alabama. A Betts aide had participated in Smith's trial, submitting frequent reports to the general about developments in the London proceedings. As the trial of a second defendant neared, Betts dispatched another assistant, Colonel Clarence Brand, to London in search of a settlement. Brand promised light sentences for Johnson's clients and an admission from the army that the defendants had been following their superiors' policies if they would plead guilty to minor charges. When this ploy failed, General Betts himself flew to London and met with Johnson and his clients. "General Betts came down," Johnson remembers, "and he says, 'Now, who is this? . . . If he pleads guilty, he'll get this much; if [that one] pleads guilty, he'll get this much,' " offering each defendant leniency in exchange for his plea.[44]

Betts's maneuver would influence the course of the Lichfield trials, but not in the direction the general had hoped. Hotly rejecting any settlement, Johnson charged that Betts's offer and related army efforts to bring the cases to a swift conclusion were clear evidence that the army was exerting an undue, and illegal, influence over the proceedings. Despite warnings from his superiors, he next began preparing a challenge to the court's composition and announced plans to call a number of high-ranking officers, including Major General John T. Lewis, commanding general for the European theater's Western Base Section, as witnesses to support his contentions.

The second trial began in London on April 9. Assisting Johnson at the defense table was Morris McGee, a short, thin, small-shouldered Alabamian who previously had won twenty-three court-martial acquittals and later would become something of an institution teaching law at the University. The accused was Sergeant James M. Jones of Muskogee, Oklahoma, a former Lichfield guard and holder of the Bronze Star, later to be described by a staff judge advocate as "an honest, frank, and clean-cut American boy." Sergeant Jones was charged with eight counts of assault, but his alleged offenses quickly faded into the background as Frank and McGee challenged the court's president, most of its members, and its law member, and charged that the defendants were being "railroaded" as part of a scheme to "whitewash" senior officers.[45]

In an effort to establish undue influence over the proceedings, the defense called Colonel Brand and other officers involved in the efforts to secure a settlement of the cases. Brand conceded that an offer had been made, but insisted that he had acted only in an "advisory" capacity and solely to expedite the trials of the enlisted men so that they could appear as witnesses in proceedings against the growing number of officers (now six, including Colonel Kilian) charged with Lichfield-related offenses. Major Richard D. Kearney, staff judge advocate for the London area, made similar admissions. But when Johnson pressed Kearney to admit that he had promised "drastic action" in the event that Johnson embarrassed his superior officers, Major Benito Gaguine, the court's law member, came to Kearney's rescue, largely obstructing that line of defense questioning. McGee then asked the court to declare Kearney a hostile witness, and when his request was denied, took over defense questioning of the witness. When he asked Kearney about military efforts to make enlisted men "the goats" in the proceedings, however, McGee, too, became embroiled in a battle with Gaguine.

Law Member: Let us have some facts on that. The line of questioning which you are now taking is in no way germane to that issue. That question is considered irrelevant, and it will not be answered. . . .
Defense (Lt. McGee): Here is our position——
Law Member: I have ruled.
Defense (Lt. McGee): May I say this——?
Law Member: No.
Defense (Lt. McGee): You mean I cannot say anything?
Law Member: That is right.
Defense (Lt. McGee): I cannot say a thing[?] I will just quit right now.

Turning to Johnson McGee asked, "Will you go ahead and run the case?" At this point, the president of the court declared a recess, apparently none too soon.

After the recess, the questioning proceeded more smoothly, but not for long. The next morning, the defense called General Lewis to the witness stand. As the general, resplendent in shiny boots and carrying a riding crop, strode to the witness chair, the president of the court jumped up and saluted—a violation of protocol and, for Johnson and McGee, one more indication of where control over the proceedings actually lay.[46]

Shortly after the Lichfield case arose, General Eisenhower had ordered Lewis to investigate conditions at Lichfield. Lewis had visited the stockade and filed a glowing report about its operations.[47] There was also considerable evidence that his office had attempted to influence the direction of the court-martial proceedings. On the witness stand, however, he insisted repeatedly that he had been concerned purely with the case's administrative status. When Johnson pressed the issue, inquiring of Lewis whether the general had complied with orders to inspect conditions at the Lichfield stockade, Major Gaguine again intervened, disallowing as irrelevant an increasingly frustrated defense counsel's probing questions.

The next day's editions of American newspapers gave Johnson's confrontation with General Lewis considerable coverage ("An army lieutenant looked a general in the eye . . ."). As Mrs. Johnson was leaving her office building for lunch that day, she heard a Washington newsboy for a tabloid hawking his product. "Extra! Extra! Read all about it. Lieutenant tells off General!" She was not surprised. "Even over in Lichfield," she would later smile and say, "he was stirring up trouble."[48]

The evidence of undue influence on the court was substantial. In fact, even before Sergeant Jones's trial began, Captain Earl J. Carroll, the assistant prosecutor in the case, had called the trials a "whitewash" of higher echelon officers and, in a searing, seven-page letter to army headquarters, had requested—and promptly received—a release from further participation in the proceedings. Though unsuccessful, the chief prosecutor had made the same request, and for essentially the same reasons. In the end, however, only the president of the court was required—via a peremptory challenge from the defense—to step down. After extensive testimony, Johnson withdrew challenges against five of the court's six members. And while he and McGee argued vehemently that Major Gaguine was prejudiced—and given to "leering" when overruling defense motions—the court found no basis for the law member's disqualification. But the defense had achieved its objective. "They had given us a hard time on Sergeant Smith," Johnson would later say, "and we were trying to repay them on Sergeant Jones, . . . and we did."[49]

In the wake of the battle over the court's composition, the portion of the trial devoted to the charges against Sergeant Jones seemed anticlimactic. Amid frequent clashes with Gaguine and the court's president, Frank and McGee attacked weaknesses in the prosecution's evidence and charged that Jones, like Smith, had merely been following orders. They also appealed to the court's respect for faithful soldiers and contempt for deserters, suggesting that the Lichfield inmates were cowards who deserved their treatment.

Whether because of this "the victims deserved it" defense, the "I was only following orders" rationale, the adverse publicity given the army's handling of the case, or a combination of such factors, Jones emerged from the trial with little more than a token punishment. Convicted on three of the eight counts of assault, he was sentenced to six months at hard labor and given a small fine. Later, half his prison sentence was suspended, the reviewing officer reasoning that, after all, his victims were "incorrigibles."

The site for the remaining trials was transferred to Bad Nauheim, Germany. During the summer of 1946, other enlisted men and several officers were convicted of Lichfield-related offenses and given light sentences. In early September, Colonel Kilian was found not guilty of "knowingly" condoning brutalities against Lichfield's inmates, but convicted of "permitting" them. He was given a reprimand and fined $500.[50]

By this time, however, Johnson had long since returned to civilian life. The army had delayed his discharge six months to allow him to participate in the Smith and Jones trials. But after the second trial, his superiors were more than happy to see him out of the army. One well may wonder whether Judge Johnson would have tolerated in his courtroom some of the tactics Counselor Johnson employed in his defense of the Lichfield defendants. In a review of the case, moreover, a staff judge advocate would term Johnson's challenge to the court a "fishing expedition" "heretofore unknown to military justice or courts-martial procedure," and characterize the record of Jones's trial as "replete with wrangling, bickering, caustic comments, horseplay, and childish clashes of personality, particularly by the defense counsel, the president, and law member of the court." In later years, however, Johnson would offer a different assessment. "I tried it like a lawyer," he said, "and the military wasn't accustomed to that."[51]

Twentieth-Century Slavery

Their military service completed, the Johnsons returned to Alabama in the spring of 1946. He joined the law firm of Curtis and Maddox in Jasper, a small coal-mining town nestled in the hills of rural Walker County about midway between Birmingham and Haleyville. The firm's aging senior partner, Judge James J. Curtis, was a close family friend and native of Double Springs who had served briefly as mayor of Haleyville before Johnson's birth. Long active in the Republican politics of northwestern Alabama, Curtis had been a delegate to the Republican national conventions of 1908, 1912, and 1920 and had held a circuit judgeship for twelve years early in his career. As the war ended, he was completing over thirty years of law practice in Jasper. He had long looked forward to having Johnson join his firm.[1]

The Johnsons first moved into a small apartment owned by a family friend from Winston County. But in 1948, they built a home; and in December of that year, they adopted a son. Unable to have children themselves, they were thrilled when they learned that a baby boy, less than a week old, was available for adoption in New York City. Mrs. Johnson went to New York to get their son—named James Curtis in honor of the judge but soon to be called Johnny—extremely excited finally to have a baby and so concerned about his welfare that she had hotel personnel where they were staying bring his formula to her room so that she could prepare it herself.[2]

At the time of Johnny's adoption, Mrs. Johnson was teaching in a Jasper public school. Unable to bear leaving her baby with a sitter, she gave up the teaching position and the badly needed income it had provided the young family. But Johnson's law practice grew steadily, the couple developed a warm circle of close friends, and their life in Jasper soon settled into a satisfying routine. Like most small-town lawyers, Johnson involved himself in a variety of civic activities. He joined the local Rotary Club and served for a time on its board of directors. One year, he headed the local cancer fund drive. He also became heavily involved in GOP politics; and it was through his party activities, ironically, that he formed an enduring friendship with one of the county's leading Democrats.[3]

In the fall of 1946, Lecil Gray was making a successful first bid for the office of probate judge in Walker County; and Johnson, a newcomer to the community, was campaigning on behalf of Republican candidates. Gray later recalled,

> I made a speech on the radio where I talked about the Depression and just gave Hoover and the Republicans generally hell, and after the speech I was driving down to Dora, I had my radio on in the car, and I heard them say, "We'll now bring you a paid political speech by the Republican party represented by Mr. Frank Johnson answering Lecil Gray's speech for the Democrats." And some young fellow—it was obvious to me he was just a kid—just gave me unshirted hell, not about his party and the issues, he just gave me unshirted hell. And I worried about that all afternoon, thinking, "Who is that kid?" We had a Frank Johnson who was beat comitteeman, a good, old-line Democrat. And I wondered if he had a boy who had gone astray.

Gray made a point of meeting Johnson that day "to straighten him out on his politics," and the two quickly became close friends, playful political opponents, and fishing partners.[4]

Lecil Gray was a short, chubby fellow with a cherubic face—and sparkling eyes always twinkling with devilment—the embodiment of the stereotypical small-town politician. He and Johnson took their politics seriously—but not too seriously. When Gray was seeking reelection as probate judge in 1952, he recused himself from participating on the local board that would appoint officials to supervise the upcoming election, and Johnson's law partner Herman Maddox was appointed to take his place. Later that same day, Judge Gray found some of the GOP hierarchy talking and drinking coffee around a table in the rear of a local drugstore. In their hearing, Gray informed a Democratic crony that the Republicans had sent him a list of people they wanted to have appointed as election officials, adding, "And I'm not gonna appoint a damn one of 'em." Johnson, the Republican county chairman, and the party secretary soon stormed into Gray's office, citing precedents to the effect that some Republicans would have to be appointed. Gray calmly responded that he would make no Republican appointments—then, when the delegation had worked itself into an appropriate state of agitation, explained that he was off the board and thus would make no appointments of Republicans or anyone else. On that occasion, he would recall with a smile, "Frank got pretty excited."[5]

In that same election year, Democratic and Republican women put up stickers supporting the national party tickets on the doors of the county courthouse, but every night someone took down the "I Like Ike" stickers. The GOP women believed that Judge Gray was the culprit, and after many complaints he asked the county commission to ban all political stickers from the courthouse. Later, he learned that Johnson had been having the women put up the Republican stickers—and that he was the one going to the courthouse each night and tearing them down. "Those women nearly ran me out of town, and it was all Frank's fault."[6]

Johnson and his law partners had a wide-ranging practice that covered most of the counties of northwestern Alabama. "I came from Winston County, and Maddox came from Lamar County, and Judge Curtis had lived in Winston, and he had been a circuit judge in Winston and Walker and Cullman, and we ran our rears off going to circuit courts in different places." The firm had a broad partisan appeal. Herman Maddox was an active Democrat who later would serve as Jasper's mayor, and Johnson and Judge Curtis, of course, were staunch Republicans. The variety of party attachments in the firm probably helped to attract clients, but while Johnson was in the firm the partners avoided active candidacy for office. "We had a real basic philosophy," he recalls, "that you can fool with it if you want to, but let it be somebody else's race. Don't you ever get involved in it as a candidate."[7]

Judge Curtis died in 1947, and Johnson and Herman Maddox continued alone, building a large and varied practice. They represented numerous clients barely able—or unable—to pay for their services. The firm also represented, however, a number of solvent clients—banks, savings and loan associations, railroads—and tried a large number of criminal cases, the field of practice Frank perhaps enjoyed most.[8]

One of Johnson's earliest criminal cases was tried in neighboring Marion County before Judge Curtis's death. Two war veterans, Noah and Ethridge Dodd, were accused of murdering a deputy sheriff, and they retained Johnson and Judge Curtis to defend them. The defendants were convicted after a week-long trial, but the Alabama Supreme Court reversed. By this point, Judge Curtis had died, and Johnson prepared for a second trial alone.[9]

Serving as special prosecutors in the case were members of Marion County's most prominent family, Ernest Fite and his son Rankin. The Fites controlled the county's principal bank, and both Ernest and Rankin served repeated terms in the Alabama House of Representatives, Rankin as Speaker. Johnson moved to quash the jury venire in the case, and a hearing was held on the motion. "The evidence reflected that the jury commissioners were appointed upon the recommendation of the Fites, that the secretary to the jury commission was a cashier in the Fite bank, that they didn't pretend to follow the law as to filling the jury box or maintaining the jury rolls, that a large percentage of those that were on the jury rolls were indebted to the Fites, who owned the banks." Judge Roy Mayhall, a fellow Jasper resident who served for years as chairman of the state Democratic party, was presiding in the case. Mayhall accepted Johnson's motion. When a new venire had been selected, the case was tried, but the jury deadlocked eleven to one for acquittal. A retrial was never held.[10]

Like any attorney, Frank sometimes had difficulty coaching his clients for trial. Once he defended a poor white tenant farmer named Willie Sutherland, accused of killing his landlord, an old man named Cantrell, on a farm near Double Springs. Willie and Cantrell had gotten into an argument in front of Willie's shack. According to Willie, Cantrell had threatened him with a hawk-bill knife and Willie had seized his own pocket knife and slit the elderly man's throat. Cantrell had walked a mile back to the house, collapsed on his front porch, and died.[11]

Willie's family got together enough money to retain Johnson, and since Cantrell had cut Sutherland superficially during the argument, a case for self-defense seemed strong. Johnson soon learned, however, that his client would be a difficult witness. "Willie Sutherland was uneducated and not the most intelligent person I've ever known. He wasn't anything except a tenant farmer with a bunch of kids." Willie could discuss certain aspects of the case calmly and rationally with Johnson. "But when he would get down to the point that he actually cut the old man, he'd grit his teeth and his eyes would flash and roll around, and he'd stand up and say, 'I slashed at him!' And he'd come around with that knife, and it would just nearly make you get under the table. I warned him about that half a dozen times. I said, 'You just go ahead and tell it like it happened, and don't give me any of those theatrics, just hold your hands down.' "[12]

When Johnson was questioning Willie on the witness stand, he led his client up to the point in his testimony at which he was to begin describing the fatal blows, then asked the judge for a brief recess and took Willie into an anteroom for another coaching session. "I said, 'Now, Willie, when you get on to where you cut Mr. Cantrell, go ahead and tell it like it was, but hold your hands down in your lap, and don't grit your teeth, and don't give it any emphasis at all.' We got back in the courtroom, and I led him on to the critical point in his testimony, and he stood all the way up in the witness box, slinging those arms! My jurors were dodging and everything. . . . Yeah, he was convicted [of first-degree manslaughter]. If he hadn't done that, I believe they wouldn't have given him anything." As it turned out, Willie served only a year of a three-year sentence and was allowed to serve that on a road gang near his family.[13]

In the fall of 1951, Johnson and Herman Maddox represented a client in a murder case involving a Jasper policeman and a member of a prominent local family. Thomas Hardcastle was the black sheep of his family, a narcotics addict desperate for funds. In September 1951, Hardcastle was arrested following a burglary of a local furniture warehouse when Jasper police learned that he had sold some blankets stolen during the burglary. While in jail, Hardcastle developed a high fever, had to be carried to the local hospital on several occasions, and finally died at the hospital. His body bore a number of bruises, and rumors were soon circulating through Jasper that city policemen had beaten him to death.[14]

Johnson was then serving as city attorney for Jasper, and he conducted an investigation into the circumstances of Hardcastle's death. A local physician who initially examined the body acknowledged that there were bruises on Hardcastle's head but said that none was sufficiently serious, in his judgment, to have caused the prisoner's death. He attributed the death to pneumonia. Hospital personnel said that the bruises had occurred when Hardcastle, delirious from a 108-degree fever, had run into a heavy hospital door, and an orderly who had been with Hardcastle said he saw no cuts or bruises on the prisoner prior to that time. Thomas H. Bromley, a federal narcotics agent stationed in Birmingham, had visited Hardcastle at the city jail. He told Frank that Hardcastle had become addicted to narcotics in 1947, initially by drinking paregoric. He also said that Hardcastle had not complained of mistreatment at the jail and bore no cuts or bruises at the time of Bromley's visit. Finally, two prisoners who had shared a cell with Hardcastle signed statements indicating that their jailmate had not been beaten and that drug abuse might have contributed to his death. When his investigation was completed, Johnson issued a statement exonerating the police of any wrongdoing in the case. "We have found absolutely no evidence," he said, "to support rumors that Hardcastle was mistreated by local police. In fact, all evidence supports the fact that our policemen were considerate and most careful. It's a shame that our police department has been victimized by these rumors, but now we think it is cleared up once and for all."[15]

But the case was far from over. Members of Hardcastle's family had lived in Walker County many years, they were socially prominent, and they were not at all satisfied with Johnson's conclusions. At the family's request, a state toxicologist performed a second autopsy, and further investigation was begun into the circumstances of the prisoner's death. The county solicitor, filling in for the circuit solicitor who was related to Jasper's police chief, conducted the investigation with the assistance of an attorney furnished by the state attorney general's office. Their findings were presented to a grand jury, and less than a week later, the grand jury returned a first-degree murder indictment against John Brom, a young war veteran with four years' service in the Jasper police department. Trial was set for early December.[16]

Brom's five-day trial produced few prosecution surprises. A state toxicologist who had examined Hardcastle's body at the second autopsy testified that the metal guards on the dead man's hospital bed could not have caused the injuries on his body, as the defense was suggesting. But the toxicologist was not a practicing physician or a graduate of an accredited medical school, and Johnson challenged his credentials as an expert witness and produced the physician who had performed the first examination of the body, attributing death to pneumonia. Johnson also called three witnesses who testified that they saw Hardcastle run down a hospital corridor and crash into a door and that there were no cuts or bruises on his body prior to the collision. Thomas Bromley, the federal narcotics agent who had assisted in the initial investigation of Hardcastle's death, testified that the prisoner had offered to serve as an informer for his office and for Brom and other policemen investigating the local narcotics traffic. Bromley was called as a prosecution witness, but his testimony tended to support a key defense theme that Hardcastle was planning to serve Brom as an informer and the policeman would thus have had little reason to beat the prisoner. The defense was effective. After less than an hour's deliberation, the jury acquitted the young policeman—and Brom promptly fainted. "The jury turned him loose," Johnson recalls, "and we had to send for the fire department with their breathing apparatus to revive him, he had been under such pressure."[17]

The Johnsons were happy with life in Jasper. "This was going to be my home forever, Jasper was it," Ruth Johnson later said. "And I was perfectly content and happy to have it that way." In 1952, however, Dwight D. Eisenhower was elected president; his election would dramatically change their lives.[18]

Johnson's father had served as a delegate to the Republican national conventions in 1936, 1940, and 1944; and Johnson secured a slot in the 1948 and 1952 delegations. Like his father, Johnson was committed to Governor Thomas E. Dewey of New York, the GOP's 1948 nominee. Dewey's moderate Republican positions on the issues were compatible with Johnson's, and Johnson was strongly attracted to Herbert Brownell, Dewey's southern campaign manager. Johnson campaigned for the unsuccessful Dewey ticket in Alabama, serving as state chairman of a Republican veterans organization. When Dewey and his key supporters backed General Eisenhower against Senator Robert Taft of Ohio at the 1952 convention, Johnson went along.

> After Dewey joined the forces to keep Taft from getting the nomination, Brownell went with him and so did all the old Dewey people we'd been in the nest with for a long time, and it was just natural that we would, too. We didn't think Taft would be good for the country. We thought he was just too conservative to make the necessary progress that we thought ought to be made. . . . Taft was pretty well an isolationist in foreign policy and we didn't like that either. We had lot rather bought Wendell Willkie's 'One World' theory than Taft's semi-isolationist viewpoint. The other reason we went with Eisenhower, and this is a real pragmatic reason—all politicians are pretty pragmatic, you know—we thought Eisenhower could get elected and Taft couldn't.[19]

The Alabama delegation split nine to five for Senator Taft at the 1952 convention, until General Eisenhower's nomination was a certainty; but Johnson supported the Eisenhower candidacy from the first. And when Eisenhower was nominated, he was described by one Birmingham newspaper as "one of the strongest of the Republican Ike-likers" in Alabama. By that time, he had become a member of the state Republican committee. In that capacity and as state chairman of Veterans for Eisenhower, he made numerous speeches and performed other services in behalf of the GOP ticket.[20]

Eisenhower's 1952 victory returned the Republicans to the White House for the first time in twenty years, and in each state there was patronage to be dispensed. In Alabama, it was soon obvious that the Eisenhower administration would leave most patronage questions in the hands of Claude O. Vardaman, the state Republican chairman; and Vardaman offered Johnson the post of U.S. attorney for the Northern District of Alabama. Also in Johnson's corner was Eisenhower's new attorney general, Herbert Brownell, a key figure in the selection process because U.S. attorneys are part of the Justice Department.[21]

Initially, Johnson was reluctant to accept the appointment and leave a lucrative law practice. When he finally did agree to accept the administration's offer, he emphasized that for him the appointment was to be temporary. He would take only a two-year leave of absence from the firm; he would not give up his Jasper home but instead would commute to his new office in Birmingham. Above all, he was to be a prime contender for any federal judgeship vacancy arising in Alabama. The Eisenhower people accepted his conditions, and on August 18, 1953, he took the oath of office as U.S. attorney.[22]

Frank Johnson must have been the hardest working U.S. attorney the personnel and clientele of Alabama's Northern District had ever encountered. U.S. attorneys rarely appear in court, leaving the prosecution of cases largely to their assistants. Johnson's predecessor had prosecuted only one case; his successor would prosecute only one. But Johnson personally prosecuted every case he considered important, including a substantial number of bank robbery, liquor, and income tax cases in every part of the district.[23]

Characteristically, he placed a high premium on speed and efficiency. He and Seybourn H. Lynne, the district's chief judge, worked out an elaborate and highly successful plea bargain arrangement under which virtually every defendant with retained counsel would be invited to meet with them prior to trial for a plea negotiation session. Their procedure clearly would violate present federal rules of procedure and probably was somewhat inconsistent with the rules prevailing at the time. But the number of trials was reduced substantially; during one year of Johnson's service, in fact, there were only three trials in all seven of the district's divisions. District operating costs naturally fell well below the national median for comparable districts.[24]

Johnson had not been in office long before what was to become his most significant case as U.S. attorney began to unfold. In early May of 1953, the body of a black tenant farmer was brought to the Weatherly Funeral Home in York, a rural western Alabama community. The body bore evidence of severe beatings, and when local authorities appeared to be taking no action in the case, the black couple who operated the funeral home notified Johnson. He asked FBI agents to investigate, and their investigation revealed that, the Thirteenth Amendment notwithstanding, slavery was not yet dead in rural Alabama.[25]

The dead man was identified as Herbert (Monk) Thompson, a worker on farms owned by Fred Dial, member of a prominent Sumter County family with extensive landholdings on the edge of Alabama's Black Belt. The FBI investigation produced evidence that Fred and certain other members of the Dial family had found an inexpensive source of farm labor. They would go to neighboring Mississippi jails and prison camps, pay the fines of blacks imprisoned for relatively minor offenses, then force them to work in the fields on one of the Dial plantations. Those who attempted to escape or otherwise displeased their masters were beaten. "Monk" Thompson had apparently been the victim of one such beating.

When the FBI investigation had been completed, Johnson sought indictments against seven members of the family, and on September 4, 1953, a grand jury returned a twelve-count indictment charging slavery and involuntary servitude, peonage, the use of interstate travel for such offenses, and conspiracy. Charged in one or more counts were four brothers—Oscar Edwin, Fred Nichle, Grady Clarence, and Robert Mitchell Dial. Also charged were two cousins—Lindsey Winyard Dial and Arnold Dial—and Francis Hopper, a Mississippi relative.[26]

The defendants retained attorney Thomas F. Seale, Jr., of Livingston, the Sumter County seat, to represent them. Their principal defense, however, was to be provided by the firm of Birmingham attorney Roderick Beddow. Beddow, Alabama's preeminent practitioner of criminal law, was a formidable courtroom adversary. His clients over a three-decade career had ranged from Ku Klux Klansmen to a poor black youth whose trial for murdering a prominent white woman required national guard protection.

During preparations for the trial, members of Beddow's firm were invited to the Dial plantations for a deer hunt and became better acquainted with their clients. Beddow's son, Roderick, Jr., then a relatively new member of the firm, recalls that the Dials were a rather wild lot. But they treated their Birmingham visitors royally, feting them with quail for breakfast and other indulgences of gracious plantation living. The visitors in turn were duly impressed with their clients' hospitality and the massive size of their landholdings. Economically, if not culturally, their clients clearly did not fit the stereotype of redneck southern yeomen.[27]

The case was to be tried before Judge Lynne. A 1946 Truman appointee, Lynne was a member of one of northern Alabama's oldest families and one with impeccable confederate credentials. Like most "enlightened" southerners of the day, he believed that segregation was acceptable—even desirable—if equal facilities were provided for both races. He had no sympathy, however, for those who brutalized blacks. Despite marked contrasts in their backgrounds, Lynne and Frank Johnson had a strong affinity for each other. Johnson was learning federal practice in Judge Lynne's court and later would pattern his own courtroom approach as a district judge largely after Judge Lynne's. Lynne greatly admired his young U.S. attorney's legal skill, tenacity, and conscientiousness, remarking more than once that Frank Johnson was "without a doubt the finest U.S. attorney I ever saw in action, without a doubt. He worked real hard."[28]

The Dial case went to trial in Birmingham's white stone federal building on the morning of May 10, 1954. The trial would last five days. In the early 1950s, criminal cases involving white atrocities against blacks in the South rarely attracted extensive public attention, and the Dial case was no exception. Stories about the trial were generally relegated to the inner pages of Birmingham papers, and the case received scant treatment in the national press. Trial sessions were well attended but never packed with spectators. In keeping with his reputation for running a tight courtroom, Judge Lynne maintained firm control over the proceedings and all sessions were orderly. The defendants, well coached by Roderick Beddow, a master at client and witness preparation, were neatly dressed and poised, in appearance the very antithesis of the vicious brutes depicted in the government's indictment.[29]

As the trial began, Beddow announced to the press that a large number of character witnesses, including several state legislators and judges, would appear in his clients' behalf. He also noted that Mississippi U.S. Senator John Stennis, who was acquainted with the defendants, had offered earlier to appear as a defense witness but now would probably be unable to attend the trial because of pressing Washington duties. Both the defense and the government initially planned to call more than 120 witnesses, but Judge Lynne eventually limited the number of witnesses each side could call.[30]

After empaneling of a jury and opening statements by counsel, Frank Johnson began a procession of prosecution witnesses whose testimony painted a grim picture of the defendants and conditions for workers on their plantations. Fred and Oscar, two of the four brothers charged in the case, were mentioned in most counts of the indictment; and the major portion of prosecution testimony related to their treatment of black workers. In fact, on the second day of the trial, Johnson asked that certain counts in the indictment be dismissed for lack of evidence; and this action, coupled with Judge Lynne's earlier severance of the only counts involving Grady Dial and Francis Hopper for later trial, had the effect of removing all defendants but Fred and Oscar from the trial.[31]

Johnson's first prosecution witness was Coy Lee Tanksley, a twenty-four-year-old Klondike, Mississippi, black who had worked on the Dial farms about two and a half months in early 1953, then became ill and was allowed to leave. Tanksley testified that in January of 1953, Oscar Dial had paid $21.25 to secure his release from a Meridian, Mississippi, jail where he was serving a sentence on a public drunkenness charge. He agreed to go to Oscar's Boyd, Alabama, farm and work after Dial promised to "treat me good." Dial, he testified, had promised to pay him $3 a day but never paid him. About a week after his arrival at the farm, moreover, he was beaten for staying out late on a Sunday night. Some three weeks later, Oscar Dial turned from talking to another worker and saw Tanksley looking at him—at that time a serious violation of racial etiquette in the Black Belt South. Tanksley apologized and averted his eyes, but Dial hit him in the head with the singletree from a plow. The black later recovered consciousness in his tenant shack, but shortly thereafter Oscar, Fred Dial, and J. E. Eads, a black worker, came in, put a chain around his neck, and chained him to his bed. Then, Eads, Fred, and Oscar took turns hitting him with a rope. Still later, the three put Tanksley into a truck and took him to the Fred Dial farm where he was beaten further by five persons, then returned to his sleeping quarters where he lay for several days while his wounds healed. One of the beatings was so severe that Fred Dial had carried him to a York physician for treatment.[32]

The testimony of other prosecution witnesses covered events leading up to "Monk" Thompson's death. On March 28, 1953, Fred Dial had gone to Lauderdale County, Mississippi, paid Thompson's $55 fine, and carried him back to Sumter County to work. Thompson had worked at the Fred Dial farm in Boyd until May 7, then attempted to run away. Fred and Oscar caught him and brought him back to a barn on Fred's farm. Fred then held a shotgun on a worker and ordered him to tie Thompson to a bale of hay. When the worker refused, Fred ordered him to hold Thompson while he tied him to the bale. Fred and six black workers then beat Thompson with a rope, and while Fred was beating him, Leon (Red) Rutledge, a teenaged white worker who testified for the prosecution, held a shotgun on the blacks. After the beatings, Fred and Rutledge carried Thompson to a tenant shack where, two days later, he died.[33]

Counts of the indictment eliminated during the trial charged offenses against John Henry Lowe, a black working on the farm of Clarence Dial, the brothers' father. Johnson asked that these counts be dismissed for insufficient evidence, but only after putting before the jury testimony from Lowe and others that Lowe, too, had been whipped.

Johnson completed the government's case on the trial's second day, and the defense team took over. Beddow presented numerous witnesses who attested to the defendants' good character and testified that black workers on the Dial plantations had free run of the farms and the surrounding area and had never complained of mistreatment.

The testimony of character witnesses went relatively well for the defense until J. W. Boyd, an elderly Livingston farmer, took the witness stand in the defendants' behalf. It was Frank Johnson's normal policy not to cross-examine character witnesses because questioning ordinarily simply provided them with further opportunity for extolling the defendant's virtues. In Boyd's case, however, he made an exception. "I got the impression from just watching him," he later said, "that the old gentleman was honest and candid."[34]

Johnson first let Boyd elaborate on the Dial brothers' fine qualities. Yes, he had known Fred and Oscar since they were kids. Yes, he knew their character and reputations and they were fine boys, the salt of the earth. Johnson then moved cautiously into questions about their treatment of blacks on the Dial farms, and finally he asked the witness offhandedly whether Fred and Oscar had reputations for beating their black workers. Amazingly, Boyd replied: "Yes, I've heard about that."[35]

Roderick Beddow was furious. Calling for a recess, he followed the old man into the courtroom corridor, collared him, and cried: "You old son of a bitch! I told all you witnesses this morning that if you knew anything bad about the Dial boys to tell me. I knew Frank Johnson would bring it out." "But Mr. Beddow," the crestfallen old man replied with an innocence reflecting his heritage, "whupping a nigger ain't bad in Sumter County."[36]

Defense efforts to challenge evidence that "Monk" Thompson had died as a result of beatings ultimately proved equally disastrous for the brothers. Nelson Grubb, a state toxicologist, had performed an autopsy on Thompson's body at the funeral home in York two days after the black worker's death. He testified for the defense that pneumonia was the immediate cause of death but that Thompson's body bore deep gashes on the front of the legs and a four-by-eight-inch bruise on the left hip. The leg wounds, Grubb said, could have been caused by beatings with a wire or similar material, but none of the marks, in his judgment, had been made with a rope. Under questioning by defense counsel, he suggested, in fact, that the marks on Thompson's body could have been the result not of beatings but of "skin slippage," the pulling apart of skin and flesh caused by body deterioration after death. (In a grim variation on Grubb's theory, someone connected with the case would facetiously suggest years after the trial that "that's all it was, just a little slippage. That black had been swimming, he'd swum too long, and his skin just sort of roughed up from the swimming.")[37]

Johnson and Roderick Beddow had a strong mutual attraction, and each considered the other a strong courtroom adversary. But Johnson was singularly unimpressed with the skin slippage thesis ("All that was hogwash. Rod Beddow's capable of better than that"). During cross-examination he proceeded to demolish the theory with ammunition Grubb had supplied. No elaborate questioning of the witness was required. Instead, Johnson simply introduced into evidence three grisly photographs Grubb had taken of Thompson's body during the autopsy and circulated them among the jurors. The photos demonstrated clearly to everyone present, including the defense team, that the dead man had been subjected to a heinous beating shortly before his death.[38]

Again Beddow had been caught off guard. At that time, the federal rules for evidence discovery were extremely restrictive, and he had not seen the photos until they were introduced into evidence. The Dial brothers had repeatedly assured him, moreover, that they had not beaten Thompson. After the court session ended for the day, Beddow stormed back to his office in a rage and called Fred and Oscar in for an all-night session. He told his clients that he could provide them an adequate defense only if they told him the truth and urged them to be candid with him. But Fred and Oscar continued to protest their innocence, asserting repeatedly that the marks on Thompson's body must have been caused by skin slippage, that they had not beaten him.[39]

The remaining defense testimony was designed primarily to discredit prosecution witnesses. Fred and Oscar took the witness stand and denied all charges. Mrs. Oscar Dial testified that Coy Tanksley had been cursing drunkenly around her and her children, and when he refused her husband's order to stop, Oscar had hit him with a stick. Like her husband, though, Mrs. Dial denied that Oscar had beaten Tanksley with a singletree. W. C. Temple, a Mississippi jail guard, said that Thompson had wanted to go to Alabama with Fred Dial. John Ivory, a black defense witness, testified that he once had gone with Fred Dial and two other persons to Mobile to return John Henry Lowe to the Dial farms, but said that he understood Lowe had written the Dials earlier that he wanted to return.[40]

On cross-examination, Johnson continued to chip away at defense testimony. Pressing Ivory for details about Lowe's return to the farms from Mobile, for example, he asked at one point: "Was he promised that if he returned he would not be whipped?" "No, sir," Ivory answered, revealing more about his employers than he—or Beddow—had perhaps intended, "I'd told Mr. Clarence [Clarence Dial, father of the defendants] that if they was going to whip him, I wasn't going along. He said they wouldn't whip Lowe." (Earlier, Lowe and other government witnesses had testified that he was beaten with a rope after being brought back to the farms from Mobile.)[41]

In closing arguments to the jury, defense counsel attacked weaknesses in the prosecution's case and the credibility of government witnesses, several of whom had jail records. Beddow's associate Robert Gwin also complained about the timing of Johnson's request that two counts in the indictment be dropped for inadequate evidence—a request made only after two days of prosecution testimony, some of which related to the dropped charges. Accusing the government of "taking a weak case and trying to bolster it by indicting everyone in the neighborhood named Dial," Gwin asserted that Johnson had used the additional charges simply as "window dressing" to get damaging testimony before the jury that could not otherwise have been introduced. To their credit, however, the defense team largely avoided the sort of jury race-baiting that could well have been expected in such a case. "Beddow defended the case on a high plane," Johnson later remarked.[42]

Judge Lynne had allowed each side an hour for final arguments in the case, and Johnson made a strong summation, putting the issues, one official later recalled, "right on the line." He devoted much of his allotted time to impressing upon the all-white jury its obligation to return a verdict based solely on the evidence. "The victims in this case can't protect themselves," he told the jurors, "because of their positions in society." Only the government could protect them; only the jury could provide redress for the abuses to which they had been subjected. Nor, he added, should the jail records of two of the victims affect the jurors' deliberations. "That is the kind of people you might expect would be victims. The Government will never be asked to defend people like yourselves, or me, from slavery or involuntary servitude."[43]

In a forceful charge to the jury, Judge Lynne also stressed the jurors' ultimate duty in the case. Characterizing the federal statutes on which the charges had been based as "a wonderful guarantee for the dignity of the individual," Lynne cautioned the jurors: "If you do believe the defendants are guilty of one of the offenses charged in this indictment beyond a reasonable doubt, then I think it may be fairly observed that such flagrant violations of the law and such shameless inhumanity and brutality, such base dishonor to American citizenship can be deliberately practiced in a civilized and Christian community by intelligent men, is a reproach to our civilization. It's a challenge for instant and vigorous protest and action by all right-minded men."[44]

The case went to the jury at 2:30 P. M. on Thursday, May 13. While the jury was beginning its deliberations, Johnson strolled out into the courtroom corridor and found Roderick Beddow and his clients sitting on a bench. Ordinarily, given the contrasts in the protagonists' race and station, the odds would have weighed heavily against conviction. But Johnson had built a good case, and his summation to the jury, like Judge Lynne's charge, had been exceptionally strong. Then, too, there were the damning photographs of the pathetic "Monk" Thompson's battered body. The defendants and their counsel had considerable cause for concern.

Nevertheless, Beddow was in a playful mood. "Frank," he said with a malicious smile playing across his face, "Oscar and Fred don't have any hard feelings toward you. They know you had a job to do, and you did it and you did it fair. In fact, to show you they have no hard feelings, they're having a deer hunt down on their plantation, and they want you to come down as their invited guest. They want to take you out in the woods deer hunting with them." Johnson laughed—and declined the invitation.[45]

Late the following night, after more than fifteen hours of deliberation, the jury announced that it had reached a verdict. Fred and Oscar were found guilty of involuntary servitude, Fred alone of forcing "Monk" Thompson into peonage. Fred faced a maximum sentence of fifteen years, Oscar a ten-year sentence. Both men were subject to a maximum of $5,000 in fines.

After the verdict had been rendered but before sentencing, a number of prominent Sumter County citizens urged Judge Lynne to place Fred and Oscar on probation. Lynne rejected probation for the defendants but did agree to allow them to serve their sentences at different times. In that way, one brother could continue to manage the family's extensive farm holdings while the other was away in prison. Since Fred was being treated for a malignant growth on an ear, Oscar was scheduled to serve his sentence first.[46]

On December 16, Judge Lynne sentenced both men to eighteen months in the federal prison at Tallahassee, Florida. Lynne had been firmly convinced of the brothers' guilt and outraged at the brutality of their offenses. The light sentences meted in the case are thus somewhat difficult to explain. They may have been influenced by Lynne's own cultural and racial biases, the state toxicologist's finding that pneumonia had been the immediate cause of "Monk" Thompson's death, or any number of other factors. But the lenient sentences probably simply reflected Judge Lynne's feeling that Clarence Dial, the clan patriarch, who had died while the case was pending, was in a sense the real culprit in the case, not his sons. Courtroom gossip circulated during the trial and portions of the government testimony had depicted the elder Dial as a harsh taskmaster who had the habit of riding horseback over his domain, whip in hand, administering summary punishment to any worker caught lazing or otherwise misbehaving. Judge Lynne was convinced that, indirectly at least, Fred and Oscar were largely following their father's instructions in their treatment of blacks on the Dial farms.[47]

Ultimately, only Oscar Dial ever went to prison in the case. Oscar developed an exemplary prison record, but the federal board of pardon and parole denied his petition for parole. The chairman of the board at the time was a black and, given the nature of the defendant's offense, he was adamant that Oscar serve his full sentence. Angered by the board's posture, Judge Lynne, on May 1, 1956, set aside Fred's sentence and placed him on five years' probation. Untried counts in the indictment were dismissed at Frank Johnson's recommendation in January of 1955. The last item in the court record of the case was filed in September 1961, when Oscar Dial, who had interfered with the enjoyment of basic citizenship rights by others, wrote the clerk of the Northern District as an ex-felon seeking assistance in recovering his own.[48]

The convictions in the Dial case represented one of the very few occasions since Reconstruction that white defendants in Alabama had been convicted of subjecting blacks to involuntary servitude. Ironically, had the timing of the trial been slightly different, the Dials might not have been convicted. On May 17, just three days after the jury's verdict in the Dial case, the Supreme Court announced its "Black Monday" decision in *Brown* v. *Board of Education*, outlawing segregation in public schools. Roderick Beddow insisted that had the Alabama case gone to the jury after the *Brown* decision rather than before, his clients would never have been convicted. As the experiences of Frank Johnson and others to be caught up in the cause of racial justice in Alabama would soon suggest, he was probably right.[49]

The Judgeship

Each state has from one to four federal judicial districts with a U.S. district court and one or more judges exercising jurisdiction in each. Augmenting Alabama's Northern District are the Southern and Middle Districts. Despite the labels, the territory of both the latter districts extends from the central portion of the state to its southern border, with the Middle District covering twenty-three counties in southeastern Alabama. The Middle District is predominantly rural. Though small towns with such exotic sounding names as Dothan, Opelika, Wetumpka, Tuskegee, and Clio dot its landscape, Montgomery is its only major city. In the mid-1950s, the black population of the district's counties ranged from 13.2 percent in Geneva County to 84.4 percent in Macon, with the counties of lowest nonwhite population situated in the extreme northern portion of the district and in the wiregrass region along its southern border. Six counties in the district had a nonwhite population of over 50 percent; of these, three were clearly deserving of Black Belt status both in terms of soil texture and the size of their black populations: Macon, with the largest percentage of blacks among the state's counties; Lowndes (82.2 percent black), and Bullock (73.6 percent).

Montgomery is the seat of the Middle District. In the 1950s, Montgomery's population numbered well over a hundred thousand, yet it retained a small-town atmosphere. Its major landmark in the heart of the downtown business district was Court Square, once the site of the county courthouse, and earlier the location for the city's principal slave block. Within easy walking distance of the square were the city's centers of commerce and government; and several blocks up Dexter Avenue, high atop Goat Hill, were Alabama's Greek Revival capitol and other state office buildings. Culturally and psychologically the city had remained the "Cradle of the Confederacy." Like the rest of the Middle District and the South of the 1950s, its public life and much of its private life were thoroughly segregated. Less than 10 percent of its voting-age blacks were registered to vote.

When Frank Johnson was appointed U.S. attorney, the Middle District court had been presided over for almost a quarter century by Judge Charles Brents Kennamer. Johnson's career had paralleled Judge Kennamer's in a number of ways. A north Alabamian, Kennamer was an active Republican who had been a delegate to the party's national conventions in 1916, 1920, 1924, and 1928. One Republican president had appointed him U.S. attorney for the Northern District in 1922, another to the Middle District court in 1931. When Judge Kennamer died in early 1955, Johnson sought to take the parallels one step further by seeking the vacant judgeship.

Support for Johnson's selection came from a variety of sources. Remembering his promise that the young U.S. attorney would be a top contender for any federal judgeship vacancy, Claude Vardaman announced to the press shortly after Kennamer's death that Johnson was "far and away the leading" contender for the vacant seat. Vardaman worked hard to secure the appointment for Johnson, and GOP national committeeman Marvin Mostellar of Mobile also endorsed his selection. Among state party officials, however, the most loyal was the party's secretary-treasurer Oscar Drake of Haleyville, a longtime family friend, fellow mountain Republican, and Dewey-Eisenhower man.[1]

A brochure was prepared listing Johnson's qualifications, and his home in Jasper became a makeshift campaign headquarters. Drake and Ruth Johnson stuffed envelopes and mailed the brochure and other supportive material to party leaders throughout the state. The campaign was effective. Johnson eventually received the endorsement of most of Alabama's GOP leadership, including 95 percent of the state party committee's membership. At the U.S. Justice Department, through which federal judicial appointments are processed, Attorney General Brownell could also be counted on for support, given the two men's earlier political ties and Brownell's growing admiration for Johnson's record as U.S. attorney.[2]

Johnson's Justice Department file was soon filled with supportive letters from judges before whom he had practiced, fellow attorneys, and other prominent Alabamians.[3] Lecil Gray did his part, too. When the Justice Department received few supportive letters from the Middle District, Judge Gray persuaded a number of his fellow probate judges in the district to submit enthusiastic endorsements of Johnson's candidacy. Needless to say, they were none too pleased with Gray when the candidate they had so strongly endorsed at their colleague's request began rendering liberal decisions in civil rights cases. At the time, however, his effort helped to lend an appearance, at least, of Middle District support for the appointment.[4]

Opposition to Johnson's appointment came essentially from supporters of other contenders for the vacancy and from Middle District residents who opposed the appointment of any northern Alabamian to the post. A number of Republicans, including Judge Kennamer's son Ralph, who had been clerk of his father's court, made at least a token effort to secure the appointment. Probably the most active of the Republican contenders, however, was J. Foy Guin of Russellville, vice-chairman of the state GOP and a northern Alabamian. But there were two major obstacles to Guin's appointment: he was too old for the job, and he—and his principal backer, GOP national committeeman Curtis Atkins—had made the mistake of supporting Senator Taft in 1952.[5]

Johnson also had to contend with the aspirations of the "Eisenhower Democrats." In an effort to enlarge the GOP's narrow southern voting base, Eisenhower strategists had made a significant effort to woo the votes of Democrats disenchanted with their national party's social policies. In 1952, Eisenhower Democrats turned out in impressive numbers to support the general, and after the election their leadership struggled with the Republican "regulars" in the South for a share of federal patronage. Certain GOP organizations made an effort, however, to attract the continued support of dissident Democrats; and when Judge Kennamer died, the Montgomery County Republican committee endorsed Eisenhower Democrat Thomas Bowen Hill, a prominent Montgomery attorney with solid social and professional credentials who also was a cousin of Lister Hill, Alabama's senior U.S. senator.

Given the influence senators of a president's party have over selections to federal district judgeships, T. B. Hill's relationship to the senator, under different circumstances, might have enhanced his chances for appointment. But Senator Hill was not of the appointing president's party; in fact, he was one of Eisenhower's more aggressive Senate critics. More significantly, he was a loyal Democrat who viewed the Eisenhower Democrat movement with considerable distaste; he and John Sparkman, Alabama's junior senator, had vowed to oppose the appointment of any turncoat Democrat to federal office. Finally, Senator Hill's relations with his cousin had been strained since the 1940s. When asked by reporters what candidate he was supporting for the position, the senator replied that the appointment was entirely in the hands of the Republican administration, adding: "I am not going to make any comment on any of the candidates." When reminded that his cousin was among the hopefuls, he gave the same response.[6]

Johnson's appointment was also opposed by those in the Middle District who believed that a native son—or at the very least a resident of the district—should be tapped as Judge Kennamer's replacement. Traditionally, Alabama politics has been characterized by intense political rivalry between northern and southern Alabama, and to Montgomerians, as one distinguished member of the city's bar would explain years after the fight over Judge Kennamer's seat, "anything just north of Montgomery is north Alabama." Shortly after Claude Vardaman announced that Johnson was the leading contender for the vacant position, the Montgomery Advertiser, which had endorsed Eisenhower in 1952, published a stinging rejoinder that brought the issue of regional bias into sharp focus. Complaining that Johnson was largely unknown in the Middle District, the *Advertiser* urged appointment of a "Middle District lawyer whose attainments are beyond controversy," and warned: "If in spite of public opinion, we get Johnson, the ADVER-TISER will consider that it has Vardaman's word for it that in Alabama the Republican Party is still just a game of post office. We shall bear the hoots as best we can."[7]

From the perspective of the GOP's continued development in Alabama, appointment of an Eisenhower Democrat and resident of the Middle District to the vacancy probably made good political sense. But Claude Vardaman and other northern Alabama Republican regulars had waited a long time for a chance at presidential patronage, and they had no desire to share the major spoils of office with Johnny-come-late-lys. Vardaman was insistent, moreover, that Johnson be the Republican beneficiary of the party's most recent patronage opportunity. Since the FBI's security check had produced no skeletons in Johnson's closet, and Attorney General Brownell enthusiastically endorsed his appointment, the issue was settled. Announcement of the appointment ultimately was simply a matter of time.[8]

Through the summer and early fall of 1955, the Eisenhower administration took no action on the appointment, in part because the president was stricken with a serious heart illness. Oscar Drake and Johnson's other supporters were reasonably confident that the appointment was forthcoming, but as the weeks passed they became increasingly discouraged. Then, on October 22, Attorney General Brownell conferred with the recuperating president in a Denver hospital. After the meeting, Brownell announced to the press that the first of a series of documents signed by the president that day—the first since his illness, in fact—was Johnson's appointment as judge for the Middle District. At thirty-seven, Frank Johnson would become the nation's youngest federal judge.[9]

On November 7, Judge Lynne administered the oath of office at installation ceremonies in Montgomery. Before his family and several hundred well-wishers, federal and state jurists welcomed their young colleague into the judicial fraternity and praised his "outstanding war record," "patriotism," and "maturity of experience." For his part, Johnson quoted President Eisenhower's admonition that "when the people . . . lose faith in [the] courts, they have lost faith in [the] country" and dedicated himself to the "high ideals of the courts."[11]

By law, the Senate must confirm all presidential nominations to federal district judgeships, but the president may make temporary recess appointments when the Senate is not in session. Since Attorney General Brownell had announced Johnson's selection after Senate adjournment, his first months on the bench were served under the recess arrangement. When Congress reconvened in January of 1956, however, his appointment was quickly confirmed without debate either in the Judiciary Committee or on the Senate floor.

By this time, of course, Judge Johnson and his family had begun adapting to life in Montgomery. Like other upwardly mobile newcomers, they joined the Montgomery Country Club and established a church membership with his parents' congregation at the First Baptist Church. They also purchased a home, an unpretentious but spacious and comfortable red brick on Haardt Drive in the city's southern section. Over the years, real estate values in the neighborhood would steadily decline as "marginal" (that is, black) residential housing moved closer and closer to the area; but when the Johnsons first moved to Montgomery, the neighborhood was considered prime residential property. More important, Bellingrath public school, which Johnny would attend during their first years in Montgomery, was only a stone's throw away, and the neighborhood was filled with young children— twenty-two by one count. Johnson's parents lived on Southmont Drive, a few blocks away.[12]

Especially during the Johnsons' early years in Montgomery, the neighborhood was the scene of frequent parties, and although the atmosphere cooled somewhat after Judge Johnson's civil rights stance became apparent, he and Mrs. Johnson established enduring friendships with a number of neighbors. Their circle of friends would extend, however, well beyond their immediate neighborhood. Even before his civil rights decisions began to strain his relations with certain segments of the community, Johnson attempted to limit his contacts with members of the local bar to avoid any appearance of impropriety. But he and Mrs. Johnson would number among their closer friends several local attorneys and their families, including former law clerks who established practices in the Montgomery area. Over the years, they also developed a growing number of friendships with those in the community who sympathized with the judge's decisions, including Earl Pippen, a Montgomery lobbyist who for years was a leader in the Alabama AFL-CIO, and Ray Jenkins, a Montgomery journalist who has given the judge's decisions thoughtful—though not always sympathetic—coverage for almost two decades. Ironically, however, one of Judge Johnson's closest Montgomery friends was to be a wealthy funeral home operator, who was years the judge's senior and had little interest in politics or law. Sam Durden had been one of Judge Lynne's college classmates, and when Johnson was installed as district judge, Lynne invited Durden to attend the ceremony and asked that Durden help the Johnsons get settled in Montgomery. Over the years, Durden and Judge Johnson developed a comfortable relationship, occasionally attending football games together, having dinner, or relaxing for a Sunday after-

noon of games on the judge's television. Though not always sympathetic with Judge Johnson's racial decisions ("You know how we
southerners feel"), Durden became one of Johnson's most ardent defenders. The affection was mutual. "I soon discovered," Judge Johnson
has remarked, "that Sam Durden didn't want anything from me and
would never ask me for anything, that all he was looking for was
friendship. I buy that sort of thing."[13]

Beyond their friends, the Johnsons would also have the company of
the Johnson clan. Along with his parents, Jimmy Johnson had moved to
Montgomery in 1946, where he began a series of small loan operations
and other profitable business ventures. In time, Ellen Ruth would also
move to Montgomery with her husband, an Alabama Power Company
executive. For some years, Wallace Johnson practiced law there and
lobbied for small loan interests at the capitol.[14]

Finally, of course, there were Judge Johnson's court personnel. With
the exception of U.S. attorneys and federal marshals, their assistants
and deputies, district judges, as a form of patronage, appoint the
magistrates, clerks, bailiffs, court criers, secretarial staff, and other
personnel attached to their courts. Especially in the beginning, Johnson
filled a number of positions with Winston County friends; and in early
January of 1959, his boyhood friend Lee Dodd became a bailiff, court
crier, and special deputy marshal at the court, remaining with him over
a decade. Like Dodd, other members of Judge Johnson's staff have been
extremely loyal. Leon Hopper, now a bankruptcy judge attached to the
court, had worked with the judge in Birmingham and went with him to
Montgomery in 1955. The judge's first secretary, Helen Cosper, had
been his secretary in Birmingham and would serve him in that capacity
in Montgomery until her retirement in the early 1970s. Her replacement, Dorothy Perry, would be equally loyal and protective. The
judge's principal court reporter, Glynn Henderson, was also with him
almost from the beginning. When Judge Johnson was first appointed,
Henderson was a reporter in the Georgia court system who occasionally
filled in as the judge's reporter when he was on temporary assignment
in Atlanta. In 1957, he went with the judge permanently. At one point,
a member of the marshal's office resigned in protest over Judge Johnson's civil rights rulings, moved to Mississippi, and began selling
Volkswagens. But that incident stands in marked contrast to the obvious loyalty and devotion of most of his personnel—feelings that clearly
run much more deeply than their patronage ties to the court.[15]

Rounding out a district judge's official family are his law clerks—recent law graduates who do research, digest case files, draft opinions,
and perform related services for their judge. Until 1971, Judge Johnson
was authorized one clerk a year, after that, two. Some served for two
years, but the normal tenure has been one year. Most have been male,

but some of his very best clerks have been women. Most were drawn from his alma mater, particularly during his first years on the bench. As his reputation grew, however, applications began to flow in from campuses across the country, and a larger number were selected from Yale, Stanford, and other prestigious schools. Successful candidates were chosen for their outstanding academic performance and typing skills. A few minutes after offering him a clerkship, one former clerk recalls, "Judge called me back and said, 'I forgot to ask you, can you type?' and I said, 'Oh yeah, I sure can.' Never had typed a damn thing in my life. Immediately went out and enrolled in a typing course. I later found out that the clerk who preceded me did not type, and the judge swore he'd never hire another law clerk who couldn't type." Usually, he has been successful in ferreting out the nontypists.[16]

The daily work routine which Judge Johnson established early in his career varied little over the years. He arrives at his office in Montgomery's federal building, handiwork of a Depression-era public works project, shortly after seven each morning—and expects his staff to begin the work day early. When court is not in session, he devotes much of each day to reviewing briefs and memorandums submitted by law clerks, writing opinions, and conducting in-chambers conferences with attorneys involved in pending litigation. Proceedings in his large, ornate courtroom were normally broken into fifty-minute sessions, followed by ten-minute recesses. For a variety of reasons, including a distaste for restaurant food, he generally goes home for lunch; and each work day ends around 5:30. Remarkably, in view of the sheer volume of his caseload, he rarely takes work home in the evening or on weekends.[17]

From the beginning, Judge Johnson's opinion-drafting habits have varied with the circumstances. On occasion, he writes opinion drafts out in longhand; more often, he dictates brief opinions directly to his secretary and longer ones into a dictaphone, later polishing a typed draft into final form. Some of his more eloquent opinions, however, have been delivered verbally from the bench immediately following completion of a hearing. At times, he has allowed law clerks to draft opinions and, on rare occasions, has adopted a clerk's version as his own, with only minor revisions. One clerk began his duties, for example, shortly before the judge ordered reinstatement of a Montgomery high school teacher dicharged for assigning her students a short story by Kurt Vonnegut. "I hadn't been there ten minutes," the clerk remembers, "and Judge Johnson said, 'I'm going out of town; I want you to draft an opinion.' And I said, 'Well, is there any particular way you want me to go,' and he said, 'Not really, but I want the teacher to have her job back,' or something to that effect." The clerk had once worked with the general counsel to the National Education Association and had a strong grounding in teacher rights litigation. Judge Johnson accepted his draft with no substantive changes; the teacher got her job back.[18]

From the beginning, the judge's opinions tended to be brief, formal, generally lacking in literary flair. More significantly, they were confined largely to detailed findings of fact and legal conclusions, rarely revealing to any extensive degree their author's reasoning processes. Partly, this pattern was designed to insulate his rulings from reversal, but it also was a consequence of his heavy caseload and his conviction that parties before a district judge are "not entitled to a dissertation" on the legal questions at issue.[19]

Judge Johnson's judicial duties were not confined to Montgomery. The Middle District is divided into three divisions, and court is held not only in the division encompassing Montgomery, but also in Opelika (for the eastern division) and Dothan (for the southern division). Until 1971, he held court twice a year in Opelika and Dothan. In that year, the Middle District received an additional judge, Robert Varner, and Varner took over the Opelika duties in addition to a share of the Montgomery caseload. Especially in the early years, Johnson was also frequently called to temporary duty on district courts in Georgia, Florida, Mississippi, and the District of Columbia, hearing in Miami, for example, the income tax trial of heavyweight boxer Ingemar Johansson. On many occasions, too, he sat on three-judge panels of the Court of Appeals for the Fifth Circuit, whose vast appellate jurisdiction includes the federal district courts of Alabama and other Deep South states; and in 1972, Chief Justice Warren Burger appointed him to the Temporary Emergency Court of Appeals, a tribunal established to hear disputes over federal wage and price regulations. Finally, as a member of the federal judicial bureaucracy, he was assigned a number of administrative and related duties. In 1969, for example, Chief Justice Burger named him to a three-man ethics committee set up to oversee the off-the-bench earnings of lower federal court judges.[20]

Shortly after coming to the Middle District, Judge Johnson instituted a number of administrative reforms designed to enhance the court's efficiency and professionalism. The clerk's office was reorganized, modern docket procedures introduced, and trained probation officers recruited. In contrast to the freewheeling approach he had developed with Judge Lynne in the Northern District, plea bargaining in his court was severely restricted. Federal prosecutors are allowed to drop certain charges against a defendant in exchange for a guilty plea to other counts; beyond this, plea negotiations were taboo in the Middle District.[21]

Within his first few years of service, Judge Johnson had acquired a reputation as a hardworking, efficient, fair jurist who ran his court the way a court should be run. He was rarely reversed and developed a remarkable record for expediting his caseload. Invariably, lawyers found him well prepared. Hearings and in-chambers conferences always began on time. Tardy jurors and witnesses would receive stern lectures about citizen responsibility in a constitutional democracy, then be told: "There's one other point I want to make to you. Don't you ever be late to this court again without an acceptable reason." On at least one occasion, a poorly prepared government lawyer was abruptly interrupted by the judge's apology to the jury "for the obvious ill-preparation of this case by the prosecuting attorney." On the bench, he never used a gavel to maintain order; his voice always had the desired effect.[22]

Until required to, he ordinarily refused to wear a robe in his courtroom, but looked every bit the judge nevertheless. Initially, he was attired almost invariably in black suit, white shirt, and black tie, succumbing only in later years to shirts and ties with a touch of color and pattern and suits in rakish gray or dark blue. His erect bearing and rugged physical features enhanced his judicial image. After several years on the bench, he began wearing half-moon reading glasses in his chambers and on the bench. Peering over those glasses, he would have a sobering effect on more than one attorney.

An advocate long active in Middle District civil liberties cases has captured the scene in Johnson's court very colorfully.

> Nobody like him in America. No courtroom I've ever been in that's run as well. No courtroom I'm prouder to be in. . . . If he says you're going to be there at eight o'clock that doesn't mean one minute to eight, or one minute after eight. It means eight o'clock. It's simple. He just means what he says when he says it. You don't talk in Frank Johnson's courtroom. You stand up when you talk to Frank Johnson. But he's no tyrant. He sets no higher standards for lawyers and witnesses in his court than he sets for himself. And . . . that's the way it ought to be. It's business, the people's business, and he conducts it like the people's business. Ain't no deals in Frank Johnson's courtroom. Nobody ever walks up to the bench and whispers in Frank Johnson's court like they do in every other court in the country. No whispering in that courtroom. Everybody hears it. You can hear it on the back row, every damned word that's said. Early in my career, my clients would see me up at the bench whispering with a judge, and say, "You wuddn't up there selling me out with the judge, was you?" I became sensitive to that at a very early age, and his is the only courtroom in which, by God, all the public's business is conducted in public. That's the way it ought to be. If you could design every court in America on Frank Johnson's court, you wouldn't hear the words "judicial reform." There wouldn't be any need for judicial reform if everybody ran their courts like Frank Johnson does.[23]

Nor was there any hint of scandal in the operations of his court. For a time, his brother Wallace practiced before him, and rumors soon began

circulating that Wallace was assuring potential clients special treatment in Middle District cases if they would retain him as counsel.
When Judge Johnson learned that the rumors were accurate, he barred
his brother from all practice in his court. Later, Wallace was convicted
on federal charges of conspiracy to transport stolen automobiles interstate and served a brief prison sentence. He has been in and out of
veterans hospitals with a variety of physical and psychological problems and now lives in Texas; he has severed almost all ties with his
family.[24]

Almost from the beginning, of course, there were complaints about
the way Judge Johnson ran his court, particularly from those alarmed at
his decisions in controversial civil rights cases. Some contended that
the judge's quest for speed and efficiency at times denied attorneys an
adequate opportunity to develop their cases. Others complained of
general highhandedness. GOP Congressman William Dickinson, a beneficiary of the 1964 Goldwater landslide in Alabama, now serves the
Montgomery area in the U.S. House of Representatives. During Judge
Johnson's early years in the Middle District, however, Dickinson held a
state judgeship; and while he believes that the judge has "mellowed"
somewhat over the years, his recollections of Johnson's initial judicial
style are far from positive.

> Hell, we'd have a regular court session set—it's set by statute—and I'd
> hold court as prescribed. Well, he knew that we had court at a certain
> time, but it didn't make any difference to him. He'd subpoena jurors that
> maybe would be on my venire, and he wouldn't excuse them. They were
> supposed to be in two places at one time. There was just very little
> consideration shown at that time. . . . One of the things that he did when
> he first started, . . . he'd get involved in the settlement of cases, and just
> tell one side, "If you get more than such and so, I'll give a remittitur and
> reduce the amount of the judgment," and tell the other side, "If you don't
> pay him this amount of money, I'm gonna direct a verdict against you."
> He just got the parties together and wouldn't even give them a chance to
> try the case![25]

Whatever the weight of such complaints, press profiles served largely
to enhance his developing "larger than life" image as a tough, fair-
minded, no-nonsense, uncompromising "super judge." As early as
1959, Time magazine noted that he had "inherited the nickname
'Straight Edge' from his great-grandfather, Fayette County's first Republican sheriff and a man widely known for his directness and sharpcut-
ting edge. . . . Johnson inherited the traits as well as the name." Over
the years, moreover, numerous profiles quoted the observation of an
Alabama attorney who said of the judge: "If you have a good case, you
don't have to worry. The judge will rule with you. If you don't have a
case you don't have to worry either. He'll throw it out before you

unpack your briefcase." Nor, seemingly, would the journalists ever tire of describing the way, early in his career, he had summarily dealt with a form of racial injustice in his own arena. On one occasion, four blacks and a white were on trial for stealing peanuts owned by the Commodity Credit Corporation from a warehouse. The white defendant, who had hired the blacks to load the peanuts on his truck, was acquitted, but the blacks were convicted. Judge Johnson could have imposed a five-year sentence on the convicted blacks, but instead sentenced them to thirty minutes in the custody of the U.S. marshal, just time enough for them to get their belongings together and leave. The U.S. attorney's office concurred in the token sentence because the white man had been absolved of all guilt and the blacks' guilt had hinged on his. Repeatedly, through the years—with occasional variations and embellishments—the press would recount this refusal of "the court and the prosecutor . . . to be the instrument of rank injustice."[26]

A very private person, Judge Johnson rarely granted interviews with reporters. The statements that he did make, however, were entirely compatible with his developing public image. Confronted by a newsman with the popular impression that he was "tough as hell—but fair," he responded, "I'll stand on that." For those who charged that his liberal decisions in racial cases were a reflection of his personal predilections, or complained because his rulings did not mirror the racial sentiments of most white southerners, he provided journalists with ready retorts. "I'm not a segregationist," he once remarked, "but I'm no crusader either. I don't make the law. I don't create the facts. I just interpret the law." And when journalists exhausted their supply of his statements, they could use the paperweight inscription on the desk in his chambers, a quotation from Abraham Lincoln: "I'll do the very best I know how—the very best I can; and I mean to keep doing so until the end. If the end brings me out all right, what is said against me won't amount to anything. If the end brings me out wrong, ten angels swearing I was right would make no difference."[27]

On at least one occasion, the judge's image may have prompted his assignment to conduct a bizarre criminal prosecution in another district. In 1958, one Dock Perry Glenn and several henchmen were indicted on federal charges arising out of a scheme to fake automobile accidents in Georgia and file fraudulent insurance claims. A Fifth Circuit panel reversed the defendants' first convictions, and the cases were set for retrial. During the first round of proceedings, however, several judges connected with the case and their families had been subjected to an intensive campaign of harassment, including threatening phone calls and letters, and the elderly judge who had presided at the first trial refused to continue. The chief judge of the Fifth Circuit asked Judge Johnson to preside. The judge agreed, and he and some of his staff members journeyed to Tallahassee, Florida, for the trial. Before the trial began, however, he established some ground rules with Glenn and his counsel. "Judge called the ring-tail leader of that gang into his chambers," Lee Dodd recalls. "I was present and the court reporter. A record was made of it. . . . Judge told him that several of the judges' families had been harassed by him and his gang, and he told him that the first harassment that he and his family got, he was going to have to deal with him personally, that he wasn't going to put up with it."[28]

From the first, Glenn refused to cooperate with his court-appointed attorneys, criticized counsel for the other defendants, and filed several motions on his own. He also mailed inflammatory letters to his attorneys' families and finally persuaded Judge Johnson to discharge his counsel (probably to their everlasting relief) and let him conduct his own defense. There was no harassment of Judge Johnson or his family, however, and the Fifth Circuit upheld the second set of convictions against numerous challenges—including Glenn's complaint that he had been denied benefit of counsel![29]

His stern courtroom style and superficial journalistic profiles combined to suggest that Judge Johnson was not only efficient and uncompromising, but also cold and aloof. In public and with strangers, he was reserved, almost guarded, in demeanor. But his friends and co-workers found the private man entirely human. He enjoyed golf and bowling with friends; continued his love for carpentry and woodwork, handcrafting items of furniture and, with Glynn Henderson's help, exquisite grandfather clocks for his home and office; worked with flowers; and got away whenever he could for fishing at Lake Martin and along the Gulf Coast. When his duties carried him away from Montgomery, as they frequently did during his early years on the bench, Lee Dodd and other staff members who joined him found the judge an enjoyable companion. Although he preferred small and intimate parties, he could also be a charming host or guest.[30]

Most of his working day was spent either in the courtroom or in chambers, but he often found time to chat or joke with his co-workers, and his supply of rustic humor from the hills of Winston County seemed inexhaustible. On extremely rare occasions, his humor would find its way into his opinions. In 1962, for example, he tried a suit against Proctor and Gamble for damages growing out of a plaintiff's hypersensitivity to Crest toothpaste, one of the company's leading products. The case was tried before a jury, but Judge Johnson directed a verdict in favor of the defendant company, and the plaintiff filed notice of appeal. After a trial transcript had been filed in the case, James Garrett, the defendant's attorney and a popular Montgomery advocate, asked that part of the transcript be eliminated from the record. Garrett was concerned about portions in which he, and in one instance, a juror, were recorded by the reporter as laughing ("Ha, ha, ha"). The sounds made were not laughter, Garrett insisted, and their presence in the transcript would serve merely to clutter the record on appeal. Judge Johnson denied Garrett's motion with a touch of humor of his own. Far from cluttering the record, he suggested, the challenged portions of the record simply demonstrated Garrett's proficiency "as a past master in the art of suggestive psychology" and "auditory stimulation." Some time later, the *New Yorker* duly noted the incident, in a piece entitled "The Legal (ha ha) Mind at Work."[31]

At least in the court setting, however, Judge Johnson's humanity came through most clearly perhaps in his decisions and in his relationships with his law clerks. His clerks almost invariably left his service with strong feelings of respect bordering on adoration for his knowledge of the law, diligence, courage, integrity, sense of justice, and courtroom presence. "To me," one clerk has said, "he lends more dignity to a courtroom than anybody else I've ever seen. . . . Judge Johnson looks like a judge. He just embodies what a judge ought to be in terms of appearance and demeanor. When you get ordinary guys who are judges, you just don't have the same feeling in the courtroom. Just watching him, you have the feeling that you are someplace." He was their friend, father confessor, and—for the rare lazy or sloppy clerk—a stern dutch uncle. "He's almost like a father figure. To me he was. I remember one occasion, he said, 'Now, you can talk to me like a father.' And I did feel like that toward him—and still do. He's godfather to my fourth child."[32]

At times, too, he could extend them a large measure of patience. Howard Mandell, a Montgomery attorney who specializes in civil liberties cases, served as Judge Johnson's clerk for a year beginning in the late spring of 1970. During Mandell's first weeks at the court, the judge, attempting to reduce a heavy backlog of cases, asked him to prepare a memorandum for *Smith v. YMCA*, a suit contesting racial discrimination in the Y's Montgomery operations. Mandell had planned to attend a sister's wedding in Rhode Island that weekend and stop off in New York for a visit with an old girl friend. He had decided to take the *YMCA* file with him to study during the trip. On the ride from the airport in New York, he and his girl friend renewed acquaintances in the back seat of a taxi—and left the case file in the taxi when they arrived at her apartment. Through the weekend, he tried desperately to retrieve the lost file—placing ads in newspapers, offering a reward, notifying the police and the cab company—all to no avail. "I wanted that weekend to last forever, but unfortunately here it was 7:30 Monday morning, and I had to go into the judge's office to explain the situation to him. I knocked on the door very timidly and walked in. He just sat there smiling, said he understood, appreciated my industrious-

ness, called in the clerk and had the lawyers reconstruct the file."
Mandell was amazed at the judge's good-natured, sympathetic reaction.
Only later did he learn that he had been furious over the incident.[33]

If the warm private individual his friends describe is closer to the
true man, however, the hard, cold, aloof public image—an image Judge
Johnson obviously helped to cultivate—probably served him better on
the bench. His rulings in racial cases would strike at the very core of
deeply rooted southern traditions and attitudes—feelings so deeply felt
that an earlier federal affront to them had embroiled the nation in
violent civil war. If such revolutionary rulings were to be enforced, the
judge would have to convince his audience not only that he had the
legal authority to render them, but also the cold-steel fortitude to assure
their compliance.

Bus Boycotts and Pariahs

Judge Johnson's background and personal racial views offered mixed cues to his probable stance in the civil rights cases that flowed into his court soon after his appointment. During his youth, Johnson had accepted racial segregation as one of the realities of southern social life, never really questioning its propriety.

> I wasn't confronted with it like I would have been had I been growing up down in the Black Belt, in Lowndes County or Macon County or some-place like that. I grew up there in the hills of northwest Alabama, and there were maybe fifty or sixty blacks in Winston County. Two or three of them at the most voted. Those that lived there in Haleyville where I grew up as a kid, their parents worked on the railroad, or some of them worked as domestics in the homes that could afford domestics, and there weren't many of those. But we didn't go to school together, we didn't socialize, and it never occurred to me that that was good or bad. It was just there.

Ironically, even today, he includes no blacks among his close social acquaintances—an arrangement calculated in part, perhaps, to inhibit charges of favoritism toward blacks in civil rights cases, but largely simply a reflection of personal preference.[1]

If life in Winston County had insulated Johnson somewhat from the harsher conditions of segregated society, however, its small black population and traditional ties with the Republicans—according to V. O. Key, "historically the party of emancipation, reconstruction, and civil rights for Negroes"[2]—may also have helped to free him from the "Negrophobia" that often afflicted Black Belt whites. Moreover, over the years he had become increasingly sensitive to the injustices con-fronting Alabama blacks. As a boy, he had been shocked by rumors that a black suspected of a crime in neighboring Fayette County had been taken into the swamps and murdered, and he listened with approval as his grandparents told how, as sheriff, his great-grandfather had driven the post–Civil War Ku Klux Klan from Fayette County.

> The Klan came to his house one night while he and his deputies were away. Great-Grandma was there by herself when they rode up on their horses wearing their robes. When she saw they were dressed as klans-men, she pulled the latchstring to the front door in, got a gun and stuck it out the latch hole, and told them her husband was not at home. When he and his deputies came back later that night, she told them she had

recognized one of the riders, a man with a peg leg, and they went out and got him, hung him up over a well, head down, and made him tell who the other members of his organization were. I don't guess they gave him any *Miranda* warnings, or anything, but that broke up the Klan in Fayette County. I don't think they've had one since then.[3]

In college and law school, his racial education had continued. With the possible exception of George Wallace, none of his law school classmates could have been considered racial liberals. But one of them was the son of Judge James E. Horton, a state circuit judge until he sacrificed a promising political future and overturned one set of rape convictions handed the "Scottsboro boys" by Alabama juries in the 1930s. The trials, which became an international symbol of racial injustice in the United States, had no immediate effect on Johnson, who was a teenager during the years the cases were moving through the courts. As a law student, however, he was moved by Judge Horton's courage in the face of political reprisal. His years as an attorney in Jasper had made him acutely aware, moreover, of discrimination against blacks in the courts of Alabama; and his experiences in the Dial peonage case had given him a close look at the horrors of discrimination in its starkest form.[4]

Early in his adult life at least, Johnson had also come to reject completely the notion that blacks are inherently inferior to whites. "I believe people are inferior to me if it's evident in their conduct. Inferior to me if it's evident in some ridiculous philosophy like the philosophy that blacks are inherently inferior. It's people like that I feel are inferior to me, intellectually and morally. But not by reason of their color."[5] The political route he had taken to a federal judgeship had freed him of any necessity even to give lip service to the idea of black inferiority and the virtues of segregation. As an appointed U.S. attorney, he could avoid the race-baiting then required of candidates for southern elective office—rhetoric that might have reinforced any latent racial biases and influenced his later performance on the bench.

In addition, he was influenced by his wife. Until her service with the navy during World War II, Ruth Johnson had never questioned the segregated society in which she lived. One day while stationed in Miami, however, she and a friend had boarded a crowded municipal bus. The friend suggested that they sit in the only vacant seats, next to an elderly black woman. Ruth abruptly refused. She then looked back at the old woman and saw tears streaming down her lined, weary face. That incident had a profound effect on her subsequent racial attitudes. "Even back in the Jasper days," she recalls, "I was known as a 'nigger lover.' A group of friends and I made it possible for the blacks to use the public library, but they wouldn't use it because they were intimidated by the idea. So we built up a block building over in what was called 'nigger quarters' . . . poverty-ridden huts where no human being should be allowed to live . . . and we had a rotating system with books over there, and manned it." When Alabama's college facilities were finally desegregated under federal court order, Mrs. Johnson enrolled in a graduate program in library science at Montgomery's formerly all-black Alabama State College and became one of the first white women to receive a degree there. Her first public school teaching assignment was to an all-black school.[6]

Personal social preferences aside, at least by the time of his appointment to the federal bench, Judge Johnson could probably be best described as a man for whom race had little significance. As a Montgomery attorney remarked years later, "I think he's really without any consciousness of race. . . . I think he just doesn't have any consciousness of it, and he's not even patronizing about it, as a lot of, quote, enlightened, unquote, southerners are—those people who say, 'We've got to help those pore folks, those pore colored folks.' " Whatever his personal racial beliefs, moreover, he went to Alabama's Middle District convinced that *Plessy* v. *Ferguson*, the Supreme Court's 1896 endorsement of racial segregation, had been wrongly decided. Like the first Justice John Marshall Harlan, the former Kentucky slaveholder who had dissented alone in *Plessy*, Judge Johnson believed that the Constitution was completely color-blind. Before his first year on the federal bench was over, Montgomery officials were well aware of this element in his constitutional philosophy.[7]

Almost immediately after the Supreme Court's ruling in *Brown* v. *Board of Education* that the *Plessy* doctrine of "separate but equal" had no place in the field of public education, attempts were made to extend the ruling to other public service areas, including intrastate transportation. In South Carolina, a black woman forced to leave a bus when she refused to move to the black section filed a damage suit, *Flemming* v. *South Carolina Electric and Gas Co.*, against operators of the bus line on which she had been riding. Relying on *Plessy*, which had approved segregation on common carriers and thus had not been specifically overruled in the *Brown* case, a federal district court dismissed the suit. The U.S. Court of Appeals for the Fourth Circuit reversed, extending the *Brown* precedent to segregation in intrastate transportation and remanding the case to the lower court for further proceedings consistent with its ruling. Before remand proceedings could begin, however, the South Carolina company appealed the appellate court's decision to the Supreme Court. The Supreme Court dismissed the appeal, but did so simply on the basis of a 1929 case in which appeal had been sought prematurely before proper remand proceedings could be undertaken. Thus, the Court did not rule on the constitutionality of segregated local buses.[8]

GARDNER WEBB COLLEGE LIBRARY

By the time the Supreme Court dismissed the appeal in the South Carolina case, a movement to end segregation on Montgomery buses had been in progress several months. On the night of December 1, 1955, Rosa Parks, a black seamstress at a local men's clothing store and former secretary of the Montgomery chapter of the National Association for the Advancement of Colored People (NAACP), had been arrested when she refused to give up her seat on a Montgomery bus to a white passenger. Earlier in the year, three other black women had been arrested, jailed, and fined under regulations requiring segregation on public transportation facilities when they, too, had refused to give up bus seats to whites. The arrest of one of the women, a high school student, had aroused sufficient sympathy and anger in the black community that a committee of black leaders had gone to bus company officials to discuss reforms in seating arrangements and more courteous treatment for black riders. But the committee's efforts had produced virtually no results.[9]

Rosa Parks's arrest and subsequent conviction were to have a decidedly more significant impact. Incensed to action, black leaders called for a one-day boycott of Montgomery's buses. When that effort proved 99 percent successful, boycott leaders created a permanent organization, the Montgomery Improvement Association (MIA), to press for racial reform, and named as its leader Martin Luther King, Jr., the young pastor of the city's black Dexter Avenue Baptist Church. Despite his youth—he was but twenty-seven when the movement began—and an initial reluctance to assume a leadership role, King's selection seemed a wise choice even at the time. Montgomery was well stocked with outspoken black ministers, but Dexter Avenue's minister was special in a number of respects. He held several academic degrees, including a recently earned doctorate from Boston College, and was extremely articulate—easily a match for Montgomery's white power structure. An Atlanta native, he had lived in Montgomery less than a year, not long enough to have become involved in factional disputes dividing the black community. Finally, he was a commanding, almost charismatic leader, combining in just the right amounts for his audience refined scholarly delivery and intense, evangelical zeal. In King's hands, the MIA boycott would become the impetus for the modern revolution in civil rights.[10]

Shortly after its organization, the MIA compiled a list of three demands: a guarantee of courtesy from the bus drivers; a "first-come, first-served" seating policy with whites boarding from the front, blacks from the rear; and jobs for black drivers on bus routes in predominantly black neighborhoods. When city and bus company officials refused to comply, the boycott continued. Under King's leadership, moreover, an extremely effective car pool was organized for those blacks otherwise dependent on Montgomery's buses.[11]

The boycott placed a severe strain on the city and its bus line. Before the boycott, thirty thousand blacks had ridden Montgomery's buses daily. Now, only three to four hundred were riding. The income of the city transit line had dropped by over 65 percent. As the weeks passed, white Alabamians viewed the boycott with increasing alarm. In a letter to the *Montgomery Advertiser*, for example, one exasperated resident of rural Georgiana asked of Montgomery's blacks, "Where is your appreciation, your sense of duty?" for the benevolence the city's whites had shown them in the past. On their editorial pages and in editorials masquerading as news articles, the local press frequently castigated the boycott leaders and reporters who flocked into Montgomery from around the world to cover the movement. Whenever legal charges were brought against boycott participants, the papers not only published their names and addresses, but also their places of employment, perhaps to inform employers about the sort of workers they had hired.[12]

Some persons expressed distaste for the boycott in less civilized ways. One night toward the end of January, a bomb exploded on the front porch of King's home; two nights later, dynamite exploded in another MIA leader's yard. No one was hurt in either incident, and King was able to dissuade those in the movement who wished to return violence with violence. But the already tense situation grew even more strained.[13]

Official Montgomery also went on the offensive. King was arrested for driving thirty-five miles per hour in a twenty-five-mile zone and fined $14; other participants in the car pool were arrested repeatedly on traffic and other minor charges. More and more MIA money became tied up in bail bonds, and some volunteers complained of being beaten by city policemen on the ride to the jail. Vehicles used in the car pool were frequently cited for safety violations and towed away for repair, at considerable expense to the owner. On February 21, moreover, a county grand jury indicted 115 blacks under a little-used statute banning conspiracies to initiate boycotts having no "just cause or legal excuse." About a month later, King was convicted and given a sentence of $500 or 140 days in jail, plus court costs of $500 or 246 additional days in jail. Pending appeal of his conviction, King was released on bond, and trials for the other defendants were continued pending the outcome of his appeal.[14]

When the conspiracy prosecutions failed to halt the boycott, Montgomery mayor W. A. Gayle, increasingly concerned about the financial burden the boycott was creating for the city and its bus line, appointed a biracial committee of eight blacks and eight whites to work out a compromise. The white members of the committee agreed to ensure courtesy toward black riders with periodic checks by black and white inspectors, and they offered to reserve only the first ten spaces for whites and the last ten for blacks with the middle of each bus to be filled on a "first-come, first-served" basis. But blacks on the committee were adamant now that "first-come, first-served" be the rule throughout every bus and insisted on the employment of black as well as white drivers. When neither group would yield, the compromise effort collapsed.[15]

As the boycott continued, its leaders were obliged to cope increasingly with internal dissension, including a black minister's charge—later withdrawn—that MIA leaders were misappropriating movement funds. By mid-June, however, the challenge to segregation on Montgomery's buses had received a major boost from another source. Rosa Parks's attorney was Fred Gray, one of two black Montgomery lawyers. Gray had been concerned that a constitutional challenge to the segregation laws via an appeal of Mrs. Parks's conviction through the state courts—with no certainty of U.S. Supreme Court review—might be a painfully slow, and ultimately futile, process. In early February, therefore, he had filed a federal suit in Judge Johnson's court on behalf of Aurelia S. Browder and several other black women who had been required to comply with the segregated seating arrangement on Montgomery's buses or arrested and fined for refusing to comply. The suit, styled *Browder* v. *Gayle,* requested a declaratory judgment from the court that the segregation requirements were unconstitutional and an injunction prohibiting their further enforcement. Federal law then provided that lawsuits seeking an injunction against state statutes claimed to be unconstitutional must be heard before a special three-judge district court panel. Judge Johnson and Judge Seybourn H. Lynne were assigned to two of the seats on the panel. The panel's third member was Judge Richard Taylor Rives of the U.S. Court of Appeals for the Fifth Circuit.[16]

Judge Rives was born in 1895, and his family had lived in Montgomery since 1819. When appointed to the Fifth Circuit in 1947, he was a partner in Hill, Hill, Whiting, and Rives, Montgomery's most prestigious firm. Although New Orleans was the seat of the Fifth Circuit, Rives maintained offices in Montgomery's federal building. Over the years, he and Judge Johnson would sit together on many significant three-judge panels.[17]

Segregationist white Montgomerians unacquainted with Judge Rives may have thought that they had a ready ally in one so firmly rooted in the city and its traditions. But those who knew him well would not have been so confident. In his youth, Judge Rives "had just accepted it as a way of life that blacks shouldn't vote, that they were to be treated almost as a different species of people from the whites." While practicing law in Montgomery, moreover, he had represented state and local officials in a number of cases involving claims of racial discrimination in the voter registration process. Even Judge Rives's parents were not of one mind, however, regarding the propriety of southern racial mores. His mother, Rives would recall, "was an unreconstructed rebel all her life," but his father exerted a different influence on their three sons. "He had come up in the difficult period right after the War between the States, but he felt that blacks should be given opportunities at least to go as far as they could, and he told us that he thought perhaps it was a good thing the Yankees won the war." In the mid-1940s, moreover, Rives had become convinced that eligible voters should be given access to the ballot without regard to color; and when Alabama sought to preserve white supremacy at the polls after the Supreme Court's invalidation of the white primary in 1944, he joined others in an unsuccessful effort to defeat the Boswell Amendment, a state constitutional provision denying the suffrage to voter applicants who could not "understand and interpret" a provision of the state constitution, were not of "good character," and did not understand "the duties and obligations of good citizenship."[18]

In time, in fact, Rives had begun to question the propriety of racial segregation itself. His son Dick had a profound effect on his changing posture. "Dick had been to Harvard and was very liberal in his views on racial questions. He had served his time in the second World War, and had been in the hospital with blacks, and he felt like they should have equal opportunities to vote, to go to school, and to advance in life how they could." On numerous occasions in the late 1940s, Dick and his father discussed the propriety of southern racial norms, with Dick invariably urging reform. While on holiday from the University of Michigan law school in 1948, Dick was killed in an automobile accident. But his influence on his father would endure. Rives had revered his son, and in later years his comments about his own racial views would include frequent references to his son's ideas and influence. Some would suggest, in fact, that the liberal reputation he was to forge in racial cases on the Fifth Circuit was to a degree his way of letting his son's ideals live on in his decisions and opinions. In any event, when *Browder* v. *Gayle* arose in Montgomery, Judge Rives, like Judge Johnson, was no friend of the *Plessy* doctrine.[19]

A hearing in the case was set for May 11. Before the hearing, however, the boycott movement received an additional temporary setback. One of the women whom Fred Gray had originally included among the plaintiffs in the federal suit was a cook in the home of a relative of Mayor Gayle. She swore that Gray had not secured her permission to file a suit in her behalf, and Gray was charged in a state court with unlawful legal practice. On the day set for a trial of the charge, however, the prosecutor moved for a dismissal, ostensibly on the ground that the offense had occurred on federal property and thus was beyond state jurisdiction.[20]

Then, two days before the federal hearing was to begin, Judge Johnson was walking into a Montgomery cafeteria with the other members of the panel when he spotted a newspaper headline to the effect that Judge Walter B. Jones, a prominent state jurist and avowed segregationist, had upheld state and local laws requiring segregated local busing. When the U.S. Supreme Court had dismissed the state's appeal in the South Carolina bus case, an official of National City Lines, the Chicago-based parent company of the Montgomery line, had ordered its drivers to cease enforcing segregation on Montgomery's buses. The Montgomery City Commission had immediately filed a suit in Judge Jones's court seeking an injunction to restrain compliance with the bus company's directive. Almost as quickly, Judge Jones had provided the requested relief, observing: "The decision of the Fourth Circuit Court of Appeals in the Flemming case is not well reasoned, is not sound law and certainly a State court in Alabama is not bound by the unsound reasoning, or rather lack of reasoning of this court's opinion."[21]

Judge Jones had spoken. Now, it was the federal panel's turn. The federal hearing was relatively brief and uneventful. Each of the plaintiffs testified, and their counsel argued that the state and local laws at issue offended the Fourteenth Amendment's guarantee to equal protection of the laws. Gordon Madison, an assistant attorney general for the state, predicted that a lifting of segregation barriers would make "violence . . . the order of the day." Judge Rives dismissed Madison's contention with a pointed observation of his own: "Can you command one man to surrender his constitutional rights, if they are his constitutional rights, to prevent another man from committing a crime?" But both Rives and Judge Lynne repeatedly emphasized from the bench that the Supreme Court had not yet specifically outlawed segregation in intrastate transportation. Judge Johnson said nothing.[22]

A number of Alabama newspapers speculated after the hearing that Rives and Lynne might vote to uphold segregated seating on Montgomery's buses. In the end, though, only Judge Lynne would assume that position. While personally comfortable with a segregated society, Lynne realized that the Plessy doctrine was doomed. He believed, however, that the Supreme Court should administer the last rites. In his judgment, lower federal courts had no business anticipating new trends in the direction of Supreme Court precedent; until Plessy was explicitly overruled, it should be considered controlling by lower courts. [23]

Judge Lynne made little effort to persuade Judge Rives that the suit should be dismissed. He admired Rives as "a great lawyer and great judge," but believed that once Rives had become fixed in his position on an issue, "no earthly power could shake him." And Lynne was convinced that Rives would vote to grant the plaintiffs relief. He did his best to convert Judge Johnson to his approach, even writing his young colleague a lengthy letter defending his position early in the litigation. But Judge Johnson, like Judge Rives, believed that *Plessy* had been wrongly decided; and shortly after the suit was filed, the two had met in Judge Rives's chambers and agreed that they would wait until the case had been briefed and argued before deciding whether *Plessy* should be considered controlling. For a time after the May 11 hearing, each believed that the other might side with Judge Lynne. Ultimately, however, they formed a majority to overrule *Plessy*—and segregation on Alabama buses.[24]

The two-to-one decision was announced in an opinion by Judge Rives on June 5. After tracing the long line of Supreme Court and lower federal court decisions weakening the *Plessy* doctrine, Judge Rives concluded: "We cannot in good conscience perform our duty as judges by blindly following the precedent of Plessy v. Ferguson . . . when our study leaves us in complete agreement with the Fourth Circuit's opinion in Flemming . . . that the separate but equal doctrine can no longer be safely followed as a correct statement of the law." Judge Lynne registered a forceful dissent—his first in nearly ten years of service in the federal judiciary and one which Judge Rives then considered the most cogent he had ever read. Lynne condemned as "pernicious" the notion that trial judges may disregard precedent "if they perceive 'a pronounced new doctrinal trend' " and cited a recent Rives opinion echoing his sentiments. The *Plessy* doctrine of separate but equal, Lynne contended, had not yet been repudiated; in *Brown*, the Supreme Court had merely concluded that it had no place in the field of public education and that racially segregated schools simply could not be made equal. The *Brown* Court had thus suggested, Lynne asserted, "that there still remains an area within our constitutional scheme of state and federal governments wherein that doctrine may be applied even though its applications are always constitutionally suspect and for sixty years it may have been more honored in the breach than in the observance." To Lynne, local transportation was such a field.[25]

State and city officials appealed the panel's decision to the Supreme Court, and MIA leaders announced that the bus boycott would continue pending the outcome of the appeal. At the NAACP's annual convention in San Francisco, King suggested that a black boycott of segregated southern schools might help speed compliance with *Brown*, but his proposal received a cool reception from NAACP leaders, who preferred litigation to mass action in promoting racial reform. Asked by a reporter to comment on King's suggestion, the association's chief counsel Thurgood Marshall dryly responded: "I don't approve of using children to do men's work."[26]

In Montgomery, boycott leaders attempted to cope with now familiar forms of harassment and a number of new ones. Although no one was injured, dynamite bombs were occasionally tossed into the yards of homes in black neighborhoods, and MIA leaders continued to receive threatening phone calls and letters. For a time, moreover, it appeared that the car pool would be forced to operate without liability insurance, if at all. Although the pool had functioned without serious accidents, insurance companies repeatedly canceled liability policies until Lloyds of London finally rescued MIA leaders with extensive coverage.[27]

Then, in late October, Montgomery officials initiated a court attack on the car pool. Pressed for action by a trade union group, city commissioners announced that they intended "to maintain the way of life which has existed here in Montgomery since its origin, so far as we are legally able" and asked a state court to enjoin operation of the car pool unless it secured a city franchise. A hearing in the case was set for November 13. That day, however, the U.S. Supreme Court affirmed the three-judge panel's decision in a brief per curiam opinion that merely cited Brown and subsequent rulings invalidating segregation laws. Later, the Court denied state and local officials a rehearing in the case, and on December 20, just over a year after the boycott began, its mandate reached Montgomery. At that point, the boycott—and segregated seating on Montgomery's buses—came to an end.[28]

Martin Luther King had termed the desegregation of Montgomery's buses "a victory for democracy and the forces of justice." The reaction of white officials was no more restrained, but had a markedly different tenor. C. C. (Jack) Owen—president of the Alabama Public Service Commission, a defendant in Browder, and an ardent segregationist—expressed "shock" at the three-judge panel's ruling, calling it an affront to "principles and customs we have been taught throughout our lives." When the Supreme Court's mandate reached Montgomery, Judge Jones dissolved his injunction against integration of the city's buses, but attacked the Supreme Court's "evil construction" of the Fourteenth Amendment.[29]

Opposition to the ruling was not confined to verbal outbursts against the federal courts. After several days of peaceful compliance with the court order, buses and homes became the targets of sporadic sniper fire in poorly lighted sections of the city, a young black girl was beaten by white thugs as she got off a bus, and a pregnant black was shot in the leg. On several occasions, moreover, white-robed klansmen marched into black neighborhoods. Then came more bombings. On January 9, 1956, the Reverend Ralph Abernathy's home and church were bombed. Also bombed that night were three other black churches and the home of a white Lutheran minister, the only white on the MIA executive committee and one of the few Montgomery whites active in the boycott movement. Later, a black-owned service station in King's neighborhood and the residence of an elderly black neighbor were bombed, and a bundle of dynamite was found beneath King's porch. No one was injured in the blasts, but the FBI conducted an intensive investigation, and seven men were eventually charged with the bombings. At their trials, the seven were represented by John Blue Hill, an extremely skillful attorney and yet another member of Montgomery's most prestigious political family, and all were acquitted. Finally, however, the bombings and related incidents subsided—a consequence, some would say, more of the size of Hill's legal fees than the FBI's diligence.[30]

MIA leaders and others in the black community were not the only Montgomerians subjected to reprisals in the wake of the bus decision. "There was tremendous opposition to it," Judge Rives recalls.

> I got phone calls throughout the night, night after night, nearly all of which was just simply to harass us apparently, because they would wake us up at all hours and then hang up the phone. In my absence, . . . my wife would get phone calls and they would make such statements to her as, "You'd better prepare for widowhood," and "Your husband is soon to be killed," and things of that kind. Those that constituted threats I would report to the FBI. I got a tremendous amount of fan mail. . . . I paid no attention to it and didn't report any of it except that which was threatening and a violation of the criminal law, and I felt it necessary to report that. . . . The commissioner of police called and asked if I wanted a guard around my house, and he said would I object to having the place patrolled. I said, "No, but please don't send them out to my place. Just patrol the blocks, and don't let my neighbors know that I'm under that kind of situation." I did tell him . . . that I had my old shotgun and I could take care of anyone that worried around my house. But I never had any real trouble.[31]

Judge Rives took the phone calls and hate letters in stride, never feeling seriously threatened. On one occasion, however, his tormentors were unusually cruel. Judge Rives had taken his son's death extremely hard. "You just wouldn't know what a traumatic thing this was for Judge Rives," Ray Jenkins said years later, "losing his only son. He still speaks of Dick, Jr., almost as if it were only yesterday that he was alive." Dick had been killed eight years before the bus boycott began, but Judge Rives still made frequent visits to his grave. On one visit shortly after the desegregation of Montgomery's buses, he found his son's gravestone smeared with red paint (those soft on race, ran the segregationist dogma of the day, must be soft on communism) and the grave littered with garbage. The cemetery sexton reported the vandalism to local authorities, but those responsible were never apprehended.[32]

Opposition to the *Browder* ruling and to his later civil rights decisions extended, of course, to Judge Rives's own circle of acquaintances, many of whom simply could not comprehend how a native son could render such decisions. Some stopped speaking; some refused to sit near him in church or at other social gatherings. He was never especially concerned about the ostracism ("they were just missing speaking to a fellow they ought to speak to") and dissuaded two close friends who offered to speak out in his behalf ("I've got a lifetime job, but you'd be committing financial suicide almost to speak out"). Judge Rives is a deeply religious man, however, and when in the early 1960s his Presbyterian congregation resisted black attempts to integrate Montgomery's churches, ultimately breaking its ties with its national organization over church racial policy, he moved his membership to another congregation.[33]

Judge Rives is a kindly and gracious man—almost to a fault. Despite adverse reactions to his decisions and the slights of acquaintances, he maintained an optimistic confidence in the basic fairness of Montgomery's white citizens throughout the tense years of racial turmoil in Alabama. "I've lived here all my life," he would say, "my parents have lived here, and my grandparents have lived here on both sides all their lives. I never did think people here were fundamentally unfair, and I felt like when they understood things, that they would take a fair attitude of it." Nor did he blame members of the local bar for failing to speak out ("I don't think, if I had put myself in their positions, I'd spoken out either"). And when Time condemned Alabamians for mistreating him, he rose quickly—and characteristically—to their defense. In 1964, Time published an article on the judges of the Fifth Circuit and adverse reaction to their civil rights rulings. In discussing the treatment accorded Judge Rives in his native state, the article's author observed: "After his son's death in an auto accident, Judge Richard T. Rives was honored by his fellow Alabamians—they threw garbage on his son's grave." In a letter to the editor, Judge Rives gently rebuked the magazine for its "[un]intended" but "serious injustice to my fellow Alabamians . . . , the overwhelming majority of whom are as fine, decent, and fair-minded people as can be found anywhere."[34]

Although shocked that a native son could turn his back on Montgomery's racial traditions, white Montgomerians may not have been surprised—as Ruth Johnson later suggested—that "a young upstart from north Alabama" would vote to desegregate their buses. Surprised or not, they subjected Judge Johnson and his family to much the same treatment they accorded Judge Rives. On the evening of December 21, 1956, one day after the Supreme Court's desegregation order reached Montgomery, the Johnsons attended a Christmas party at a neighbor's home while Judge Johnson's mother babysat with Johnny. During the party, someone reported a disturbance at their home. Judge Johnson borrowed a pistol from his host, went to investigate, and found a crude cross blazing in his yard. Later, two teenagers, aged sixteen and seventeen, were charged with violating federal statutes prohibiting intimidation of federal judges and related offenses.[35]

Judge Johnson dismissed the cross-burning as a harmless prank and intervened to assure the youths considerate treatment. Instead of arresting them, the FBI called their homes and asked that their parents bring them in for questioning and proceedings before a federal commissioner. Because of their youth, their names were never released to the press. On Judge Johnson's recommendation, they were placed on two years' probation and never sent to jail.[36]

Unfortunately, the harassment of the Johnsons was not to be limited to an isolated childish prank. Like Judge and Mrs. Rives, the Johnsons received threatening phone calls ("We're going to get you, you nigger-loving son of a bitch"; "Tell the judge he's going to be sorry") and hate mail. Judge Johnson's parents also received abusive calls. Ruth Johnson could tolerate the calls easily enough, and Judge Johnson's father even attempted to engage the callers in friendly debate. But "Frank," Mrs. Johnson recalls, "didn't like them at all" and got an unlisted number.[37]

Judge Johnson is a powerfully built man, easily capable of defending himself and his family in a fair fight. When the threats and harassment continued, however, the Justice Department placed him in protective custody. A dusk-to-dawn guard was established at his home, and when Lee Dodd came to work with him in early 1959, Dodd was made special deputy marshal, armed, and given an office next to the judge's chambers. Manned initially by Dodd and others connected with the court and later, when the press of their Middle District duties became too great, by off-duty Montgomery policemen, the guard detail remained at his home intermittently for eighteen years.[38]

Particularly when discussing the first decade of his judicial career, journalists have devoted considerable attention to Judge Johnson's pariah status in Alabama, reporting that after the bus decision he and his family were virtually driven from the First Baptist Church and largely excluded from the city's active social life. Some of these press reports—based on the comments of well-meaning but confused friends—are factually erroneous. The Johnsons were not, for example, ostracized by members of their church congregation. Judge Johnson had taught a Sunday school class in Jasper and, for a time after their move to Montgomery, he taught one there also. Eventually, he stopped teaching the class, and later he and his family ceased attending church altogether. He and Mrs. Johnson had been treated cordially, however, during their years at the church. They stopped attending, they later insisted, because, like Judge Rives, they could not countenance their congregation's hostility to black attendance and they had no satisfactory answers when young Johnny asked why, if Jesus loved "all the little children of the world, red, yellow, black, and white," as the child's song said, blacks were not allowed to attend their church. "My wife and I still are as religious as anyone, I think," Judge Johnson now explains. "But we practice our religion instead of just verbalizing it."[39]

Nevertheless, Judge Johnson's civil rights decisions obviously did strain his family's relations with certain segments of the community. Behind his back and in the press, he and his rulings were subjected to vitriolic abuse; relations with certain neighbors cooled noticeably; and at times even his friends and employees were made to feel the community's resentment. A young Montgomery lawyer, who served as Judge Johnson's law clerk when the judge was well into his second decade on the bench and public outcry against his rulings had subsided somewhat, recalls, for example: "When I first came here, the first place I lived was an apartment complex. There was a retired army colonel living there. Here I was, a new man in town, and he was friendly and had me over for dinner to meet his family. And he said, 'Young man, what do you do here, are you with the federal government?' figuring I was with the air force or something. And I said, 'Yes sir, I am,' and he said, 'Well, who are you working with?' And I said, 'I'm working down at the federal court here,' and he said, 'Well, who in particular?' I said, 'Judge Johnson.' From that point on, his whole attitude changed."[40]

Despite the often hostile climate and presence of armed guards, however, the Johnsons were able to lead reasonably normal lives even after the bus decision. In fact, they later insisted that the stories of community ostracism were vastly overdrawn. They had the support of friends who either sympathized with Judge Johnson's stance or refused to let disagreement with his decisions affect their personal relationship. They maintained a membership in the Montgomery Country Club, but if the atmosphere there was at times uncomfortable, it made little difference; Judge Johnson preferred the facilities of the officers' club at Maxwell Air Base. Beyond this, the Johnsons by nature were not the sort of people who could be seriously concerned about being excluded from the Montgomery social whirl. "We belonged to the Country Club and any other club that we wanted," he now contends.

> We turned down invitations to every one of the masked ball clubs in Montgomery. Instead of our being socially ostracized, we did the ostracizing, because my wife and I are just not socially inclined. We weren't when I was practicing law. I'm probably the only lawyer that ever resigned from the Rotary Club in Jasper, Alabama, a long time before I became a federal judge. I'd rather be on the river fishing than to be at a masked ball. That's just the long and the short of it. Had I been socially inclined, it would have been bad. But you can't ostracize a person who does his own ostracizing, and that's just the way we are.[41]

Despite the sentiments of his fellow white Montgomerians, in the years immediately following the *Browder* decision, Judge Johnson ordered the desegregation of other city facilities. Late in 1958, Montgomery blacks brought a class action requesting an end to segregation in the city's parks. Although the city commission quickly adopted a resolution closing all public parks in the city to all persons, regardless of color, Judge Johnson permanently enjoined city officials from enforcing any ordinance, custom, or practice that would deny blacks the use of any public park. In 1962, moreover, he enjoined enforcement of a city policy excluding blacks from the public library system and city museum. Earlier, he had ordered desegregation of interstate and intrastate motor carriers and the facilities and services of bus terminals located in Montgomery and other cities under his jurisdiction. The same year, he ordered Dannelly Field, Montgomery's airport, desegregated in accordance with the nondiscrimination provisions of the Federal Aviation Act. In all these cases, of course, he was ruling according to firmly established Supreme Court precedent. By this point, the *Plessy* doctrine had been overruled in virtually every public field.[42]

The Big Judge and the Little Judge

While the federal courts were beginning to attack segregation in the schools and other public facilities, Congress made a first feeble modern attempt to eliminate racial discrimination in voting. On September 9, 1957, in its first civil rights legislation in almost a century, Congress authorized the Justice Department to seek federal injunctions against voting registrars guilty of discriminatory registration practices. It also established a Commission on Civil Rights with authority to "investigate allegations . . . that certain citizens of the United States are being deprived of their right to vote . . . by reason of their color, race, religion, or national origin."[1] The commission's first confrontation with Alabama officials would soon embroil Judge Johnson in a bizarre courtroom battle with his bantam-weight law school chum George Corley Wallace.

After law school and military service in the Pacific, George Wallace had returned to Barbour County to practice law and indulge his first love, politics. He served for a time in the Alabama legislature, achieving a minor reputation as a progressive legislator in the mold of the state's populist governor James E. (Big Jim) Folsom, then was elected to a state circuit judgeship. As his term as circuit judge was ending in 1958, he made an unsuccessful first bid for the Democratic gubernatorial nomination, securing a slot in the runoff primary but losing by 64,902 votes in the June runoff to Alabama's popular young attorney general John Patterson.

In the years before Judge Johnson's appointment to the federal bench, he and Wallace had occasionally joined forces in state bar politics. In 1946, for example, Wallace agreed to support Johnson's law partner Herman Maddox for president of the Alabama Bar Association's junior bar section, and Johnson put Wallace's name in nomination for the position at the next election. In recent years, however, the two had had little contact.[2]

For about a year after its creation, the Civil Rights Commission took little action. Then, in September 1958, its chairman, Michigan State University president John A. Hannah, announced that the commission was beginning an investigation into complaints of discrimination against prospective black voters in several southern states, including Alabama. Shortly thereafter, Colonel A. H. Rosenfeld, director of the commission's Office of Complaints, Information, and Surveys, requested access to voter registration records in six Alabama counties, including Macon, Barbour, and Bullock in Judge Johnson's jurisdiction. But voter registrars in the counties refused to cooperate. Attorney General Patterson had advised them that the documents requested were not public records and thus not subject to scrutiny by the federal agency.[3]

Failing to secure voluntary compliance, the commission announced that it had decided to hold public hearings in Montgomery and compel disclosure of voter registration records by use of its subpoena powers. Several days before the hearings were to begin in early December 1958, however, Judge Wallace impounded the Barbour and Bullock county voting files, ostensibly for a grand jury investigation of charges that unqualified persons had been fraudulently registered to vote in the two counties; and later, hastily assembled grand juries impounded the records of two other counties under investigation, Dallas and Wilcox. Although no similar action was taken in Macon County, the chairman of its board of registrars promised that no records would be surrendered to the commission without Attorney General Patterson's approval.[4]

At this point in his career, George Wallace's racial posture was cloudy at best. At his urging, Governor Folsom had appointed him to the board of trustees of Tuskegee Institute; and during his unsuccessful 1958 bid for governor, he had actively sought the support of black voters, accused Patterson of being "wrapped in the robes of the Ku Klux Klan," and condemned the tactics of the secret society. Already, though, Wallace had come to realize the potential political value of a hard line on the segregation issue and strident attacks on the federal courts and other federal institutions. In 1956, when the FBI announced that it was beginning an investigation of jury selection practices in Cobb County, Georgia, two hundred miles from Wallace's court, he had warned: "I will jail every member of the FBI or other federal police if they try to inspect my records." Later, the Bullock County grand jury commended his action, and Wallace phoned the Associated Press, telling the dismayed personnel there how he had frightened the "feds." When he lost his 1958 gubernatorial bid, he reportedly attributed his defeat to his opponent's harsher stance on the segregation issue and promised never to be "out-niggered" again. But even during that campaign, his speeches were liberally sprinkled with anti-civil rights rhetoric. Opening his campaign in the little village of Ozark, in a forty-mile-an-hour wind that threatened to blow him from the speaker's platform, he promised to preserve "our way of life" and condemned federal interference in the state's race relations, adding: "You have enough good and honest people right here in Ozark to decide on matters such as that, and you sure don't have to rely on any imported federal and district judges."[5]

The Civil Rights Commission seemed a likely target for "fed-baiting" ("We knew we could talk big," a Wallace crony later explained, "because the commission had no power to punish"), and when the Montgomery hearings were announced, Wallace quickly maneuvered himself into a position of potential confrontation with commission officials. Earlier, he had dismissed a challenge to a local election involving charges that blacks had been improperly registered as voters by the winning candidate's supporters. But when the Montgomery hearings were scheduled, he told a close friend, Barbour County attorney Crews Johnston, to make up some charges against black voters "like that old suit I dismissed." Johnston filed a complaint claiming that a number of unidentified voters were improperly registered and, at Wallace's request, another crony filed a similar complaint in Bullock County. Wallace then impounded the counties' voting records ostensibly for a future grand jury investigation of the charges and declined a commission subpoena that he produce the records at the Montgomery hearings. "We have an investigation pending," he solemnly intoned, "which we feel is more important than the Civil Rights Commission hearing." More characteristically, he later threatened to jail any "civil rights agent" attempting to seize the records in his possession.[6]

When the commission hearings began on December 8 in a small courtroom on the fourth floor of the Montgomery federal building, Attorney General Patterson, now the state's governor-elect, was there with a number of staff members to provide legal advice for the subpoenaed voting officials. In 1954, John Patterson's father had won the Democratic nomination for attorney general on a "law and order" platform, promising to clean up vice-ridden Phenix City, his home town, and remove racketeering elements from influence in state government. Shortly after his nomination, the elder Patterson was shot down outside his Phenix City law office, and John moved into his slot on the ticket, winning handily in the general election with a vow to drive organized crime from Alabama.[7]

John Patterson had gained considerable mileage from his crime-busting image, but soon learned that a hard line on race was a political necessity for ambitious politicians in post-Brown Alabama. "It wasn't long after I got involved in the governor's race that race became the key issue. This was not any of my making. But you had to take a stand on that issue. If you didn't, you were through. We knew that there was no way by which we could ultimately prevail constitutionally . . . that we were ultimately going to lose. But we just didn't have the political mechanisms to bring the change about. It was political suicide to offer any moderate approach. . . . The whole attitude on the question polarized, and . . . anybody who said anything to indicate that he was weak on that point was finished."[8]

Patterson later said that he found attacks on federal institutions distasteful, and he was an early and ardent supporter of John F. Kennedy's presidential nomination in 1960. Even so, he recognized the political value of a segregationist role. "Alabamians are gullible for that kind of thing. In essence, I did the same thing. Give the people something to dislike and hate, create a straw man for them to fight. They'd rather be against something than for something. As long as our people are of that frame of mind and like their politics with that brand, then we're going to have people to take advantage of that kind of situation." In the main, however, Patterson's style was somewhat more subtle than Wallace's or that of Arkansas Governor Orval Faubus and certain of their other unreconstructed contemporaries in southern statehouses. Though clearly not above race-baiting on the stump, Patterson preferred legal maneuvers and delay to an appearance of outright defiance of federal authority.[9]

Eight Alabama registrars and five probate judges attended the Montgomery hearings. On Patterson's advice, five of the registrars refused to take the oath required of witnesses, and a sixth would not testify on the ground that the Civil Rights Commission had no power to interrogate an official of the state judiciary. Although willing to testify, the probate judges were of little assistance because they were merely the custodians of lists of voters already certified by the registrars. George Wallace refused even to attend.[10]

It was now apparent to members of the Civil Rights Commission that court action would be the only means of securing information about voting discrimination in Alabama. Federal law authorized any U.S. district court with jurisdiction to issue orders requiring those persons failing to respond to a subpoena to produce evidence or give testimony relating to any matter under commission investigation, and Judge Wallace and the six registrars who had refused to testify before the commission were within Judge Johnson's jurisdiction. On December 10, U.S. attorney Hartwell Davis and Justice Department attorneys Joseph Ryan and Robert Owen asked Johnson to order Wallace and the registrars to appear before the commission on December 19 and produce evidence and testimony.[11]

The following day Judge Johnson issued the order, but on December 16 Patterson filed a motion to quash the order with respect to all parties but Wallace, charging that the 1957 Civil Rights Act and the subpoenas were unconstitutional, portions of the subpoenas were inconsistent with the act, and the subpoenas would require the voting registrars "to appear at a hearing stripped of all dignity and to subject themselves to television broadcasts and other publicity staged by or with the sanction of publicity agents hired by the Commission." Wallace and Patterson also signed a motion challenging Judge Johnson's jurisdiction over the voting records in Wallace's possession. Though convinced that some of the contentions were frivolous, Judge Johnson scheduled a hearing on the motions.

The hearing was set for January 5, but on that morning Justice Department attorneys and the defendants' counsel met in Judge Johnson's chambers and worked out a compromise. Under the agreement, the Civil Rights Commission abandoned attempts to force the registrars to testify about complaints of voting discrimination, and Judge Johnson modified his December 11 production order to provide that commission agents could "inspect official voter registration records in Barbour, Bullock, and Macon County to the extent that they [were] relevant to the Commission's inquiry." Inspection was to be carried out where the records were kept at a time mutually agreed to by their custodians and commission agents, and the inspection was not "to interfere with the proper judicial processes of the State of Alabama."

John Patterson was pleased with the compromise. He recalls that, in chambers, Judge Johnson had made it clear to the Justice Department attorneys that the records were to be examined as quickly as possible and with minimum inconvenience to state officials. "He said, 'Now, I want you to get in there and I want you to photostat what you want and I want you to get out.' . . . He got a little rough with them, I thought. . . . And everybody felt pretty good about that."[12]

The Macon County records were quickly made available to commission agents in their entirety, but Judge Wallace was considerably less cooperative. He avoided commission investigators when they first sought access to the voting records in his possession on January 7. On the morning of January 8, Charles Clark and another commission agent again drove to Clayton, the Barbour County seat, and asked Wallace to let them examine the records. Wallace told them that he considered their request in the manner of a judicial proceeding subject to the test of relevancy and asked that they prepare a written itemization of the records sought, the number and identity of the Barbour and Bullock county complainants, and a showing of the records' relevance to the commission's investigation. Clark and his associate compiled a list of the records and the names of four complainants, all of whom had already testified at the December hearings in Montgomery. Wallace marked this material "filed," then adjourned the meeting to confer with his brother Jack and Seymour Trammell, his circuit solicitor. Finally, at 7:15 that evening, after a day of stalling, Wallace permitted the two agents to examine a registration book containing the name of a George Morris, listed as registered, and the registration applications of Morris and an Andrew Jones. At about 8:00, Clark met Jack Wallace and Seymour Trammell in Union Springs, the Bullock County seat, where he was permitted to examine two registration applications of an Aaron

Sellers. That was the extent of the little judge's compliance, and a showdown with the big judge seemed increasingly likely.[13]

On Friday, January 9, Justice Department attorney Ryan related the previous days' events to Judge Johnson and requested further assistance. Preston Clayton, an attorney representing Wallace, attempted to explain that Judge Johnson's order had not defined "what were and what were not relevant records" and that his client had merely surrendered those records he believed relevant to the commission's investigation. Judge Johnson was unimpressed. Rejecting Wallace's claims to judicial immunity from federal process and continued challenges to the commission's authority, Johnson ordered him to make relevant records available to commission agents between 10:00 A.M. and 4:00 P.M., Monday and Tuesday, January 12 and 13. "Relevant records," he pointedly added, meant "all the voting and registration records in" Judge Wallace's custody.

From his home in Wetumpka, twenty miles north of Montgomery, the two protagonists' law school classmate Glen Curlee had been watching developments in the case with growing concern. As a member of Elmore County's courthouse gang, Curlee was obviously familiar with the finer points of racial politics in Alabama. He had been president of the county's chapter of the Citizens Council (purely to keep the "radicals" from taking control, he later explained) and held the number one card in the organization until it disbanded. But Wallace seemed to be taking matters a bit far. "I said to myself, you know, this thing is more serious than George thinks it is. They have the authority to place him in contempt, put him in jail." Yet Wallace had declined to say whether he would comply with Judge Johnson's latest order.[14]

On Sunday, January 11, the day before commission agents were scheduled to begin inspecting the Barbour and Bullock records, Curlee and a Wetumpka friend drove to Wallace's home in Clayton. "I told George, I said, 'You've been doing all this bragging and talking and now the showdown's come, and in my judgment and opinion you're in trouble.' He said, 'You really think so?' I said, 'I know so. I'll tell you what. We'd better figure out a way to get you out of this predicament that you're in.' He said, 'Well, what do you suggest?' I said, 'Well, the only thing I know to do, let's go see Frank tonight if he'll see you.' Course, time was of the essence. He said, 'All right.' "[15]

Curlee then drove to Judge Johnson's Haardt Drive home to try and work out a meeting, but the Johnsons and Johnny were out for dinner. When they returned home about 7:30 that evening, Judge Johnson recalls,

> Curlee was waiting there at the house in his automobile, and came in, and chewed around on his cigar awhile, and finally told me that little

George—that's what we called him—wanted to talk to me. I told him I'd talk with him. So he called me back on the telephone fifteen minutes after he left the house and said George's on his way, he's having to drive up from Clayton. So I sat around and read, and Mrs. Johnson went on to bed. I guess he got to the house about 11:30. The doorbell rang and I went to the door. First statement he made—and my wife heard this because the doorbell woke her up—he says, "Judge, my ass is in a crack." I invited him on in and we went in the kitchen and sat. He asked if I could give him just a ten- or fifteen-day sentence, that that would help him politically. And I told him no, that if he defied that order I was going to give him a longer sentence, and he said he didn't think his wife would care much, but a longer sentence would kill his mama, and he just couldn't stand to be incarcerated. I told him that the option was his, that I didn't have any options; he would have to comply with the order. Finally, he asks, "Well, if I get them to them indirectly, will that be all right?" I said, "If you get them to them by the deadline, I don't care if you go by the moon."[16]

It was well after midnight when Wallace and Curlee left Judge Johnson's house. Curlee was present during only portions of the conversation, but the essence of what Judge Johnson had told Wallace was painfully clear ("You're either going to produce the records or you're going to jail"). As he and Wallace left the judge's house, they began to map out a strategy. Curlee recalls,

I said, "Now, Judge has done put the bee on you, and you're going to have to outfox the judge." He said, "How can I do that?" I said, "Well, the grand jury turned over the records to you to keep. That's all. You're custodian of the records. You call the grand jury, turn the records back over to them, and whatever they want to do with them, it's up to them. Then, you can't be held in contempt, because you're no longer custodian of the records. You haven't given them to the federals. . . . You've made your point, and the judge has carried his point, and the only thing he can do is not find you in contempt because you don't have the records."[17]

At about 2:00 that morning Seymour Trammell was awakened by a phone call from Wallace. Wallace told Trammell his plan and instructed his circuit solicitor to make arrangements for an early morning session of the Barbour County grand jury. By 8:00, the grand jury was in session. "This is a grave matter," Wallace told the bleary-eyed jurors. "Today I am turning these records over to you. I have kept them intact and inviolate. . . . I have no apologies to make for my actions and I am ready to face any consequences I may have to bear." For the slow-witted, he added: "When I turn the voter registration records over to you I realize I have no control over them. What you do is your business. Who you make them available to is your business."[18]

There followed three days of comical—and, for Civil Rights Commission agents, frustrating—maneuvering in which Wallace attempted to

assure that the agents obtained the subpoenaed voter records, but via
the Barbour and Bullock county grand juries, while Colonel Rosenfeld
attempted to make just as certain that the records came ultimately from
Wallace alone, whatever the route. By Wednesday, January 14, commission agents had been given all the records they sought. It was now
one day after the deadline set in Judge Johnson's order of the previous
Friday. Technically, therefore, Wallace was in contempt. But Frank
Johnson was not about to make a martyr of his little friend.

The following day, government attorneys and counsel for the defendants met with Judge Johnson. Justice Department attorney Ryan reported that the Barbour and Bullock voter registrars had cooperated
fully with commission agents, then said: "Although the agents were
harassed by dilatory tactics and questionable and rather childish conduct on the part of the persons who were ordered to cooperate and to
produce the records . . . as a matter of fact . . . the purpose of this
court's order was effectuated in that all of the records were produced
for inspection finally, if in jumbled-up form, and there was inspection
permitted." Commission agents had not had time to make a thorough
examination of the records, he added, but a spot check had revealed the
sort of patterns under investigation and the agents did not feel that
additional inspection time was needed. The government was requesting, therefore, that the civil suit against Wallace be dismissed.

Judge Johnson agreed to the government's motion. Noting, however,
that Wallace, "possibly" had "failed and refused to technically comply
with the order of this court," he then ordered Ryan to institute criminal
contempt proceedings "as early as possible." When charges were
prepared, Judge Johnson ordered Wallace to appear before him on
January 26 and show cause why he should not be cited for criminal
contempt.

Much of the national press expressed shock and dismay at Wallace's
maneuvering. "Things have come to a deplorable pass in this country,"
editorialized the Washington *Evening Star*, "when a State judge, in
effect, challenges a Federal judge to send him to jail." But in Alabama,
defense committees immediately sprang up around the state to raise
funds in Wallace's behalf; and Wallace, whose term as circuit judge
was ending, continued to feed defiant statements to reporters. At one
point, he told newsmen that he would jail any civil rights investigators
seeking to subpoena any records from his court. Yes, he conceded, he
was leaving office the next day, and yes, to his knowledge no federal
agents had expressed any interest in examining the records of his court.
But he wanted to "let the anti-South politicians in Washington know
that any efforts by the Civil Rights Commission to intimidate us will be
resisted to the fullest extent legally."[19]

The January 26 hearing was a strange affair. Wallace's attorneys
presented no witnesses in his behalf. Instead, they filed an answer to

the show cause order in which their client pleaded "guilty to failing to deliver the voter registration records to agents of the Civil Rights Commission and . . . not guilty of contempt of court in that his duties as Circuit Judge prevented his compliance with the order of the Court." Government attorneys, on the other hand, sought to show that Wallace had merely pretended to defy Judge Johnson's order while actually complying in every way.

The government first called Colonel Rosenfeld as a witness. Rosenfeld described in copious detail the frustrating events preceding inspection of the Barbour and Bullock records; and when he completed his testimony, four additional witnesses were called to substantiate his assertion that the civil rights investigators had not requested the records from either of the grand juries, thereby increasing the probability that Wallace himself ordered the records surrendered and thus in effect had complied with the court's order. Such testimony conflicted with publicized reports by both grand juries to the effect that Rosenfeld had requested the records from them.

Most of the witnesses called did substantiate Rosenfeld's version of the events, but Roy Holmes, the Bullock County grand jury foreman, implied in his testimony that no one had ordered his grand jury to surrender the records—that Rosenfeld had requested them. Under pointed questioning from Judge Johnson, however, Holmes conceded that he had phoned Colonel Rosenfeld and offered to make the subpoenaed records available to the commission and had never met Rosenfeld prior to that point. Holmes also acknowledgd that Rosenfeld had not requested the records from the grand jury, formally or informally, directly or indirectly.

Shortly after 2:00 that afternoon, Judge Johnson announced his verdict, finding Wallace not guilty of criminal contempt. He also sought to put the defendant's maneuvering in proper perspective. While attempting "to give the impression that he was defying this Court's order by turning [the voter] records over to hastily summoned grand juries," said Johnson, Wallace had actually retained control of the records and assisted Civil Rights Commission agents. The reasons for such "devious methods," Johnson added, were "judicially unknown" to the court. But the judge could speculate nevertheless. "If [they] were in good faith considered by Wallace to be essential to the proper exercise of his state judicial functions, then this court will not and should not comment upon these methods. However, if these devious means were for political purposes, then this court refuses to allow its authority and dignity to be bent or swayed by such politically generated whirlwinds."[20]

A sizable crowd of spectators, many wearing "Win with Wallace" campaign buttons and promising to pay any fine imposed on the defendant, had gathered in the courtroom. Wallace appeared ill at ease standing before his law school classmate to hear the verdict, but the roar of approval from the crowd when the verdict was announced brought a smile to his face—and a stern warning from the bench for order. Smoking a cigar and accompanied by his wife Lurleen, his lawyers, about twenty supporters, newsmen, and photographers, he walked down the street toward the Jefferson Davis Hotel, then turned with his attorneys and went over to his counsel's law office. About ninety minutes later, he returned to the hotel and read a prepared statement in the glare of television lights.[21]

The six-paragraph statement was what could now be called vintage Wallace, reflecting his personal self-sacrifice ("I was willing to risk my freedom"); an exalted view of the issues ("there was a grave constitutional question involved"), contempt for federal officials ("these characters from the evil Civil Rights Commission and Justice Department"), his amazing capacity for wresting an appearance of victory from the jaws of defeat ("they were defied and backed down. . . . This 1959 attempt to have a second Sherman's March to the Sea has been stopped in the Cradle of the Confederacy"), and what cynics might call a loose regard for the truth ("As to the alleged statement of 'whirlwind politics,' there is no testimony before the court on this subject either directly or indirectly"). He was indeed guilty, he said, of failing to deliver the voter records to commission agents, and no witness had testified otherwise. "I did my duty and plead guilty to the failure to bow to the wishes of the court and if the judge holds this is not a contempt, then I have no control over such conclusion." But he was not trying to hide anything from the commission; to the contrary, he had simply done his duty as a circuit judge, turning the records "over to the grand jury to do with as they saw fit." The court's reference to "devious methods" merely reflected its "lack of understanding of the independence and procedure of our state courts."

The statement was not Wallace's last word on the case, even for the moment. Four days after his acquittal, he went into his old office at the courthouse in Clayton—now occupied by his brother Jack, the new circuit judge—sat down at a typewriter, and pecked out a final report for the Barbour County grand jury. The grand jury foreman later signed the report and filed it officially with the circuit court clerk. It read: "We commend the courageous action of the Honorable George C. Wallace, who risked his very freedom in the federal courts in carrying out the duties and oath of office as a Circuit Judge. . . . The great need of the South today is for more men of the foresight and determination of Judge George C. Wallace."[22]

The morning after Wallace's acquittal, the *Montgomery Advertiser* criticized Judge Johnson editorially for apparently allowing politics to influence his verdict in the case. "Let us concede for argument that Wallace did indeed practice contumacy for political considerations. The fact is that Johnson likewise made his ruling upon the basis of political consideration, and so proclaims. The point before the court was whether Wallace had acted in contempt of court. The motive for the contempt was not the matter." In Judge Johnson's view, however, the case for contempt had been weak. "I guess technically he was guilty of contempt," he remarked years later, "but I never have used the contempt authority very much. I didn't have any desire to use it then unless I just absolutely had to. I saw a way that I could preserve what I thought was the authority and integrity of the court without finding him guilty of contempt, in that he had indirectly furnished all of the records that he was supposed to, . . . and that's the finding I made."[23]

The *Advertiser* had also editorialized: "Denying Wallace the role of martyred politician, Johnson sent him on his way—probably the most distressed acquitted man ever to appear before the court." In fact, Wallace was probably relieved at the outcome (recall Georgia Governor Marvin Griffin's response when asked whether he would be willing to go to jail in the cause of states' rights: "Being in jail sorta crimps a governor's style"). But he was also angered by Judge Johnson's charge that he had merely pretended defiance while actually cooperating with federal authorities—and haunted perhaps by the fear that Alabama voters might believe the accusation.[24]

Glen Curlee shared Wallace's irritation and concern. "Frank could have handled it more diplomatically in my judgment and opinion from what he did. He could have just said, 'Well, as long as the records are available. . . . ' But he went on to talk in his decision about 'devious means' and so forth." Was that not an accurate assessment? "Yeah, but he didn't have to say it, you know what I mean. . . . It was just politics. . . . That was the beginning of the breakup. Well, that was the breakup of a long-standing relationship."[25]

CHAPTER 6

Black Voters and Freedom Riders

George Wallace's voter records charade was Judge Johnson's second experience with resistance to black registration in the Middle District. His first had been no less bizarre.

The racial composition of Macon County in the late 1950s was typical of rural Black Belt counties. But its black population was anything but typical of Black Belt blacks—or most Alabama whites. Many Macon blacks residing in or around Tuskegee worked at Tuskegee Institute or in the county's federal Veterans Administration hospital. They were well-educated, economically comfortable, and politically motivated. In 1954, one of their number, Jessie P. Guzman, Tuskegee Institute's director of records and research, had run for the Tuskegee seat on the county board of education. Mrs. Guzman fell far short of victory, but the very fact of her candidacy disturbed Tuskegee whites. And when voting rights legislation began moving toward congressional passage in early 1957, they had become convinced that Tuskegee's electoral Armageddon was just around the corner and prevailed on their state senator Sam Engelhardt to save them from the prospect of black control at the polls.[1]

As a staunch segregationist and former head of the Alabama Association of White Citizens Councils, Senator Engelhardt was happy to oblige. Under his sponsorship, the legislature—unanimously and without debate—enacted Alabama Act 140, providing for an alteration of Tuskegee's boundaries. Prior to 140's passage, Tuskegee had been essentially square in shape, with a population of 5,397 blacks and 1,316 whites. Afterward, its boundaries had twenty-eight sides and resembled a stylized sea horse. More critically, the boundary change placed Tuskegee Institute and all but ten of Tuskegee's 420 black voters outside the city limits—while affecting none of its approximately 600 white voters.[2]

Tuskegee blacks were then organized in the Tuskegee Civic Association, patterned along the same lines as Martin Luther King's Montgomery Improvement Association. Its president was Charles G. Gomillion, chairman of Tuskegee Institute's Division of Social Sciences. After Act 140's enactment, Gomillion and other association members met and decided to initiate a lawsuit. On August 4, 1957, Fred Gray filed suit in Judge Johnson's court against Tuskegee mayor Phil Lightfoot and other city officials. Enforcement of Act 140, Gray claimed, would violate equal protection, due process, and the Fifteenth Amendment's ban on racial discrimination in voting.[3]

At first blush, *Gomillion* v. *Lightfoot* seemed a simple case, involving the most blatant discrimination. But a variety of Supreme Court precedents muddied the constitutional waters. For years, the high Court had been denying relief to the urban victims of congressional and state legislative malapportionment. For decades also, it had emphasized that counties, cities, and towns were purely the creatures of the state legislature and subject to sweeping legislative control. In addition, numerous rulings forbade judicial inquiry into legislative motive. Confronted with such decisions, Judge Johnson concluded that he had no alternative but to deny the plaintiffs relief. Whatever the motivation underlying Act 140's passage, he held, "This Court has no control over, no supervision over and no power to change any boundaries of municipal corporations fixed by a duly convened and elected legislative body, acting for the people in the State of Alabama."[4]

Senator Engelhardt was naturally pleased with the ruling. "I am mighty happy," he told newsmen, "and I know the people of Tuskegee are, too. There is not much I can say. Judge Johnson took the words right out of my mouth." A number of state papers shared the senator's elation. "The newest decision is encouraging," editorialized the *Birmingham News*. "As we have said many times before, the southern legal mind is keen, the avenues of maneuver are many, so be of good cheer, all is not yet lost."[5]

Tuskegee's blacks appealed, but at first to no avail. Two members of a Fifth Circuit panel upheld Judge Johnson and state legislative supremacy over municipal boundaries, holding that federal court intervention was proper in such cases only where "racial or class discrimination appear[ed] on the face of the statute." In a concurring opinion, moreover, Judge John Minor Wisdom asserted—as Judge Johnson had contended earlier—that in the *Gomillion* case, as in the legislative malapportionment cases, no effective relief could be given. The only result that could flow from a ruling that Act 140 was unconstitutional, Wisdom suggested, would be the enactment of additional statutes and an exacerbation of federal-state relations. One member of the panel disagreed, however, with his colleagues' rationale and Judge Johnson's ruling. In an eloquent dissent, Judge John R. Brown observed: "State legislatures are accorded, and rightfully so, great respect and a far ranging latitude in their legislative programs. Occasionally there comes a time however, when legislation oversteps its bounds. . . . In such times the courts are the only haven for those citizens in the minority. I believe this is such a time."[6]

A unanimous Supreme Court agreed with Judge Brown. Justice Felix Frankfurter, ironically the Court's most vocal critic of judicial intervention in the "political thicket" of legislative malapportionment, authored the Court's opinion. For Frankfurter, Act 140's obvious racial purpose and effect distinguished the constitutional claims raised in *Gomillion* from those at issue in malapportionment cases. Though extensive, said Frankfurter, a state legislature's power over municipal boundaries did not exceed the Fifteenth Amendment's provisions—and Act 140 clearly breached these provisions.[7]

In a separate opinion, Justice Charles Evans Whittaker challenged Frankfurter's conclusion that the Tuskegee gerrymander had violated the plaintiffs' "right to vote." "One's right to vote in Division A," Whittaker reasoned, "is not abridged by a redistricting that places his residence in Division B, if he there enjoys the same voting privileges as others in that Division." But Whittaker concurred in the Court's ruling nevertheless. It was clear to him that "fencing Negro citizens out of" Tuskegee constituted racial segregation in conflict with the Fourteenth Amendment's guarantee of equal protection.[8]

At the Supreme Court's direction, the *Gomillion* case went back to Judge Johnson's court for final disposition. In a strongly worded opinion, the judge sustained Fred Gray's motion to enjoin Act 140's enforcement, citing "the undisputed facts . . . supplemented by the law of [the] case as laid down by the Supreme Court." On this occasion, he had welcomed defeat in the higher courts.[9]

In December 1957, Alabama's voters had approved a constitutional amendment permitting the legislature to abolish Macon County. But after submitting the proposal to the electorate and winning its approval, the legislature refused to exercise the power its enactment conferred. "Everybody took that as a joke," John Patterson recalls, "except the fellas who introduced it." None of the surrounding counties, it seemed, were at all anxious to share Macon's racial problems.[10]

Although the racial gerrymander thus met the same fate as the white primary, southern voter registrars retained a formidable arsenal of weapons in the fight to preserve white supremacy at the polls. Several states, including Alabama, employed a "voucher" system under which each voter applicant had to be properly identified by a registered voter as a prerequisite to registration. There were strict limits on the number of times a voter could serve as a voucher in any given year (twice was the limit in Alabama), and in counties with few black voters—or none, as in Lowndes and Wilcox County, Alabama—securing a voucher often proved an insurmountable barrier to black registration. And unlike vouchers for white applicants—who not infrequently were provided to forgetful applicants by helpful registrars—vouchers for black applicants found the process extremely demanding, requiring detailed knowledge of the applicant's background.

If the black applicant overcame the voucher hurdle, he faced others. He could still be disqualified for minor technical errors on the complex application form, or for failing to provide the "correct" answers to open-ended questions about the "duties and obligations of good citizenship," or for failure to "pass" educational tests for which there was no uniform minimum score, or for any of a number of other "defects." In fact, just getting a chance to fill out an application form was no small matter for the hopeful black applicant. In each Deep South state, the number of days allotted for voter registration was limited drastically; in Alabama, for example, two days each month, at most, were set aside for registration. When black applicants appeared, moreover, the normally lengthy process became extremely time-consuming—or the registrar simply closed the office for the day. Generally, only one application would be processed at a time, and not infrequently white applicants were given a priority position on the waiting list over blacks who had arrived earlier. And, too, if a black applicant surmounted such hurdles and was registered, there was always the chance he might neglect to pay his poll tax.[11]

When the Civil Rights Commission held its December 1958 hearings in Montgomery, a parade of witnesses accused Black Belt Alabama registrars of such discriminatory practices. Macon County—where less than 10 percent of voting-age blacks, and virtually all whites, were registered to vote—was the principal target of allegations. In all, twenty-seven Macon witnesses testified—professors, public school teachers, medical technicians, ministers, businessmen. When the hearings ended, one fact appeared obvious: Macon County's registrars seemed certain candidates for a Justice Department suit.[12]

On February 5, 1959, Justice Department attorneys filed suit in Judge Johnson's court seeking an injunction against what was termed the Macon board of registrars' systematic discrimination "for many years" against black voter applicants. The Macon suit was the department's second under the 1957 Civil Rights Act. The first had been filed against the registrars of Terrell County, Georgia. In April, the district judge in the Georgia case dismissed the government's complaint and declared the 1957 statute's injunctive provisions unconstitutional. Under the Fourteenth and Fifteenth Amendments, he reasoned, Congress had power to prevent only *governmental* interferences with federal voting rights, yet the 1957 law allowed injunctions against "any person" engaged in such practices. True, all the Terrell County defendants were government officials, but to the judge that factor was of no significance. Since private persons *could* be enjoined under the law, its injunction provision was unconstitutional "on its face."[13]

Judge Johnson was hardly bound by the Georgia judge's strange reasoning. But initially the Justice Department's Macon County suit was to have rough sledding in his court also. Injunctions against public officials ordinarily extend to the office as well as the individual. Under the 1957 Civil Rights Act, however, only voter registrars, not their offices, could be enjoined. At the time of the Civil Rights Commission's Montgomery hearings, E. P. Livingston, a Citizens Council member and brother of the chief justice of the Alabama Supreme Court, was chairman of the Macon board. But five days after the hearings, Livingston had resigned. The other two seats on the board were now also vacant. When the Justice Department filed its suit, therefore, Alabama's new attorney general MacDonald Gallion moved for a dismissal, claiming that there were no Macon registrars left for Judge Johnson to enjoin.[14]

The Justice Department's attorneys claimed the obvious—that the resignations were a "transparent device" to frustrate federal efforts in behalf of voting rights. But Judge Johnson agreed with Gallion. In an opinion dismissing the suit against each defendant, he concluded that "in using only the word 'person' " in the 1957 statute, Congress had "deliberately restricted the authority of the Attorney General to institute" voting suits.[15]

Alabama officials praised Judge Johnson's ruling in glowing terms, Governor Patterson calling it "a victory for the people and our constitutional form of government," and Attorney General Gallion naming it the "greatest breakthrough so far in the fight to preserve states rights" and a "sound defeat for the South-hating federal civil rights meddlers." The Justice Department appealed the decision to the Fifth Circuit, but an appellate panel upheld Judge Johnson. An appeal was then taken to the Supreme Court, but in the face of Alabama's legal argument, the chances for victory there seemed slight at best. In dismissing the case, Judge Johnson had suggested that the plaintiffs might initiate mandamus proceedings to compel appointment of new registrars if the seats on the Macon board remained vacant. But no action was taken along those lines either. Where registrars were willing to resign, then, further action under the 1957 act seemed doomed to failure.[16]

While the appeal of Judge Johnson's ruling was pending before the Supreme Court, however, President Eisenhower signed the 1960 Civil Rights Act into law. Essentially a series of amendments to plug up loopholes in the 1957 statute, the new legislation made voter records public and required their preservation for twenty-two months following any general or special election. It also authorized district judges to appoint federal voting referees in any jurisdiction found to have engaged in a "pattern or practice" of racial discrimination in voting. Finally, it made a shambles of Alabama's defense in the Macon County case by allowing district courts to proceed against the office whenever registrars resigned in the face of a voter suit.[17]

In Alabama, there was quick reaction to the new statute. In the recent past, Governor Patterson had bemoaned the problems he had encountered in attempting to fill the vacant seats on the Macon board. "Our job is difficult," said Patterson, "because of the unwarranted harassment

by the federal government and . . . the Civil Rights Commission." On
the day the 1960 legislation was signed into law, however, Patterson
located two civic-minded souls to serve as Macon registrars. The reason
for his haste was not difficult to fathom: under the 1960 statute,
vacancies on local election boards constituted a ground for the appointment of federal voting referees.[18]

The Justice Department's response to the new legislation was almost
as prompt as Governor Patterson's. Renewing their efforts to halt voting
discrimination in Macon County, government attorneys petitioned
Judge Johnson for an order allowing further inspection of the county's
voter records. In an opinion denying a state motion to dismiss, Johnson
granted the petition and upheld the constitutionality of the 1957 and
1960 Civil Rights Acts. When the inspection was completed, the
government's attorneys filed a motion for an injunction against Macon
County's newly appointed registrars—and against the state of Alabama.
They also petitioned for the appointment of federal voting referees.[19]

During a hearing on the Justice Department's motion, discriminatory
practices were established in at least six phases of the Macon registration process: (1) *The order of accepting applications.* Invariably, white
applicants had been given priority over blacks on the waiting list.
(2) *Assistance rendered to white applicants.* White applicants had
often received assistance in completing their application forms, while
blacks with high school and college educations were denied assistance
and rejected repeatedly because of minor errors in their forms. (3) *The
writing test.* Blacks had been required to copy a provision of the United
States Constitution, usually an extremely long one. White applicants,
on the other hand, had often been permitted to prove their ability to
read and write by copying a shorter passage or been allowed to
complete the registration process with no writing test at all. (4) *Grading
applications.* Blacks had often been rejected for registration because of
formal, inconsequential errors in their application forms, while white
applicants whose forms contained the same sorts of errors had been
registered. (5) *Failure to mail registration certificates to black applicants.* When registrars had acted favorably toward a black applicant,
they had often failed to notify the applicant of his certification as a
voter. (6) *Non-notification of rejected applications.* Black applicants
frequently received no notice that their applications had been rejected
and that they should reapply if they wished to register.

Testimony and documentary evidence underscored the nature and
consequences of such practices. After a great upsurge in black applications following enactment of the 1960 Civil Rights Act, Macon's registrars engaged in "slowdown" tactics. The maximum number of
applications processed in one day during 1960 was five, in contrast
with eight times that number in 1958. Since white applicants were

given priority, the slowdown meant that few blacks got an opportunity to complete an application form. In 1960, some four hundred blacks had signed the Macon priority list, but only eighteen were allowed to apply. At that rate, government witnesses estimated, it would take over twenty years for the Macon board even to process the applications of blacks who had sought to apply for registration in 1960. Fifteen black witnesses testified that they had attempted to register in 1957-58. Of the twelve whose applications were rejected, seven had completed at least one letter-perfect application form. One had a Ph.D., two had completed at least a year of study on a master's degree, three had B.S. degrees, two had completed at least two years of college, two were high school graduates, and two had at least two years of high school work. Not only were the state's attorneys unable to explain away such findings; they were unwilling even to allow the defendant registrars to testify. Judge Johnson obtained their testimony by calling them as witnesses for the court.

On March 17, 1961, Judge Johnson announced a decision in the Macon County case. Finding the evidence "overwhelmingly" supportive of the Justice Department's case, he enjoined the defendants from engaging in further discriminatory registration practices. Quoting from a 1939 Supreme Court ruling, he also reminded the defendants that the Fifteenth Amendment reaches "sophisticated as well as simple-minded modes of discrimination" and "onerous procedural requirements which effectively handicap exercises of the franchise by the colored race although [leaving] the abstract right to vote . . . unrestricted as to race." He refused, however, to appoint a federal voting referee. Instead, he expressed hope that, in the future, the registrars would act in good faith and ordered the defendants to place the names of sixty-four apparently qualified blacks on the Macon voting rolls. Although that figure was reduced when ten of the blacks were later found to be unqualified, he later ordered additional blacks added to the county's rolls and tightened the terms of his injunction against the defendants.[20]

Judge Johnson's decision to order blacks registered rather than appoint a federal voting referee for that purpose probably reflected as much—or more—his concern about alleviating federal-state tensions as his confidence in the Macon registrars' good faith. Concurrently with the Macon voter order, he held that in all future civil rights cases heard in his court, at least one attorney for each party must reside in the Middle District and the U.S. attorney was to play an active role in all stages of such litigation. The new rule, he explained, was based in part on his awareness "not only of the legal but of the social problems involved" in civil rights cases.[21]

Alabama response to the Macon County ruling was fixed. The *Bir-*

mingham News conceded "that there are probably numbers of white Alabama voters whose qualifications really could not stand the white glare of publicity." But state officials were not nearly so conciliatory. The federal government, Governor Patterson charged, was attempting to "deliver the reins of government to the Negroes by forced mass registration of Negro voters." Within a few months, however, Patterson and other Alabama officials, accompanied by a choir of state newspapers, would be praising Judge Johnson's resolution of another phase in the state's continuing civil rights crisis.[22]

While Justice Department attorneys were attacking voting discrimination in the courts, the Congress of Racial Equality (CORE) and other civil rights groups had initiated "freedom rides" into southern states to test segregation in bus station waiting rooms, restrooms, and lunch counters. When the freedom riders reached Alabama, violence erupted. On Mother's Day 1961, a Greyhound bus carrying a group of freedom riders was burned near Anniston; and a mob attacked another busload at a Trailways terminal in Birmingham. There were also sporadic outbreaks of nightrider violence. In a secluded field in one rural county, a white couple were forced to strip naked and viciously beaten; later, a white father was whipped in his home. All were accused of having allowed black maids to punish their children.[23]

On the Saturday morning following the Anniston and Birmingham violence, yet another busload of riders pulled into Montgomery's Greyhound station. A mob of some two hundred whites was waiting for them. When the bus came to a halt in the terminal, its driver announced over a public address system, "Here comes the freedom riders to tame the South," and the mob charged the bus, beating the riders with metal pipes, sticks, and fists.

The bus arrived around 10:30 A.M. Earlier, Floyd Mann, Alabama's director of public safety, had warned Montgomery's commissioner of public safety, L. B. Sullivan, of the impending arrival of the bus, but city police had taken no precautions to assure the riders' safety. At 10:37 and again at 10:39, a police car was sent to the area "to investigate"; at 11:24, two policemen arrived in another patrol car to "direct traffic." Initially, however, none of the officers made any effort to contain the mounting mayhem. Commissioner Sullivan sat in a car watching the mob. When asked by a newsman what his men intended to do about the violence all around them, Sullivan replied: "We have no intention of standing guard for a bunch of trouble-makers coming into our city and making trouble."[24]

Floyd Mann did his best to restore order, wading into the mob at one point with pistol drawn to rescue a black who had been beaten to the ground, on another occasion forcing white thugs to release a television reporter. But Mann was no match for the mob. At least four out-of-town reporters and photographers were beaten, others had their cameras smashed. A Justice Department observer was hospitalized after being hit from behind while attempting to rescue a white girl from the mob. Several of the riders were severely beaten. The chaos continued for hours, the mob swelling at times to over a thousand. Finally, city police used tear gas to restore order.[25]

In Washington, the Kennedy administration reacted swiftly to the Montgomery violence. President Kennedy issued a statement deploring the attacks and urging Governor Patterson to maintain order. The president also sent a request to the Interstate Commerce Commission (ICC) for a ban on segregation in interstate transportation facilities. Attorney General Robert Kennedy ordered four hundred federal marshals to Montgomery and announced that the Justice Department would ask Judge Johnson to enjoin Klan groups and the National States Rights party from further violence, along with others believed to have been involved in the attacks on the freedom riders.[26]

The next night, there was further violence in Montgomery. King and fifteen hundred blacks and white sympathizers with the civil rights movement gathered in a black church to voice support for the freedom rides. A mob soon surrounded the church, threatening to overwhelm the detachment of marshals sent there to protect King and his followers. Characteristically, Governor Patterson denounced the riders and the federal "interlopers." But when the marshals seemed inadequate to the task of restoring order, he declared martial law and called out the national guard. With the sweeping powers authorized them by the governor, the guard quickly scattered the mob and restored order.[27]

While the mob was still raging, Judge Johnson had issued a temporary restraining order against further Klan violence. A temporary order expires in ten days. But after a five-day hearing, May 29–June 2, Judge Johnson granted the Justice Department's motion for a preliminary injunction against the Klan and Montgomery police, prohibiting further interference with the free flow of interstate commerce. At the same time, however, he granted Commissioner Sullivan's request for a temporary restraining order against CORE, King, and a host of other groups and individuals, banning further organized freedom rides pending a hearing on the issue. "Those who sponsor, finance and encourage [freedom rides] with the knowledge that such publicized trips will foment violence," he asserted, "are just as effective in causing an obstruction to the movement of bona fide interstate bus passengers as are those defendants named in the Government's complaint." The freedom riders may be engaged in the exercise of a legal right, he conceded, but in his view, "the right of the public to be protected from the evils of their conduct [was] a greater and more important right." In short, pending further hearings, there was to be no action by either side that might inspire a repeat of the earlier violence. "If there are any such incidents as this again," he warned from the bench, "I am going to put some Klansmen, some city officials, some city policemen and some Negro preachers in the Federal penitentiary."

The violence against the freedom riders had further blackened Alabama's racial image, and the state's politicians and newspapers applauded Judge Johnson's ruling. "With one stroke of the pen," said the *Alabama Journal*'s city editor, the judge had "ceased to be the villain and became the hero of the hour" with "injunctions against just about everybody—from the Klan wizard to Martin Luther King"—"somehow . . . precisely what an exhausted populace wanted." But a number of Alabama and national papers questioned the propriety of the judge's ban on the freedom rides. While praising Johnson's desire to prevent further violence, the *New York Times* complained, for example, that his order had "the effect of equating persons seeking to exercise their legal rights and others who are violating the law by trying to prevent such exercise." To the *Times*, such a position seemed clearly inconsistent with the Supreme Court's 1958 ruling that the climate of resistance created by Governor Faubus and other Arkansas officials was inadequate to justify even a temporary delay in the desegregation of Little Rock's Central High School.[28]

As Judge Johnson had pointed out in banning further freedom rides, the rights at issue in the Little Rock case had been firmly established by federal court order, whereas no specific order had yet been issued regarding the status of Montgomery's bus terminals. Naturally, however, counsel for the freedom riders and the Justice Department shared the *Times*'s concerns. The temporary restraining order against the riders lapsed after ten days, but Commissioner Sullivan sought a permanent ban. At a July 17 hearing, Louis Pollak, the riders' counsel, asked Judge Johnson to dismiss Sullivan's motion. Reminding Pollak that a freedom rider suit challenging bus station segregation was then pending before the court, Johnson responded to Pollak's motion with a question and a pointed observation: "Why do [your clients] continue to agitate when you have a case filed here in the Court? . . . It is unheard of, people that file a law suit in a court and ask the court to adjudicate their rights, and then continue to agitate to get them by agitation and not wait for the Court."

While obviously displeased that the freedom riders wanted to continue their "agitation" even though a lawsuit to challenge bus terminal segregation was then pending in his court, Judge Johnson also seemed unimpressed with Commissioner Sullivan's position. Calvin Whitesell, the commissioner's attorney, complained that the freedom riders—and "an element in Alabama that resists with violent means these people coming in here to demonstrate"—had caused a serious disruption of bus services. Of the riders, Whitesell said: "They put a burden on our police department. They put a burden on our highway patrol. And they put a burden on the FBI. All because they insist upon a right to ride a bus." "I see nothing wrong with that," Judge Johnson retorted. "That is what your police are for. That is what the patrol is for; that is what the FBI is for; I don't see that helps your case at all." But Whitesell pressed on: "I don't know that it is their duty to escort every bus that comes into the State of Alabama." "It is their duty," the judge shot back, "to maintain law and order."

Ultimately, neither side would win. After the July hearing, Judge Johnson simply sat on the issue until it disappeared. On November 1, the ICC issued orders requiring desegregation of interstate transportation facilities; and on the same day, Judge Johnson issued a ruling along the same lines desegregating Montgomery's bus terminals. Calling the decision "an insult to every citizen of Alabama," Governor Patterson warned freedom riders to stay out of his state. "If they continue to invade our state and continue to try to run over us," Patterson promised, "we want to serve notice that we are going to defend ourselves and we are not going to take it lying down." From then on, however, there was no further freedom rider violence in the Middle District.[29]

During the freedom rider interlude, a Fifth Circuit panel had begun considering Alabama's appeal of the Macon County ruling. On June 1, 1962, the panel voted two to one to affirm Judge Johnson's order. Only that portion of the order requiring the addition of blacks to the Macon voting rolls posed any difficulty for the majority, and that problem was by no means insurmountable. The 1957 and 1960 Civil Rights Acts had not specifically authorized such orders. The 1957 act had stipulated, however, that district judges could provide relief in voting discrimination cases through issuance of an injunction "or other order." For the majority, that provision was adequate to justify Judge Johnson's action.[30]

The lone dissenter was Judge Benjamin Franklin Cameron, a Meridian, Mississippi, native and the Fifth Circuit's most thoroughly unreconstructed southerner. By this point, the circuit was developing a moderate-to-liberal image in civil rights cases, largely as a result of the presence on the court of Judge Rives and three Eisenhower appointees—Elbert P. Tuttle, a California native, Cornell law graduate, and former chairman of the Georgia GOP, since 1961 the court's chief judge; John Minor Wisdom, a New Orleans corporation lawyer and former Republican national committeeman; and John R. Brown, a Houston attorney until his appointment in 1955. Judge Cameron was also an Eisenhower appointee (1955), but there the similarity to his moderate-to-liberal brethren ended. To Cameron the southern states were "conquered provinces" again under siege, Justice Department attorneys "invaders," and the federal judge's proper role that of interpreting the United States Constitution according to the "ethos of the people" (presumably, the white people) within the judge's jurisdiction. He had repeatedly voiced such themes in stinging dissents, even where the majority stance rested firmly on clear Supreme Court precedent. On occasion, moreover, he had complained vehemently (and apparently with some justification) that his chief judge was stacking the circuit's civil rights panels with at most one conservative and two racial moderates, thereby prejudicing the outcome of sensitive cases.[31]

In the Macon County case, Judge Cameron challenged the majority's assumption that federal judges have power to add names to voting rolls, arguing with some force that the 1957 and 1960 legislation authorized only preventive relief. He also delivered another sermon on the evils of federal power, quoting the late Justice Robert H. Jackson's warning that federal abuse of authority poses a greater threat to individual liberty than state excesses. Whatever the validity of Judge Cameron's broad attacks on federal power, his specific challenge to Judge Johnson's addition of names to the Macon voting rolls carried considerable force. One may well appreciate the strategy behind Johnson's reluctance to appoint voting referees, and implementation of the referee procedure itself posed substantial difficulties. But the 1960 civil rights legislation seemed a doubtful basis for Judge Johnson's order. The principal study of the legislation's adoption in no way suggests, for example, that the "other order[s]" beyond injunctive relief which district judges could impose in voting cases could include a method for bypassing the referee mechanism while achieving the same result.[32]

Even so, later in the year the Supreme Court upheld Judge Johnson and the Fifth Circuit majority. Two years earlier, the high Court had overturned the district court challenge to the 1957 Civil Rights Act in the Terrell County, Georgia, case. Of the judge's conclusion in that case that the 1957 act was invalid because it was vulnerable to unconstitutional applications, Justice William Brennan remarked for a unanimous Court: "The delicate power of pronouncing an Act of Congress unconstitutional is not to be exercised with reference to hypothetical cases thus imagined." With judicial power under the 1957 and 1960 legislation thus firmly entrenched, the Macon County registrars continued to function under Judge Johnson's watchful eyes.[33]

While the Macon litigation had been in progress, Justice Department attorneys had filed complaints in Judge Johnson's court to end voting discrimination in Montgomery and Bullock counties—but not before considerable maneuvering by state officials and the counties' registrars. In May 1960, the Justice Department attempted to inspect the voting files of Montgomery County. Judge Walter B. Jones was no George Wallace. As the Montgomery bus boycott litigation had demonstrated, however, he was more than willing to assist state officials caught up in civil rights battles. When the Justice Department made its move, Attorney General Gallion turned to Judge Jones for help, and the judge promptly issued an injunction preventing the inspection of the Montgomery records. Shortly thereafter, Justice Department counsel filed separate motions before Judge Johnson for orders dissolving Jones's injunction and authorizing inspection of the records. Rejecting any notion that state courts had any share in judicial authority granted under the 1957 and 1960 Civil Rights Acts and citing the "basic legal principle" that state courts have no power to enjoin the actions of federal officers, Judge Johnson promptly granted both motions. When the inspection was completed, the Justice Department sought an injunction against Montgomery County's registrars. A few months earlier, a similar suit had been filed against discriminatory registration practices in Bullock County.[34]

In the Bullock case, Judge Johnson ultimately banned the use of the voucher system and a number of other discriminatory practices. When the Bullock registrars continued to reject black applicants at an alarming rate, moreover, he called them in for hard-nosed lectures on their constitutional responsibilities and threats to appoint federal referees if they failed to mend their ways. "I can't and I am not going to permit these people to be denied registration because of some technical error or omission in their application," he warned at one point. "Now once we can reach a meeting of the minds on that, we'll get along all right. But we haven't so far in . . . Bullock County." In both the Bullock and Montgomery cases, he also enjoined a relatively new form of voting discrimination—a "freezing tactic" under which registrars had attempted to perpetuate white supremacy at the polls by adopting a single but extremely strict set of standards applicable to both races. Virtually no applicant, whatever his race, could meet such requirements; in fact, in Montgomery County white applicants rejected under the device included the law partner of one of the defense attorneys in the case, a retired general and West Point graduate, and the college graduate son of a former Alabama attorney general. Since, however, few blacks and most voting-age whites were then registered to vote in the two counties, the racially discriminatory effect of the new standards was obvious—and, for Judge Johnson, a clear constitutional violation. Finally, in the Montgomery County case, Judge Johnson followed his Macon precedent. On November 20, 1962, he ordered 1,072 qualified black applicants added to the county's voting rolls and rebuked Alabama's officials for continuing in the belief that "some contrivance" could successfully be adopted to deny black citizens the right to vote.[35]

Had all southern federal judges approached the task of eliminating voting discrimination with Judge Johnson's determination, further resistance would indeed have seemed futile. But a substantial minority of southern district judges did not share Judge Johnson's willingness to enforce the law in voting rights cases—or, for that matter, in any field of civil rights. Consider, for example, the case of W. Harold Cox, Mississippi Senator James Eastland's college roommate. In 1961, President Kennedy was compelled by the dictates of senatorial courtesy to appoint Cox to a district judgeship in Mississippi—the president's first southern judicial appointment, but by no means his last selection of an avowed segregationist for the federal bench. Judge Cox likened blacks to "chimpanzees" who "ought to be in the movies rather than being registered to vote." During his early tenure on the bench, he rendered decisions in thirteen voting rights cases—two in favor of the Justice Department, one ambiguous in outcome, ten in favor of defendant registrars. On more than one occasion, moreover, he rebuked the Justice Department for making him "spend most of my time in fooling with lousy cases brought before me by your Department."[36]

Judge Cox, Judge Cameron, and a select few others were in a class all their own, but they were not alone. Of thirty-seven southern district judges who sat on three or more civil rights cases, 1954–62, seven rendered pro-black decisions in less than 10 percent of the cases, eighteen in less than 60 percent, despite the obvious constitutional violations at issue. Moreover, although most southern district judges could perhaps be characterized as "judicial gradualists" who supported segregation but could be expected to follow higher court precedents once their initial antiblack decisions had been reversed, their examples generally offered little cause for optimism that the judicial approach to civil rights reform in the South would be adequate to the task. Judge Daniel Thomas, Judge Johnson's counterpart in Alabama's Southern District, was one such moderate segregationist. While Judge Johnson was busy issuing comprehensive injunctions, ordering black names added to county voting rolls, and threatening recalcitrant registrars with contempt proceedings and the appointment of federal referees, Judge Thomas was pursuing a decidedly more deliberate pace. In the Justice Department's Dallas County (Selma) voting suit, for example, Judge Thomas conceded that many qualified blacks had been denied registration and many unqualified whites had been registered between 1952 and 1960. Even so, he denied injunctive relief, explaining that he was confident that a new board of registrars would show good faith. "These problems," he pointedly added, "must be resolved and should be resolved by the people and not by the courts." Only after two Fifth Circuit reversals did Judge Thomas begin to provide effective relief in Dallas County.[37]

In truth, of course, Deep South politicians attempting to ride the crest of southern racial unrest probably preferred the aggressiveness of a

Judge Johnson to the obliging complicity of a Judge Thomas—and none more so than George Wallace. After his gubernatorial defeat and contempt acquittal, Wallace had exiled himself to Barbour County for the duration of the Patterson years in Montgomery. In early 1962, however, he was off and running in a second bid for the Democratic gubernatorial nomination. He faced a field of eight opponents, including Attorney General Gallion and former Governor Folsom. But it soon became obvious who his principal targets would be. The United States, he told crowd after crowd of enthusiastic spectators, "has the sorriest federal court system in the world. They're telling us who we're going to live with, who we're going to swim with, who we're going to play with, [and] who we're going to eat with. They're trying to run the country by their own rules and I'm sick and tired of it." "I don't like what has been done by those courts at all, do you?" he would ask the crowds. "No, no, no," they invariably responded. Although never referring to him by name, Wallace singled Judge Johnson out for special treatment. "This race-mixing federal judge down at Montgomery," he charged repeatedly, was an "integrating, scalawagging, carpet-bagging, race-mixing, bald-faced liar" who "hasn't ever done anything for Alabama except to help destroy it." If elected, Wallace promised, "this state is not going to be big enough for him and me running the schools."[38]

At one point in the campaign, an unsportsmanlike organization of mysterious origin, dubbed the League for Truth in Government, placed advertisements in state newspapers, ridiculing the "Little Judge" and reprinting those portions of Judge Johnson's contempt order detailing the candidate's clandestine cooperation with Civil Rights Commission agents. But Wallace kept pounding away with his own version of the events. "What did the federal judge do? He turned me loose. Why? He knew the people were not going to stand for arresting public officials. . . . But when they backed down they said some nasty things about me. . . . I would like to remind anyone who says I didn't back down the federal court that he is an integrating, race-mixing, scalawagging liar." Invariably, such harangues were his chief crowd-pleasers.[39]

No candidate won the majority needed for a first primary victory, but Wallace made it into a runoff with state Senator Ryan DeGraffenried, a handsome, articulate scion of an aristocratic Tuscaloosa family. DeGraffenried ran on a pledge to improve Alabama's national image. "The only way we'll ever be able to preserve our customs and traditions," he told his audiences, "is to go on the offensive and sell Alabama to the rest of the nation." But white Alabamians preferred Wallace's promise of a second Civil War. To them, Marshall Frady has explained in his fascinating study of the Wallace phenomenon, "Wallace was an enthralling, giddy, irresistible temptation. He vowed he would place his body in the door of any schoolhouse ordered to integrate, and before long DeGraffenried was left protesting the honesty and aggressiveness of his own segregationist beliefs." Wallace won the runoff with a comfortable 56 percent of the vote.[40]

Even after his primary victory—which was tantamount to election in solidly Democratic Alabama—Wallace continued attacking his law school classmate. But at a Selma Citizens Council rally and barbeque in October, Wallace's finance director-designee Seymour Trammell out-did the master. Standing in for Wallace at the rally, Trammell called the Kennedys "power crazy . . . vote-counters looking for the bloc vote" and urged "responsible Southerners" to blacklist federal judges, their families, and friends. "The cloak and dagger federal judges are more dangerous than Khrushchev," he exclaimed, "and we know how to deal with him as our enemy. We also know how to deal with those scalawagging federal judges who are our enemies."[41]

A number of Alabama newspapers published scathing editorials condemning Trammell's harangue. While finding "no cause for tears over the lot of [lifetime] federal judges," the Montgomery Advertiser, for example, called Trammell's proposal "infantile," adding: "The idea of taking it out on the women and children of a judge hardly qualifies as Southern gallantry." But to Judge Rives's surprise, he later recalled, some Montgomerians followed Trammell's suggestion.[42]

If such attacks had any effect on Judge Johnson, obviously they did not weaken his resolve in civil rights cases. His strongest Bullock County ruling was issued shortly after the 1962 primaries, his Mont-gomery County ruling less than two months after Trammell's tirade. In 1964, moreover, he would enjoin use of a newly developed question-naire designed to test prospective voters' knowledge of federal and state political institutions—a questionnaire to which white applicants had not been subjected in the past. In the same year, he would grant injunctive relief against the registrars of Elmore County, rejecting whatever defense Glen Curlee was able to muster in his clients' behalf. Building a case in Elmore County had posed more of a problem for the Justice Department than their development of cases in other Middle District counties. When the Elmore County registrars learned of the impending federal investigation into their practices, they had simply carried the county's voter records to the Wetumpka city dump and burned them. The case that was developed, however, had the same ring as the others. Eighty-nine percent of the county's voting-age whites were registered, 7.5 percent of its blacks. Black applicants rejected for registration included public school teachers. Among whites accepted for registration were an illiterate man with a fourth grade education, whose sister had completed the application form; a man with a sixth grade education, whose son filled out his father's form; and a man with a second grade education, whose wife completed his form in a hallway outside the registrars' office. Judge Johnson issued an injunction and ordered a hundred black names added to the Elmore County rolls. By this point, however, the Wallace era of confrontation politics was well under way, and the focus of controversy had moved from the ballot box to the schoolhouse door.[43]

 Schools

For more than a decade after the *Brown* decision, school desegregation remained largely a promise unfulfilled, obstructed on all fronts by the varieties of massive resistance. Bolstered by the inherent vagueness of the Supreme Court's initial mandates, southern legislatures invoked the historic—though entirely discredited—doctrines of nullification and interposition, declaring the Court's orders and decisions null and void. Statutes requiring racial segregation in southern schools were replaced with more subtle controls eliminating the policy, but not the practice, of segregated schooling. Citizens' groups cynically shipped poor black families off on reverse freedom rides, promising paradise in "enlightened" northern communities. Membership in Citizens Councils and their more militant segregationist counterparts, the National States Rights party and Klan organizations, grew rapidly—as did incidents of racial violence and the number of southern politicians willing to fuel the flames of white discontent. Perhaps the most visible manifestations of massive resistance, however, were George Wallace's confrontations with Judge Johnson's desegregation orders. Certainly, for Wallace they would prove the most politically rewarding.[1]

Like the Justice Department's attempts to eliminate discriminatory voter registration practices, efforts to desegregate Alabama's public schools had their first feeble beginnings in Macon County. In the summer of 1955, thirty-two parents of black schoolchildren had submitted a petition to the Macon board of education demanding "immediate steps to reorganize the [county's] public schools . . . on a non-discriminatory basis." Citing the Supreme Court's requirement of "good faith compliance" with its *Brown* mandate "at the earliest practicable date," the petitioners insisted that the school board was "duty bound to take immediate concrete steps leading to early elimination of segregation in the [Macon] public schools."[2]

In Alabama in 1955, however, they might as well have been asking for the moon. "Personally," said Macon's school superintendent C. A. Pruitt, "I feel the majority of Negroes in Macon County do not want integration any more than white people. . . . I will work for equally good educational facilities for both races which will have equally good programs. [But] I hope the fine relations which have existed between the races in Macon County will not be destroyed by a few hotheads of both races." Senator Engelhardt was more direct: "We will have segregation in the public schools of Macon County or there will be no public schools."[3]

Other early desegregation efforts in Alabama proved equally futile. In 1955, Judge Hobart Grooms, Judge Lynne's colleague in the Northern District, ordered Autherine Lucy admitted to the University of Alabama. When rioting erupted there following Miss Lucy's admission in early 1956, however, Judge Grooms upheld the school when it first barred her temporarily from the campus as a safety measure, then permanently expelled her for "outrageous, false and baseless accusations" against university officials. Later, Grooms joined Judges Rives and Lynne in rejecting a claim that Alabama's public placement law was unconstitutional on its face. Under the statute's provisions, students were not formally assigned to schools on the basis of race; but school officials were allowed to consider such factors as a student's "psychological qualifications," the "physical effect" upon the pupil of attendance at a particular school, the possibility of threat or disorder, economic retaliation, and "the maintenance or severance of established social and psychological relationships with other pupils and teachers." Despite such obvious racial overtones, the three-judge panel cited the traditional judicial reluctance to inquire into legislative motive and ruled that the statute was susceptible to constitutional application.[4]

To the layman reading the statute in the context of those turbulent times, such judicial blindness to legislative motive may have bordered on the ludicrous. Even so, the Supreme Court upheld the panel's ruling. And on that cold, bleak January day in 1963, when George Wallace took the oath as governor, Alabama's schools remained totally segregated. But not for long. Even as Wallace symbolically drew the "line in the dust and toss[ed] the gauntlet before the feet of tyranny," pledging "Segregation now! Segregation tomorrow! Segregation forever!" his administration was already moving toward the first of a long series of civil rights defeats in Alabama's federal courts.[5]

In the week following Wallace's inauguration, black parents petitioned Judge Johnson to end segregation in the Macon County school system. On August 13, the judge concluded that "an honest and fair application" of the state pupil placement law would "result in the immediate admission of a number of qualified Negro students" and ordered the Macon board to begin desegregation of the county's schools by the fall term and to submit a general desegregation plan by mid-December. The board, he emphasized, had the primary responsibility for "bringing to an end the operation of a school system that violates the constitutional rights of a large majority of the citizens in Macon County."[6]

By this point, Macon's white officialdom was no longer in a fighting mood. Blacks outnumbered whites twenty-two thousand to five thousand, county officials faced an articulate and increasingly aggressive black leadership, and the county was still suffering the effects of a black boycott that had closed sixteen white-owned businesses in the wake of the Tuskegee gerrymander. Instead of appealing Judge Johnson's ruling, the school board agreed to accept thirteen of forty-eight black applicants for admission to the all-white Tuskegee High School. After considerable prodding from the Fifth Circuit, Judge Lynne and Judge Thomas ordered the Birmingham and Mobile school systems to begin desegregating also.[7]

By the fall term of 1963, then, three Alabama school systems were under court order to desegregate. In Huntsville, moreover, the board of education had adopted a voluntary plan of token desegregation. Governor Wallace's futile "stand in the schoolhouse door" to prevent desegregation of the University of Alabama the previous spring had made it clear, however, that the transition was likely to be anything but smooth. And when the public schools opened in the fall, Wallace embarked on another round of "schoolhouse door" politics—albeit this time through stand-ins. In Macon County, state troopers under the command of Colonel Albert J. Lingo, Wallace's director of public safety, ringed the Tuskegee High School campus, allowing no one but the principal to enter. At Wallace's request, Huntsville officials agreed to delay the opening of schools slated for desegregation there. Mobile officials followed suit, although two blacks were registered for formerly all-white schools at the offices of the city school board. In Birmingham, the schools under order to desegregate opened on schedule; but when rioting erupted and the home of a black attorney was bombed, they were quickly closed. Later, when Huntsville officials refused to delay the opening of school any longer, state troopers ringed the campus of each Huntsville school scheduled to desegregate, barring all but a few determined white students from entering. In Mobile, Wallace's troopers ultimately permitted a high school slated for desegregation to open, but only after exacting a promise that no black students would attend.[8]

Such direct intervention in local affairs by a politician known for his defense of states' rights provoked widespread public outcry. In Tuskegee, the president of the local bank, a father of three "distressed" children, condemned Wallace's tactics and speculated that 90 percent of the town's white citizens shared his sentiments. In Huntsville, the home of the nation's space program and a northern Alabama city with a large non-native population, feelings were particularly bitter. Parent after parent turned away from the doors of Huntsville's schools recommended that Wallace be hanged, or worse. Birmingham's two dailies also published stinging editorials decrying the ultimate futility of the governor's course. And in southern Alabama, even Grover Hall, Jr., editor of the *Montgomery Advertiser* and a staunch Wallaceite, joined the critics' growing ranks: "The Advertiser must sorrowfully conclude that, in this instance, its friend has gone wild. Alabama is not a banana republic. It is in no need of an adventurer to ride down upon local authority."[9]

But Wallace was moving once again toward near-martyrdom and was not to be dissuaded. On Monday, September 9, he allowed Huntsville's schools to open on a desegregated basis, but in a series of executive orders issued the same day directed Macon, Birmingham, and Mobile school officials to maintain segregation. "Integration of the public schools," he declared, "will totally disrupt and effectively destroy the educational process and constitutes an abridgement of the civil rights of other children attending the schools, and deprives them of the equal protection of the laws and constitutes the deprivation of their rights, liberty and property without due process of law."[10]

These events formed the background for the "Big Judge's" second confrontation with the "Little Judge." After the September 9 orders were issued, Justice Department attorneys requested and received a temporary restraining order against the governor, prohibiting not only resistance to public school desegregation in Alabama, but also any failure to maintain "peace . . . within and around the schools" subject to court order. In issuing the order, which each of Alabama's federal district judges signed, Judge Johnson asserted: "Unless a temporary injunction is issued without notice the plaintiffs will suffer immediate and irreparable injury consisting of the impairment of the integrity of the judicial process of the United States Courts, the destruction of due administration of justice and the deprivation of rights under the Constitution and laws of the United States."[11]

Instead of complying with the court order, Governor Wallace ordered marshals attempting to serve it off the capitol grounds and dispatched national guardsmen to the schools to preserve segregation—and, perhaps, to be conveniently available in case President Kennedy might wish to overwhelm him with military force, thus winning the governor a few more segregationist votes. At this point, the president signed a cease and desist order against the "obstruction of Justice in Alabama" and federalized the national guard to enforce the order. At the same time, however, he attempted to obstruct Wallace's plans for martyrdom. Immediately after the guardsmen had been placed under his authority, he ordered them back to their armories, leaving only local police at the school sites. But this modification of the facts prompted no change in the Wallace scenario. On Tuesday, twenty blacks attended formerly all-white schools in Tuskegee, Birmingham, and Mobile. Asked by reporters about his second desegregation defeat in three months, Wallace quickly retorted: "I can't fight bayonets with my bare hands."[12]

The desegregation accomplished, Justice Department attorneys and Fred Gray, counsel for the parents of the Macon schoolchildren, asked Judge Johnson and Alabama's other district judges to enlarge the restraining order into a more permanently binding preliminary injunction. Before a hearing on the motion could be held, however, Wallace filed his own motion—that Judge Johnson disqualify himself from further participation in the case. Citing his public attacks on the judge, Wallace charged Johnson with "personal bias and prejudice." A federal judge's decision to withdraw himself from participation in a given case is largely a matter of personal judgment, and Judge Johnson was clearly unpersuaded by the force of Wallace's strange logic. "If statements made by a defendant against a judge could constitute a legal basis for asking a judge to disqualify himself," he retorted, "then any defendant could at his own will render the judge disqualified by making public statements about him." In fact, "a defendant could make statements about all federal judges and thereby such judges would become biased and prejudiced against him." Had he any "personal feelings of prejudice" against Wallace, he icily added, "a voluntary recusation would have occurred—no motion would have been necessary." When the hearing was conducted on September 24, Judge Johnson was among the participants.[13]

In an attempt to legitimize his maneuvering, Wallace on September 9 had asked the Alabama Supreme Court for an advisory opinion as to his power to close the schools and maintain segregation. On the day set for the federal hearing, the justices issued an opinion upholding the governor. While finding no specific power to close the schools, much less preserve segregated schools, the justices concluded: "If closing of the schools be the actual and incidental result of keeping the peace, the power to keep the peace is not restricted." At the federal hearing, Wallace's legal counsel and political adviser John Kohn advanced the same thesis. Citing Wallace's public declarations that he would no longer interfere with school desegregation efforts, Kohn also charged that issuance of an injunction in the face of such assurances would be "an implied insult to the chief executive of this state." But the governor's counsel did not confine his defense entirely to such narrow contentions. Urging the judges to rule on the Fourteenth Amendment's validity, he denounced its provisions as "conceived in hate, born in the aftermath of war, and carried through at the point of the bayonet." Justice Department attorney John Doar contended, on the other hand, that failure to issue a preliminary injunction would mean that Wallace's executive order had become "a higher law than the Constitution." Scoffing at Kohn's assertion that the governor was motivated by a desire to prevent violence, Doar charged that there was little evidence—only an opinion—that a threat of violence existed. Wallace, he asserted, was simply "using state power to paralyze the supreme law of the land."[14]

Alabama's five district judges agreed with Doar. In a replica of Judge Johnson's earlier restraining order, they enjoined Wallace, Albert Lingo, and other state officials from further interference and failure to maintain peace and order. Late that evening, U.S. marshals delivered the injunction to John Kohn's Woodley Road home in Montgomery after having no success in reaching the governor.[15]

Judge Johnson's school desegregation battles, of course, were just beginning. In early November, he ordered a black admitted to graduate study at Auburn University. Officially, Harold A. Franklin had been denied admission not because of his race, but because he had not graduated-from an accredited undergraduate college. Since Alabama maintained no accredited black colleges, the accreditation requirement effectively barred all black admissions. In granting relief, Judge Johnson observed: "The effect of this rule . . . is necessarily to preclude him from securing a post-graduate education at Auburn University solely because the State of Alabama discriminated against him in its undergraduate schools. Such racial discrimination . . . amounts to a clear denial of the equal protection of the laws." Franklin was slated for admission in early January 1964; but before his admission, Judge Johnson was again forced to intervene, this time to order university officials to provide Franklin with on-campus housing. This last order proved too inviting a target for Wallace. Calling Judge Johnson a "judicial tyrant," Wallace charged that the judge "not only insults the people of this state [but] evidently relishes such." On this occasion, however, his opposition was purely verbal. On January 2, 1964, Franklin enrolled at Auburn without incident.[16]

Following resolution of the Auburn case, Wallace began maneuvering toward yet another confrontation over the desegregation of Macon County's schools. After the black students had entered Tuskegee High School under Judge Johnson's court order in September, all the school's white students had eventually withdrawn, about 150 transferring to high schools in the rural communities of Shorter and Notasulga, the remainder enrolling at Macon Academy, a hastily created "private" school financed largely with state funds—and transportation provided by Alabama state troopers. As a result, only the black students and thirteen teachers had attended Tuskegee High the balance of the fall term. In late January, Wallace decided to take advantage of the situation. At his request, the state board of education adopted a resolution ordering the closing of Tuskegee High School, the transfer of its teachers to other Macon County schools, and the transfer of the black students to "other schools in the Tuskegee area." The board rested the resolution on grounds of finances and efficiency. By limiting the black pupils to "other schools in the Tuskegee area," however, the resolution had the effect of requiring them to return to the all-black Tuskegee Institute High School. Thus, when they were denied admission to Tuskegee High on February 4, Judge Johnson issued a restraining order. While refusing to prevent Tuskegee High's closing for economic reasons, he ordered the blacks admitted to the Shorter and Notasulga schools on the same basis as the white students who had transferred from Tuskegee High when the blacks had first entered there. He also asked the Fifth Circuit's chief judge to form a three-judge panel to hear the plaintiffs' request for another preliminary injunction against the governor (as president of the state board of education), members of the state board, and the Macon County board.[17]

The restraining order infuriated Wallace. Adding a new twist to his now familiar attacks, he termed the order a "judicial tantrum" and recommended Judge Johnson's impeachment. "The action of this Federal judge," said Wallace, "is rash, headstrong and vindictive. . . . This Federal judge is attempting to run this state by a usurpation of authority and the threat of bayonets. . . . As the governor of Alabama I resent it. . . . In my judgment this judge ought to be impeached."[18]

On the day the restraining order was issued, Wallace called the members of the state board of education in for a meeting to authorize appointment of attorneys for the forthcoming federal hearing. During the session, the board adopted a resolution condemning the restraining order and pledging continued efforts to maintain segregation in Alabama's public schools. The board also ordered the Macon school board to provide financial assistance for the students at Macon Academy.[19]

After the meeting, Wallace told newsmen that he doubted state funding of segregated private schools would lead to increased federal court intervention, but added sarcastically: "Federal judges make the law as they go along. They may make a law to hang you and I tomorrow." Of Judge Johnson, he said: "Some people need an examination. I think you know who I'm talking about." Noting that Johnson had ordered Macon school officials to provide transportation for black students attending the Shorter and Notasulga schools, he accused the judge of forced "busing"—thereby becoming perhaps the first in a long line of politicians to raise that now overworked complaint against members of the federal judiciary. He also had some unkind words for the sort of schooling Johnny Johnson was receiving. Both to insulate their son from abuse in the public schools and to shield him from the problems of school desegregation, the Johnsons by this point had enrolled Johnny in the Montgomery Academy, a segregated private school they had helped to establish. Though saying that he intended no criticism of Johnny ("a fine young man"), Wallace scored the judge for sending his son to an expensive private school while those less fortunate had to cope with the problems of court-ordered desegregation.[20]

Despite Wallace's rhetoric, Macon school officials moved promptly to comply with Judge Johnson's order. Six of the black students were ordered transferred to Shorter High School, the rest to the Macon County High School in Notasulga, a rural community with a population of about a thousand situated some fifty miles east of Montgomery. Local whites accepted neither the court order nor the board's good-faith efforts to comply. Nightriders burned two barns on a farm owned by a member of the board. And though the six black students assigned to Shorter were admitted peacefully on February 5, those who boarded a yellow school bus for the trip to Notasulga met total resistance. A Confederate flag flew over the school, and a crowd of fifty whites waited across the street. State troopers under Colonel Lingo ringed the campus. Augmenting the troopers were members of Notasulga's small police force and mounted sheriff's deputies under the command of James Clark, the sheriff of Dallas County and a rising star in the ranks of Alabama's anti-civil rights leadership. Clark and his men were there at the invitation of Notasulga's young mayor James Rea.[21]

When the bus reached the Macon County High School, Mayor Rea embarked on a variation of Wallace's earlier ploy at the University of Alabama. Apart from the black students and a black bus driver, the only occupant of the bus was a young free-lance photographer. Sheriff Clark and a Notasulga policeman quickly dragged the stowaway photographer from the bus and threw him to the ground. Mayor Rea then stood in the doorway of the bus and denied the blacks entry to the school. Wallace had invoked the historic (though entirely discredited) doctrine of interposition in his university stand, but Rea made a more modest claim: the students' presence in the school would constitute a fire hazard. Ten days earlier, it seemed, the community had adopted a fire ordinance designating Rea to serve as fire and safety inspector. In his new capacity, the mayor had promptly decided that the school could safely accommodate no more than 175 persons. The facilities were currently occupied by 174 white students and staff. Thus, said the mayor, enrollment of the black students would threaten the safety and lives of all concerned.[22]

His "stand in the school bus door" brought Rea brief national notoriety, but the mayor was no George Wallace. After turning the students away, he stressed to newsmen his willingness to comply with Judge Johnson's orders. "I have all the respect in the world for the courts in this country," he assured them. "I wouldn't think of defying a court order." Within a week, he got a chance to prove his commitment. Acting on a Justice Department request, Judge Johnson found that the fire ordinance had been enacted as a devious tool for obstructing desegregation and enjoined Rea from employing it or any other ordinance to prevent the black students' admission to the Macon County High School. At that point, the mayor's defiance came to an abrupt end.[23]

On February 21, Judge Johnson, Judge Rives, and Judge Grooms convened a hearing in Opelika on Fred Gray's motion that the restraining order against Wallace, the state board of education, and the Macon school board be enlarged into another preliminary injunction. The hearing quickly turned into a statewide attack on segregation in Alabama's public schools. For a number of years, school officials had claimed that Alabama had no state school system, but only independent local schools. In the post-*Brown* era, the practical significance of such an arrangement was obvious: any court order requiring desegregation of Alabama schools would apply to but one of the state's more than one hundred school districts, and desegregation of all the state's schools would require expensive and time-consuming litigation in virtually every district.

Seizing on Wallace's recent Macon County antics, Fred Gray and NAACP attorneys charged that the state's conception of Alabama's school system was a mere fiction, that in fact state officials had long exercised extensive control over Alabama's local school boards, and that Wallace, the state board, and other state officials should be permanently enjoined from operating biracial schools not only in Macon County, but anywhere in the state. In addition, they moved for an order requiring the state board to submit a plan for the complete reorganization of Alabama's public schools on a nonracial basis. Finally, they asked that an injunction be issued against state funding of "private," segregated schools, charging that the clear purpose of such arrangements was circumvention of federal court desegregation orders.

Though recent events belied their claim, attorneys for the defendants sought to establish that the state board had no control over Alabama's local school boards, even though they had "mistakenly" exercised such powers in the recent past. In support of their contention, they submitted yet another advisory opinion from the ever-helpful justices of the Alabama Supreme Court. When Wallace had begun to realize the use to which the Macon County plaintiffs planned to put his most recent maneuvers, his attorneys had made a frantic rush to the state high court for an advisory opinion on the legitimacy of the state board's actions. The justices quickly produced the answer Wallace undoubtedly wanted. "The authority and power which you assume . . . to be in the State Board of Education," they said, "is not in that Board, but in the . . . local boards."[24]

Again, however, the Alabama court's post hoc advice was to be of no assistance to Wallace and his cohorts in the federal courts. The hearing lasted two days. During the next fifty days, counsel for the parties and the Justice Department submitted briefs relative to the key issues raised at the hearing. Then, on July 13, 1964, the panel issued a ruling in an unsigned per curiam opinion Judge Johnson had drafted. Finding that the state board of education had indeed exercised extensive control over Alabama's local school systems "to prevent or impede any deseg-regation," the panel enjoined the board, and Wallace as its president, from further "interfering with Court-ordered desegregation anywhere in the State of Alabama." It also banned further state financing of private, segregated schools. For the time being, however, the panel declined to order desegregation of every Alabama public school "upon the assumption that the Governor, the State Superintendent of Educa-tion and the State Board of Education will comply in good faith with the injunction."[25]

Not surprisingly, Alabama officials were at least mildly elated by the ruling. As Alabama Attorney General Richmond Flowers, a racial moderate and Wallace opponent, had warned before the decision was announced, the intervention of Wallace and the board of education in Macon County had been a "terrible blunder" which quite conceivably could have involved "the entire state and every school board in the state" in a single desegregation order. In time, Flowers's words would prove prophetic. In the interim, however, court-ordered desegregation in Alabama proceeded on a district-by-district basis. In the summer of 1964, Judge Johnson ordered the school boards of Montgomery and Bullock counties to begin desegregating. Macon County, of course, also remained under Judge Johnson's jurisdiction. But there desegregation now existed only on paper. With the arrival of black students at the Shorter and Notasulga schools, all the white students had withdrawn and begun attending one of Macon's two private academies. On April 17, arsonists had burned the Notasulga school. Left smeared on the walls of the gutted building were a variety of racial epithets and the words: "Judge Johnson's and Bobby Kennedy's school . . . Godfathers of all Niggers."[26]

Unfortunately, such statements reflected the sentiments of many Alabamians—including those too "refined" to utter them in public, much less resort to the tactics of the Klan. But if such feelings made life any more difficult for the Johnsons, they rarely revealed their concern. Johnny Johnson was separated by only a few days in age from the son of the Jack Vanns, two of the Johnsons' more loyal Haardt Drive neigh-bors. Johnny and Dick Vann had become almost inseparable boyhood chums; and for several summers, the boys and their fathers took long boat trips, fishing during the day and camping at night on the banks of the river. After moving to Montgomery, the Johnsons had also rented a cottage at Lake Martin and the cottage became a favorite haven from the turmoil of Alabama's racial politics. Johnny soon became adept at skiing and other water sports, and the Johnsons enjoyed fishing and relaxing. Often, too, they entertained friends there. "When our sons were seniors," Jack Vann recalls of one such outing,

> Johnny entertained . . . the boys of his senior class, and invited Dick along. Dick was at [Sidney] Lanier [High School] then, and Johnny was at the Montgomery Academy. I was also invited to help Lee Dodd with the chaperoning and cooking. . . . After we got the boys to bed about midnight, we went out on the lake to catch striped bass. . . . I caught a fish. . . . Pretty soon, I caught another one. . . . Oh, I guess I caught four or five fish before either Dodd or the judge caught the first one. Then, Dodd caught one or two, but I was well ahead. And pretty soon, we had the fish stacked up under the boat seat like cordwood. I had caught . . . at least fifteen fish, and Judge by then had caught about five or six, and Dodd maybe ten or twelve. Then, Dodd said softly, "Look, you know the judge is not going to leave this spot as long as we're ahead of him. You take that minnow off your hook and throw out an empty hook. . . ." So that's pretty much what we did. We stalled around until the judge caught up with us, then cranked up the motor to go back to camp just before daybreak—and spent the morning cleaning all those fish. . . . He's very competitive.[27]

Frank M. Johnson Jr., at eighteen months.

Frank at age four with his mother. A family friend has remarked that Alabama Long Johnson "is a woman of strong character. And Frank inherited an awful lot of that. He has always shown the courage of his convictions—sometimes to a fault."

Frank M. Johnson, Sr. During the 1930s and early 1940s, Judge Johnson's father was "Mr. Republican" in Winston County, Alabama's lone GOP stronghold.

Left to right, Wallace, Bill, and Frank Johnson with family setter. As the eldest of seven children, Frank had more than his fair share of babysitting chores.

Frank M. Johnson, Jr.
A law school photograph.

As law school classmates, Frank Johnson and George Wallace clearly enjoyed more than a passing acquaintance. Here, Frank and Ruth Johnson attend a school dance with Wallace, future Wallace political crony Glen Curlee, and their dates.

Johnson and co-counsel Morris McGee (right) secured a light sentence for S/Sgt. James M. Jones (center), one of several guards charged with brutality against American deserters and other inmates of the army prison barracks in Lichfield, England.

Johnson and son Johnny clown for the camera during a mountain vacation.

Peering over his half-moon glasses, Judge Johnson would have a sobering effect on more than one lawyer.

Judge Johnson and federal appeals court judge Richard T. Rives at a banquet honoring Johnson's twentieth anniversary on the bench. A member of a prominent Montgomery family, Rives infuriated fellow white Montgomerians when he and Johnson voted to desegregate the city's buses.

Even while recuperating from the surgery that prompted his withdrawal as director-nom-inee of the FBI, the judge could fix visitors to his chambers with a characteristic penetrating gaze.

The times do change. In 1979, former segregationist governor John Patterson welcomed Judge Johnson into the Alabama Academy of Honor, a society recognizing outstanding contributions to the state and its citizens. Patterson now considers the judge "about the best valve for bringing about change that couldn't be done politically I've ever seen."

After taking the oath of office as judge of the U.S. Court of Appeals for the Fifth Circuit, Judge Johnson spoke of those in Alabama "who understood the spirit—the spirit as well as the letter of the law, who ventured forward while others did not." His example was fellow Alabamian Supreme Court Justice Hugo L. Black. On this occasion, however, his words brought to mind his own career.

 Selma

While Alabama was experiencing the first tremors of court-ordered school desegregation, the president and Congress had again entered the civil rights thicket. In the spring of 1963, civil rights activists under the leadership of Martin Luther King, Jr., had rocked Birmingham with a series of sit-ins and mass demonstrations protesting discrimination in the city's thoroughly segregated restaurants, lunch counters, and theaters. As a shocked nation watched on television, Birmingham's commissioner of public safety Eugene (Bull) Connor had responded in predictable "Simon Legree" fashion, complete with snarling police dogs, fire hoses, mass arrests, and a ready supply of vitriolic segregationist rhetoric and crude racial humor for attentive newsmen. The massive civil rights march on Washington followed in the late summer. Then, on a quiet Sunday morning in mid-September, a dynamite bomb had exploded in a black Birmingham church, killing four little girls and igniting further racial unrest in the troubled city.[1]

Prodded by the Birmingham demonstrations—and national revulsion at the reaction of the city's white officialdom—the Kennedy administration had pushed Congress to enact an omnibus civil rights statute covering a variety of fields, but aimed primarily at discrimination in places of public accommodation and employment. In November, President Kennedy had made his fateful trip to Dallas. But his successor had quickly made it clear that, if anything, he would be a more forceful advocate of civil rights reform than the dead president. As a southerner, Lyndon Johnson no doubt felt a special need to convey to black voters his commitment to their cause. As one of the Senate's more effective majority leaders of the recent past, he was an old hand at ramming legislation through the Congress. On July 2, 1964, he signed into law the most far-reaching civil rights legislation enacted by Congress since Reconstruction. While focusing on public accommodations and employment, the Civil Rights Act of 1964 had included a number of voting provisions. Equal voter registration standards were to be applied to white and black alike. No voter applicant was to be disqualified for technical errors on his voter application form. A sixth grade education was to constitute a rebuttable presumption of literacy.[2]

The principal responsibility for enforcing voting equality was left, however, with the federal courts. Even in counties under the jurisdiction of Judge Johnson or one of the few other southern federal judges willing to act aggressively against discriminatory voting officials, the progress of court-backed black registration had been slow. In those districts manned by more passive jurists, it had progressed at a snail's pace, or not at all. In the Black Belt counties of Judge Thomas's Southern District, for example, the percentage of black adults registered to vote in 1964 ranged from zero in Wilcox County, to less than 3 percent in Dallas and less than 4 percent in Hale, to slightly over 7 percent in Choctaw and Perry. By contrast, white registration was well over 90 percent in each of these counties except Dallas (where 66.3 percent of whites of voting age were registered). And in Wilcox—where white voters apparently remained extremely civic-minded even after death—over 100 percent (2,959 of 2,647 voting-age residents as of late 1963) were registered.[3]

During the early weeks of 1965, King's Southern Christian Leadership Conference (SCLC) and the more militant Student Non-Violent Coordinating Committee (SNCC) under John Lewis organized demonstrations and a voter registration drive in six Southern District Black Belt counties. The focal point of the movement was Selma, the Dallas County seat. In Selma, county and city officials were confronted daily for weeks with marches and demands that discrimination in voter registration be abolished. Demonstrations were also conducted in Marion, the Perry County seat. On a number of occasions, the Selma and Marion protests erupted in violent clashes between the protesting blacks and state and local authorities. During one Marion incident, a black demonstrator, Jimmie Lee Jackson, was killed.[4]

Selma is located fifty miles west of Montgomery. The two communities are connected by U.S. Highway 80. After the voter drive had continued for seven weeks, King announced a "Freedom March" from Selma to the state capitol in Montgomery to dramatize black demands for an end to voting discrimination—and to denounce the police brutality to which participants in the voter drive had been subjected.[5]

Governor Wallace had been watching the developments in Selma closely, and his reaction to King's announcement was characteristic. On March 6, Wallace held a televised press conference at the capitol. The voter drive, he announced, had caused "disorderly interruption of the normal functions of government" for weeks. The "so-called" march would not be "conducive" to the free flow of traffic and commerce and would not be tolerated.

The protesters chose to ignore the ban. On Sunday, March 7, some 650 blacks gathered at the Brown's Chapel church in Selma, headquarters for the voter registration drive. After hymn-singing and speechmaking, the group set out toward Montgomery with camping equipment and extra clothing. Without incident, they proceeded through Selma's business district and across the Edmund Pettus bridge. On the Montgomery side of the bridge, however, they were met by a phalanx of state and county law officers. Awaiting their approach on Highway 80 were sixty to seventy troopers under the command of Colonel Albert Lingo and Dallas County sheriff James Clark, flanked by his deputies and mounted "possemen." During the voter drive, Selma's police chief Wilson Baker had earned a reputation for professional, restrained control of protest demonstrations. But Sheriff Clark was a different story. Frequently in the preceding weeks, he and Lingo's troopers had employed unwarranted force against the protesters. Today would be no exception. State trooper Major John Cloud gave the marchers two minutes to disperse. After about a minute, the troopers moved among the marchers, pushing and jabbing them with billy clubs, then routing them with canisters of gas. Sheriff Clark's mounted posse-men, wielding whips and clubs, then joined the troopers, riding their horses into the marchers and pressing them back over the Pettus bridge. The drive did not end until the bleeding and choking blacks had retreated through the streets of Selma to the safety of the Brown's Chapel church. By the time the rout was over, seventeen blacks re-quired hospitalization; another sixty-seven had been injured. White thugs had also attacked an FBI agent, seizing his camera.[6]

National reaction to the incident at the Pettus bridge was swift. In Washington, a thousand civil rights activists—and a handful of Ameri-can Nazis defending Governor Wallace's approach to race relations—staged demonstrations at the White House and Justice Department. In Detroit, ten thousand persons joined Governor George Romney and Detroit Mayor James Cavanaugh in a protest march down Woodward Avenue. Thousands of demonstrators blocked rush-hour traffic in Chi-cago's Loop area. Three thousand gathered at a CORE rally on the University of California's Berkeley campus. In cities and on college campuses throughout the country—and in a number of foreign coun-tries as well—the pattern was repeated.[7]

Back in Alabama, Governor Wallace denied that the troopers and sheriff's deputies had used excessive force and asserted that their action might actually have saved some of the marchers' lives. Had they been allowed to continue, he explained, police could not have pro-tected them from irate whites. Besides, he added, not nearly as many had been injured in Selma as in recent northern racial incidents. Wallace and his lieutenants also charged—once again—biased report-ing by the national media. Edited film clips, complained one Wallace aide, had made it "look like [the police] didn't give the niggers any time to obey the command to disperse."[8]

In Selma, Mayor Joseph Smitherman noted that King had not been present for the Sunday march and accused King and other top civil rights leaders of deserting their flock during times of crisis. Local wits circulated their own proposal for stopping any future march to Montgomery: just place a diving board at the crest of the Pettus bridge, they suggested, and erect a sign beside it reading "Whites Only." But the Selma Times-Journal provided its readers with a thorough, straightforward account of the Sunday incident, describing the clubbings and gassing in copious detail. Other state papers generally followed a similar pattern, and a number published highly critical editorials about the state's handling of the situation. Still other papers appealed to Wallace's political common sense. In an editorial entitled "Let Them March," for example, the Birmingham Post-Herald urged Wallace to provide the protesters adequate police protection, noted that King and his followers "thrive on violence," and predicted that violence against them would simply mean additional federal interference in the state's race relations.[9]

The editorial was perceptive—but the advice a bit late. On March 15, President Johnson went before a joint session of Congress and pledged to overcome the nation's "crippling legacy of bigotry and injustice," adding with special emphasis: "And we ... shall ... overcome." Accompanying his pledge was the most comprehensive voting rights legislation ever submitted for congressional consideration.[10]

While the nation reacted, King and SNCC leaders vowed to march to Montgomery despite the Wallace ban. Early Monday morning following Sunday's violence at the bridge, civil rights lawyers were in Judge Johnson's court seeking an injunction to prevent further state interference with their clients' activities. The judge was expecting them. Several days earlier, he had instructed his law clerk Walter Turner to begin researching the constitutional issues such a march might raise.[11]

Issuance of an injunction would require a hearing, but counsel for the would-be marchers also requested a temporary restraining order preventing state interference pending the hearing's outcome. Judge Johnson denied the request and instead enjoined further attempts to march. "In order to protect the integrity of this Court and to prevent the judicial processes from being frustrated by the plaintiffs and other members of their class continuing to attempt to enforce the rights they seek to have judicially determined in this Court," he ruled, "it appears that it will be to the best interest of all concerned and will work no irreparable injury or harm to plaintiffs, or members of their class, if they are ordered to refrain from attempting to exercise what they claim to be a constitutional right to march, until the matter can be judicially determined at an early hearing." A hearing was set to begin at 9:00 A.M. the following Thursday.

Judge Johnson's order put King in a bind. He admired the judge's courage and dedication to human rights, but considered the order unjust. "I was very upset," he would say later. "I felt it was like condemning the robbed man for being robbed." King feared, too, that his compliance with the order would serve further to enlarge the influence of SNCC leaders and militants within his own organization who had become increasingly critical of his nonviolent philosophy. His followers, he sensed, were tired of being on the receiving end of whips, clubs, and cattle prods—and were ripe for conversion to a more militant stance. Another march could serve as a safety valve for their growing frustrations.

In the 1964 Civil Rights Act, Congress had created a Community Relations Service to seek informal solutions to local racial problems. President Johnson had selected former Florida governor and racial moderate Leroy Collins as the service's first director, and Collins was serving as the president's chief administrative spokesman during the Alabama crisis. Collins attempted to persuade King to observe the terms of Judge Johnson's order and forego another march pending outcome of the hearing. Though his efforts proved futile, he was able to work out a compromise with King and Alabama's officialdom. King's group would attempt to march in defiance of the order, but be turned back—peacefully this time—by a line of troopers. King could satisfy his followers, the governor his, and violence could be avoided. King agreed to the arrangement; so did Wallace. And on Tuesday, March 9, the scenario unfolded largely according to the script. As a New York *Herald Tribune* newsman wrote the next day: "For 20 tense minutes yesterday, the Rev. Dr. Martin Luther King, Jr., and 2,000 civil rights marchers confronted this segregationist state's armed might, and then both sides retreated."[12]

Not everyone, of course, had been pleased with the arrangement. That night, five thugs clubbed three Unitarian clerics on a Selma street corner. Several days later, one of the ministers, the Reverend James Reeb, died in a Birmingham hospital. Civil rights militants saw the compromise as yet another sign of King's impotence. At the other end of the political spectrum, attorneys for Sheriff Clark petitioned Judge Johnson to cite King for contempt of the court order. The judge quickly made it clear, however, that any contempt proceedings would be a matter between King and the court and were "not any business of James Clark." While not actually revealing in open court that he had approved the compromise in advance, Judge Johnson drew testimony outlining its terms from King and other witnesses and concluded that there had been only an appearance of defiance. "It was a symbolic sort of thing," he later explained, "to save face for King."[13]

The hearing on the civil rights leaders' motion for an injunction lasted almost five days. Twenty-one attorneys were present as counsel for the parties. Fred Gray, joined by Jack Greenberg of the NAACP's

Legal Defense Fund, led a team representing the would-be marchers. Three lawyers represented Wallace and Colonel Lingo. John Kohn was also on hand to represent Lingo. Four Selma attorneys represented Sheriff Clark. On the day before the hearing was to begin, the federal government also entered the case; John Doar, a Justice Department colleague, and U.S. attorney Ben Hardeman were present to represent the United States.

Much of the testimony and numerous photographs introduced at the hearing focused on the violence of the previous Sunday, but a number of witnesses told of other confrontations during the voter drive. Sallie Rodgers, a nineteen-year-old student at an all-black Selma college, described, for example, a February 10 demonstration by black teenagers at the Dallas County courthouse. After she and two hundred others had been there about forty-five minutes, police ordered them to "Left face" and "March." "We started to marching, and we went out in the streets; we thought we was going to the jail, but we wasn't." With troopers and sheriff's deputies following in state cars, the youths were driven into the countryside. When they began to tire, the officers "beat some of them, cattle prod some of them, and they cursed some of them, hit some of them."

State and local officials provided other evidence of the treatment accorded the demonstrators. Colonel Lingo acknowledged, for the first time, that one of his troopers had killed Jimmie Lee Jackson, the youth shot in the February 18 violence at Marion. Lingo's other testimony was equally revealing. "Governor Wallace had proclaimed that there was to be no march," he testified at one point. "I interpreted this to mean that I was to restrain the marchers." "Regardless of what it meant to do it?" Judge Johnson asked. "No," Lingo replied, "I did not mean to kill them." A Dallas County sheriff's deputy conceded on cross-examination, moreover, that Sheriff Clark had apparently knocked a black minister to the ground during one confrontation.[14]

Counsel for the defendants scored few points for their side during the hearing. Over the plaintiffs' objections, they were allowed to call state troopers who testified that a march from Selma to Montgomery over winding Highway 80 would pose serious traffic hazards. But Judge Johnson rebuffed their efforts to introduce a Defense Department film on crowd control designed to support their claim that the defendants had followed standard procedures in the confrontation at the Pettus bridge. The film, he noted, depicted techniques employed by the military to control armed rioters in foreign countries and was hardly germane to the case before the court. The judge was equally impatient with sporadic defense efforts to browbeat the plaintiffs' witnesses. Are you not being paid to "agitate"? John Kohn asked a black Selma minister, teacher, and president of the county voters league. "It shouldn't have been necessary," the judge wearily interrupted, "but it has been necessary once during this trial for me to advise counsel that when they examine they are to—they are to demonstrate common courtesies to all of these witnesses, regardless of who they are or what color they are." Kohn withdrew the question.[15]

As the hearing drew to a close, Judge Johnson pondered what decision he should render. "The judge would come down on one side of the case for awhile," Walter Turner recalls, "and then he would come down on the other side. We would sit in his chambers and he would use me as a sounding board. He would outline the basic rights of the state to protect the citizens and maintain the integrity of the highways, and then he would outline the great injustices that had been done to the blacks in Selma, and the basic constitutional rights that had been denied to them." At home, too, Ruth Johnson remembers, he "agonized" over a ruling. Judge Johnson admired King's philosophy of nonviolence and his leadership abilities, but preferred the courts and the ballot box to the streets as tools of political and social change. While blacks lacked the vote, he believed, their marches and demonstrations would have little ultimate impact. With the vote, many of their problems would disappear. At the same time, he obviously realized that black access to the ballot *was* the march's ultimate goal; and he knew, in any event, that a judge should not allow personal predilections to influence his judicial decisions.[16]

Whatever his misgivings, Judge Johnson acted decisively when the hearing ended. The plaintiffs had submitted a plan of march to the court. The judge approved the plan to the extent that it related to movement along Highway 80 from Selma to Montgomery. He also ordered Governor Wallace and the other defendants to provide the marchers with adequate police protection. The freedom of petition, he reasoned, obviously could be exercised by large groups. In fact, for "coerced, harassed, and intimidated" minorities, group association seemed "the only realistic way of exercising such rights." Moreover, though there were limits to its exercise, the scope of the freedom must be "commensurate with the enormity of the wrongs protested and petitioned against," particularly where "the usual, basic and constitutionally-provided means of protesting in our American way—voting— have been deprived." The plan of march proposed by the plaintiffs admittedly reached "to the outer limits of what is constitutionally allowed." But the "enormous" injustices heaped on them and others like them by Alabama's officialdom had "clearly exceeded—and continue[d] to exceed—" constitutional limits. The proposed march was thus a "reasonable" exercise of a right guaranteed by the Constitution.[17]

By the time Judge Johnson rendered judgment on the propriety of the Selma march, the Supreme Court had itself decided a fair number of cases arising out of civil rights protest demonstrations in southern states. Building on decisions from the 1930s and 1940s about government's power to control expression in public places, the Court had concluded that the right of protest must be weighed against competing societal interests. The Court's stance seemed a far cry, however, from Judge Johnson's apparent assumption that the scope of a group's freedom to protest its grievances depended on the virtue of its cause. Moreover, the protective burden his order imposed on government officials far exceeded anything the high Court had yet countenanced.[18]

Even so, Judge Johnson's ruling would never receive a full airing in the appellate courts. He announced his decision on Wednesday, March 17. Two days later, he denied the defendants' request for a stay of the order pending appeal to the Fifth Circuit. Citing the federal government's professed willingness to provide Alabama assistance in protecting the marchers if so requested by Governor Wallace, he also rejected the defendants' claim that the state lacked adequate manpower and resources to comply with the order. The only question remaining, he asserted, was "whether the State of Alabama authorities [were] willing to . . . preserve peace and order." He did inform the defendants that a Fifth Circuit panel stood ready to grant an immediate review of his decision to deny a stay, and the defendants quickly appealed. Almost as promptly, however, the panel denied a stay. Further appeal seemed futile; within a week, the issue would be moot.

Reaction to the court order in Alabama was typical. Arthur Hanes, a former Birmingham mayor and diehard segregationist, announced plans for a white countermarch from Selma to Montgomery. In Montgomery, moreover, two hundred angry whites marched five blocks through the business district and held a rally on the steps of the capitol. Black and white SNCC demonstrators were picketing on the capitol steps when the whites arrived, and a cordon of police moved between the two groups. After about an hour, the whites left. Police then arrested members of the SNCC group for parading without a permit. In Birmingham, the resident bishop of the Methodist church termed the march "a great disservice to the cause of human freedom." A number of Episcopal and Catholic clerics were equally negative.[19]

State newspapers were also generally critical of the order. As always, however, Alabama's press was no match for its governor. On national television the evening following issuance of the order, Wallace addressed a joint session of the legislature and delivered a twenty-minute tirade against Judge Johnson, the media, and the demonstrators. Johnson, he charged, was a man "hypocritically wearing the robes" of a judge while "presiding over a mock court" and "prostitut[ing] our law in favor of mob rule." The communist-inspired, "collectivist press" were "propagandists masquerading as newsmen," the demonstrators knife-wielding "mobs employing the street-warfare tactics of the Communists" and abetted by every "left-wing, pro-Communist fellow traveler and Communist in the country." Alabama's solons were quickly caught up in the spirit of the evening. Before Wallace left the chamber, they had passed a resolution calling the march "asinine" and dangerous and urging President Johnson and Attorney General Nicholas Katzenbach to persuade the marchers to "cease and desist." Later, Wallace would claim in a television interview that Judge Johnson's order had been dictated by the Justice Department.[20]

But, again, the governor would stop short of outright defiance of a Johnson order. Instead, he chose to plead state poverty and indulge in what the press quickly termed "financial interposition." In a telegram requesting the president to send "federal civilian forces" to Alabama, he claimed that Alabama was simply too poor to comply with the order. Compliance, he estimated, would require 6,000 men, 489 automobiles, 15 buses, and necessary support units, but at best, the state could provide only a few hundred troopers, conservation officers, and Alcoholic Beverage Control agents to protect the "so-called" march.[21]

The ploy worked. Reminding the governor that he had over ten thousand Alabama national guardsmen at his disposal and that an "Alabama judge" had approved the march, President Johnson administered another Wallace-type lecture on the necessity for "law and order" and refused to provide civilian protection for the marchers. He conceded, however, that if Wallace failed to mobilize the guard, even though conditions warranted it, he would.[22]

The Selma march did not, of course, mark the first deployment of troops in racial crises. But the protection furnished the Selma marchers was among the most ambitious and costly ever undertaken. Ultimately, they were shepherded by a federally financed force of 1,863 Alabama guardsmen, a thousand regular army troops, a hundred FBI agents, and an equal number of federal marshals.[23]

On Sunday, March 21, two weeks after their fateful first attempt, the marchers, over three thousand strong and three hours behind schedule, began their trek to Montgomery. As they moved out of Selma, white onlookers—some bearing signs on their cars reading "I Hate Niggers," "Go Home King," and "Meredian, Mississippi Hates Niggers"—watched and complained bitterly to newsmen about integregation, a government willing to waste taxpayer dollars while our boys were fighting in Vietnam, and blacks in general. But this time there was no violence. Troops were stationed every hundred yards along Highway 80; army helicopters hovered overhead.[24]

The march to the outskirts of Montgomery took four days. At times, the number of marchers dwindled to less than two hundred; only a relatively few sore-footed stalwarts would complete the entire journey.

In the evening, sympathetic actors, singers, and musicians provided entertainment. At night, the marchers slept under tents in pastures along the highway.²⁵

While the marchers made slow and steady progress, Governor Wallace complained that their trek would cost the American taxpayer at least a million dollars. Alabama's congressional delegation made similar estimates, and Montgomery's first-term GOP Congressman William Dickinson charged on the floor of the House of Representatives that the marchers were defecating in public and engaging nightly in interracial sex orgies. Asked about Dickinson's allegations, SNCC head John Lewis replied: "All these segregationists can think of is fornication," adding, "that's why there are so many different shades of Negroes."²⁶

The marchers reached Montgomery on Wednesday, March 24. Whatever one's philosophical perspective, the procession to the capitol was an impressive affair. Led by King and bearers carrying two United States flags and the flag of the United Nations, over twenty-five thousand marchers, many carrying flags and banners, converged on Dexter Avenue and moved up Goat Hill toward the capitol. Almost two hours passed from the time the head of the march reached the foot of the capitol steps to the arrival of the last marchers at the end of the throng, which extended all the way down Dexter Avenue to Court Square.²⁷

Throughout the week, the marshal's office had provided Judge Johnson with frequent reports of the march's progress. And as the marchers moved toward the capitol, the judge, Walter Turner, and other court personnel joined Judge Rives in Rives's chambers to get a firsthand view. They watched the procession for over an hour. At one point, John Doar came by to report that so far there had been no serious problems and to remark that the march was "a beautiful sight." As the seemingly endless mass of humanity paraded by below, Judge Rives began to smile. Finally, he turned to his colleague and grinned. "This," he said, "does indeed reach the outer perimeters of what is constitutionally allowed."²⁸

When the march leaders reached the top of Goat Hill, they were met at the capitol steps by a line of seventy riot-equipped state troopers. Other troopers, Alabama legislators, and office workers watched from capitol windows. Governor Wallace had declared a legal holiday for all women employees, and it was assumed that he, too, would stay away from the capitol that day. His press secretary had announced, however, that he would be in the office "as usual." And, occasionally, he could be seen peering through the blinds of an office window at the state's uninvited guests. He refused, however, the march leaders' request for a meeting.²⁹

Their unwilling host's inhospitality would not dampen the marchers' spirits. Joining King and Ralph Bunche of the United Nations on a speaker's platform were representatives of every persuasion on the civil rights spectrum, from Whitney Young of the Urban League, to Roy Wilkins of the NAACP, to SNCC's John Lewis. While the nation watched on network television, the marchers celebrated the occasion with speeches and hymn-singing. "We are not about to turn around," King told his followers. "We are on the move now. Yes, we are on the move and no wave of racism can stop us."[30]

White Montgomerians, of course, generally did not share the marchers' enthusiasm. In their plan, the marchers had indicated that the demonstration at the capitol would end at 3:00 P.M. Judge Johnson had not specifically incorporated any time limit into his order. But when 3:00 passed and the marchers remained in the streets, the phone in his office began to ring incessantly. "Do you have the time?" "Wasn't this thing to be over with by now?" invariably anonymous callers asked. Mixed in with the inquiries were the usual death threats. While they never failed to unnerve the judge's secretary Miss Cosper—and she had Walter Turner answer these—crank calls had become an accepted part of the routine at Judge Johnson's court by this point. And on this occasion, the calls were the extent of the judge's harassment. The day was equally uneventful for Ruth. While the marchers converged on the capitol, she and several friends walked the links of the Montgomery Country Club.[31]

In the days following the march, a variety of critics, from Governor Wallace and Congressman Dickinson to the Imperial Wizard of the Ku Klux Klan, continued to raise charges of communist influence and sexual improprieties among the demonstrators; and the *Birmingham News* reported that an admitted communist "was right there with King and other leaders in the march to Montgomery." In time, Alabama's Sovereignty Commission funded a fifty-eight-minute filmed "exposé" of the march, but the finished product may have been a disappointment to those awaiting its release. About one-third of the film was devoted to the march itself, the rest to excerpts from the speeches of civil rights leaders and close-ups of individual marchers—with a heavy emphasis on those with bearded chins. No sex orgies—or anything approaching them—were depicted. The Sovereignty Commission had films of such activities in its possession, the film's co-producer explained, but they were simply too strong for viewing by a family audience. The film received a few showings, principally at Citizen Council gatherings around the state. By late December, however, news stories of the production were concerned solely with the film's alarmingly high cost; its exhibition grew increasingly rare, then ceased altogether.[32]

If Judge Johnson's march order had created the impression that he generally condoned civil disobedience or disruptive marches—civil rights or otherwise—his subsequent rulings quickly dispelled any such notion. On the Supreme Court, Justice Hugo L. Black of Alabama had begun to warn—with increasing vehemence—of the threat the current varieties of protest posed for the rule of law and an orderly society. In Black's view, such activities were conduct, not speech, and thus beyond the reach of the First Amendment's protective cloak. Judge Johnson found his senior colleague's attempts to distinguish speech and conduct both artificial and unworkable. But he shared many of the justice's concerns about the growing emphasis on street protest as a vehicle of social reform and reflected those concerns in his post-Selma protest rulings.[33]

Before, during, and following the march to Montgomery, civil rights protesters were arrested frequently in Montgomery and elsewhere in the Middle District for trespass, breach of the peace, parading without a permit, and a variety of other offenses. Invariably, they petitioned Judge Johnson to remove their state prosecutions to his court and protect their right of protest. Where the protests had been peaceful, and there had been no interference with vehicle or pedestrian traffic, the judge was willing to provide relief. But hundreds of demonstrators had blocked streets and sidewalks without first seeking a parade permit, and others had taken over the offices of the president of Alabama State College, ignoring orders to disperse. For those petitioners, Judge Johnson had no relief, only some strong language about the limits of free expression—and the dangers of civil disobedience—in an orderly society. Directly confronting King's thesis that "unjust" laws should be disobeyed, he charged: "The philosophy that a person may—if his cause is labeled 'civil rights' or 'states rights'—determine for himself what laws and court decisions are morally right or wrong and either obey or refuse to obey them according to his own determination, is a philosophy that is foreign to our 'rule-of-law' theory of government." For several years, Judge Johnson would frequently repeat and expand these themes in law school addresses, at Law Day citizenship proceedings, and in other settings, always reminding his audience that there may be moral—though never legal—justifications for civil disobedience, but stressing, too, that "unqualified" doctrines of disobedience were simply "more sophisticated" ways of "saying that a man is entitled to take the law into his own hands."[34]

If the Selma march seemed to violate Judge Johnson's own basic precepts, it was because he considered it a unique, onetime affair, "the last hurrah," so to speak, of the direct-action approach to civil rights reform that had had its birth in the Montgomery bus boycott. Time would prove him correct. As the civil rights movement merged with antiwar protest and other social concerns—and its focus shifted from the South to northern cities and suburbs—protest demonstrations became increasingly counterproductive.[35]

The impact of the Selma movement was nevertheless undeniable. As President Johnson's voting rights bill moved steadily through the congressional mill, Alabama officials made a desperate attempt to show that there was no need for voting rights safeguards. County registrars, who previously had met only two days a month, were given additional time for registration; Governor Wallace proclaimed his support for registration of every "eligible citizen"; and in Lowndes County, registrars enrolled the first black voter since Reconstruction. But the effort was too little and too late. In early August of 1965, the president signed the Voting Rights Act into law. Under its provisions, all voter tests were suspended in Alabama and other Deep South states; and the attorney general was authorized to send in federal examiners to register voters and assure that they would not be intimidated. The legislation proved extremely effective. By the summer of 1968, almost 60 percent of Alabama's black population was registered to vote; and the increase in some of the state's Black Belt counties was even greater. In Dallas County, for example, 71.8 percent were registered. As Congressman Dickinson would lament years later: "George [Wallace] did more to bring about what he professed to oppose than any other three people I can name. Standing in the schoolhouse door—well, that gave him nationwide attention. But it sure did integrate our schools faster than any other state in the South. And this adamant, defiant attitude on the Selma march thing—whatever point they were trying to make, George just made it for 'em."[36]

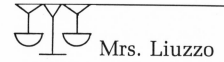 Mrs. Liuzzo

Even before the Selma voter drive and the deaths of Jimmie Lee Jackson and the Reverend Reeb, killings in connection with civil rights demonstrations and racial crises had become a relatively common occurrence. A French newsman and an Oxford, Mississippi, television repairman had died in the 1962 violence at the University of Mississippi. In April 1963, a Baltimore postman on a solitary civil rights trek to Alabama's capital was shot to death near Anniston; two months later, an auto mechanic had died from a rifle bullet fired into a crowd of whites at Lexington, North Carolina. The following April, a minister was crushed to death beneath a bulldozer during a demonstration against de facto segregation at a school construction site in a black Cleveland, Ohio, neighborhood. In July 1964, Lemuel Penn, a black Washington, D.C., assistant school superintendent, was shotgunned to death near Colbert, Georgia, as he and two black companions returned from army reserve duty at Fort Benning. The previous month, James Chaney, a black, and Michael Schwerner and Andrew Goodman, both white, had disappeared after brief confinement in a Mississippi jail on a trumped-up traffic charge. Like hundreds of other young people from over the nation, they had come to the South to participate in voter registration drives. On August 4, their bodies were recovered from an earthen dam near Philadelphia, Mississippi.[1]

The freedom march to Montgomery had seemed a likely occasion for an increase in those grim statistics, and when the tense final day's activities had drawn to a close without serious incident in Alabama's capital city, Judge Johnson and the federal officers responsible for the marchers' protection breathed a collective sigh of relief. But the feeling would be short-lived. That evening, the Justice Department's John Doar had relaxed for a late dinner—his first meal of the day—at Montgomery's Elite Cafe, a few blocks from the federal building. At 11:30, he was summoned to the phone. A few minutes later, he returned to his companions with painful news. "It was the FBI. A Mrs. Liuzzo has been killed on the road back to Selma."[2]

Viola Gregg Liuzzo was a white, middle-aged Detroit housewife and mother, her husband a minor teamsters union official. At Selma, she had been a member of the march transportation committee. On March 25, the march's last day in Montgomery, she and Leroy Moton, a black

SCLC worker, drove march participants back to Selma in her blue 1963 Oldsmobile. During the day there had been several minor encounters with whites. Once, a car had bumped her car from behind, almost forcing it off the road. Twice, when she and Moton had stopped for gas, bystanders had shouted insults. Early that evening, a car pulled alongside them, and its occupants fired pistol shots into the Olds, hitting Mrs. Liuzzo. Moton escaped and reported the incident to the FBI and Selma police. Later, two Alabama state troopers went to the scene of the shooting to investigate. They found six bullet holes in the Olds, the car's windows shattered, blood "all over," and Mrs. Liuzzo's body. She had been shot in the head with a thirty-eight caliber pistol.[3]

For the second time in less than a month, Alabama was the target of national outrage. Michigan Congresswoman Martha Griffiths charged that the state was "on trial." If its officials did not quickly try and convict Mrs. Liuzzo's killers, she asserted, they would prove to the world that there was not "as much courage in the whole state of Alabama as in the heart of Viola Gregg Liuzzo." Others placed responsibility for Mrs. Liuzzo's death on Governor Wallace, charging that his defiant attitude and demagoguery had encouraged hoodlums to believe that they were immune from punishment for violence against blacks and whites sympathetic to the cause of civil rights. And in Anniston, five hundred business and civic leaders signed a newspaper resolution calling for "responsible, realistic and thoughtful" responses to black demands.[4]

Governor Wallace was his usual combative self. He was no more responsible for Mrs. Liuzzo's death, he told reporters, than New York Governor Nelson Rockefeller had been for the shooting of the Muslim leader Malcolm X in Harlem the previous month. Alabama's highways, he added, were safer than New York's streets. Wallace did agree, however, that the murder was an "outrageous" and "cowardly" act that should not go unpunished. He also offered the state's standard reward—$1,000—for information leading to the arrest of Mrs. Liuzzo's assailants and instructed state authorities to cooperate with federal agents in the investigation.[5]

Even before Wallace's statements, however, the FBI had announced the arrest of four members of the Ku Klux Klan in connection with the shooting. Arrested were Eugene Thomas, forty-three, a steel worker with three children; William Orville Eaton, forty-one, a steel worker and father of five, retired with a medical disability; Collie Leroy Wilkins, twenty-one, a self-employed auto mechanic; and Gary Thomas Rowe, divorced, the father of four, presently unemployed, the FBI reported. Rowe was a native of Savannah, Georgia, and a Birmingham resident. The others lived in Fairfield and Bessemer, blue-collar Birmingham suburbs. In November 1964, Wilkins had been convicted in

Birmingham federal court for possession of an unregistered shotgun and placed on two years probation. In 1960, he had been convicted of petty larceny and destruction of property, fined $30, and given a six-month sentence. The other suspects had no prior criminal record. There is no general federal law covering murder. The four would be charged with conspiring to violate the Selma marchers' civil rights under Title 18, Section 241 of the U.S. Code, a little-used Reconstruction-era statute enacted in 1870 to combat Klan violence against the newly freed slaves. If convicted, they faced a maximum sentence of ten years in prison, a $5,000 fine, or both.[6]

The evening following the shooting, President Johnson, with FBI Director J. Edgar Hoover at his side, announced the arrests on national television. The president also reviewed the Klan's history of violence and offered the suspects' associates some advice: Get out of the "hooded society of bigots" before "it is too late."[7]

While newsmen speculated about the reasons behind the FBI's rapid arrest of suspects, Robert Shelton, a former Tuscaloosa service station attendant now serving as the imperial wizard of the United Klans of America, Inc., the nation's largest KKK outfit, held a bizarre press conference. Calling the president a "damn liar," Shelton presented his own theories about the deaths of Mrs. Liuzzo and the Reverend Reeb. While declining to say whether he was personally acquainted with any of the suspects, he assured newsmen that they had played no role in the killings, and that, in any event, Reeb was already dying of cancer when he was beaten in Selma. Their deaths, the imperial wizard explained, were actually part of a communist plot to denigrate the Klan and "destroy the right wing in America." President Johnson was simply using trumped-up criminal charges to eliminate anyone who spoke out against him. In fact, said Shelton, the FBI had offered Gary Thomas Rowe $160,000 and a farm in Minnesota if he would sign a statement implicating the imperial wizard in the Liuzzo shooting.[8]

As a probationer, Collie Leroy Wilkins was denied the privilege of bail. Bond was set at $50,000 for each of the other suspects, but within hours of their arrests, they were released. Klan Imperial Klonsel Matt H. Murphy, Jr., explained that he, Shelton, and Alabama's grand dragon Robert Creel, together with "some other of our friends," had raised the bail money. On April 7, Wilkins, Eaton, and Thomas were indicted by a federal grand jury for later trial in Judge Johnson's court. When Murphy asked why Rowe had not been indicted also, he got no reply. But none was necessary. By this point, he, Shelton, and the defendants had begun to suspect the worst: Gary Thomas Rowe was an FBI undercover agent preparing to appear as a prosecution witness.[9]

State murder charges followed close behind the federal indictment. After the violence at the Pettus bridge, Attorney General Flowers had charged that Alabama was "being ruled by race hatred and defiance." And in the wake of Mrs. Liuzzo's shooting, he pledged that his office would conduct a thorough investigation into the circumstances behind her death. Mrs. Liuzzo had been shot near Lowndesboro, a tiny Lowndes County community located midway between Selma and Montgomery. When the Lowndes County grand jury met to consider charges against the Klansmen, Flowers's assistant attorney general Joseph Gantt, aided by local prosecutors, presented the state's case. To avoid any appearance of federal influence over the proceedings, Gantt called no federal officials as witnesses, relying instead on the testimony of Rowe and Moton—and on the murder weapon, a thirty-eight caliber pistol found in Eugene Thomas's car the morning after the shooting. On April 22, the grand jury returned murder indictments against Thomas, Eaton, and Wilkins. Each defendant was then freed on $10,000 bond, amid complaints that bond had rarely been set so low in an Alabama murder case.[10]

In early May, Wilkins went to trial on the state charges at the Lowndes County courthouse in Hayneville. Circuit Judge T. Werth Thagard, a white-haired, genial little man, presided. Circuit Solicitor Arthur Gamble, assisted by Lowndes County's solicitor Carlton Perdue, was in charge of the prosecution. But Joseph Gantt would play a major role in the state's presentation. Matt Murphy represented the defendant. Throughout the four-day proceeding, Shelton and Creel sat near the defense table, providing Wilkins with the invisible empire's moral support. Except for newsmen, there were few other spectators in the high-ceilinged courtroom.[11]

Wilkins's trial ended in a deadlocked jury. Gary Thomas Rowe offered eyewitness testimony implicating Wilkins in Mrs. Liuzzo's death, while Gantt and Carlton Perdue made strong appeals to what they hoped would be the jurors' sense of honor, outrage, and regard for law and order, Gantt reminding the jury during his closing arguments that Governor Wallace had called the shooting "a cowardly act that should not go unpunished." But Imperial Klonsel Murphy's vitriolic attacks on Rowe ("a Judas Iscariot"), Leroy Moton (an insolent "nigger"), the civil rights movement (a "communistic" conspiracy), and the victim ("White woman? Hah! Where's that NAACP card?") apparently had the desired effect. Murphy's racist appeal insulted some of the jurors. "He must have thought we were very, very ignorant," said one, "to be taken in by that act." Even so, the jury voted against conviction even for second-degree murder and divided ten to two for conviction on a first-degree manslaughter count. One of the holdouts for acquittal was a member of the Citizens Council, the other a former member. They had been concerned, they said, about Rowe's integrity. After all, he had admitted violating the Klan's oath of secrecy.[12]

The outcome of a second trial the following October would be even more disappointing for state prosecutors. On this occasion, Attorney General Flowers, who had become increasingly outspoken about the climate of racial hatred in Alabama, took personal charge of the prosecution. But, if anything, the atmosphere in Lowndes County was even less conducive to a conviction in October than at the time of the first trial. By that point, Congress had enacted the 1965 Voting Rights Act, suspending all voter registration tests in Alabama and other jurisdictions with a history of discriminatory voter practices and empowering the attorney general to dispatch federal voting examiners to register voters in such areas. The House Un-American Activities Committee, moreover, had momentarily forgotten the communists and begun an intensive investigation into the KKK and its leadership. In late August, Los Angeles blacks had rioted in Watts. And in Hayneville, Thomas Coleman, a sheriff's deputy and member of a prominent Lowndes County family, had shotgunned to death Jonathan Daniels, a white Episcopal seminarian, and seriously wounded a Catholic priest from Chicago as they stood with two black friends in front of a small Hayneville grocery store. Daniels and his friends had been participating in a voter registration drive, and the shooting had further inflamed the racial climate in Lowndes County. Then, too, some may have resented Flowers's interference in local affairs. In his closing argument, Flowers warned the jurors: "If you do not convict this man, you might as well lock up the courthouse, open up the jail, and throw away the keys." But to no avail. The all-white jury, including eight present or former Citizens Council members and six self-professed white supremacists, deliberated an hour and thirty-five minutes, then acquitted Wilkins. In contrast to the first trial, the courtroom was filled with white spectators. When the verdict was announced, several applauded.[13]

The focus of events in the Liuzzo case shifted next to Judge Johnson's court. Arthur Hanes, the former mayor of Brimingham who had attempted to organize a white countermarch to the Selma marchers, had taken over Wilkins's defense in Hayneville after Matt Murphy was killed in an automobile accident following the first state trial. Hanes would represent the defendants in the Montgomery proceedings; and John Doar would lead prosecution forces. A Republican, Doar had joined the Justice Department in 1960 as number two man in the Civil Rights Division. As a member of the division, Doar had removed himself entirely from politics. And when President Kennedy named Burke Marshall to head the division, Marshall kept Doar on. In December 1964, President Johnson had appointed him to succeed Marshall. During his Justice Department tenure, Doar had become a familiar figure in southern racial crises and had appeared frequently before

Judge Johnson in behalf of the United States. He admired the judge's courage, integrity, and judicial skill. There were three men, he would tell his associates in later years, whom he considered touchstones of fairness; Frank Johnson was one of them. The feeling was mutual. "Doar," Judge Johnson has said, probably "has the strongest sense of what's right and wrong, and personal integrity, [of any person] I've ever met."[14]

The federal trial was set to begin on November 29. But on November 18, Judge Johnson held a pretrail hearing to consider a defense motion that the indictment be dismissed. Title 18, Section 241, the U.S. Code provision the defendants were charged with violating, punishes conspiracies to interfere with rights "secured . . . by the Constitution or laws of the United States." At the hearing, Arthur Hanes claimed that the indictment charged his clients with a conspiracy to violate Fourteenth Amendment rights of due process and equal protection, then challenged the assumption that Section 241 reached interferences with such rights.[15]

To the layman reading Section 241's language, Hanes's contention may have seemed strange. But a number of legal scholars and lower courts had long contended that the provision covered only a narrow category of U.S. citizenship rights, such as a voter's right to cast a vote in a federal election, the freedom of interstate travel, and the right to petition the federal government for a redress of grievances. The Supreme Court had never directly ruled on the issue, the justices dividing equally when the question was last raised before them in a 1951 case. In Mississippi, however, Judge Harold Cox had recently dismissed Section 241 charges against eighteen defendants indicted in the Philadelphia, Mississippi, civil rights killings, citing the very arguments Hanes was now raising. And in Georgia, another district judge had taken the same stance in preventing a federal prosecution of six Klansmen charged with violating Lemuel Penn's civil rights. Judge Johnson, Hanes contended, should follow their example.[16]

John Doar attempted to distinguish the Mississippi and Georgia cases. While agreeing that Fourteenth Amendment rights were implicated in the indictment, he also contended that the conspiracy charged had interfered with citizenship guarantees clearly covered by Section 241, including voting rights and "the right to travel freely in interstate commerce." Involved, too, he said, was "the fact that the Negro citizens and the people involved in the march from Selma to Montgomery were acting and operating under an order of this court. They had rights that came from this court to engage in that march. . . . And that is a right that is not a Fourteenth Amendment right; it is a right that flows from the Federal Government; flows from the Court. . . . That right is right in the middle of Section 241. . . . If private citizens can with impunity against the Federal Government then interfere with that right through violence, then 241 doesn't mean anything."

Judge Johnson tended to agree. There was no need, he concluded, to reach the Fourteenth Amendment issue. The indictment charged a conspiracy to interfere with "rights under the laws of the United States as was determined by the order of this court"; and Section 241, he asserted, covered interference with federal court orders. "If 241 doesn't apply in this particular case," he asked, "where does it apply, Mr. Hanes?" Hanes next weakly suggested ("no reflection to you intended") that perhaps the march order itself had been unconstitutional. But to no avail. The order was not at issue, the judge reminded him. Besides, it had been affirmed by the Fifth Circuit; and a review of the order before the Supreme Court had not been sought. "So," he added, "it is pretty good law."

Trying to salvage something from the hearing, Hanes then attempted to secure more detailed information about the nature of the government's case, calling the indictment against his clients "one of the vaguest and broadest and [most] uncertain" he had ever seen. That effort, too, was fruitless. As the hearing concluded, he remarked lamely that because of his late involvement in the case, he had learned only that day that the trial was scheduled for the twenty-ninth. "Regardless of how I rule," Judge Johnson jokingly responded, "you got something from filing your motion." Later, the judge entered an order denying the motion to dismiss.

On November 29, the attorneys again met with Judge Johnson in his chambers to discuss ground rules for the trial, including questions the judge and counsel might employ to exclude potentially biased jurors. The Mississippi and Georgia cases were then pending before the Supreme Court. But Judge Johnson denied Hanes's request that his clients' trial be delayed pending a Supreme Court ruling on the Section 241 issue. "Let's just try it," he said, as the conference ended, "like a law suit; I don't want it to sound so novel."

Later in the day, a jury was selected. The fifty-nine-member jury venire contained the names of six blacks, but a random selection process produced no blacks among the prospective jurors. When a black was called to replace an alternate challenged by the government, Hanes had him excused. As agreed during the pretrial conference, Judge Johnson probed the prospective jurors about their knowledge of the case and organizational affiliations and a number were excused because of their responses. The government, for example, excluded a former Citizens Council member, Hanes an NAACP member selected as a possible alternate juror. The all-male jury eventually selected consisted of nine businessmen, a school superintendent, and two farmers; nearly all of them were from small towns. A Montgomery housewife and another farmer were selected as alternates. Once impaneled, Judge Johnson warned them repeatedly that they were to rid their minds of preconceived notions about the case and strive for a fair verdict. "And by fair verdict," he added meaningfully, "I mean a verdict that is fair to both sides, the Government and the defense."

In his opening statement to the jury, John Doar outlined the federal rights violations charged in the indictment and summarized the evidence the government planned to introduce. Arthur Hanes described himself as a "small time lawyer from Birmingham" (and Doar as a federal lawyer "from Washington"), then told the jurors that his clients' defense would be based principally on weaknesses and omissions in the government's case. He might have added that there would be no race-baiting in Judge Johnson's courtroom. "Art was very cooperative," Judge Johnson's law clerk Walter Turner recalls. "I expected him to be more of a Klansman than he was. I expected some unpleasantness that could've developed," but did not. Nor, in Judge Johnson's tightly run courtroom, would there be any spectator demonstrations of support for the defendants'—or government's—cause. Collie Leroy Wilkins seemed arrogant and contemptuous of the proceedings, but only in his facial expression. His co-defendants were completely docile throughout the trial.[17]

Again, Gary Rowe would be the prosecution's chief witness; and for the first time Judge Johnson heard his account of the events surrounding the shooting. Rowe had joined the Klan at the FBI's request; at the time of Mrs. Liuzzo's death, he had been working as the agency's paid informer for six years. On the first day of the Selma march, the defendants had participated in a Montgomery Klan rally in protest against Judge Johnson's order. On the last day of the march in Montgomery, Rowe testified, he and the defendants had driven from Bessemer to the capital. There, they spent several hours harassing marchers in a number of minor skirmishes. Later, they drove to Selma, discussing "head knocking" and "skinning heads." At Selma, they had a beer at a local cafe and happened on a friend, one of the men charged earlier in the Reverend Reeb's death. The man walked up to Eugene Thomas and put his arm around Thomas's shoulder. "God bless you, boys," he said, "you go do your job. I have already did mine."

Rowe and the defendants had then driven around Selma looking for march participants. Once, they started to "take" two "colored people," but were frightened off by an army truck. Shortly thereafter, Wilkins spotted Mrs. Liuzzo and Leroy Moton in Mrs. Liuzzo's blue Olds. "Looka there!" Wilkins exclaimed. "I will be damned! Looka there, babe brother, looka there!"

As the Liuzzo auto left Selma on the highway toward Montgomery, Thomas suggested that they "follow them and take them." They were just going out on the highway to "make love." "We're going to take them tonight," he said repeatedly.

Eventually, the defendants' car caught up with Mrs. Liuzzo's Olds. Thomas gave Wilkins his thirty-eight pistol. "Get your guns out," he told the others, "we're going to take them." As they passed the Olds, Wilkins stuck his arm out his window nearly to elbow length. "The woman turned her head and kind of looked over toward the automobile." In rapid succession, Wilkins fired two shots into the Olds driver's window. "Shoot the hell out of them," Thomas shouted, "everybody shoot the hell out of them!" As Wilkins continued firing, Thomas sped up to pass, and Eaton began firing. Rowe put his pistol out the window but, he testified, had fired no shots.

After their car had passed, Rowe looked back. Mrs. Liuzzo's Olds appeared to be following them. "Good God!" he exclaimed. "You missed . . . they are following us now." Wilkins slapped Rowe on the knee and laughed. "Baby brother, don't worry. I don't miss . . . that bitch and bastard are both dead and in hell." The Liuzzo car then swerved off the road. Their task completed, the defendants raced back to Bessemer to establish an alibi. Later, Rowe slipped to a phone and called the FBI.

During cross-examination, Hanes tried once again to raise doubts about the FBI informer's character. Under the defense counsel's questioning, Rowe conceded that, yes, he had violated the Klan oath to "die rather than divulge" information about the group's activities. Hanes also elicited admissions that Rowe was not supporting his five children from two previous marriages; that his pay as an informer was based on the extent of his activity for the FBI; that he had participated in the Mother's Day 1961 beatings of the freedom riders in Birmingham. Hanes was unsuccessful, however, in his attempts to get Rowe to concede that he had encouraged Klan violence, even though, years later, Rowe would testify before a congressional committee that he had engaged in such activity.[18]

In his summation to the jury, Hanes continued to hit hard at Rowe's testimony, citing internal conflicts in his statements and his status as a "silver merchant." He also drew the now familiar allusions to Judas's betrayal of Christ. Mrs. Liuzzo's death, he said, was "a terrible thing . . . a hideous crime . . . not to be condoned." But her murderers were not in the courtroom. "I suspect," Hanes concluded, "that they are somewhere laughing at the poor simple people of Alabama . . . and looking for their next victim."

John Doar delivered the "most brilliant" summation Walter Turner had ever heard, outlining clearly the jurors' responsibility.[19] He knew, Doar said, that the jurors had put "aside a number of things, things you don't like, your emotions, feelings, anger perhaps, and determined that you would decide this case loyal to only one thing, your oath." But the closing argument of their fellow Alabamiam Ben Hardeman may have had a greater impact on the jurors. "Are we," Hardeman asked them, "going to permit a star chamber court, by persons unknown at times and places unknown, who are their own investigators, their own witnesses, their judges, their own jury, and yes, their own executioner? Are we going to have a government of law or of men? We take the flat position that all of these matters should be settled within the halls of a temple of justice such as this one."

Judge Johnson's charge to the jurors would consume twenty-seven pages of transcript. Emphasizing the importance of "our free and independent court system," he lectured them on "the principles of justice and supremacy of the law." Those ideals, he observed, must "override any political or sociological causes or movements." In short, the jurors were to render a verdict based solely on the evidence.

The jury deliberated through most of the day on December 2 and retired for the evening without reaching a verdict. Judge Johnson had been incensed by the outcome of Wilkins's state trials and hoped that the federal proceedings were not moving toward the same conclusion. "I think we're going to have to give the jury a little dynamite," he told Walter Turner. "Get me the *Allen* charge."

In *Allen v. United States*, an 1896 case, the U.S. Supreme Court had upheld a supplemental charge to a jury in a murder case prosecuted in Indian territory. In attempting to break a deadlocked jury, the trial judge in *Allen* had cautioned the jurors that absolute certainty of a defendant's guilt or innocence rarely could be expected; that although each jury member must render his own verdict, not merely acquiescing in the views of the other jurors, he should have a proper regard and deference for their opinions; that each juror should listen to the arguments of other jurors with a disposition toward being convinced; that if a much larger number of jurors favored conviction, a dissenting juror should consider whether his own doubts about the defendant's guilt were reasonable; that if a majority were for acquittal, the minority should ask themselves whether they might not reasonably doubt their own judgment. Critics charged that such instructions violated the accused's right to a fair trial. But in post-*Allen* cases, the courts had reaffirmed their use. Where federal jurors deadlocked, it was permissible for the judge to put a little "dynamite," so to speak, under their feet. As the Liuzzo jurors deliberated, Judge Johnson prepared for them a heavy dose of "dynamite."[20]

At 10:09 A.M., December 3, the jurors filed back into the courtroom to announce that they were hopelessly deadlocked. Judge Johnson recalled that forty to fifty witnesses had been called and approximately fifty exhibits introduced in evidence. "So you haven't commenced to deliberate the case long enough," he added, "to reach the conclusion that you are hopelessly deadlocked." Over Arthur Hanes's objections, he then reminded the jurors that the trial had been long and expensive, gave them a stern lecture incorporating essentials of the *Allen* charge, and asserted: "There is no reason to suppose that the case will ever be submitted to twelve more intelligent, more impartial, or more competent to decide it, or that more or clearer evidence will be produced on one side or the other."

The charge had the desired effect. At 2:08 that afternoon, the jury returned to the courtroom with guilty verdicts; and Judge Johnson imposed the maximum sentence on each defendant.

Attorney General Katzenbach hailed the convictions as "a victory for equal justice in the South." John Doar said the court and the jury had "done their duty," adding: "I'm very proud of the system of justice in this country." Judge Johnson was equally pleased and relieved. After the jury foreman had announced its verdicts, he had told the jurors: "All right, gentlemen, if it is worth anything to you, in my opinion that was the only verdict that you could possibly reach in this case and still reach a fair and honest and just verdict." He did not reveal to the jury another impression he had of the case—that the defendants were not the only ones who should be made to answer for Mrs. Liuzzo's death. But reflecting on the case in later years, he remarked:

> I don't believe you would have any Wilkins, Thomases, or Eatons if you didn't have leadership that gave them the idea that they could do what they did and do it with immunity. Oh, you'd have some isolated instances with fanatics, maniacs. . . . But these people were not maniacs. They were employed. . . . They had families. . . . I don't mean to blame it all on John Patterson or George Wallace. I blame a lot of it on the ministers . . . [who] would condone putting what was most commonly referred to as 'goon squads' out in front of their churches to keep blacks from coming, . . . [and on] business leaders that refused to take a stand . . . , when it was obvious to everyone that the laws of the land were being violated. . . . They refused to take a stand because they feared economic repercussions and they'd rather run the risk of some nondescript black organizing a black boycott, than run the risk of being ostracized at the country club, or losing some of their white clients. I use that word deliberately, because lawyers were just as bad in failing to take a positive stand on this as anyone else.[21]

Three days after the verdicts were rendered in the Liuzzo case, the Fifth Circuit upheld Judge Johnson's use of the *Allen* charge in an earlier recent case. On April 27, 1967, another appeals panel, speaking through Judge James P. Coleman, a former governor of Mississippi, affirmed the Liuzzo convictions—but not before wading through a complicated constitutional quagmire.[22]

In 1966, the Supreme Court had finally decided the Mississippi and
Georgia variations on the Liuzzo shooting, holding in *United States* v.
Price and *United States* v. *Guest* that Section 241 reached conspiracies
to violate Fourteenth Amendment guarantees. But those rulings left the
Fifth Circuit with another thorny constitutional question: the Fourteenth Amendment's language forbids "state" interference with the
rights the Amendment guarantees. Moreover, since the *Civil Rights
Cases* of 1883, the Supreme Court had consistently rejected claims that
Congress had power to punish violations of Fourteenth Amendment
rights by such private persons as the Liuzzo defendants. And the *Price*
and *Guest* majority opinions had not rejected that doctrine. Most of the
rights mentioned in the conspiracy indictment against Wilkins,
Thomas, and Eaton were of the Fourteenth Amendment variety. In fact,
in his charge to the jury, Judge Johnson had eliminated every count
except that charging a conspiracy to interfere with the Selma march
pursuant to his court order. And "on its face," Judge Coleman conceded, the march case had been a "typical Fourteenth Amendment
proceeding."[23]

But Coleman and and his colleagues were not about to free the
defendants. An "essential ingredient" of the Selma march case, said
Coleman, had been the "right to vote in federal elections, undeniably a
right of national citizenship." Section 241 clearly reached such "attrib-
ute[s] of citizenship," he added, and Congress clearly had constitutional authority to punish private interferences with such rights.
Conviction affirmed.[24]

The defendants could be said to have interfered with the right to vote
only in the most indirect sense. No other national citizenship rights
seemed even remotely at stake in the case, however. As John Doar had
emphasized during pretrial proceedings, the courts have long recognized a national citizenship right of interstate travel; but Mrs. Liuzzo
was not traveling interstate when the shooting occurred. Years later,
Judge Johnson would contend that Section 241 covered private interferences with federal court orders; but if the court order authorizing the
Selma march reached only Fourteenth Amendment rights protected
solely from state action, it is difficult to see how the incorporation of
such guarantees into a court order could convert them into national
citizenship rights subject to protection from private as well as government interferences. Of course, the Fifth Circuit panel could have
plowed new constitutional ground, holding that Congress had the
power to punish private interferences with Fourteenth Amendment
rights and that Section 241 reached such conspiracies. But that tack
seemed extremely risky, given the Supreme Court's reluctance to
embrace such a thesis in the *Price* and *Guest* cases. Faced with these
alternatives—and apparently committed to uphold the defendants'

convictions—the panel must have seen a decision bottomed on the right to vote as the only viable option. Even so, Judge Coleman's rationale—and, thus, the basis for Judge Johnson's decision to uphold the indictments—was tortured at best, however just the outcome.[25]

Mrs. Liuzzo's death had not been entirely in vain, however. By the May 1966 Democratic primary in Alabama, the number of blacks on the state's voting rolls had swelled from 122,000 to more than 235,000. That year, a black was elected sheriff of Macon County, and blacks won two other Macon posts. In Greene County, a black was elected to the board of education. And in Dallas County, Wilson Baker, Selma's moderate police chief, beat James Clark in a race for sheriff.[26]

But the more things change, the more they seem to remain the same. In early March of 1966, William Orville Eaton had died of an apparent heart attack. But in late September, Eugene Thomas went to trial in Hayneville on state murder charges. Earlier, Judge Johnson and others on a three-judge panel had forbidden systematic discrimination against blacks in jury selection and struck down an Alabama statute excluding women from jury service. Thomas's jury was all male, but included eight blacks. Even so, after a brief trial, Thomas, like Wilkins before him, was acquitted—"a complete breakdown of justice and law and order," Attorney General Flowers termed the verdict. After Jonathan Daniels's death, Thomas Coleman was acquitted of murder. Flowers had later secured an assault charge against Coleman in connection with the assault on Daniels's companion. Several days before Eugene Thomas's acquittal, however, Judge Thagard dismissed that charge "with prejudice"—thereby preventing Coleman's further indictment and trial.[27]

Under the Alabama constitution, George Wallace was prohibited from succeeding himself as governor when his term expired at the end of 1966. And a 1965 attempt to overturn the restriction had failed. But in February 1966, Wallace announced that his wife Lurleen would be his "stand-in" candidate for governor. In the May primary, Mrs. Wallace faced nine opponents, ranging from Attorney General Flowers, to ex-Governor Folsom and populist former Congressman Carl Elliott, to Wallace senate opponent Robert Gilchrist and former Governor Patterson, to a number of also-rans, including a former postal worker with instructions "from God" to run. Richmond Flowers urged a politics of racial moderation and made direct appeals for black votes. He received 142,665 votes. Mrs. Wallace garnered almost 400,000 votes in the race, her opponents less than 365,000. But there would be no doubt who would be in charge in the governor's office. "If my wife is elected," George Wallace had explained in announcing Lurleen's candidacy, "we are frank and honest to say that I shall be by her side and shall make the policies and decisions affecting the next administration."[28]

CHAPTER 10

The Real Governor of Alabama

The Governors Wallace—"the legal and the illegal one," a Montgomery newspaper would label them—began their term in early January 1967. Two and a half years had elapsed since Judge Johnson joined Judges Rives and Grooms in enjoining further state interference with the desegregation of Alabama's public schools—a period more than sufficient to dispel any hopes that the judge and his colleagues may have entertained about the injunction's adequacy. Since its issuance, George Wallace, ably assisted by Alabama's superintendent of education Austin R. Meadows, had repeatedly pressured local school officials to keep the segregationist faith, and state educational policies had been directed consistently toward that end.[1]

Evidence of continued resistance had begun to surface less than a year after issuance of the statewide order. In December 1964, the Department of Health, Education, and Welfare published regulations aimed at assuring state and local compliance with Title VI of the 1964 Civil Rights Act. Title VI forbade discrimination in federally funded programs; and the HEW regulations required, among other things, that any application for federal funding be accompanied by an assurance that the program involved would be conducted on a nondiscriminatory basis.[2]

Although something of a political moderate by Alabama standards, Austin Meadows was an outspoken segregationist during his tenure as Alabama's school superintendent. But money was money, and on March 4, 1965, Meadows submitted to the U.S. commissioner of education Alabama's assurance of statewide compliance with federal desegregation requirements. On this occasion, however, an idle promise of compliance would be inadequate. And when Francis Keppel, the U.S. commissioner of education, questioned the sincerity of the state's assurances, Meadows's response was prompt and bitter. In a release to local school superintendents, he attacked Keppel, extolled the progress being made in segregated education in Alabama, and asked: "Will this Nation let Alabama continue its progress, nurture its fine culture, and further its goal of peaceful existence in the only way it knows to exist or will all of this be destroyed by outsiders who either do not understand or do not care enough for either race in Alabama?"

By the fall school term of 1965, George Wallace had joined Meadows in the growing fracas. In April of that year, the commissioner of education had issued the first of HEW's school desegregation "guidelines," requiring local school systems to take immediate steps to desegregate their student bodies, faculties, and programs. In response, several Alabama school districts agreed to desegregate all twelve grades for the 1965–66 school year. The governor was not pleased. In a series of telegrams—copies of which were circulated to local newspapers in the districts involved—he urged compliant school districts to limit desegregation to no more than five grades. At the same time, Meadows sent local school officials a copy of a state school board resolution condemning any compliance plan "not required by law or court order." Confronted with such pressure, a number of districts yielded.

As the 1966 school term approached, Wallace and Meadows resumed their maneuvers, attempting unsuccessfully to persuade a local school board to abandon token desegregation of its faculty. At the same time, other state officials continued to employ their powers over school construction, faculty placement, and transportation to perpetuate segregated schooling. As a result, by 1967, per pupil evaluation of school facilities was $607.12 per white child and $295.40 per black child; over 25 percent of black high schools, contrasted with only 3.4 percent of white high schools, remained unaccredited; and only seventy-six of Alabama's more than twenty-eight thousand public school teachers had been assigned to schools traditionally attended by students of another race.

Then, too, there had been a further state attempt to fund segregated private schooling. Under the scheme invalidated by Judge Johnson and his colleagues in 1964, private school tuition grants were made available to any parent who withdrew his child from a "school in which the races are commingled." Under a new statutory arrangement, the same assistance was extended to those parents who believed that public school attendance would impair their children's "physical and emotional health." No one could doubt the legislation's intent. In 1965–66, every dollar paid under the program had gone to students who enrolled in all-white private schools established when Alabama's public schools were first required to desegregate.

In short, by Mrs. Wallace's inauguration, the need for additional judicial intervention seemed compelling. It was not long in coming. On March 22, 1967, the three-judge panel imposed a statewide desegregation decree on the new governor, Austin Meadows's successor, and members of the state board of education. As in 1964, Judge Johnson authored the panel's unsigned opinion.

Under the order, the defendants and their agents were to use their financial and related controls over school construction and consolidation, teacher placement, and transportation to encourage desegregation.

Moreover, the superintendent of education was to notify each school district not previously covered by court order to adopt a desegregation plan for all grades, effective with the 1967–68 school year. Attached to the order were detailed standards to which each local plan was to conform, including a copy of an explanatory letter to be sent to the parents of affected children. Finally, the panel relegated the new tuition scheme to its predecessor's fate and cautioned the defendants against further efforts to fund segregated education. "If the state persists," Judge Johnson warned, "and its involvement with the private school system continues to be 'significant,' then this 'private' system will have become a state actor within the meaning of the Fourteenth Amendment and will need to be brought under this Court's state-wide desegregation order."[3]

To this point, federal courts had invariably opted for the "freedom of choice" approach to school desegregation, and the panel's statewide order incorporated such a formula. Increasingly, however, freedom of choice had come under attack as promoting, at best, only token integration. In his opinion, Judge Johnson emphasized that "freedom of choice is a fantasy" if "choice influencing factors are not eliminated," stressed the interim nature of such an approach, and asserted: "The measure of a freedom of choice plan—or, for that matter, any school plan designed to eliminate discrimination based on race—is whether it is effective." Within a year, the United States Supreme Court would assume essentially the same stance.[4]

On the evening of March 30, the stand-in governor responded to the latest order in a now-familiar Wallace forum, the floor of the Alabama legislature. Perhaps out of respect for Mrs. Wallace's gender, unusual decorum prevailed. The solons kept their coats on, and the peanut vendors who normally enjoyed free access to the floor were nowhere to be seen. The governor's "Number One Adviser" watched the proceedings on television in his capitol office, but his wife's address, delivered in the intense, deliberate style of a high school oratorical contestant, clearly bore his imprint. Predicting that Alabamians would go to jail before permitting their children to attend desegregated schools, she condemned the judges' decree as "the final step toward a complete takeover of [our children's] hearts and minds" and equated the panel's action with the tactics of Hitler. Promising to use "whatever power I possess . . . to prevent the destruction of our public school system," she urged the legislators to issue a "cease and desist" order against Judge Johnson and his colleagues. Then, evoking the memory of President Andrew Jackson's reaction to an unpopular Supreme Court decision, she stamped her foot and defiantly declared: "They have made their decree. Now let them enforce it!"[5]

Though her demure appearance and manner of delivery gave the governor's fiery words a mildly ludicrous air, Alabama's legislators were appropriately enthusiastic. Whooping and stomping their feet at every new volley she fired at the feds, they repeatedly interrupted her with deafening applause and rebel yells. Her chief adviser was pleased.[6]

Unfortunately, however, on this occasion, as on earlier similar ones, adverse reaction to the decree was not confined to speechmaking. In April, the three-judge panel refused to delay enforcement of its order. Ten days later, opponents of desegregation retaliated. Judge Johnson's father had died in 1965, and his mother now lived alone in the family's Montgomery house. Intermittently during racial crises, the judge's home had remained under guard; and occasionally in the recent past, a guard had been placed on his mother's home as well. On April 25, however, Mrs. Johnson's house was unguarded. At about 10:00 that evening, a bomb exploded there. Judge Johnson arrived soon after the explosion, angrily searching the area with a flashlight borrowed from a fireman. Neither he nor federal and state agents assigned to the case discovered any useful evidence, however, and the culprits were never apprehended.[7]

Although the impact of the blast shattered several windows, no one was injured. In fact, the bomb—a small dynamite device buried in the ground near the rear of Mrs. Johnson's house—seemed clearly designed to frighten rather than to maim or kill. Whatever its purpose, the explosion had no discernible effect on Alabama Johnson. Although now under heavy guard, she insisted on remaining in her house alone. And while demolition experts combed the property for clues the morning after the bombing, she worked quietly in her yard—"the calmest person on the block," the *Montgomery Advertiser* reported. Nor did the bombing affect the desegregation decisions of Judge Johnson and his colleagues. In July, the Johnson, Rives, Grooms trio did refuse to allow HEW to terminate federal funds to school districts making a good-faith effort to comply with court-imposed desegregation orders. In May, however, Judge Johnson and Judge Rives, joined on this occasion by Judge Virgil Pittman of the Southern District, overturned a bizarre Alabama statute purporting to nullify federal school desegregation guidelines and the assurances of compliance which local boards had filed with HEW.[8]

Even so, the explosion did have one significant impact: to a degree unprecedented in Judge Johnson's career, it put Alabama's press and bar on the offensive against the Wallace brand of court-baiting. After the bombing, Mrs. Wallace had offered a $5,400 reward for information leading to the culprit's arrest, found it "difficult to find words to express my abhorrence and scorn" for the "cowardly" act, and declared: "This is not the American way or the Alabama way to protest

[court] decisions." The *Birmingham Post-Herald* quickly rejoined:
"This newspaper also believes that verbal assaults on the courts and
undocumented charges of lying against Federal judges are unAmerican.
We wish they were unAlabamian." In a scathing editorial entitled
"Who Bears the Guilt?" Ray Jenkins's *Alabama Journal* was more
direct: "Every society, of course, has its deranged element capable of
criminal violence. But the test is whether the whole community will
endorse the act by allowing the criminal to go free. When we do this,
we allow madmen to speak for all of us."[9]

Segments of the state legal profession also rose, timidly, to Judge
Johnson's defense. At the time of the bombing, the president of the state
bar association was content with a public expression of outrage against
"this cowardly act of violence perpetrated upon a defenseless lady."
But in the fall, when a letter to a Montgomery paper attacked the judge,
the county bar's executive committee responded with a letter defending Judge Johnson and the rule of law, though tactfully avoiding a
direct assault on the Wallaces. For the *Advertiser-Journal*, the combined Sunday edition of Montgomery's major dailies, the effort was too
little, too late. Excoriating George Wallace for "outrageous attacks" and
"shameless court-baiting, which has infected the minds of thousands of
Alabamians," the paper scored the state's "lawyers in solemn assem-
bly" for failing—outside "the relative security of fashionable cocktail
parties"—to identify "the poisoner by name." In public statements,
scoffed the editor, members of the bar "confine themselves to shooting
minnows in a barrel. That doesn't require much."[10]

One may well doubt that George Wallace conceded any personal
responsibility for the volatile atmosphere then prevailing in Alabama.
Certainly, the bombing and public reaction had no discernible effect on
his political rhetoric. In 1968, however, Mrs. Wallace died, a victim of
the cancer already ravaging her body when her husband and his
advisers persuaded her to become his stand-in. Her successor, Lieutenant Governor Albert Brewer, would serve out her term, then lose to
Wallace in a bloody 1970 fight to hold the governorship. During
Wallace's first term, Brewer had served as the governor's hand-picked
Speaker of the Alabama House of Representatives. But during his
tenure as governor, he studiously avoided the Wallace brand of court-
baiting. Thus, for a time, Judge Johnson and the state's other federal
judges proceeded with the desegregation of Alabama's schools free of
statehouse harangues.[11]

By this point in his career, of course, Judge Johnson had long since
developed a massive body of human rights decisions reaching well
beyond the voter registration and school desegregation contexts. Following the Supreme Court's landmark 1962 ruling in *Baker v. Carr*, the
federal courts had devoted increasing attention to the reapportionment

issue, and the Middle District was no exception. Alabama's legislature had not been reapportioned since 1901, and pre-*Baker* malapportionment was egregious. The largest senate district in the state was forty-one times more populous than the smallest, the most populous house district sixteen times larger than the least populous district. As one critic of the arrangement remarked, "The voice of the boll weevil in Barbour, Lowndes, and Wilcox counties is heard louder than the voice of the urban voter in the Alabama legislature." In the summer of 1962, close on the heels of *Baker*, Judges Johnson, Rives, and Grooms declared the scheme unconstitutional and became the first federal jurists to accomplish legislative reapportionment by direct judicial order. In 1964, the Supreme Court used the Alabama case as the vehicle for extending the "one man, one vote" principle to both houses of state legislatures; and for eight years thereafter, Judge Johnson and his colleagues pressed Alabama officials to adopt an apportionment system compatible with the equality standard—imposing a plan proposed by urban plaintiffs in 1972 only when continued state recalcitrance seemed inevitable. Acting alone or as a member of other three-judge panels, moreover, he supervised reapportionment of Alabama's congressional districts, extended the one person, one vote rule to local units of government, and invalidated a number of racially discriminatory apportionment schemes, including a reapportionment plan for the Alabama House of Representatives under which predominantly black and predominantly white counties were grouped together to dilute the black vote.[12]

While the attack on Alabama's governmental structure was being completed, Judge Johnson and his colleagues also upheld a challenge to the state's property tax system. Under Alabama law, property was to be evaluated, assessed at a fixed percentage of its market value, then taxed at its assessed value. Language in the state's constitution and statutes stipulated that property be assessed and taxed uniformly. But the law also allowed local revenue boards wide discretion in the assessment of property, and gross inequities abounded. A 1969 state revenue department study had revealed, for example, median assessment ratios ranging from lows of 6.7 and 7 percent of fair market value in rural Hale and Washington counties to highs of 23.1 and 26.8 percent in urban Madison (Huntsville) and Jefferson (Birmingham) counties. Finding no rational basis for such disparities, a Middle District panel on which Judge Johnson participated found the arrangement fraught with equal protection and due process violations.[13]

The services and personnel practices of state administrative agencies have also felt the brunt of Middle District oversight. In 1967, Judge Johnson and others on a three-judge panel overturned Alabama's "substitute father" regulation under which assistance through Aid to Families with Dependent Children (AFDC) could be denied a child because of the mother's immoral conduct. And in 1975, equal protection violations were found in the disparity of benefits going to predominantly black AFDC recipients and predominantly white recipients of old-age assistance. Alabama's attempt to preserve a segregated agricultural extension service met the same fate.[14]

In 1978, Judge Johnson would invalidate discrimination against whites in the hiring, firing, promotion, and tenure practices of predominantly black Alabama State University. Emphasizing that the school's labor pool was overwhelmingly white, he found no adequate justification for its relatively few white faculty and staff and attributed discrimination against white faculty largely to the "arbitrary whim and caprice" of the university president, whom the judge characterized as "an administrative tyrant." During his district court career, Judge Johnson would not be confronted with the sort of "affirmative action" or "reverse discrimination" program at issue in the Bakke case—an announced policy of preferential treatment for the disadvantaged over better qualified whites in university admissions programs. Privately, however, he agrees with those on the Supreme Court who have contended that such programs are a permissible tool for assuring diverse student bodies and faculties. In the field of employment, on the other hand, his position is somewhat different. There, he believes that valid employment tests should be applied equally to blacks and whites alike. He clearly endorses, however, preferential hiring of minorities over equally qualified whites as an appropriate means of correcting the effects of past discrimination ("playing catch-up," he calls it). In 1972, for example, he outlawed discriminatory employment practices in the state police and required preferential hiring of black troopers. Under his decree, 25 percent of Alabama's trooper trainees were to be black; and one black was to be hired for every white employed until blacks constituted at least a quarter of the trooper force. While motivated more by an interest in eliminating segregated schooling than correcting the effects of past hiring practices, he also imposed quotas for the hiring of black school teachers. And in United States v. Frazer, a protracted challenge to discriminatory hiring in federally funded state programs, he moved gradually toward the same approach.[15]

Not all of Judge Johnson's discrimination caseload, of course, was confined to the racial and voting contexts. In Frontiero v. Laird, decided in 1972, he registered a rare dissent when Judge Rives, joined by a Northern District judge, voted to uphold a federal military regulation under which a married male member of the uniformed services automatically received a dependency allowance for his spouse, while a female member was first required to establish her husband's dependency. The previous year, in Reed v. Reed, the Supreme Court had invalidated a gender discrimination for the first time in the Court's history, but had declined to hold that discrimination based on sex, like that based on race, religion, or national origin, was "inherently suspect" and subject to the most exacting judicial scrutiny. Instead, Chief Justice Burger had suggested for the Court that gender regulations need have only somewhat more justification than discriminatory commercial regulations; and the latter had long been immune from all but the most nominal judicial review. In his *Frontiero* opinion, Judge Rives gave *Reed* a reading extremely deferential to government and concluded that the challenged regulation was rationally related to the government's interest in saving administrative time and expense. Judge Johnson, on the other hand, construed *Reed* to mean "that administrative convenience is not a shibboleth, the mere recitation of which dictates constitutionality." In his view, any administrative convenience the regulation served should be balanced against its "impact upon the subject class and the arbitrariness of the classification." Applying such a formula, Judge Johnson found the regulation wanting. And in 1973, a majority on the Supreme Court agreed. Only Justice William H. Rehnquist, the lone dissenter, adopted Judge Rives's stance.[16]

With the present Supreme Court majority, Judge Johnson rejects the notion that sex is a "suspect" basis of classification. Privately, in fact, he has expressed doubt whether racial and related classifications should any longer be considered constitutional suspects—an attitude explained, in part, perhaps, by the difficulty race as a suspect poses for race-based affirmative action programs. Most forms of discrimination, he contends, need have only a rational basis. In private conversation, however, it quickly becomes clear that, for Judge Johnson, the regulation must have a *sufficient degree* of rationality to satisfy his conception of what is fair and reasonable. And for one of that persuasion, it makes little difference whether or not a particular form of discrimination is deemed constitutionally "suspect."[17]

While most of Judge Johnson's school decisions, like those rendered in other human rights settings, have rested on equal protection grounds, he has also decided several significant cases involving the First Amendment, privacy, and procedural rights of college and high school students and faculty. In terms of the events and personalities involved, perhaps the most provocative to date has been *Dickey v. Alabama State Board of Education*. In early April of 1967, a number of state legislators had attacked Frank Rose, president of the University of Alabama, for his refusal to censor a campus student publication. "Emphasis 67, A World in Revolution" had served as the program for a campus series of speakers and panels on contemporary international politics. In keeping with its theme, the publication included excerpts from speeches by the communist Bettina Aptheker and by Stokely Carmichael, then a noisy advocate of violent worldwide revolution. "Emphasis 67" had also carried articles by noted antirevolutionaries, including the chairman of the Joint Chiefs of Staff; but the legislators charged Rose with fomenting subversive activity on the university campus. Far from yielding, Rose defended the publication and academic freedom in a strongly worded speech to the Birmingham Bar Association.[18]

Gary Clinton Dickey was then editor in chief of the *Tropolitan*, the student newspaper at Troy State College, a small south Alabama school. Dickey wrote an editorial supporting Rose, but campus officials, including Troy president Ralph Adams, refused to approve the editorial for publication. Adams—a longtime Wallace crony and college rooming house companion with little in his background but a wise choice of friends to recommend him for an academic post—explained that a newspaper could not criticize its owners and that the Alabama legislature and governor "owned" Troy State and its newspaper. The *Tropolitan's* faculty adviser suggested that Dickey substitute an article on dog-raising in North Carolina for the offensive editorial. Instead, Dickey published the editorial's title, "A Lament for Dr. Rose," and left the remaining editorial space blank—except for the word "Censored" running diagonally across the space. For his offense, Dickey was charged with "willful and deliberate insubordination" and summarily denied admission to school the following fall. On a petition from Dickey's counsel, Judge Johnson quickly intervened, first voiding Dickey's suspension without a hearing, then holding that Dickey's second suspension after a hearing violated his First and Fourteenth Amendment free expression rights. The judge did not doubt that college officials could discharge an editor, choose not to operate a student newspaper, or impose reasonable regulations on student papers as a means of controlling substantial interferences with the educational process and student discipline. But he termed "superficial" Troy State's argument that Dickey's admission would jeopardize school discipline.[19]

Several of Judge Johnson's Middle District First Amendment cases would arise, of course, outside the academic setting. He has enforced the Supreme Court's ban on devotional exercises in the public schools and joined a three-judge panel in overturning the phrase "so help me God" in the oath taken by Alabama bar applicants. In two cases, moreover, he has confronted the intractable obscenity problem. Judge Johnson is clearly impatient with Supreme Court efforts to define what is "obscene." He has remarked,

I've thought for a long time that the Supreme Court did the lower courts and the people that were having to deal with this thing at their peril a great injustice in not deciding what I think will ultimately be decided and made the law of the land on obscenity. And that is, if you're a mature, consenting adult, there can be no censorship. . . . If people want to read those girlie magazines . . . where minors can't get to them, then who am I to say they can't? If they're mature and if they're consenting, then courts shouldn't censor it. And I think the Supreme Court should have said this years and years ago and stopped fooling around with what is and isn't obscene.

He views as "ridiculous," at best, moreover, the Supreme Court's present notion that what is obscene may vary from community to community. His two Middle District obscenity decisions reflected this skepticism about government controls over erotica. In a 1968 case, he upheld the right of a Montgomery newsstand operator to sell sexually explicit books and magazines to an adult clientele, remarking during the hearing in the case that, in his judgment, a dealer could put "neon lights on his girlie magazines," as long as minors were unable to buy them. And after police, acting on Governor Brewer's instructions, made warrantless raids on local adult theaters throughout Alabama, first viewing then seizing sex films and arresting theater operators, he joined a three-judge panel in invalidating the seizures and enjoining further such antics.[20]

Other Middle District human rights rulings also rested on nonequal protection grounds. In a number of cases, Judge Johnson extended to Alabama the Supreme Court's rulings forbidding justices of the peace to participate in decisions in which they have a pecuniary interest in the outcome. In 1971, moreover, he intervened in behalf of a national guard major who had been harassed by his superiors after failing to contribute to George Wallace's 1970 gubernatorial bid. As a participant on three-judge panels, he also voted to overturn Alabama "ethics" legislation requiring newsmen covering the capitol to reveal their economic interests and employers and intervened to assure due process for a legislator subjected to expulsion proceedings. Even after adoption of the 1965 Voting Rights Act, however, voting discrimination cases would remain a regular part of the court's docket. In a series of three-judge rulings, for example, Alabama's poll tax was overturned, its lengthy residency requirements for voting invalidated, and an injunction issued against extension of a Bullock County commissioner's term as a transparent device for blunting the impact of black voter increases. Judge Johnson and others on a three-judge panel also intervened repeatedly in behalf of Alabama's predominantly black National Democratic party, at one point holding state officials in civil contempt when they refused to place the party's candidates for local offices on the ballot. Sitting alone, moreover, Judge Johnson imposed a $300 criminal contempt fine on a Greene County circuit judge involved in the same ploy.[21]

Judge Johnson has been equally willing to impose constitutional obligations on organizations that are ostensibly private in nature, but actually are permeated with state involvement. The Montgomery YMCA case provides the most clear-cut illustration. After he had ordered desegregation of Montgomery's parks and recreational facilities, city officials closed them and embarked upon a cooperative scheme with the city's thoroughly segregated YMCA. Under the arrangement, the YMCA was given free use of the city's parks, playgrounds, and lighting equipment for its athletic programs; the city furnished free water for the association's swimming pools; and the organization was allowed to recruit members in the Montgomery public schools. Over the claims of association officials and city fathers that the YMCA was merely a private organization and thus immune from equal protection obligations, Judge Johnson found unconstitutional "state action" and ordered the association's immediate desegregation. Moreover, in the event that the appellate courts might disagree with his rejection of the YMCA's claim to private status, he further held that the association constituted a place of public entertainment within the scope of the 1964 Civil Rights Act's ban on discrimination in most such facilities. In 1972, he closed the door a bit further, forbidding segregated private schools and other groups to use Montgomery's recreational facilities. Until the Supreme Court ruled differently, however, he refused to extend to private action the provisions of Title 42, Section 1981 of the United States Code, which, among other things, grants all persons equal rights with white citizens in contract transactions. So reasoning, he ignored recent decisions of other lower courts and rejected a 1981 challenge to the all-white society section of Montgomery's jointly owned major newspapers, only to be reversed by the Fifth Circuit.[22]

As the foregoing indicates, three-judge panels rendered some of the more significant and controversial Middle District human rights decisions during Judge Johnson's tenure there. Formally, the judge was merely a single participant in collegial decisions on such panels. In the public mind, however, he was the jurist most readily associated with the Middle District's brand of judicial activism. And by the beginning of George Wallace's second (legitimate) term, Johnson had become, in the minds of friend and foe alike in the state, Alabama's de facto governor.

As the image of his power grew in the minds of Alabamians, so also did his national stature. In the wake of the bombing of his mother's home, Time put his portrait on its cover and published an admiring account of his Alabama exploits. By the early 1970s, moreover, he had begun to amass a variety of national honors, including honorary doctorates from Notre Dame ("a man who has shown us that 'law and order' does not have to be a shorthand reference to indignity or oppression") and Princeton ("his courtroom has been a sanctuary of integrity, fairness, and decency"). For civil rights sympathizers around the nation, he had become a last bastion against the forces of darkness in the Deep South.[23]

With belated national recognition came consideration for higher judicial office. When Supreme Court Justice Abe Fortas resigned under fire in 1969, Judge Johnson was mentioned often as a possible replacement—and increasingly so when President Nixon's initial two nominees for the post met defeat in Senate confirmation proceedings. Civil rights activists warmly endorsed a Johnson appointment; and, though asking that his letter be kept confidential, a northwest Alabama Democratic congressman with conservative credentials wrote the Justice Department supporting his nomination. But Alabama Republicans viewed the prospect of a Johnson appointment with growing alarm. "What with us the fledgling party that we were in the state," Montgomery's GOP Congressman William Dickinson later remarked, "politically it would [have been] devastating to the Republican party [in Alabama] if, the first crack out of the box, Nixon appointed Judge Johnson, who is an outstanding judge, but was certainly an activist in the civil rights movement. I mean, he was way out front looking around to see if anybody else was following him." At one point, Nixon's Attorney General John Mitchell telephoned Dickinson and his Alabama Republican colleagues about the possibility of a Johnson appointment. Each praised the judge's legal talents but predicted that his selection would be political suicide for the party in Alabama and detrimental to GOP efforts elsewhere in the South.[24]

Before newsmen, Dickinson later applauded Judge Johnson as "an extremely capable jurist," termed him "a conservative and a strict constructionist" in all constitutional fields but civil rights, and predicted "that down the road people are going to come to find out that by stepping out in front, he will save Alabama some grief in the long run." Dickinson dismissed as "the wildest story I've ever heard," however, the rumor that Judge Johnson's name had topped the administration's list of prospective nominees and conceded that "on the political side we'd have to be negative," adding: "If Nixon is trying to appease the side of the South, he'd be defeating his purpose there if he appointed Johnson." Dickinson's congressional colleagues and other state GOP leaders assumed the same stance, and eventually the presidential nod went to Harry A. Blackmun, an obscure veteran of the Eighth Circuit court of appeals.[25]

With the retirements and deaths of Justices Black and John Marshall Harlan in the fall of 1971, two additional vacancies arose on the high Court. Again, Judge Johnson's name received prominent play, particularly as a replacement for his fellow Alabamian Justice Black; again, he was passed over for other choices. He took the president's decision philosophically. "Nixon never was about to appoint me to the Supreme Court," he would later say. "By that time, the philosophy of the Nixon administration was pretty evident, so I never did pack my suitcase to go to Washington."[26]

On this occasion especially, however, Judge Johnson's possible nomination attracted considerable support, and from a number of unlikely sources. Not unexpectedly, Fred Gray and twenty-five other civil rights advocates and black officials from around the nation sent the president a warm endorsement, as did a number of law school faculties and student groups, including those at Duke and the judge's alma mater. But his supporters also included the bar associations of Montgomery County and five other Middle District counties, conservative Black Belt congressman and Wallace ally George Andrews, and a variety of Montgomery officials. Congressman Dickinson sent a supporting letter, too, then paid a visit to Judge Johnson's chambers to explain the obvious—that his earlier opposition had been prompted by the dictates of political expediency.[27]

Several southern newspapers with a racially liberal editorial posture also joined the ranks of Johnson supporters. In Montgomery, the *Advertiser* editorialized, "Why Not Judge Johnson?" and the *Journal* praised him as a "law and order" jurist, "strict constructionist," and "fiscal conservative." The *Advertiser* and *Journal* support was no surprise. Both papers had published similar editorials when the Fortas vacancy arose and had been increasingly—though not consistently— friendly to Johnson rulings. What did appear surprising was the editorial support Judge Johnson received elsewhere in the state. Bullock County's Union Springs *Herald* maintained, for example, that no one could "accuse Judge Johnson of being 'political' in his decisions," and declared—enthusiastically, if not accurately—that "he has never been overruled by a higher court."[28]

This mellowing of local feeling was probably attributable to a variety of factors, including the temporary lessening of court-baiting occasioned by Wallace's hiatus from the statehouse, a general decline of racial tension in Alabama, the increasingly nonracial focus of the judge's human rights caseload, civic pride in a down-home boy—and no doubt the feeling among some new-found admirers that a Supreme Court appointment would at least get their old nemesis out of the state. Perhaps the most significant factor, however, was Judge Johnson's moderate stance on school desegregation, and particularly his distaste for court-ordered school busing.

After imposing their statewide desegregation decree in 1967, Judges Johnson, Rives, and Grooms had begun supervising its implementation.

For a lengthy period, Friday became "School Board Day" at the court. Meeting in Judge Johnson's chambers, the panel conferred with school officials and attorneys from around the state, reviewing compliance plans. In that setting, former law clerk Howard Mandell recalls, "Judge Johnson . . . was the motivating force. He was the one who was familiar with every single school board's plan; he was the one who would make the recommendations." Beyond overseeing implementation of the statewide decree, Judge Johnson and his colleagues also invalidated the state's operation of racially separate high school athletic associations and other discriminatory features of Alabama education. In 1968, moreover, he tightened standards for Montgomery's consolidated school system. Scoring the school board's failure to convert freedom of choice into an effective tool of desegregation, he erected safeguards to assure that school construction and transportation policies did not perpetuate segregation and imposed hiring ratios to assure faculty and staff desegregation. (Privately, he also criticized the Supreme Court's virtual ban on interdistrict desegregation plans. While hoping that he would be spared such a case, he contended that the Court's regard for local autonomy in the educational field flies in the face of the extensive state controls that have long existed and justify court disregard of school district lines.)[29]

It soon became evident, however, that Judge Johnson was no friend of court-ordered busing and the notion that the Constitution requires racial balance in the public schools. In 1970, he approved an interim Montgomery desegregation plan that largely incorporated the neighborhood school concept and resulted in only limited busing of students, most of whom were black, from rural areas to city schools. In 1971, the Supreme Court approved extensive use of busing to achieve desegregation. But in 1974, Judge Johnson rejected two plans calling for substantial busing of Montgomery schoolchildren, adopting instead a school board plan that allowed most students to attend the school nearest their homes and thus, given the city's strict patterns of residential segregation, did not completely eliminate the system's predominantly black schools.[30]

In short, Judge Johnson's sympathies rested with those parents who resent the busing of their children to remote areas of a school district. For him, busing is simply not worth the price of potentially disrupting the educational process and further exacerbating racial tensions. In the Middle District, therefore, there was little court-ordered busing. As Judge Johnson has remarked, "We have less busing now than we did before I started messing with it."[31]

Tied to a growing local appreciation of his antibusing posture may have been a modicum of gratitude that, by acting forcefully in early civil rights battles, Judge Johnson had insulated his moderate school desegregation stance from aggressive appellate review. By the late 1960s, appellate courts often praised Judge Johnson's rulings. In upholding his 1968 order in the Montgomery school case—and overturning a Fifth Circuit modification of the order—the Supreme Court, speaking through Justice Black, had applauded, for example, the judge's "patience and wisdom," adding: "It is good to be able to decide a case with the feelings we have about this one." It seems likely, therefore, that over the years Judge Johnson's decisions in racial cases became increasingly immune from the close appellate scrutiny accorded most of his southern peers' rulings and that Alabamians were duly grateful. In supporting Judge Johnson for the Supreme Court in 1970 and 1971, for example, the *Montgomery Advertiser* contrasted the judge's appellate batting average with those of his Alabama counterparts and editorialized: "The appellate court has let him alone, in the main, while rocketing missiles at the other districts. Result: these areas are worse off by far than we are."[32]

Judge Johnson continued to receive his share of hate mail. After his 1968 order tightening Montgomery desegregation requirements, for example, an anonymous critic wrote, in a crudely printed note, "You are a buzzard of a man. . . . You must love your money more than you love God or you'd quit. No love and less respect from. *A True Patriot*." But increasingly his mail was complimentary or at least ambivalent in tone. (The latter included a Christmas card depicting a black Christ cradling a black lamb, which carried the message, "Thought of you when I saw this card!") When George Wallace returned to power in 1971, moreover, the governor's rhetoric lacked its former vehemence. Wallace's attacks on Judge Johnson had always been part and parcel of his racial politics. And after 1971, the governor, ever attentive to the winds of change, had become noticeably solicitous of black votes, appointing blacks to cabinet offices, posing awkwardly for pictures with the University of Alabama's first black homecoming queen, even appearing unannounced at Dexter Avenue Baptist Church to proclaim his love for black folks. By September of 1974, Alabama's racial climate had calmed to the point that the guards could be removed from Judge Johnson's home and his mother's house as well.[33]

As hatred of his civil rights stance subsided, however, Judge Johnson's decisions in other human rights fields began to attract the wrath of another set of critics. On this occasion, traditional foes of the Wallace stripe would be joined by legal scholars concerned about judicial activism in the lower federal courts. Their principal targets would be the judge's landmark decisions requiring reform of Alabama's mental institutions and prisons.

CHAPTER 11

Human Warehouses

The state of Alabama maintains three major institutions for the mentally ill and retarded—Bryce Hospital in Tuscaloosa; Searcy Hospital in Mt. Vernon; and Partlow State School and Hospital, also located in Tuscaloosa. Bryce was built in the 1850s and initially enjoyed an excellent reputation as one of the nation's more enlightened "insane asylums." It was the first mental institution in the United States, for example, to remove shackles from patients. Even by 1875, however, its head Dr. Peter F. Bryce had conceded that the facility had become little more than an almshouse and old folks' home. By 1970, conditions there had reached a crisis stage; daily food allowance per patient, for example, was less than fifty cents. If anything, conditions at Partlow, the state school and hospital for the retarded, were even more pathetic; as more than one state mental health official had remarked, Partlow was truly the "stepchild" of the system. Worst of the lot, however, was Searcy Hospital, a nineteenth-century fort and military barracks converted in 1900 into a mental institution for blacks. By 1970, the state had begun pumping additional funds into the facility, but for years Searcy was considered a classic example of an unbelievably poor mental hospital. In 1968, for example, there was but one licensed physician and a few unlicensed Cuban refugee doctors on the staff for twenty-two hundred patients.[1]

Not surprisingly, Judge Johnson's first official confrontation with what Justice Department officials would later term Alabama's "misnomered" mental health system had come in the context of a racial segregation case. Provisions of Alabama law required assignment of the mentally ill and retarded on the basis of race or color. Bryce was operated principally for white patients (approximately forty-seven hundred in 1969, compared with four hundred blacks), Searcy totally for blacks. Only those black patients residing north of U.S. Highway 80 and diagnosed as having acute impairments could be admitted to Bryce, and the races were segregated within the facility. All white patients were housed at the main Bryce complex. Some blacks were assigned to Bryce Treatment Center Number Two, a segregated facility located eight miles from the main complex. The remainder lived in Ward X and the Lodge, segregated buildings in the main complex, and the Colony, a facility adjacent to Bryce Number Two. Partlow served white and black mentally retarded patients, but on a strictly segregated basis. Physical facilities provided black patients were clearly inferior to those provided whites; the Lodge, which housed blacks at the main Bryce complex, for example, was a converted stable at the rear—naturally—of the facility.[2]

On February 11, 1969, Judge Johnson and others on a three-judge panel invalidated as "separate and unequal" the segregation and discrimination in the state's mental health facilities, giving Alabama officials twelve months to desegregate Bryce and Searcy, three months to bring Partlow into compliance. Speaking for the panel, Judge Johnson agreed that "medical discriminations which take racial factors, such as patients' fears and delusions, into account" were permissible, but added: "Racial classifications are always suspect, however, and if such actions are challenged, the burden will be on the officials to demonstrate that the discrimination is medically justified."[3]

The challenge to racial discrimination at Bryce, Searcy, and Partlow did not touch, of course, upon the deplorable conditions at each institution. In fact, Judge Johnson gave a rather glowing report of the facilities being provided white patients, remarking at one point in his opinion: "Bryce has many recreational programs and craft shops; Searcy has a television set, dominoes, and cards, if requested, and a weekly visit from the recreation department." Within months of the panel's discrimination decision, however, conditions at the facilities would become his court's principal concern.[4]

In the late summer of 1970, over a hundred Bryce employees, including a number of psychologists and other professional personnel, were told that they were to be discharged within a few months. A reduction in revenue caused by a cut in the state cigarette tax was cited as the major reason for the cutback.

Faculty in Alabama's universities and colleges, along with many other state citizens, had long been concerned about conditions in the state's mental institutions, and they viewed this latest development with considerable alarm. Shortly after learning of the impending cutback, for example, concerned citizens held a meeting at Canterbury Chapel on The University of Alabama campus to consider ways of protecting the threatened positions. Raymond Fowler, head of the university's psychology department and a specialist in correctional psychology, was among those most incensed by the announced cutbacks, particularly because a number of the professionals to be discharged were his former students. Fowler also doubted that revenue strictures were the real cause for at least a portion of the announced reduction in staff. Stonewall Stickney, the state commissioner of mental health, was grooming Dr. James Folsom, a relative of former Governor Folsom, as Bryce's next superintendent. Folsom, a native of Marengo County, had completed his graduate training at the University of Vienna and the Menninger Institute and was then serving as director of the VA hospital in Tuscaloosa. Folsom placed great emphasis on the use of paraprofessionals in the treatment of the mentally ill, and in Fowler's judgment, the cutback was actually designed to get rid of those professionals who opposed extensive use of paraprofessionals and objected to other recent changes in Bryce's approach to the delivery of medical services—particularly the move to a unit system in which patients from the same geographical area in the state would be assigned to a particular unit in the hospital.[5]

When Fowler went home that evening after hearing of the forthcoming cutbacks, he and his wife Nancy told their neighbors Jay and Alberta Murphy what was to happen at Bryce. Jay, an Illinois native, had come to The University of Alabama in 1947 to teach constitutional and labor law in the university's law school. Alberta, a tall, handsome Texas native with a penchant for broad-brimmed hats and flashy cars, was also an attorney and, like her husband, an outspoken liberal. In 1972 and 1974, she would seek the Democratic nomination for Congress against the district's conservative representative Walter Flowers, and though branded a "communist, atheist, nigger" (the Murphys are white) would receive 38 percent of the vote on each attempt. The Murphys had long been concerned about conditions at Bryce and the other state mental institutions, and the Fowlers believed their friends might not only share their sense of outrage at the cutbacks, but also offer some helpful legal advice.[6]

Fortunately for the Fowlers—and ultimately for Alabama's mental patients—the Murphys had a house guest that evening. George Dean was a Montgomery native then residing in Florida. In recent years especially, he had devoted his law practice largely to voting and other civil rights cases. Tall, tanned, with patrician features, the molasses voice of southern gentry, and prematurely graying hair, Dean cut a flamboyant and outspoken figure, both in and out of the courtroom. In 1967, Lurleen Wallace had toured Alabama's mental health facilities with tears in her eyes and later persuaded the legislature to enact a $15 million bond issue to upgrade the facilities. The funds were quickly gobbled up by buildings and inflation; nothing had gone to improved therapy for the patients. Dean was incensed by conditions at Bryce, Searcy, and Partlow and singularly unimpressed with the state's modest reform efforts. Of Lurleen's mental health reforms, he scoffed, "Shortest sentence in the Wallace Bible: 'Lurleen wept.' " He had no hope that George Wallace, who had just won renomination to the governorship over Albert Brewer, would do much better. In fact, he rejected completely the thesis that, at heart, Wallace is a progressive interested in social reform. "George Wallace is just a bad little evil man. He's just a simple demagogue in the classic Greek definition. Absolutely nothing but whatever madness the crowd wants to hear at the time, George Wallace feeds to them. That's all he is. He has no philosophy. He's never had any philosophy. . . . If we had not had the word demagogue we would have had to invent one for George."[7]

At the Murphys' house that evening, Dean and the others soon agreed to promote a federal suit tying protection of the employees' jobs to their patients' civil rights. "It's hard to believe," he recalls, "that within twenty or thirty minutes we had conceptualized that there had to be a constitutional right to treatment. Then the corollary was that you can't treat without treaters. . . . We sat there and talked that evening about the case, and everyone knew that it would have an enormous, profound effect on our lives because we just knew god-damn well, from our knowledge of Bryce, its horrible conditions, the reduction of staff, the involuntary nature of the commitment process in Alabama, that the case could be just what we could make it. . . . I never had the slightest doubts that it would be a major case."[8]

After the meeting, Dean received signed retainers from the professionals and other staff personnel who were to be discharged and from the guardians of a number of Bryce patients, none of whom he would ever meet. All told, he received about forty retainers. He then began preparing to file a complaint. Among federal judges in Alabama, there was no doubt in whose court the suit would be filed.[9]

A distasteful incident involving Judge Johnson's brother Jimmy had prompted Dean largely to avoid practice in the Middle District court early in his career. When Dean first returned to Montgomery and set up law practice, he and other young attorneys in the junior bar section of the Alabama Bar Association became interested in reforming the state's usury laws under which loan sharks were allowed virtually unlimited discretion in setting interest rates. At the time, Jimmy was engaged in a thriving loan business. One day, John Henry Thomas, a black garbage-man, came by Dean's office, said that he wanted to file for bankruptcy, and asked that Dean represent him in court. Dean soon learned that his client had recently filed for bankruptcy but that his debts to Jimmy Johnson had been reinstated shortly thereafter. His client explained that Jimmy had told him his brother was a federal judge and he would have to reinstate his debts to him despite the bankruptcy proceedings. At the federal courthouse Dean found twenty-four other cases where recent bankrupts had reinstated their debts to Jimmy. After interviewing them, Dean sued Jimmy for fraud in state court.[10]

Some time later, Dean went to the bankruptcy court to check on another case and learned that Judge Johnson had ordered the files closed because, the clerk told him, "that lawyer George Dean has been using these cases to solicit business." "Being young, foolish, and having no god-damn sense, I went to see Judge Johnson, the first time I ever remember seeing him. It was a long way from his secretary all the way back to that desk in his chambers." When Dean complained about the closing of the files, Judge Johnson's response was brief: "If the shoe fits, wear it." Dean then stormed upstairs to see Judge Rives, bent on filing a formal complaint. Rives agreed to have a meeting of the Fifth Circuit judicial council convened. Dean thought about it for a day, then asked Judge Rives to forget it.[11]

A few days later, Dean received a call from a local lawyer, a patient in a Montgomery hospital, asking him to come for a talk. When Dean arrived, the attorney had pulled back the covers on his bed, revealing two large sacks of money. "See how much you need out of those sacks to settle the John Henry Thomas case," the lawyer instructed. Dean took out $2,500, conferred with his client, and had the fraud case against Jimmy dismissed.[12]

Though Dean admired Judge Johnson's courageous handling of civil rights cases and respected his judicial talents, he tried to avoid practice in the judge's court for several years after the incident with Jimmy. "I just didn't know Judge Johnson well enough to know how he would react. I knew he was crazy about Jimmy, crazy about his family, and I didn't think I ought to put myself in a position of letting Judge Johnson get even, until it had buried itself pretty well." He had played a minor role in the initial Alabama reapportionment cases, however, and in recent years had tried a number of major civil liberties cases in the judge's court. He and Charles Morgan of the ACLU had helped represent the plaintiffs in a Middle District suit attacking state and local harassment of Black Muslims, which had begun after Muslims had attempted to establish a community in rural St. Clair County near Birmingham. In June 1970, Judge Johnson and others on a three-judge panel had invalidated as unduly vague and sweeping in scope a state statute requiring the Muslims to register with state officials. The panel had also enjoined pending criminal prosecutions under the statute on the ground that the law's very existence imposed a chilling effect on the group's associational rights.[13]

Ironically, given the nature of the complaint he was about to file in Judge Johnson's court, Dean had once had a more indirect contact with the judge's family in the context of a civil commitment to Bryce. When Johnny Johnson was twelve or thirteen, he had learned that he was adopted, and the experience had been traumatic. When Johnny was sixteen, he suffered a nervous breakdown; and in the years that followed he had been admitted on a number of occasions to sanitariums in Birmingham and North Carolina for electrotherapy and other treatment for psychological and emotional problems—treatment some friends believe later would affect his father's approach in mental health litigation.[14]

Johnny had a winning personality and many friends, but the realization that he was adopted, the pressures on his father, and occasional involvement with drugs had taken their toll. Judge Johnson and Ruth also attributed many of their son's problems to his relationship with a Montgomery matron, which began when he was finishing high school and lasted almost nine years. The woman's husband had died early in their marriage, leaving his widow with a comfortable trust fund, one of Montgomery's larger homes, and young children. Johnny became enamored of her, and when the Johnsons attempted to turn his interests in other directions, she was, in their judgment, no help. To the contrary, she appeared to work against them, encouraging the relationship. At times, she would phone the Johnsons' home in the middle of the night, and they would attempt to reason with her. When that had no effect, Judge Johnson sent lawyers to her and threatened to attempt to have her committed to Bryce.[15]

Eventually, the woman's family did have her committed, and at this point George Dean entered the picture. From Bryce, she wrote a friend, asking that he contact Dean in her behalf. Over her prominent father's strong objections, Dean secured her release. "If I had been Johnny's daddy, I'd have been upset about it. . . . But the woman didn't belong in jail by my standards, in prison or in the hospital, so I got her out."[16]

On October 23, 1970, Dean filed a complaint in the Bryce case with Judge Johnson's court. In civil liberties cases, he and Charles Morgan attempted to style their cases with a touch of humor. One of the plaintiffs in the Muslim case, for example, had been a John Wallace, and the principal defendant was Governor Brewer. Naturally, the case was styled *Wallace* v. *Brewer*, in honor of the state's two leading contenders for the Governor's Mansion. Other civil rights cases with which Dean had been connected included *Washington* v. *Lee* and *White* v. *Crook*. In the Bryce case, the name of the state's mental health commissioner—Stonewall Stickney—offered immense opportunities, of course, but none of the plaintiffs' names was very encouraging. Finally, Dean told a secretary to simply pick any plaintiff's name in styling the case. She picked Ricky Wyatt, a sixteen-year-old Bryce patient since 1969, whose aunt and guardian was an aide at the hospital. Thus, the case was filed as *Wyatt* v. *Stickney*.[17]

The initial focus of the case was on protecting the jobs of the Bryce personnel. In fact, on the day the complaint was filed, Dean also moved for a temporary restraining order to prevent the defendants from modifying or interrupting services and probate judges from committing additional patients, pending further proceedings. Affidavits from Bryce personnel supporting the plaintiffs' case also emphasized this element of the complaint.

When Dean approached the judge about a restraining order to keep the personnel on, however, "Judge Johnson indicated rather promptly," Dean recalls, "that he wasn't gonna fool with that aspect of it." Howard Mandell was then serving as Johnson's law clerk, and he well remembers the meeting at which Dean inquired about the possibility of a restraining order.

> George came in and gave the judge a fifteen or twenty-minute presentation and . . . his argument reflected that he was interested primarily, at that time, in the rights of the employees and their families. And the judge listened, then said: "I am concerned about the rights of those people, but what about the rights of the patients?" And George stood silent for a couple of minutes and collected his thoughts, and as an extremely fine advocate, seemed to realize that this was another peg that maybe he could put the hat on, and all cf a sudden George started emphasizing the rights of the patients. . . . Judge looked at him and said, "I'm even more interested in those rights, Mr. Dean." And that was just the turning point right there. . . . Now, I'm not saying . . . that George did not intend, at some point, to make the rights of the patients part of his claim, but his initial argument was addressed primarily to the rights of [the staff]. . . . George lived, ate, and slept that case for three years, and the amount of work he put into that case only shows his compassion. But I think that the judge . . . gave him a . . . push in the right direction right off the bat.[18]

Even at this point, of course, Dean clearly was concerned with patient rights, if only as a constitutional basis for protecting the staff's interests. His meeting with Judge Johnson convinced him, however, that the employee plaintiffs should be dropped, and the case was pursued from that point purely as a class action in behalf of Bryce's patients. Later, the employees retained Tuscaloosa counsel who eventually saved their positions through a state court suit.[19]

The January hearing was devoted largely to testimony by personnel in Alabama's mental health system. Two months after the hearing, on March 12, Judge Johnson issued his first opinion in the case. He concluded that patients involuntarily committed to a mental institution for treatment have a constitutional right to "adequate" treatment and that the treatment accorded Bryce patients was constitutionally inadequate. He reserved for the time being, however, the plaintiffs' petition for proceedings to establish what constitutes adequate treatment. Instead, he gave the defendants ninety days to prepare a plan for adequate treatment of Bryce patients and six months to implement a treatment program that would give a Bryce patient "a realistic opportunity to be cured or to improve his or her mental condition." Failure to implement such a program, he warned, would prompt further intervention.[20]

Judge Johnson could cite precious little precedent to support his finding of a constitutional right to adequate treatment. In recent years, split panels on the District of Columbia court of appeals had recognized a right to treatment. In *Rouse* v. *Cameron*, for example, Chief Judge

David L. Bazelon had declared for a divided panel that "the purpose of involuntary hospitalization is treatment, not punishment," and concluded that Congress had created a statutory "right to treatment" for mental patients involuntarily committed to District of Columbia facilities. While referring to the "considerable constitutional problems that arise because 'institutionalized patients receive only custodial care,' " Judge Bazelon had bottomed Rouse's right to treatment not on the Constitution but on a statute—and one that had no application in Alabama. The case thus offered Judge Johnson a slender reed on which to hang a constitutional right of treatment. But *Rouse* was about all he had, so he cited Judge Bazelon's ruling there, plus an earlier D.C. circuit decision touching on the issue, and announced a new constitutional principle: "The purpose of involuntary hospitalization for treatment purposes is *treatment* and not mere custodial care or punishment. . . . There can be no legal (or moral) justification for the State of Alabama failing to afford treatment—and adequate treatment from a medical standpoint—to the several thousand patients who have been civilly committed to Bryce's for treatment purposes. To deprive any citizen of his or her liberty upon the altruistic theory that the confinement is for human therapeutic reasons and then fail to provide adequate treatment violates the very fundamentals of due process."[21]

At first glance, Judge Johnson's position seemed to reflect merely the widely accepted traditional notion that, under due process, the state must follow established law when depriving the individual of his liberty: if the law allowed civil commitment for treatment, due process required treatment for those committed. Actually, however, Judge Johnson was announcing a much broader constitutional doctrine. Not only was treatment required; it was to be "adequate." And judges, guided presumably by medical expertise, were to determine the adequacy of treatment programs. In that sense, his decision was in line with Supreme Court rulings of an earlier era which had employed due process to create economic rights mentioned nowhere in the Constitution's text and with modern rulings utilizing due process in recognizing a variety of privacy rights. In terms of the judicial supervision required for implementation, moreover, Judge Johnson's right of adequate treatment promised unprecedented judicial involvement in administrative policy decisions.[22]

In his March 12 opinion, Judge Johnson requested that Justice Department and HEW officials come into the case as amici curiae (friends of the court). Later, the American Psychological Association, ACLU, American Orthopsychiatric Association, American Association on Mental Deficiency, National Legal Aid and Defenders Association, and Center for Law and Social Policy would be given permission to appear as amici also. By early summer of 1971, the Justice Department had assigned two young attorneys from its Civil Rights Division fulltime to the litigation, and the FBI was providing investigative assistance. Of government attorneys involved in the case, however, the Middle District's U.S. attorney Ira DeMent was to become most active in the litigation.

Ira DeMent is a Birmingham native and graduate of the University of Alabama law school. After clerking for the Alabama Supreme Court in 1958–59, he had served briefly as an assistant state attorney general and assistant U.S. attorney, then set up a law practice in Montgomery. For a time, he had also served as legal adviser to the city's police and fire departments.

In 1969, President Nixon had appointed DeMent U.S. attorney for the Middle District. The appointment aroused considerable controversy. Rumors circulated that DeMent, a Republican, had supported George Wallace's presidential aspirations. Moreover, in 1968, he had defended members of Crenshaw County's Ku Klux Klan unit when Judge Johnson had enjoined them from interfering with school desegregation in the county. DeMent had also encountered stiff competition. His chief sponsor was William L. Dickinson, Montgomery's GOP congressman. But the most potent Republican in the area was Winton M. (Red) Blount—multimillionaire builder, heavy GOP contributor, and the Nixon administration's new postmaster general—and Blount endorsed Robert E. Varner, a prominent Montgomery attorney and descendant of a state supreme court justice, for the position.[23]

When DeMent's confirmation bogged down in the Senate, Judge Johnson appointed Leon Hopper acting U.S. attorney. Gradually, however, sympathy was aroused for DeMent. The executive committee of the Montgomery County bar association passed a resolution opposing rejection of any nominee on the basis of his clients. Robert Varner signed that resolution and issued a similar one of his own. It was also learned that DeMent had represented a variety of clients, including a Muslim and, without fee, five black children attempting to upgrade a predominantly black state reform school. At that point, the opposition subsided, and his appointment was confirmed.[24]

When DeMent and the judge first met, Johnson promptly told him with a smile that it had been DeMent's grandfather who, years before, had fined him for fighting when he had defended his father's honor against the harangue of a political opponent. The two quickly developed a close relationship. DeMent's generally calm exterior masks a pugnacious personality, but Johnson took his friend's volatile tendencies in stride. Once, before he became U.S. attorney, DeMent appeared before Judge Johnson as counsel for two teenagers who had stolen a portable radio from a fire tower in a national forest. The federal government had paid $150 for the property though a similar radio could have been bought in any discount house for $10–20. The government, not the teenagers, DeMent told the jury, should be on trial for paying $150 for a cheap radio. "Mr. DeMent," Judge Johnson cautioned with the barest trace of a smile, "I suggest that you make your John Birch speeches outside this courtroom."[25]

DeMent had seen the U.S. attorney's position as a stepping stone to an anticipated new judgeship for the Middle District. When the position was created in 1970, he became a prime contender, receiving support from a wide-ranging array of supporters, including Congressman Dickinson, President Nixon's new Law Enforcement Assistance Administration (LEAA) director Jerris Leonard, several Montgomery police officials, and many prominent state judges. Ultimately, however, the nod went to Robert Varner. Varner's critics charged that he was an undistinguished lawyer and civil rights/social conservative whose appointment would be nothing more than another plank in the Nixon administration's "Southern Strategy." Superficially at least, there was considerable substance to the charges. By a divided vote, the American Bar Association's judiciary committee had given him only a "qualified" rating, instead of one of the higher ratings reserved for "well qualified" and "exceptionally well qualified" nominees. Even the Wallace administration had expressed concern about his antipopulism and ties to Alabama's industrial and commercial elites. And when pressed by the Senate Judiciary Committee about his segregationist status, he attempted to avoid a definite answer. "That's a difficult question to respond to without being put on the spot. I must admit I'm rather gunshy about it. It means so many things to so many people down here." Because of such concerns, the Judiciary Committee delayed action on Varner's confirmation until late April 1971. On April 20, however, the committee voted to approve the nomination without a dissenting vote. The following day, the full Senate confirmed the appointment.[26]

For Alabama's mental health patients, Judge Varner's selection over Ira DeMent was to be fortuitous. DeMent and Raymond Fowler had been undergraduate roommates at the university; and in recent months, DeMent had begun helping to secure millions of dollars in federal LEAA funds for Fowler's program in correctional psychology and other university programs. DeMent and George Dean had been law school classmates and were close personal friends. "I trust him like a brother and love him like a brother," DeMent has said of Dean. "He's eccentric, erratic, and brilliant, and at times irresponsible. But when the going gets tough, I'd like to have him right with me. I greatly admire Dean and his qualities." Very shortly, Dean and Fowler would learn that their friend was to be an aggressive ally in the plaintiffs' struggle.[27]

Soon after DeMent and the attorneys from the Justice Department's Civil Rights Division entered the case as amici, Dean approached

DeMent about the possibility of an unannounced tour of Bryce as a means of publicizing mental health conditions in Alabama ("Judges read newspapers," Dean would later say). Ethically, such a move was questionable, but DeMent agreed.[28]

On Saturday, July 31, DeMent, Robert Johnson of the Civil Rights Division, and news reporters and photographers arrived at Bryce and made a lengthy tour, accompanied by an attorney for the state mental health board. After a routine morning tour of the Bryce main complex, the group drove out to Bryce Number Two, ostensibly so that DeMent could visit a friend. After the visit, in one of the center's newer sections, the group abruptly decided to tour the Jemison Building, the center's worst facility. "That's when all hell broke loose," a news source later reported.[29]

Jemison had formerly housed patients who required little if any care and worked in the fields on Bryce's vast farm holdings. Only recently had the building been converted into a treatment center for patients, and its facilities were grossly inadequate. The conditions DeMent's group uncovered there were horrifying. Human feces were caked on toilets and walls, urine saturated the aging oak floors, many beds lacked linen, some patients slept on floors, archaic shower stalls had cracked and spewing shower heads. One tiny shower closet served 131 male patients; the 75 women patients also had but one shower. Most of the patients housed at Jemison were highly tranquilized and had not been bathed in days. All appeared to lack any semblance of treatment. The stench was almost unbearable.[30]

Some of Bryce's patients, the group found, had been there for decades and had been committed under dubious circumstances. "It had become a dumping ground," DeMent later said,

> for the state's senile, who had no business ever having been put in a mental institution, for persons who were eccentric, for geriatrics with no place to go, some of whom weren't even senile. And probate judges, without any procedural safeguards, could and did commit, on a telephone call, on a letter from an M.D. who knew about as much about psychiatry as my nine-year-old son does. . . . There was one huge barracks with nothing but old people. They weren't insane. They just were old and had no place to go. I met a man up there who was celebrating his fiftieth anniversary of having been there. He was committed by an inferior court in Birmingham. . . . He had been involved in a strike in Birmingham, and he was committed to determine whether he was competent to stand trial. The court has since been abolished and the paper work on him has long since been lost, and he was celebrating his fiftieth anniversary there. And you couldn't pull him out of there with a trace chain now because he's totally and completely institutionalized.[31]

After DeMent's Saturday tour and an investigative visit to Bryce and Partlow the following week, Alabama newspapers published graphic reports and photographs of conditions in Alabama's mental health facilities. In recreation yards with virtually no grass, the press reported, one attendant attempted to supervise eighty retarded youngsters, yet allowed them to eat dirt and drink from filthy puddles of water. Women in straitjackets sat idly in courtyards, inhaling flies they were unable to fan from their faces. Is this an example of the institution's "individualized therapy program"? DeMent had asked. Temperatures at Ward X in the Bryce complex ranged between ninety and a hundred degrees, and Bryce officials had conceded that several elderly women had died in the past, at least in part because of the heat. Numerous patients—a child in a catatonic state huddled against a bundle of dirty laundry, a naked black youth cowering on a floor—were found alone and unattended. One ward housed eighty-four patients who were receiving no training at all.[32]

News reports also focused on the inadequacy of funding and facilities. Within the last decade, it was reported, state appropriations for the mentally ill and retarded had been as low as $3 per patient per day and at present were $6.72. Georgia, Florida, Tennessee, Louisiana, and Arkansas averaged $12 per patient; only Mississippi was at the bottom of the list with Alabama. As a consequence, less than 10 percent of the mentally retarded were in training programs; and Partlow's twenty-one hundred patients were under the around-the-clock care of only four physicians, sixteen registered nurses, and a single full-time psychologist.[33]

Especially moving, however, were the photographs—full pages in some papers—that accompanied the reports. Perhaps the most pitiful was a photo of a young retarded girl who sat bound in urine-soaked bed sheets while flies crawled in and out of her mouth. But each said more about the plight of Alabama's mental patients than any news story could ever convey.

Momentarily, at least, DeMent's inspection tours—"lightning assaults," one newspaper termed them—had the desired effect. Shortly after the second tour, the *Alabama Journal* called the *Wyatt* suit "a godsend"; and many other state papers followed suit. Within a week of DeMent's first visit, patients were removed from Jemison and $345,000 in emergency funds appropriated for its renovation. The state fire marshal was asked—for the first time in over a decade—to inspect the state's mental health facilities. Afterward, he reported that one building at Searcy was unsafe for human habitation and should be torn down; for the other facilities, he recommended massive improvements in fire safety standards. A number of Bryce aides were discharged for abusing patients, and there was also a brief flurry of activity in Alabama's statehouse. Governor Wallace proposed that $24 million in the teacher retirement fund be diverted to the state's mental institutions. A number of the governor's legislative leaders and a few legislators interested in the cause of mental health reform argued in support of the measure, one representative warning his colleagues: "But for the grace of God, you or I could be a patient in one of the state hospitals." And when the Alabama Education Association voiced strong opposition to the proposal, state Senator Robert Wilson, Wallace's chief legislative floor leader, went on television to complain about the state's "fat and lazy" teachers—though neglecting to mention that, earlier, Wallace had cut Dr. Stickney's budget request for an 80 percent increase in mental health funds to 38 percent. Ultimately, however, the proposal was soundly defeated, opposed in part by some of Wallace's own legislative leaders. In the house of representatives, for example, the measure was defeated 89 to 12. A later Wallace proposal to divert appropriations from school operating funds met a similar fate. "When Lurleen asked for something" for mental health, Wallace complained, "every single legislator said, 'Yes, Ma'am.' When I go and ask them for something, sometimes they say 'Uhh.' Lurleen had a woman's touch."[34]

While the governor and state legislators were bemoaning a lack of funds for improving the mental health facilities, however, George Dean filed a statement in Judge Johnson's court listing twenty groups that received a total of more than $3 million for "unnecessary or non-essential" functions, including livestock shows and beauty pageants. "Plaintiffs feel that they may have been better provided for," said Dean, "if they were athletic and photogenic cows of Confederate ancestry."

In late September, the state filed the six-month report which Judge Johnson had required in his March 12 order. As the response of the United States to the report demonstrated, the report was hardly responsive to Judge Johnson's order that the state implement a program of adequate treatment. Calling Bryce Alabama's "human warehouse" and detailing gross inadequacies in the state's mental institutions, the report concluded: "What stands out clearly from the defendants' report and the analysis by the plaintiffs and amici—as well as the history of mental treatment, or, indeed, lack of treatment, provided by the State of Alabama—is that treatment has never occurred at an Alabama mental institution—is not now occurring—and does not promise to occur in the reasonable future."

George Dean's response for the plaintiffs was equally damning. The "Patient Operated Program" of therapy discussed in the state's report, he observed, consisted of nothing more than "drugged patients helping one another in essentially make-do tasks," adding: "Plaintiffs do admit that it beats boredom and requires no staff." Bryce's program of "job placement" training he termed "in effect . . . institutional peonage," its physical facilities deplorable ("Practically every building and ward would be closed as a fire hazard by any fire department in the United

States"). After newspaper publicity about Ward X, where several elderly women had died from dehydration on particularly hot days, he
observed, Bryce officials had made but two "reforms"—ten beds were
removed, and the name was changed to Ward 37. Like the amici, Dean
urged Judge Johnson to establish constitutional standards and appoint
a panel of masters to supervise their implementation.

On December 10, Judge Johnson issued a second opinion in the case.
Public mental institutions, he wrote, must meet three "fundamental
conditions" of adequate and effective treatment—a humane psychological and physical environment, qualified staff in numbers sufficient to
administer adequate treatment, and individualized treatment plans.
Bryce, he concluded, was deficient in each area. Patients were housed
in "barn-like structures" with no privacy, given shoddy wearing ap-
parel, assigned nontherapeutic tasks, and subjected to "degrading and
humiliating" admission procedures that gave the hospital a "prison" or
"crazy house" atmosphere. Bryce's overcrowded facilities posed extreme ventilation and fire hazards, food served its patients was inferior,
the institution was grossly understaffed, its treatment program "wholly
inadequate." In late August, the class action had been enlarged to
include Searcy and Partlow; and to Judge Johnson, there were "strong
indications" that conditions at those facilities were "no better than
those at Bryce." Noting that the defendants had generally demonstrated
good faith, however, he again deferred turning over the three institutions' operations to a panel of masters. Instead, he scheduled the case
for further hearing on the sort of "medically and constitutionally
mandated standards" the institutions should be required to meet.[35]

Earlier, the defendants had agreed that any order relating to conditions at Bryce would also be binding on Searcy. The state's concession
eliminated any need for a hearing on conditions at Searcy. A hearing to
determine what standards of treatment should be required there and at
Bryce was set for early February 1972; a hearing on Partlow's conditions and the standards to be imposed there was set for the end of the
month.

In mid-January, representatives of the parties and amici met in
Atlanta. Following extensive discussion, they agreed on many of the
standards that, in their judgment, would be necessary for the provision
of minimally adequate treatment for the state's mental patients. The
stipulations, filed with Judge Johnson in two memorandums of agreement, further reduced the likely duration of the February hearings.
Even so, the Bryce/Searcy hearing would last two days, the Partlow
hearing four.

The Bryce/Searcy hearing was largely uneventful, witnesses devoting
most of their testimony to now largely subtle differences over the sorts
of treatment standards to be imposed. The plaintiffs' witness list was

filled with the names of eminent mental health specialists. But the
defendants had a prestige witness of their own—Dr. Karl Menninger of
the famed Menninger Institute, a prolific author and practicing psychiatrist for fifty-four years. Dr. Folsom had studied with Menninger,
and in the wake of Ira DeMent's tours, when the state's papers were
saturated with stories about the deplorable conditions in Alabama's
mental institutions, Folsom had invited his mentor to visit Bryce. In
late September, Menninger toured the facility and spoke at the university, praising Dr. Folsom, terming Bryce "something to be proud of,"
and predicting that "the day will come when most of the people in this
institution are here because they asked, because they begged to get in."
Later, Folsom's cousin Cornelia Wallace invited Menninger to visit
Montgomery and confer with state officials. As George Dean would
remark, it appeared that Folsom was "trying to bring the aura of the
Menningers down around him" and Alabama's mental institutions.[36]

But Dr. Menninger was then seventy-eight, and at times during the
hearing he appeared confused and disoriented. After sitting through
the proceedings until late in the afternoon on the day he was to testify,
he resisted his wife's efforts to calm him and left the courtroom,
explaining in audible tones, "I just can't stay here. . . . Why, those
young lawyers up there are asking repetitious questions." Judge Johnson cast a critical glance to the rear of the courtroom, and Dr. Folsom
dashed after his witness, finally persuading him to return. When
Menninger took the witness stand, he leaned all the way back in his
seat, looked up at Judge Johnson, and smiled. The judge smiled back.
At one point during his testimony, Judge Johnson allowed Menninger
to make a brief speech about the need for love and compassion in the
world. Later, the judge invited Menninger and opposing counsel to his
home for dinner so that Ruth and Johnny would have an opportunity to
meet the famed psychiatrist.[37]

Judge Johnson was largely unimpressed, however, with Menninger's
testimony. Expert witnesses for the parties and amici had itemized
numerous reforms required, in their judgment, to assure even minimally adequate treatment of Alabama's mental patients. Dr. Jack Ewalt,
director of the Harvard Medical School's psychiatric division and a
former Massachusetts commissioner of mental health, had told the
packed courtroom, for example, that "bare-bones" treatment of the
mentally ill in one 250-bed unit at Bryce and Searcy would require 10
occupational therapists, 4 rehabilitation counselors, 8 laboratory or
service technicians, 181 nurses, 17 social workers, 10 psychologists,
and 8 psychiatrists—at a time when there were fewer than 8 psychiatrists in the entire state mental health system. Dr. Menninger, on the
other hand, praised Folsom ("You just let Dr. Folsom handle that
hospital and the treatment will be fine"), minimized the need for

additional staff, and suggested that several hundred ministers would be
more beneficial to the patients than psychiatrists and other professional
staff personnel. More critically, from Judge Johnson's perspective, he
had suggested that what would constitute minimally adequate treatment for patients in public facilities could be considerably less than
that required for patients in private institutions.[38]

Much of the four-day Partlow hearing focused on treatment standards, but witnesses also told further horror stories about conditions
there. The testimony of Partlow's acting superintendent Dr. Peter
Blouke and others established that a number of patients had died as a
result of understaffing, lack of supervision, and brutality—one youth
after a garden hose had been inserted into his rectum for five minutes
by a working patient who was cleaning him, another who died when a
fellow patient hosed him with scalding water, a third who died when
soapy water was forced into his mouth, and a fourth who died from a
self-administered overdose of drugs that had been inadequately secured by Partlow personnel. Attendants told of youngsters being locked
away in seclusion rooms with no sanitary facilities for as long as six
years and of patients being beaten by other residents and staff members.
Dr. David Rosen, superintendent of a facility for the retarded then being
constructed in Michigan, complained about the use of electric cattle
prods—"training wands" they were called at Partlow—in an experimental program designed to control self-destructive behavior. He also
told of dining rooms staffed entirely by patients, some of them working
ten hours each day, seven days a week. Calling Partlow a "warehouse
operation," "primitive and unmanageable," Dr. Phillip Roos, the executive director of the National Association for Retarded Children, testified that some patients had worked at Partlow, without any pay, for as
long as twenty, thirty, and forty years, some at hazardous jobs. But-
tressing such testimony were written reports graphically portraying the
deplorable conditions at Partlow.

Judge Johnson was clearly moved by the testimony. At one point,
when a witness suggested that the state was capable of upgrading the
facilities without outside interference, he impatiently asked, "Why
hasn't it already been done?" And at the conclusion of the hearing, he
issued an interim emergency order designed to protect Partlow's patients. The evidence, he concluded, "has vividly and undisputably
portrayed Partlow State School and Hospital as a warehousing institution which, because of its atmosphere of psychological and physical
deprivation, is wholly incapable of furnishing treatment to the mentally retarded and is conducive only to the deterioration and the
debilitation of the residents."

Within fifteen days, he ordered, Partlow officials were to eliminate
all safety and fire hazards, install an emergency lighting system, estab-

lish a plan of evacuation in the event of fire or other disaster, survey sanitation problems with respect to food preparation and service and implement corrective measures, revamp the entire program for administering drugs, and send in a medical team to examine every patient receiving drugs. Within ten days, a team of physicians was to be engaged to conduct an immunization program for all residents. Within thirty days, the state was to hire three hundred additional employees, including mental health professionals from various disciplines; and because of the emergency, the defendants would not be required to comply with state merit system regulations or other formal hiring procedures. Arrangements were also to be made for transferring out-of-state patients to facilities in their resident states. Within forty-five days, a detailed compliance report—including the name, race, and employment status of each person hired under the order—was to be filed with the court.

Then, on April 13, Judge Johnson issued a comprehensive order and decree for Partlow,[39] another for Bryce and Searcy.[40] Appended to the Partlow order were forty-nine "Minimum Constitutional Standards for Adequate Habilitation of the Mentally Retarded." Thirty-five similar standards of "adequate treatment" were imposed on Bryce and Searcy. The standards, he emphasized, were "both medical and constitutional minimums and should be viewed as such." The judge also appointed a human rights committee for each facility to guarantee patients "constitutional and humane habilitation." After noting that the committees would have authority to review all research proposals and treatment programs to safeguard the patients' dignity and rights, advise and assist those who allege that their legal rights have been violated, inspect institutional records, interview residents and staff, and consult independent specialists, he added in a footnote: "The recitation of the licenses . . . of the committees . . . is not intended to be inclusive. The human rights committee of each mental health institution shall be authorized, within the limits of reasonableness, to pursue whatever action is necessary to accomplish its function."[41]

The treatment standards which Judge Johnson imposed were extremely elaborate and detailed, the Partlow standards later consuming thirteen double-columned pages in the *Federal Supplement*, the Bryce/Searcy standards eight pages. Under the Partlow standards, patients were to be housed in the "least restrictive" environment consistent with their treatment needs and preferably in community facilities. Individualized treatment plans were to be established for each patient, and mental health officials were to follow strict regulations regarding patient medication and behavior modification programs. Electric shock devices were to be used only "in extraordinary circumstances . . . and only after alternative techniques" had failed. Corporal punishment was prohibited; physical restraint, use of patients for work assignments and experimental research subjected to strict safeguards. Most work engaged in by patients was to be voluntary and compensated in accordance with minimum wage standards.

Numerous detailed regulations related to patient health, comfort, hygiene, and privacy: a nourishing, well-balanced diet; assistance in learning normal grooming practices; teeth brushed daily with an effective dentifrice; a daily shower or tub bath, unless medically forbidden; regularly scheduled hair cutting and styling, in an individualized manner, by trained personnel; a minimum of eighty square feet of floor space per resident in multiresident rooms, at least one hundred square feet in single rooms; a comfortable bed and adequate changes of linen; an individual closet or locker for personal belongings; appropriate furniture; screens or curtains to ensure privacy in multiresident rooms; a clean and odor-free toilet and lavatory for every six residents, a tub or shower for each eight residents. From controls over the temperature of rooms and water, to regulations about refuse, fire, and safety facilities, to those relating to housekeeping and food preparation, myriad other requirements were imposed to assure safe, sanitary conditions. Finally, there were detailed staffing ratios: one psychologist, one social worker, one vocational therapist, one recreational therapist, and one registered nurse, for example, were to be appointed for every sixty patients. With minor variations, similar staffing and other standards were imposed on Bryce and Searcy.[42]

While extremely detailed, the standards Judge Johnson had imposed were far from revolutionary; and virtually all had been agreed to by the defendants. Moreover, he reserved a ruling on the motion of the plaintiffs and amici for the appointment of a master and professional advisory committee to oversee implementation of the standards at each institution. "Federal courts," he wrote, "are reluctant to assume control of any organization, but especially one operated by a state. This Court, always having shared that reluctance, has adhered to a policy of allowing state officials one final opportunity to perform the duties imposed upon them by law." The judge also reserved rulings on the plaintiffs' motions that the mental health board be ordered to sell its extensive landholdings, and the state forbidden to spend for "non-essential functions," so that additional funds could be provided for treatment of Alabama's mentally ill and retarded. But he warned that such action would be necessary if the legislature and mental health officials failed to meet the court's standards.[43]

George Dean had petitioned Judge Johnson for an order requiring the defendants to pay the plaintiffs' lawyers reasonable attorneys' fees. Citing the "incalculable benefit" their efforts would provide "the people of Alabama"—and the defendants' "bad faith" in failing to respond earlier to mental health inadequacies—Judge Johnson granted the request. Later, he awarded Fred Gray a million dollars in fees after Gray secured an out-of-court settlement for victims of a federal experiment program testing the effects of syphilis on the human body. But Gray had requested over twice that amount, and, as George Dean has remarked, Judge Johnson is a "money conservative." Dean should know. In *Wyatt*, the judge decided that reasonable attorneys' fees should be assessed at the same rates the federal courts apply in awarding fees to counsel for indigent defendants in criminal cases. Dean had worked eighteen months full-time on the case; the judge awarded him $23,600, a small fraction of what he had requested. "People in Winston County," Judge Johnson later said, "find it hard to think in terms of large sums of money."[44]

Of course, it could have been worse. Despite obvious philosophical differences, John Patterson is Dean's friend and had advised Judge Johnson that the amount Dean had requested for *Wyatt* was reasonable. Earlier, Patterson had supported the request of Morris Dees, a Montgomery millionaire and founder of the Southern Poverty Law Center, for an award of fees in the case desegregating Montgomery's YMCA. "When I got in there," Patterson recalls, "Judge Johnson told Morris and Joe Levin, Jr., his partner, 'I think $25,000 is a reasonable fee. I think you've earned it. . . . However, I'm going to ask you to agree to something. I want you to let the Y keep your fee and use the $25,000 to pay annual dues for underprivileged black children so that they can come to the Y and use its facilities. Would you agree to that?' Old Morris turned as white as a sheet of paper. But he reluctantly agreed, because he had no choice. I thought Judge Johnson got a real kick out of that."[45]

Attorney General Bill Baxley initially announced that the state had no plans to appeal Judge Johnson's April orders to the Fifth Circuit. But Governor Wallace took time off from his presidential campaign and complained to newsmen that the orders had placed an impossible burden on the state. Wallace estimated that 80 percent of Alabama's entire annual budget would be required to secure compliance. Earlier, Dr. Stickney had told reporters that the staffing ratios imposed by Judge Johnson had actually been submitted to the court by the mental health board and approved by Governor Wallace and his advisers. And Wallace's attorneys had agreed, of course, to most of the standards well in advance of the April ruling. But the governor now denied that he had agreed to any of the standards. He had only agreed, he said, that "it would be nice to have all the money in the world to provide optimum care for mental health and all other services." Shortly thereafter, Wallace retained his own counsel and appealed the orders. In the wake of Wallace's decision, Baxley reversed himself. Baxley bemoaned the

"misery" in Alabama's mental health facilities, but cited the "dangerous precedent" of "having a judge take over the functions of state
government." He might also have noted the realities of Alabama politics.[46]

It would be over two years before a Fifth Circuit panel announced its
decision. In the intervening months, there were several further developments in the case. Shortly after Judge Johnson's April 13 orders were
issued, Dr. Stickney had been quoted as saying, "Actually, it's kind of
exhilarating to see that the courts may get the Legislature going. It's
been our experience that they'd rather spend money for highways than
mental health." Within months after the ruling, Stickney was forced to
resign under fire. Dr. Charles Aderholt replaced him briefly, then
Taylor Hardin—a lawyer, career state civil servant, general in the
Alabama national guard, and, as state finance director, Wallace's top
cabinet officer—was named to the post.[47] Hardin's tenure would be
more secure than that of his predecessors.

While *Wyatt* was pending on appeal, Alabama officials generally
took a "wait and see" attitude about compliance with the orders. But
there were a few minor improvements. Patients began receiving pay for
their work, for example. "I've been milking those cows at Bryce
Treatment Center Number Two for a long time," one resident said,
"and I ain't made a dime. It's nice to get a payday." One newspaper
article reported improvements under way at Partlow—but for renova-
tion of the superintendent's office and home, not for the sort of changes
required under the court order. In July 1972, mental health officials
asked Judge Johnson to clarify the responsibilities of the human rights
committees and complained of harassment by George Dean and committee members. Later, the judge received further similar complaints
and requests that the roles of the human rights committees be clarified.
Eventually, too, the Partlow superintendent issued an order requiring
his approval before any staff member could appear before a meeting of
the Partlow human rights committee.[48]

In September 1974, Judge Johnson entered an order clarifying the
human rights committees' role and mission. In the order, he emphasized that "free and easy communication should be established between the committees and the patients and staff" at each institution. He
also said he was "not aware of any serious [committee] interference"
with the facilities' operations. The Partlow procedure, he added, was
"completely inconsistent with both the letter and spirit of" the order.
On January 8, he had also imposed strict standards and procedural
safeguards on the sterilization of retarded patients. Two weeks earlier,
he, Judge Rives, and Judge Varner had invalidated an Alabama statute
that allowed sterilization of mentally retarded residents at the unfet-
tered discretion of a facility's superintendent or assistant superinten-

dent and contained no provision for notice, hearing, or other basic procedural safeguards. The complaint challenging the statute had claimed, among other things, that Partlow had hired an assistant medical director who had suggested that patients no longer be subjected to tubal ligation surgery, but instead "lined up against a wall" and zapped with cobalt radiation first in one ovary, then in the other.[49]

Judge Johnson, of course, was not the only federal judge being confronted with mental health suits. In neighboring Georgia, Judge Sidney O. Smith had dismissed a class action suit alleging constitutionally inadequate treatment in that state's mental institutions less than four months after Judge Johnson's April 1972 orders. In marked contrast to Judge Johnson, Smith had concluded: "It is . . . the opinion of this Court that the claimed 'duty' (i.e. to 'adequately' or 'constitutionally treat') defies judicial identity and therefore prohibits its breach from being judicially defined. The problem of mental illness is a matter of urgent social concern. The members of the community should be made aware of the existent problems and should work through their elected representatives to solve those problems. This Court, however, is not the appropriate vehicle for the stimulation of public awareness."[50]

On November 8, a Fifth Circuit panel affirmed Judge Johnson's orders and reversed Judge Smith. Judge John Minor Wisdom wrote the panel's *Wyatt* opinion. In April, Judge Wisdom and others on a different panel had recognized a right to adequate treatment for the civilly committed in *Donaldson* v. *O'Connor,* a Florida case in which a former mental patient had sought damages after almost fifteen years of involuntary confinement without treatment in a state institution. In *Wyatt,* Judge Wisdom reaffirmed *Donaldson,* thus rejecting a major contention of Governor Wallace's attorneys that a primary and constitutionally adequate function of civil commitment is the provision of custodial care to relieve the burdens of a resident's family, guardian, or friends—the "true clients," they claimed, of mental institutions. A "need to care" theory, Wisdom asserted, could not possibly justify the massive curtailments of individual liberty which civil commitment entailed. Even if an adequate justification, he added, the care provided must possess some "minimum quality." "And it is clear that, however that obligation might specifically be defined, it was not being met in the Alabama hospitals."[51]

In their briefs and oral argument, William Baxley and Wallace's lawyers had hit hard at Judge Johnson's hint that he could order the disposal of state property, alter Alabama's budget, or require other arrangements in the event the defendants did not make a good faith effort to comply with his orders. Baxley claimed, for example, that there had "never been a more definite threat to the end of federalism" and that Judge Johnson had placed himself in the position of "virtually devouring state government." Judge Wisdom conceded that such moves would raise "serious constitutional questions." But he concluded that since no orders had yet been imposed along those lines, it would be premature to make a ruling on the issue. In any event, he added, such orders would require the convening of a three-judge district court panel. Governor Wallace had also contended that the stipulations or concessions about standards which the defendants had made before Judge Johnson's orders were issued were not binding on him or the Alabama legislature. The panel agreed that the legislature had not been a party to the stipulations or the suit, but of Wallace, Wisdom said: "We hold the Governor has for his part agreed that these standards are minimally acceptable under the Constitution. . . . It is the Governor's role to propose relief to the legislature and . . . use his best efforts to accomplish the relief."[52]

For *Wyatt*, the Fifth Circuit was the last forum. The Supreme Court denied review. In 1975, the high Court did make a ruling in the *Donaldson* case, but rested its decision on narrow grounds. Speaking for all his brethren, Justice Potter Stewart announced that a state could not involuntarily commit, "without more," any person who is capable of living in freedom without harm to himself or others. (After his release, Donaldson had promptly secured a responsible position in hotel administration.)[53] The Court thus avoided the fundamental question of what constitutes constitutionally "adequate" treatment, and Judge Johnson's *Wyatt* opinions and orders remain the federal judiciary's most extensive statement on the subject and the major precedent in the developing field of mental health law.

In *Wyatt*, Judge Johnson had reviewed conditions in Alabama's mental institutions and found them sadly lacking. In *Lynch v. Baxley*, filed while *Wyatt* was pending before the Fifth Circuit, he and others on a three-judge panel were invited to find Alabama's civil commitment laws and procedures similarly inadequate. Under Alabama law, probate judges are given authority over involuntary commitments to state mental hospitals. At their discretion, certain judges impaneled a special jury of six persons to make commitment decisions; others made the decision without a jury. The only statutory standard for judge or jury read: "A person shall be adjudged insane who has been found by a proper court sufficiently deficient or defective mentally to require that, for his own or others' welfare, he be removed to the insane hospital for restraint, care and treatment." Candidates for commitment were given no notice of a hearing, were not present for the hearing, were not informed of any right of counsel, and were not appointed counsel if they were indigent.[54]

On December 14, 1974, a month after the Fifth Circuit's *Wyatt* ruling, a divided Middle District panel announced its decision in *Lynch*.

Speaking for himself and Judge Rives, Judge Johnson found virtually every element of Alabama's approach to civil commitment unconstitutional. Rejecting the state's standard for commitment, he held that a person could be committed only if found mentally ill and a substantial danger to himself or others. In addition, the danger posed must have been evidenced by a recent overt act, and treatment for the illness must be available in the state's facilities. The person to be committed was also entitled to a panoply of procedural safeguards, including notice, the right to be present at commitment proceedings, effective assistance of counsel, the opportunity to present evidence in his own behalf and cross-examine opposing witnesses, and the privilege against self-incrimination. Alabama provided a right of jury trial for those civilly committed persons who challenged their confinement in habeas corpus proceedings. If the state continued that practice, he held, a jury was also to be provided in all commitment proceedings. On occasion, emergency detention of a person believed to pose an "immediate and serious" threat of violence to himself and others would obviously be necessary. But in such cases, Judge Johnson stressed, a probable cause hearing was to be held; and detention without a hearing would be justified only for the period of time needed to schedule the hearing, and never more than seven days. All future commitments were to follow these requirements. Those committed in the past were either to be released, permitted to remain if they chose and were incapable of caring for themselves, transferred to facilities designed for the care and treatment of their illnesses, or given "new hearings attended by the full panoply of constitutional rights to which these citizens were initially entitled but of which they were deprived."[55]

Judge Varner dissented in part. Varner was convinced that certain provisions in the Alabama commitment statutes should be saved from invalidation and said he was "gravely concerned that the majority opinion would strip the State of any functional statute for commitment of any but the criminally insane and would force the release of some persons dangerous to themselves or others." He also questioned the majority's conclusion that dangerousness and treatment were the only constitutionally adequate bases for commitment. The Fifth Circuit's rejection of confinement based on a need for care in *Wyatt*, Varner contended, was only a dictum; in his judgment, commitment could be bottomed on the need for care "and training," as well as the need for treatment.[56]

Partly as a result of Judge Johnson's orders, partly because of other factors, there have been noticeable changes in Alabama's mental health system since *Wyatt* was first filed. The per patient allotment is now more than five times larger than the 1971 figure. Staff inadequacies have been reduced, living conditions made much safer and more sanitary. The stench is gone. At the community level, federal funds have been employed to establish homes where ten to twelve patients can live in pleasant and supervised settings, planning their own menus, shopping for food, preparing meals, and engaging in other routines of daily life. A number of community treatment facilities have also been built.[57]

Lecil Gray, Judge Johnson's friend and fishing buddy from the years in Jasper, has headed a Tuscaloosa insurance company in recent years. Shortly after the Fifth Circuit's ruling in *Wyatt*, Judge Johnson named him chairman of the Bryce human rights committee. Judge Gray's more colorful descriptions of the committee's impotence are unprintable, but Gray has been instrumental in the creation of an Intermediate Care Facility for former Bryce patients scheduled for eventual release or transfer to nursing homes or other facilities. He also had a major role in working out an arrangement under which a Tuscaloosa hospital now provides medical care for Bryce patients, and the totally inadequate Bryce medical unit has been closed.[58]

To date, however, the most striking consequence of *Wyatt* and *Lynch* has been a significant reduction in patient population. While *Wyatt* was pending, state mental health officials chided those who said that many, if not most, of the patients in Alabama's mental institutions did not belong there. But as a result of the hearings required under *Lynch*, and the financial burdens imposed by *Wyatt*, substantial numbers of patients have been transferred to other facilities or released. By the summer of 1976, for example, the Bryce patient population had been reduced from the approximately fifty-two hundred confined there when the *Wyatt* complaint was filed to less than fifteen hundred.

The plaintiffs' chief counsel in *Wyatt* has applauded the reduction in population. "There's not much you can do for people" in mental institutions, George Dean has remarked. "You harm people with electric shock. You harm people with drugs. All you do is make them manageable so you can take their liberty and lock them up. . . . I think Judge Johnson has a great deal of respect for doctors that I simply don't have." Dean's hope, he now emphasizes, "was that it would cost the State of Alabama so much to comply with the standards that they would do the normal, natural thing, . . . reduce the patient ratio." Raymond Fowler, who prefers community-level treatment of the mentally ill, substantially agrees. For Dean and Fowler, and certain others connected with the case, a significant reduction in patient population was a major, though largely unarticulated, goal of *Wyatt* and *Lynch*.[59]

Whatever the inherent evils of institutionalization, however, there is a darker side to the reduction in population in Alabama's mental institutions. Most of those removed from the three state hospitals have been transferred to private nursing homes. By 1975, over four thousand former mental patients financed by Medicare resided in Alabama nursing homes; and a thorough recent study of conditions in them has concluded that the treatment received by nursing home patients in 1975 was inferior to that available in the state's mental hospitals even before *Wyatt*. For those patients, Judge Johnson's orders may ultimately have done more harm than good.[60]

Beyond this, there have been numerous problems of implementation. Judge Johnson had required the treatment of patients in the "least restrictive" environment consistent with their treatment needs. Through a misinterpretation of this aspect of his orders ("intentional or otherwise," Judge Gray has wryly noted), many mental patients were allowed for a time to leave their institutions and wander about the community. A druggist whose business was located across the street from the entrance to Bryce and long had been a hangout for University of Alabama students changed locations, complaining that Bryce patients had defecated on his floors and frightened off his customers. Other merchants raised similar complaints, and several Tuscaloosa residents returned to their homes to find Bryce patients sitting at their dining tables. A local minister wrote Judge Gray a hot letter complaining that a patient was disturbing his church's Sunday evening suppers by acting boisterous, using foul language, and refusing to pay the twenty-five cent admission fee ("I told him to just treat him like the Master would," Judge Gray recalls, his eyes twinkling. "If the Master would kick him out, kick him out. If the Master would accept him, accept him"). Eventually, restrictions were imposed, but not before several Bryce patients had been struck by passing automobiles, trains, or drowned in a nearby river. Frequently, moreover, unauthorized persons have entered the grounds at Bryce or one of the other facilities, providing patients with liquor and drugs and at times abusing them sexually. From time to time, patients have continued to die under mysterious circumstances, and there have been numerous instances of patient abuse by hospital employees or other residents. Inadequate supervision has also meant that patients at times still are allowed to harm themselves. During a stay at Bryce, for example, Jean Lynch, whose earlier commitment had resulted in the imposition of procedural standards in *Lynch* v. *Baxley*, hanged herself.[61]

Critics of shortcomings in *Wyatt's* implementation cite other problems. Alberta Murphy served with Judge Gray on the Bryce human rights committee. As late as the summer of 1977, Mrs. Murphy complained that Bryce patients were still overmedicated and poorly clothed, and that, as yet, no treatment plan for Bryce patients had even approached the sort of individualized programs spelled out in Judge

Johnson's order. She, Judge Gray, and other committee members were also concerned about the quality of professional staff the state's poor salary scales have attracted.[62]

Many of the institutions' problems, Judge Gray was convinced, stemmed not from lack of funds, but from bureaucratic inefficiency. When the Intermediate Care Facility was constructed, he later recalled, mental health officials neglected to provide a kitchen; and federal funding for patient care was delayed until kitchen facilities could be provided. On another occasion, the state decided to paint the buildings at Bryce. Mental health specialists recommend that bright, cheerful colors be used and that the colors, especially for doors, be varied to assist patients in finding their way. But to save money, the state contracted to have everything, including doors and corridors 150 feet long, painted a pale green. Then, when a variety of paint colors was contracted for on a later occasion, it was learned that the contract with the painters provided that they were to paint only in one color![63]

Though sympathetic with many of the standards Judge Johnson had imposed, state mental health personnel, on the other hand, were concerned about what they considered to be unrealistic requirements in the 1972 order—and extreme interpretations given the order, in their view, by the *Wyatt* plaintiffs and amici and by the human rights committees. They considered unrealistic, for example, Judge Johnson's requirement that training programs be developed for every resident, even those who were profoundly or severely retarded. Funds consumed in futile efforts to develop meaningful training programs for such residents, they contended, could be better spent in providing the severely or profoundly retarded with enriched living environments. Mental health personnel also considered unrealistic what they saw as an implicit goal of the 1972 order—deinstitutionalization of all residents—since they believed that certain residents could never be removed from the institutional setting. They contended, too, that Judge Johnson's requirements of monthly reports on the progress of each resident and the development of postinstitutionalization plans for all residents, even those with no reasonable expectation for deinstitutionalization, were an unnecessary and unreasonable burden on institutional resources. They also opposed a misinterpretation which they believed that the plaintiffs, amici, and human rights committees were attaching to the 1972 order: in the order, Judge Johnson had required six hours of educational training per day for school-age residents; but the plaintiffs, amici, and human rights committee members had been insisting that such training was required for all residents, even the elderly. Finally, they believed that Judge Johnson's standards would have been less stringent had the state vigorously contested the claims of the plaintiffs and amici and produced nationally prominent expert witnesses whose views on the treatment of the mentally ill and retarded differed substantially from those of the expert witnesses the plaintiffs and amici had produced. Stonewall Stickney had conceded many of the plaintiff-amici contentions, they were convinced, not so much because the state accepted their views regarding treatment of the mentally ill and retarded, but because Stickney had wanted to force increased state appropriations for mental health in Alabama.[64]

While implementation efforts and disputes over the meaning of the 1972 order continued, Judge Johnson, in December 1975, allowed the parties to reopen evidence discovery for the purpose of determining the extent of state compliance with provisions of the 1972 order relating to the mentally retarded. Following the discovery process, the *Wyatt* plaintiffs and amici filed a motion for further relief, contending that there had been "substantial and serious noncompliance" with those provisions of the order that concerned creation of effective resident habilitation programs, movement of residents to the least restrictive treatment setting commensurate with resident needs, protection of resident privacy, improper administration of medication programs, protection of residents from staff abuse, and the provision of medical and dental care. In October and November of 1978, moreover, the defendants filed motions for modification of the 1972 order. Among other things, they requested that the Partlow human rights committee be divided into four separate committees and instructed not to interfere with administration of the facilities. They also proposed that severely or profoundly retarded residents be given "enriching activities" rather than subjected to continued futile efforts to provide them with effective training programs.

After hearings on the motions at which prominent expert witnesses on both sides of the issues offered testimony, Judge Johnson, on October 25, 1979, issued a memorandum opinion.[65] The "hazardous and deplorable" conditions that had pervaded Partlow in 1972, he concluded, had been ameliorated "to some degree." The severe overcrowding had been eliminated, the staff increased though shortages of trained personnel remained in certain fields, and physical conditions improved. He also agreed to certain modifications the state had requested. He adopted, for example, a state proposal that certain borderline or mildly retarded residents be retained in the state institutions if they had other severe handicaps that would preclude community placement; he allowed the state to release residents to less restrictive settings within state facilities if community placement was not feasible; he agreed that postinstitutional plans need be developed only for those residents with reasonable promise for placement outside the institution.

In many other respects, however, Judge Johnson found "serious" areas of noncompliance and refused to modify the 1972 provisions. Characterizing as a state-created "straw man" the state's interpretation of the 1972 order to require six hours per day of structured educational programming for all residents, he emphasized that this requirement was confined to school-age residents, reiterated that habilitation programs were to be tailored to the needs of individual residents, and noted that a "considerable number" of residents had not received such individualized programming. On the question of community-based treatment, he stressed that the appropriateness of community placement would be left to professional judgment, but added that a number of residents identified by the state as ready for community placement had not yet been placed in such facilities. In general, he observed, the development of community placement was proceeding "very slowly." Finally, he denied the state's motion that residents be divided between those who do not and those who do show beneficial effects from training, the latter receiving educational programming and the former "enriching activities." He did acknowledge, however, that the Partlow population had changed significantly since 1972, that 80 percent of the present population was severely or profoundly retarded and 34 percent had multiple physical handicaps, and that such a change naturally would require modification of training programs. In short, he seemed to be saying, flexibility was to be the rule and programming for certain residents might well approximate the "enriching activities" which the state had proposed.

In reacting to the October 25, 1979, order, state personnel were pleased that Judge Johnson had recognized that certain residents might never be ready for community placement, but moved instead to less restrictive settings within state institutions. They were also pleased with his instructions that the requirement of six hours per day of educational training applied only to school-age residents. They were disappointed, however, that Judge Johnson had characterized as a state-nurtured "straw man" the notion that such training was required for all residents—a misinterpretation of the 1972 order which, in their view, the plaintiffs, amici, and human rights committee members, not the state, had promoted.[66]

By this point, of course, few cries of judicial tyranny would be raised against Judge Johnson, for George Wallace was no longer a statehouse resident and the judge had already left the trial bench for a seat on the Fifth Circuit. But when, several years before, he had turned the focus of his attention from Alabama's mental institutions to its prisons, the charge of judicial tyranny that had accompanied *Wyatt* had arisen anew—and with a special intensity. After all, while people might easily doubt the propriety of judicial "meddling" in any legislative and administrative domain, few could question the need for reform in Alabama's mental institutions—and better treatment for the forgotten innocents confined there. But when the judge ordered prison reform, public concerns about judicial tyranny had merged with a more glandular opposition to "criminal coddling" judges to produce another period of brief but especially bitter resentment against the Johnson court.

Unfit for Human Habitation

Among friends and foes alike, Judge Johnson is considered a "law and order" (or, as Ira DeMent prefers, "law and order *and justice*") judge. As a district judge, he was not nearly so innovative in criminal procedure cases as in other human rights fields. In fact, he did not issue a single ruling expanding the rights of suspects and defendants that could be considered even remotely of the landmark variety. He was not known for severe sentences and was fairly generous with probation grants. After the *Wyatt* order, for example, he gave a prominent Alabama doctor convicted of illegally dispensing drugs to women patients in exchange for sexual favors an option: he could either serve a probationary period providing free medical attention to Alabama's mental patients or go to prison. But he punished white collar crime as severely as other types of crime, white defendants as harshly as blacks, blacks as harshly as whites. When, for example, a state senator and his brother were convicted of "check kiting" in Judge Johnson's court, he sentenced each to eighteen months in prison, remarking later that he could not very well send poor defendants to prison for relatively minor offenses and let prominent defendants off with little more than a slap on the wrist. Nor was he an easy mark for state defendants seeking a reversal of their convictions through federal habeas corpus proceedings. And unlike certain other district judges, he did not seek to undercut the Supreme Court's traditional opposition to federal court injunction of pending state criminal proceedings, even in the name of constitutional rights. "Were I the defendant in a criminal case," William Baxley has concluded, "I'd rather be before any other judge in the country . . . , if I were guilty."[1]

This is not to suggest, of course, that Judge Johnson was insensitive to the claims of criminal suspects and defendants. Unlike a majority on the Supreme Court—past or present—he agrees with those who contend that all the substantive and procedural guarantees of the federal Bill of Rights are binding on the states through the Fourteenth Amendment's due process clause. He opposes, moreover, recent Burger Court decisions diluting the impact of the *Miranda* and *Mapp* decisions in the fields of confessions and search and seizure. Chief Justice Burger and most of his colleagues have concluded that the *Miranda* and *Mapp* prohibitions on court use of illegally seized confessions and evidence may be ignored in certain types of proceedings. As a U.S. attorney, Judge Johnson frequently took advantage of the now defunct "silver platter" rule under which federal prosecutors were forbidden to use illegal evidence seized by their own agents, but could use tainted evidence provided them by state police. But he opposes any weakening of *Miranda* and *Mapp*. "I don't see anything wrong with *Miranda* at all," he has said; "I don't see any justification for the uproar we had throughout the country, from people engaged in law enforcement, that 'we're being unduly restricted.' Hoover started all of that. . . . If the *Miranda* rule is good at all, then it ought to be good across the board. I don't think that there should be any exceptions to it. If an illegal confession is not valid for one purpose in the prosecution's case, it shouldn't be valid for another purpose. I don't find any rational basis for using something illegal to achieve a legal purpose." While agreeing with the present Supreme Court majority that the death penalty is not unconstitutional where undue flexibility and discrimination are removed from its application, he also opposes capital punishment on moral grounds and doubts it serves either to deter crime or fulfill any other "good purpose."[2]

On the Middle District bench, he was particularly sensitive to inmate claims to improved prison conditions. When confronted with what he considered "frivolous" prisoner claims, he was quick to dismiss such suits. In 1972, for example, inmate Bobby Ford sued state officials for $500,000 damages, claiming that a guard had called him an unflattering name and prison officials had rejected his demands for a private bath, phone, visiting room, improved mail service, and assorted other amenities. In his judgment, Judge Johnson wryly observed in dismissing the suit, prison personnel had failed only in neglecting "to orient Ford to the fact that he is a prisoner and is not entitled to the privileges of a Hilton Hotel." With the Alabama penal system facing an increasing number of lawsuits, he added, it was "no wonder that one of the prison officials responded to [Ford's] demands with an epithet." On another occasion, he dismissed a suit brought by a black inmate against prison officials. When the inmate criticized his decision, the judge noted that earlier he had overturned the inmate's death sentence. "You win some, and you lose some," he added, "and you won the big one." When confronted with substantial allegations, however, Judge Johnson would intervene more aggressively in prison policies and practices than any other jurist.[3]

In 1966, Judge Johnson, joined by Judge Rives and Judge Lynne, had ordered desegregation of Alabama's prisons and jails. But the first federal court orders relating to conditions in the state's prisons were issued in the Southern District. In 1969 and 1971, Judge Virgil Pittman imposed modest requirements on living conditions in Alabama's punitive isolation units—or "doghouses" as they were commonly known in the prison system. He also assured inmates access to religious literature, placed restrictions on mail censorship regulations, and ordered notice and a hearing for inmates subjected to disciplinary action. Where prison officials had challenged inmate claims, however, Pittman was decidedly less obliging. The prisoners who had filed the Southern District suit were confined at Atmore State Prison (later to be named the G. K. Fountain Correctional Center) and Holman Prison, both located near the town of Atmore in southern Alabama. Atmore, erected in 1928, was considered the state's worst prison; and inmates housed there and at Holman had complained of filthy living conditions, beatings at the hands of guards and other prisoners, inmate possession of weapons and illicit drugs, homosexual assaults, and little semblance of medical service. Before denying inmate claims to relief from such conditions, however, Judge Pittman had made a surprise visit to the facilities and found them "in much better condition than that testified by the petitioners." In general, moreover, he found the inmates' testimony incredible. "It is the judgment and conclusion of the Court," he wrote, "that the petitioners have distorted, warped, exaggerated, and misrepresented many facts. By and large, some of them would do or say whatever they felt necessary to obtain their release, and short of this, to have their way."[4]

At the time of the hearings in the case, medical care for the nineteen hundred Holman and Atmore inmates was provided by a private physician, working part time, and by an inmate medical assistant at each institution. Pittman found no constitutional inadequacies in this level of service. The physician had since resigned, but no matter. "It is expected," Pittman noted in a footnote, "that adequate medical attention commensurate with that provided in the past will be provided." Pittman's order was not to be the last word, however, on medical care for Alabama's inmates; within sixteen months of his order, Judge Johnson imposed strict standards of medical care and treatment on the entire state penal system.[5]

Judge Johnson's opinion and order in Newman v. Alabama were issued on October 4, 1972. They painted a decidedly grimmer picture of medical care in the state's prisons than the relatively benign account Judge Pittman had provided the previous year. The almost four thousand prisoners in the Alabama system were housed in five major prisons—Atmore, Holman, Draper in Montgomery, Julia Tutwiler (for women), and the Medical and Diagnostic Center at Mt. Meigs—in a minimum security facility for young offenders, an honor farm, a prerelease center, and thirteen road camps. The Medical and Diagnostic Center served as a general hospital for the entire system, a receiving center for new inmates, and a permanent facility for about 175 inmates.

The center's hospital contained approximately eighty beds and included wards for tuberculosis and hepatitis patients. The inmates' major medical needs were provided for at the center; most of the other facilities maintained a small infirmary for minor medical services.[6]

Judge Johnson found the medical facilities poorly administered and "grossly understaffed," the physical plant and equipment "totally inadequate" except at the recently built Medical and Diagnostic Center, and a "neglect of basic medical needs of prisoners that could justly be called 'barbarous' and 'shocking to the conscience.'" The evidence seemed clearly to support his conclusions. There was no full-time physician presently employed at the center; services were provided by three private doctors working part time and by the center's medical director who also had administrative responsibilities for the entire medical care program in the prison system and maintained an extensive private practice. Three registered nurses—the only registered nurses in the entire system—worked staggered shifts at the center weekdays. At night and on weekends, no registered nurse was on duty. Most of the daily medical care at the center was provided by nine former military medics who served as medical technical assistants (MTAs) and functioned as licensed practical nurses, though not licensed by the state. At night, and frequently during the day, only one assistant was on duty to cover the entire center. A dentist provided dental care part of the day three days a week. The center had no administrator, no dietician, no registered X-ray technician, no medical records librarian, and no civilian records clerk. If facilities at the center were poor, those at the other facilities, Judge Johnson found, were deplorable. Draper, for example, had no full-time physician for its approximately 850 inmates; and a dentist was available only one-half day each week. Throughout the system, moreover, medical record-keeping was not standardized; records were often inaccurate and incomplete, lost or misplaced. Medical supplies, even simple items such as aspirin and antacids, were in chronically short supply. Because of understaffing, unsupervised and untrained inmates regularly pulled teeth, screened sick call patients, dispensed and administered medication (including dangerous drugs), gave injections, took X-rays, sutured, and even performed minor surgery.

The previous April, Judge Johnson had issued his comprehensive orders in *Wyatt v. Stickney*. The *Newman* evidence suggested that the state of mental health care in the prisons was even more critical than that provided in Alabama's mental hospitals. Expert witnesses had testified that 10 percent of the inmates were psychotic, another 60 percent sufficiently disturbed to require treatment, and that mental illness and retardation were the "most prevalent" problems in the system. Yet to diagnose and treat these approximately twenty-four hundred prisoners, the state employed one clinical psychologist one afternoon a week at the Medical and Diagnostic Center. At least one psychiatrist was employed on a contract basis to diagnose a limited number of the very worst cases. But there were no psychiatrists, social workers, or counselors on the medical staff in the entire system. Severe and dangerous psychotics were often placed in the general prison population; the vast majority of mentally disturbed inmates received "no treatment whatsoever."

Even more moving than such statistics, however, were those portions of the evidence describing some of the victims of Alabama's system of inmate medical care. A young epileptic assigned to Holman was denied medical treatment for weeks—by an untrained, unsupervised inmate on the medical staff. When finally taken to the center, he was suffering from pneumonia, running a high fever, and delirious. When no medical restraints could be found, he was handcuffed to his bed. Later, on the order of the center's business manager, the handcuffs were removed, and he was allowed to leave his bed at will and take cold showers— until his death the following day. A quadriplegic who spent many months at the center had suffered bedsores that developed into open wounds and eventually became infested with maggots. In the month before his death, he was bathed, and his bandages changed, only once. The stench from his wounds had pervaded the entire ward where he was confined.

Citing this and other evidence of neglect and abuse, Judge Johnson held that "the failure of the Board of Corrections to provide sufficient medical facilities and staff to afford inmates basic elements of adequate medical care constitutes a willful and intentional violation of the rights of prisoners guaranteed under the Eighth and Fourteenth" Amendment prohibitions against cruel and unusual punishment. The "intentional refusal" of prison officials to allow certain inmates adequate access to medical personnel, medicine, and treatment was likewise condemned. While stopping short of itemizing standards of adequate medical care, he enjoined the defendants from failing to provide such care and held that the Medical and Diagnostic Center was to comply with HEW regulations imposed on hospitals participating in the Medicare program. He also enjoined use of unqualified personnel and inmates to deliver medical services or prescribe, dispense, and administer drugs. Required, too, were regular fire inspections; written sanitation procedures; limits on access to drugs; medication or other reasonable treatment prescribed for inmates by physicians; eyeglasses, dentures, and prosthetic devices for those inmates who needed them; a system of medical records; inmate physical examinations by a physician at least once every two years; ambulances or other suitable emergency transportation at each medical facility and adequate supply of emergency equipment and supplies; medical assistants with minimum qualifications equal to that of licensed practical nurses; periodic checks and separate, uncrowded quarters for geriatrics; and prompter medical attention for inmates than that generally afforded in the past.

After *Newman*, inmate petitions began flowing into Judge Johnson's court; and in *Diamond* v. *Thompson*, decided in July of 1973, he halted arbitrary limitations on prisoner access to religious literature and held that inmates transferred to administrative segregation or punitive isolation ordinarily are entitled to notice and a hearing. He also reacted harshly, however, to what he called a "basic misunderstanding" of *Newman* on the part of both inmates and prison officials. Calling "most" of the plaintiffs "troublemakers, knowledgeable in manipulating and maneuvering others to their advantage," he warned inmates that his court did not stand "ready to intervene in the administration of the prison system whenever they complain, regardless of the charge," and assured prison officials that he would intervene only to protect constitutional rights.[7]

Judge Varner issued the Middle District's next two prison decisions. In one, he held that an inmate was not entitled to recover damages from prison officials for administrative segregation or punitive isolation imposed in violation of his rights to notice and hearing. In the other, involving the same inmate, he held that an inmate confined in administrative segregation for refusing to work was not entitled to notice and a hearing. Judge Varner's ruling in the damage suit was compatible with the present Supreme Court's position that government officials are generally immune from damages for "good faith" violations of constitutional rights. And in *Diamond* Judge Johnson had rejected the notion that inmates confined to administrative or punitive isolation were invariably entitled to notice and a hearing. But language in one of the Varner opinions may have confirmed, for some at least, the popular impression that Judge Varner clearly was no Judge Johnson in civil rights litigation. Rejecting the inmate's claim of unconstitutional treatment at the hands of prison employees, Varner wrote: "This Plaintiff has been an agitator—perhaps with some aggravation—since his transfer to Mt. Meigs. The Court files are replete with his mostly frivolous complaints. This Court reminds both parties of the Biblical admonition that, 'whatsoever a man soweth, that shall he also reap.' "[8]

Even before Judge Varner's pronouncement, however, additional prisoner complaints had been filed with the clerk of the Middle District. Two of the complaints would provide the basis for Judge Johnson's most extensive prison rulings, the most comprehensive decisions, in fact, ever entered by a judge in a prison case.[9]

The first petition had been filed January 21, 1974, by Worley James, a black Holman inmate. James was not one of God's noblest creatures.

Then eighty, he had first been sentenced to an Alabama prison in 1925, for assault with intent to murder. In 1929, he was convicted on another murderous assault charge, and in 1942 for assault with intent to ravish. Two years later, he was found guilty of carnal knowledge involving a twelve-year-old girl. In 1972, he had again been convicted of assault with intent to ravish.

As a pauper, James was entitled to file his complaint without paying a filing fee or submitting his petition in proper legal form. His barely legible and often illiterate complaint was scrawled on yellow lined legal paper. But it clearly indicated that James—or a helpful fellow inmate—understood the bare rudiments at least of effective writ writing. Relief was sought under an appropriate U.S. Code provision—Title 42, Section 1983, authorizing civil lawsuits against official interferences with federal rights. Moreover, James alleged specific constitutional violations. The "physical condictions [sic] of Plaintiff confinement," he claimed, violated the Fifth, Eighth, and Fourteenth Amendments, as did the inadequate hospital, medical, food, and recreational facilities and services at the Medical and Diagnostic Center. A year earlier, he had filed a suit for damages against a physician at Montgomery's Baptist Hospital, claiming, in effect, that surgery performed on him by the defendant had destroyed his sexual potency!

In late February 1974, the petition of Jerry Pugh, a white inmate, reached the court. Pugh's petition probably had been drafted by one of the Alabama penal system's more skillful writ writers rather than by Pugh himself. It set forth the inmate's complaints in much better form and was decidedly more articulate than the James complaint. Pugh sought a million dollars in compensatory damages and an equal amount in punitive damages from state prison commissioner L. B. Sullivan and the warden of Atmore prison. While at Atmore, he asserted, he had been assigned to a dormitory with over two hundred inmates, twenty-seven white, the rest black. When he became aware of "strong" racial tensions in the unit and saw inmates carrying a variety of weapons, including knives, steel bars, hatchets, and pick handles, he and other white prisoners had asked to be transferred to a dormitory with more whites. Atmore officials responded that such a transfer would promote racial segregation in conflict with the federal court order desegregating Alabama's prisons. According to Pugh, inmates were locked in the open dormitories from 6:00 P.M. to 5:00 A.M. each night, without any supervision by prison officials. On August 8, 1973, black inmates had "pounced on" the whites, and Pugh and thirteen other inmates had to be taken to the hospital. During the incident, one guard had been "stabbed through and through" by a black inmate, and Pugh beaten "so badly" by the blacks, he claimed, that they had "stuffed his body up under a bed for dead." Two hours after the incident, he had been taken to a private hospital in Atmore for emergency treatment and then to Mobile General Hospital the following day. His injuries had included a fractured skull and right arm, a cut across the lower part of his spine, and numerous skull abrasions and lacerations. At the time, he was told that he would require surgery and stood a chance of "losing his standard state of mind." But surgery was never performed. His treatment, he alleged, amounted to cruel and unusual punishment. Two days after Pugh's complaint arrived at the court, Judge Johnson granted him leave to proceed as a pauper and asked Robert Segall, who had represented one of the plaintiffs in the *Lynch* litigation, to serve as Pugh's counsel.[10]

One of the judge's favorite former law clerks, Segall was then a member of a prominent Montgomery firm. Although extremely interested in civil liberties litigation, he was at first reluctant to represent Pugh. "The more I looked at that complaint," he would later say, "the more I thought, 'My God, I don't want to be involved in a case that is attacking racism sort of in reverse.' " After talking with others in the firm, however, he decided that Judge Johnson was simply interested in additional prisoner rights litigation. And he found that prospect attractive. Within the firm, it was decided that the case should be converted into a class action. Segall then persuaded Joe Levin, Jr., of the Southern Poverty Law Center that the center should underwrite the litigation. On April 16, he and Levin filed an amended complaint that transposed Pugh's complaint into a class action, added the state and members of the Alabama Board of Corrections as defendants, and claimed "a constitutional right to be protected from physical injury inflicted by . . . fellow inmates." In time, they would also assert a right to inmate rehabilitation and contend that idleness and the lack of rehabilitative opportunities in Alabama's prisons contributed to the atmosphere of violence addressed in Jerry Pugh's original complaint.[11]

In July 1974, Judge Johnson granted Worley James's motion to proceed as a pauper and appointed George Peach Taylor, a University of Alabama law professor, as his counsel. Taylor soon filed an amended complaint converting James's case, like Pugh's, into a class action. On September 30, Judge Johnson denied the state's motion to dismiss. Taylor had claimed that inmates have a right of rehabilitation. Understandably, the judge rejected the notion that convicted felons could claim rights not available to other persons. "So long as treatment, rehabilitation, and reformation services and facilities may not be demanded of the state as of right by her free citizens," he wrote, "this Court is unpersuaded that such services may be demanded by convicted felons." But Judge Johnson's reading of the Constitution did recognize a right of inmates to reasonable opportunities for rehabilitating themselves; and Taylor was to be given the chance to establish a denial of that right before the court.[12]

Several months after denying the state's motion to dismiss the James complaint, Judge Johnson dismissed as "clearly frivolous" a state counterclaim filed in Jerry Pugh's case. Since Pugh was so concerned about inmate violence, the defendants asserted, Judge Johnson should simply enjoin the inmates from possessing dangerous weapons, liquor, and drugs, committing assaults, and engaging in homosexual activity. The judge was not amused. Courts, he observed, could never enjoin commission of a crime, and the defendants' claim had been "activated by bad faith" and reflected "manifest disregard of fundamental legal principles, existing statutory law, and [a] long line of authoritative case law." Alabama officials were responsible for maintaining order and discipline in the state's prisons. "It is not the province of the judiciary—and especially the federal judiciary"—he concluded, "to enforce the criminal laws of the State of Alabama." There were no more "frivolous" petitions.

By this point, Segall and Taylor were working closely in preparing the two cases for trial. The ACLU had agreed to underwrite the *James* case, and its National Prison Project (NPP) had entered the litigation as an amicus curiae. Alvin J. Bronstein of Washington, D.C., would serve in the case as the NPP's chief counsel. Although Attorney General Baxley and his office were connected with the defense, active preparation of the defendants' case fell mainly to Robert Lamar, a Montgomery attorney. Lamar had been Baxley's law school classmate at the University of Alabama, and Baxley had often retained him as a special assistant attorney general. In the recent past, Lamar had been successful in protecting prison officials from damages.[13] But in the *Pugh-James* litigation, he and his associates would be badly outgunned by attorneys for the plaintiffs and amici.

Through the early months of 1975, *Pugh* and *James* continued to develop separately as the parties exchanged interrogatories and completed other preliminaries. In late June, however, Judge Johnson consolidated the two cases for trial. At the plaintiffs' request, Ira DeMent was appointed in mid-August to represent the United States as an amicus in the case. Then, on Wednesday, August 20, the cases went to trial. The hearing would last seven days and produce 1,679 pages of transcript.

Prior to the trial, the parties had stipulated to over a thousand facts about conditions in Alabama's prisons, but attorneys for the plaintiffs and amici produced inmates, former inmates, and corrections specialists who painted an even grimmer and more graphic picture. The testimony of Horace C. Sutterer, a young Birmingham welder and Atmore (Fountain) alumnus, was typical. While at Fountain, Sutterer had worked in the fields where other inmates, called "strikers," were given control over the workers, and employed verbal abuse, threats, and beatings with hoe handles and broomsticks to keep their charges in line. He was denied soap, toothpaste, and other basic necessities and had to rely on his family to bring him warm clothing, bedding, shoes, and socks. The facility was infested with insects and rodents. On occasion, he testified, rabbits hopped through holes in the walls, and once during his confinement an owl had paid his dormitory a visit. The food was at best unsanitary and unappetizing. "The food—rice, beans—had hair. Sometimes they had bugs, flies. . . . And at one time . . . there was a rat found in a biscuit." Though there was no organized recreational activity, Fountain did have a baseball field for inmates. But "the sewage and grease trap had backed up and over-flowed on the . . . field and inmates had to wade through . . . the grease and the sewage to check out to work." Money was the "blood" of the system; it could buy "anything: drugs, marijuana, needles to shoot drugs with, weapons," or favors from guards and trusties. Sutterer earned his in part by writing term papers and completing certification examinations for prison personnel.

Fountain's homosexuals, Sutterer testified, dressed "in drag" with "hiphugger pants, high-heeled shoes, blouses, cutoff blouses, jewelry, makeup, scarves on their head, fingernail polish." Most inmates were armed, and fighting was a daily occurrence. On cold or hot nights, sleep was difficult, and "there were other nights where there was so much noise from inmates that were doing drugs, sniffing glue, homosexuals just running up and down the aisles of the barracks making noise where you couldn't sleep." Homosexual rape, he added, was not uncommon. On one occasion, he had watched as four or five blacks repeatedly raped a young white inmate.

As Bob Lamar and other attorneys for the defendants sought to show on cross-examination, the inmates' testimony may have been of doubt-ful credibility. If anything, however, the expert witnesses for the plaintiffs and amici offered a harsher indictment of conditions in Alabama prisons. The most effective expert witness, perhaps, was Charles Robert Sarver, professor of law and social work at the University of Arkansas. Sarver had served as superintendent of Arkansas's notorious Cummins prison and as commissioner of corrections in Arkansas and West Virginia, leaving each post under fire for his efforts to secure penal reform. As an expert witness in other inmate litigation, he had visited many prisons; but none, he said, could compare with the Atmore (Fountain) complex. "Very, very dirty. Unbelievably over-crowded," he testified. "Inhumanly so, I might add. I have never seen a prison as crowded as the barracks at Atmore, at G. K. Fountain; a veritable jungle where the inmates were required to live. The food at G. K. Fountain is the only institutional food I have ever refused to eat, or to even attempt it. It was the most unpalatable stuff I think I ever looked at. . . . The kitchen was terrible. It was appalling; it was shock-ing and unbelievably bad. I tried to see if I could eat the food. I try to eat something in every institution in which I go. I knew that visually I couldn't stand it, and I thought perhaps it might smell better than it looked, but it did not and, as a result, I didn't try any of it." Sarver had also visited Fountain's "doghouse." "When the door finally opened it was completely dark. The odor would make one's eyes water and throat burn from BO, feces, urine and general filth. I was shocked before I ever saw inside one of the cells; [the odor] was bad enough. I then went to Cell Number One." Five inmates, all black, were packed into the tiny cell; one was there for fourteen days, two for twenty-one days. The odor, Sarver reported, was "something I, I can't—I cannot adequately describe for you."

At times, Lamar objected, asserting that Sarver just wanted to "make another speech." But on each occasion, Judge Johnson overruled, lecturing Lamar on the differences between a lay witness and an expert witness and explaining that the latter could testify not only about what he saw and heard, but also about "the conclusions that he drew . . . and the impressions that he received from what he saw and from what he heard." "That's a classic example," he added, with some impatience, "of the difference between an expert witness and a lay witness. Classic."

Other expert witnesses joined Sarver in complaining about conditions in the state's punitive isolation units. Draper's "doghouse" came in for particularly strong criticism. As in the case of the state's other isolation units, inmates could be sent to the Draper "doghouse" for up to twenty-one days for being late to work or other minor institutional violations. Prisoners confined there were allowed only one shower a week, permitted recreation outside the windowless building one hour every eleven days, and clothed only in a pajama bottom, which they were allowed to change but once a week. One meal a day was served, each cell was four by eight feet, and the only opening in the solid metal door to each cell was covered with thick mesh screen that prevented the entry of light. There were no lights in the cells, in the summer the temperature rose well past a hundred degrees, there were no beds or furniture, only filthy mattresses. The cells contained no sinks and no soap, and the toilet in several consisted of a hole in a raised concrete platform that could only be flushed from outside the cell by a guard. As many as five inmates were confined to each cell. (Under Judge Pittman's order, as many as eight could be confined in the "doghouse" in his district.)

Under questioning from Alvin Bronstein, William George Nagel, director of the American Foundation's Institute of Corrections, termed his visit to the Draper isolation unit "a sickening experience," speculated that an hour would constitute a prolonged period of incarceration in Draper's "doghouse," and said of Draper's overcrowded conditions generally: "No man and woman, wife, husband and wife, should have to live in that intimacy, that degree of intimacy where every, every aspect of the human functioning is done in front of other human beings around the clock, and yet that's the way that institution is designed and operated. It's really, to put it simply, uncivilized." Like Sarver, Nagel and other expert witnesses also testified about inadequate medical care, deplorable hygienic conditions, prison violence, and the impact of such squalor on the inmate's chances for rehabilitation. And a U.S. public health officer testified that the major prisons were "wholly unfit for human habitation" and recommended that most of the facilities in the state penal system be closed and condemned as an imminent threat to public health.

The most moving testimony came, however, not from the experts, or even from articulate inmate witnesses, but from a twenty-year-old with the mind of a five-year-old. Stanley David Smith was Ira DeMent's witness. He had a fourth grade education; he could not read. He was in prison for burglary; he did not know the degree. On June 17, 1975, Stanley was confined at Mt. Meigs for receiving and classification. It was his first day in state prison. That night, he testified, a black inmate had persuaded him to jam a western novel in the entrance to his cell to keep the door from locking. He told Stanley he wanted to teach him to box, that he "didn't like to see people like me get fucked over." After the final lockup, the inmate called Stanley from his cell, took him to another cell, and told him to remove his clothes. He said "he had a knife and he wouldn't mind using it on me. . . . That scared me a little bit more so I pulled off my clothes." The inmate and three other blacks then took turns raping him. Later, a white inmate beat him and hung him from the bars of a cell with strips of blanket, saying "he don't like fuckboys and snitches." The inmate and a friend then decided, however, that they would take care of Stanley if he would let them "sell my ass." Stanley reported the situation to the warden, but the warden just "asked me did they get a little pussy," and said there was nothing he could do.

To those in the courtroom, the effect of the pathetic inmate's testimony on Judge Johnson was unmistakable. As Ira DeMent later remarked, Stanley's testimony would have "had a profound impact on any human being, and certainly one who's sensitive to human rights."[14]

The defendants had stipulated to so many facts about conditions in Alabama's prisons that there was little left in the plaintiffs' case for them to challenge. For the sake of appearances, Robert Lamar called Commissioner Sullivan and other prison personnel as witnesses. No doubt to impress on Judge Johnson the sort of unsavory characters he had been asked to protect, Lamar also put Worley James on the stand

and led the aged inmate through the more sordid details of his life. Counsel for the plaintiffs and amici wasted little time cross-examining James. "We . . . took the position," Ira DeMent recalls, "that, what the hell, he could be the biggest scoundrel imaginable, and he's still entitled to fair and minimal constitutional treatment at the hands of the state, even in prison."[15]

His token defense completed, Lamar made a surprise request for a conference with the judge and opposing counsel. An in-chambers conference was held on the morning of August 28. At the conference, Lamar announced that the defendants were prepared to concede Eighth Amendment violations in open court. "We think," he said, "that relief is appropriate by any conscionable judgment on the evidence under a totality concept, and that's it."

During the trial, the plaintiffs and amici had moved for immediate injunctive relief against any further confinement of inmates in Draper's "doghouse" until its facilities were substantially upgraded. They had also requested immediate relief against the severe overcrowding in the major units. Fountain, the evidence had revealed, was designed for a maximum of 632 inmates and presently held over 1,100. Overcrowding was almost as critical at Holman, Draper, and Mt. Meigs. The plaintiffs and amici wanted Judge Johnson to enjoin further admissions to the major prisons until their populations had been reduced to designed capacity.

While conceding constitutional violations, Lamar doubted whether immediate relief could or need be provided. Earlier, he and Attorney General Baxley had filed a brief with the court in which they accused the plaintiffs and amici of exaggerating conditions at Draper's "doghouse." After all, they had asserted, each cell was "scrubbed down with disinfectant on the average of once a week," guards were instructed to report suspected illnesses among the occupants, and the inmates would only try to short out any lights provided the cells, creating risks of a power shortage and the possibility that some inmates might be electrocuted.

Ira DeMent was obviously pleased that the state had thrown in the towel. But he objected to any delay in the provision of emergency relief, noting that even "a two-week delay would result in additional rapes, additional isolation at Draper . . . , additional stabbings perhaps." Judge Johnson tended to agree. He would, he said, orally enjoin continued use of punitive isolation except under certain minimum standards, then began itemizing the standards: "One man to the cell, at least sixty square feet; toilet and washbasins with running water; adequate ventilation and lighting that meet the requirements of the U.S. Public Health Service; clean bedding; a bath available at least every other day; medical attention . . . at least every third day—checking him; reading and writing materials; and other matters that, that . . . "

"Food," DeMent interjected. "Wholesome and nutritious diet three times a day," Judge Johnson responded. "There is nothing wrong insofar as the Eighth Amendment is concerned with isolation in a prison system. There is something wrong with isolation in the way that it's being run now." Would exercise be required? "At least thirty minutes a day outside in exercise." Would these standards apply only to punitive isolation? inquired Larry Newman, an assistant state attorney general. "Anytime that it's for punitive purposes or anytime that—this includes segregation of any kind, I think, Mr. Newman." And there was more—a toothbrush and toothpaste for each inmate; teeth, glasses, and other physical aids; counseling by a psychologist not less than once every three days; a custodial officer within the sight and hearing of "doghouse" inmates at all times.

As Judge Johnson talked, the defendants' counsel made some mental calculations. "Your Honor, excuse me," Newman interjected at one point. "May I say something? There—to my knowledge there is not one cell available in the Alabama prison system that is sixty square feet." When told that they were probably either six by eight feet or five by nine, Judge Johnson appeared to place a forty-five square foot minimum on cell size in the punitive isolation and segregation units. Later, DeMent noted that the limitation would eliminate all such confinement at Draper because its cells were only four by eight. "Well," the judge replied, "if it does that eliminates it. . . . I just don't think you ought to put people in a place smaller than, than five by nine. That's the smallest place for even one person."

On August 7—and after considerable prodding by a Fifth Circuit panel—Judge Brevard Hand of the Southern District had ruled in *McCray v. Sullivan* that the overcrowding and understaffing in Alabama's prisons violated the inmates' constitutional rights. But Hand had declined to provide immediate relief. "This Court is prepared to fulfill its obligations under the law by entering appropriate Orders," he had concluded; "however, this Court feels before this is done, inasmuch as the Legislature is now in session, that it, the Legislature, should be given an opportunity to undertake appropriate remedial action that would render any judicial interference moot."[16]

Alabama's legislators had taken no action, and during the in-chambers conference, DeMent asked Judge Johnson whether he would halt new admissions to the prisons until their designed capacity was reached. "I don't think so," he responded. "I would like to talk with Judge Hand. He reserved this in his case, and I don't want to put myself or this Court in the position of trying to run around him on something that he has reserved in, in a lawsuit. Otherwise, I wouldn't have any reluctance or hesitancy about doing it. But I want to talk with him first."

Later that day, Robert Lamar made the state's concessions in open

court. Leaving the courtroom afterward, he told reporters that the
plaintiffs and amici had "just proved what we knew all along. We just
didn't agree with some of their wild theories on corrections. This is
what happens," he added, "when you have a legislature that abdicates
its duties. It is a sad day when a federal court has to step in and take
control of an entire state agency." Ira DeMent agreed, but noted: "Frank
Johnson has been doing the state's work in constitutional matters for
twenty years."[17]

After Lamar had announced the state's concessions, Judge Johnson
issued a bench order requiring immediate improvements for the punitive isolation and segregation units. After conferring, he and Judge
Hand also issued a joint interim emergency order for *Pugh-James* and
McCray, enjoining any new admissions to the corrections system until
each prison's population was no greater than its designed capacity. It
would be mid-January 1976, however, before Judge Johnson was ready
to issue a comprehensive order.

Those familiar with Judge Johnson's emphasis on speed and efficiency, and aware that he sometimes dictated lengthy opinions and
orders in a matter of hours, must have expected a comprehensive
Pugh-James ruling fairly shortly after the August hearing. For Judge
Johnson, however, the fall of 1975 was to be a period of crisis—one
relatively minor but perhaps professionally disappointing, the other
personal and devastating.

In the early summer of 1975, national and state papers had begun
carrying stories that raised serious doubts about the professional standards of Judge Johnson's colleague on the Middle District court, Judge
Varner. According to one story, Varner had boasted to visitors to his
chambers that he had exaggerated by $5,000 the value of a charitable
contribution on his 1974 federal income tax return. On another occasion, court records revealed, he had sought to persuade Ira DeMent and
three assistant U.S. attorneys to eliminate blacks from the jury in an
Opelika case. The white residents of Opelika, he explained, had not yet
accepted the idea of eating and being housed with blacks, and white
jurors would resent their presence on the jury. DeMent had refused and
reported the incident to Judge Johnson.[18]

Potentially the most damaging incident, however, involved a series
of complicated transactions through which Varner had arranged to buy
more than six hundred acres of valuable land from the elderly great-
aunt of a young defendant on whom he was about to impose sentence.
On December 20, 1974, James Payton Judge III had waived trial and
pled guilty before Varner to a charge of receiving stolen property. A
1974 study conducted by the Administrative Office of the U.S. Courts
had concluded that Alabama's Middle District ranked third in the
nation in terms of the speed with which it disposed of criminal cases;

the national average was 3.9 months, the Middle District's 2.3 months. Nevertheless, January, February, and March had passed, and Judge Varner still had not set a date for Judge's sentencing.[19]

In late March, the defendants' great-aunt, Mrs. W. D. Judge, Jr., a Montgomery matron whose home was located only a block from the Governor's Mansion, phoned a local attorney, told him she was preparing to sell some Lowndes County property to Judge Varner, and asked that he handle the transaction. Mrs. Judge was a member of one of Lowndes County's oldest families. The land had been in her family for generations. It had never before been offered for sale.[20]

Apparently, the transaction moved through several stages. First, Mrs. Judge had sold the property to an Opelika resident, George P. Mann—for $31,500 less than its market value. Then, Mann had transferred title to Judge Varner and his wife Carolyn, and Varner in turn transferred 716 acres of Macon County land to Mann. Mrs. Judge's great-nephew faced a maximum sentence of five years in prison and a $5,000 fine. On April 22, Judge Varner placed him on probation. Nine days later, Varner took possession of the Judge property. According to "knowledgeable legal sources," one paper reported, one of his law clerks had done the title and abstract work connected with the transaction.[21]

In mid-October, the *Montgomery Advertiser* learned that the judges of the Fifth Circuit, who have supervisory power over district judges in the circuit, were considering the allegations against Judge Varner. In time, one of their number, Judge Paul Roney, was dispatched to Montgomery to investigate. On the basis of Roney's findings, the council eventually concluded that Judge Varner may have exercised poor judgment, but found no criminal fault and issued an order to that effect.[22] By that point, state newspaper coverage of the incident—which had always been sparse—had ended altogether. But lawyers active in the Middle District court would continue to compare Judge Varner unfavorably to Judge Johnson in terms of both judicial skill and sense of professional propriety.

In the turbulent waters in which Judge Johnson had waded for twenty years, the Varner affair could only be viewed as a mild ripple. Two days before the *Advertiser* announced the Fifth Circuit's inquiry, however, he and Ruth experienced the worst tragedy of their lives.

With the nervous breakdown, visits to sanitariums for psychological and emotional therapy, and problems with drugs, the years following high school had often been rough ones for Johnny Johnson. He had enrolled at The University of Alabama. In fact, in 1968, he had headed the campus Young Democrats there when they endorsed Senator Eugene McCarthy's presidential candidacy and adopted a resolution demanding that state officials working out of state in George Wallace's "farcical" presidential campaign return to their duties, but adding that

Wallace himself could remain away as long as he wished. Initially, however, Johnny made little progress toward a degree. Moreover, a brief marriage to a young divorcée itself ended in divorce. And although he was an excellent photographer, he apparently had difficulty establishing long-term career goals.[23]

In May 1975, however, Johnny had graduated from the university and, except for a bout with ear trouble, would have enrolled in its law school for the fall semester. Recently, too, he had worked as an aide on Attorney General Baxley's staff.[24]

On October 13, the Johnsons' neighbor Jack Vann had a Columbus Day holiday from the Air University at Maxwell Air Base. His son Dick had recently completed his dental studies, and the two had spent the morning looking for dental office space. When they returned, they spotted Johnny's Volvo in the Johnsons' driveway, and Dick remarked that he must have just returned from a vacation trip to the Bahamas. A little later, Johnny came over to the Vanns' and chatted briefly about the trip. He was tanned, smiling, cheerful, looking better, Jack Vann thought, than he had in years.[25]

About thirty minutes later, Judge Johnson knocked at the Vanns' door. He said he had been unable to get into his house and asked to use the phone to try to reach Ira DeMent. He told Jack and Dick that he was worried about Johnny and asked them to investigate. Dick and his father rushed to the Johnsons' house, and Dick broke in through a rear door. He found his friend dead. Johnny had shot himself with a borrowed shotgun.[26]

The next day, a service was conducted at one of Sam Durden's funeral homes. A rabbi delivered the eulogy. In lieu of flowers, the family asked that contributions be made to the children's fund at Partlow. Governor Wallace was touring Europe in preparation for yet another futile presidential campaign. When he returned, he asked Glen Curlee for the Johnsons' unlisted number and called to offer his sympathy and the wish that in the past "a lot of things" could have been different.[27]

The death of a child is probably the worst tragedy that can befall a parent; and in the weeks after their son's death, Judge Johnson and Ruth must have asked themselves often whether Johnny's fate might have been different had they remained in Jasper and escaped the pressures and controversy of their lives in Montgomery. They resolved, however, that they had done their best for their son and would not blame themselves for his problems. "If I had to just say one thing" about Johnny, the judge stoically told a friend, "he just wasn't tough enough to live in a pretty rough world. It's tough whether you're a federal judge's son or not." His assessment was probably accurate. Johnny "felt things very deeply and very strongly," William Baxley has said. "He had such a feeling of compassion, . . . he took things almost too much to heart."[28]

As autumn yielded to winter, Judge Johnson coped as best he could with his grief and moved toward announcement of a decision in the *Pugh-James* litigation. On January 13, 1976, he issued an opinion and order.

In general, American courts had followed a "hands-off" policy with respect to prison conditions well into the second half of this century. In isolated cases, however, judges had begun providing relief to individual inmates at least as early as 1899, when a Georgia federal judge intervened in behalf of an unruly prisoner who each night was chained by the neck to a grating in his Bibb County jail cell. Recently, moreover, federal judges outside Alabama had found constitutional violations in entire prisons or penal systems. Beginning in 1970, Judge J. Smith Henley had ordered modest reforms for the Arkansas prison system, the first state system to come under federal court scrutiny. Later, federal judges in Ohio, Louisiana, California, and Maryland had ordered improved conditions in local jails. And in 1972, Judge William C. Keady required improved medical care and living conditions, among other reforms, for inmates at Mississippi's notorious Parchman prison farm and enjoined the use of cattle prods and other forms of corporal punishment. A year later, District Judge Arthur Garrity of Boston had found a county jail constitutionally inadequate and ordered the ultimate modification—construction of a new jail. But Judge Johnson's January 13 order would be the most comprehensive yet filed.[29]

In the opinion accompanying the order, Judge Johnson summarized conditions confronting Alabama's inmates. The major institutions, he wrote, were "horrendously overcrowded," a problem aggravated by dormitory living arrangements in which bunks were often packed so closely together that there was no walking space between them. Broken and unscreened windows created serious problems with mosquitoes and flies; and the facilities were infested with vermin, including "roaches in all stages of development—a certain indicator of filthy conditions." Old and filthy cotton mattresses contributed to the spread of disease and body lice. Inmates were provided no soap or other toilet articles. Plumbing and electrical wiring were poor. In one Draper unit, housing well over two hundred inmates, there was but one functioning toilet; and many toilets either would not flush or overflowed. Some showers continually dripped or poured water; frequently, there was no hot water. An "overpowering odor" permeated the facilities. The state also lacked an effective system of inmate classification. Far too many new arrivals were given maximum security classifications; and assignments to particular prisons, units, and work details were made almost entirely on the basis of available space.[30]

The "gross inadequacies" in inmate medical care revealed in *Newman* had not yet been eliminated, and mentally disturbed inmates were still dispersed through the prison population, unidentified and untreated. The facilities were "woefully understaffed," and the overcrowding, understaffing, improper classification, and inhuman conditions had combined to create a "jungle atmosphere" of "rampant violence" which prison guards rarely entered, especially after dark. No organized recreation was provided prisoners, and the lack of any meaningful vocational, educational, and work opportunities contributed to a climate of "idleness, boredom, apathy and frustration." What opportunities were available, moreover, were arbitrarily assigned.

Having captured his reader's attention with a review of the unpleasant evidence, Judge Johnson then turned to the constitutional issue. While continuing to reject the notion that inmates have a right to rehabilitation, he concluded that prison policies were valid only when they furthered legitimate institutional goals of deterrence, rehabilitation, and security. The conditions under which Alabama's prisoners were confined, he asserted, bore no reasonable relationship to these objectives. In fact, they impeded the inmate's chances for self-generated rehabilitation, increased the likelihood of his future confinement, and jeopardized prison security. Confinement under such conditions, he held, constituted cruel and unusual punishment which must be abolished. To pass constitutional muster, Alabama's prisons were to implement "minimum constitutional standards" of inmate confinement.

The order setting forth the standards, like the *Wyatt* order, was extremely detailed. Within six months, each segregation and isolation cell was to be no less than sixty square feet, and inmates were to be confined there under conditions consistent with due process and the provisions of the August 28 emergency order. Except for escapees and parole violators, no additional inmates were to be accepted until the prison population had been reduced to designed capacity for each facility. The state corrections board was to develop and implement an inmate classification plan and contract with The University of Alabama's Department of Psychology to aid in its implementation.

Each inmate was to be supplied, without charge, toothbrushes, toothpaste, shaving cream, razors and razor blades, soap, shampoo, combs, adequate clean clothing, a storage locker with a lock, a weekly supply of clean bed linen and towels, access to household cleaning supplies, a bed off the floor, a clean mattress and blankets, and three "wholesome and nutritious meals per day, served with proper eating and drinking utensils." As could be expected, the physical facilities were the subject of numerous requirements. Units were to be adequately heated, lighted, and ventilated, windows and doors properly screened and maintained. Regular and effective control of insects and rodents was to be implemented and safe electrical wiring provided. There was to be one toilet per fifteen inmates, one urinal or one foot of urinal trough per twenty inmates, and one lavatory for every ten inmates. Food services were to be sanitary, food service supervisors to have at least a bachelor's degree level of training in dietetics or its equivalent. A nutrition consultant was also to be employed. Inmates requiring a special diet for health or religious reasons were to be provided diets corresponding to their individual needs.

Each inmate was also to be supplied postage and paper for up to five letters a week, mail censorship was to be permitted only where necessary to maintain prison security and discipline. Inmates were to be allowed visitors on "at least a weekly basis," provided "a comfortable, sheltered area for visitation," and separated physically from visitors only for documented security reasons. Each inmate was to be provided a meaningful job and the opportunity to participate in educational and vocational training programs, but no inmate was to perform household or personal tasks for others. A trained recreation director was to be employed at each facility, and adequate equipment, facilities, and space provided for recreational pursuits.

To assure protection for prisoners, aggressive, violence-prone inmates were to be segregated from the rest of the prison population; and only minimum custody inmates were to be housed in dormitories. Frequent shakedowns and other procedures were to be employed to reduce the number of weapons in possession of the inmates. To reduce illicit trafficking in contraband, most inmates were to be denied currency, and a script system was to be introduced for approved inmate purchases. At all times, guards were to be stationed inside and outside all living areas except isolation units. In the isolation units, guards were at all times to have visual and voice contact with prisoners. At no time were inmates to be used as guards or otherwise placed in positions of authority over other inmates. Accurate records were to be maintained of all incidents of inmate violence and assaults. Finally, adequate staffing was to be provided to assure order and administer programs; moreover, hiring practices were to be designed to reduce present racial and cultural disparities between the predominantly black, urban inmate population and the largely white, rural prison staffs.

Following the *Wyatt* pattern, Judge Johnson created a human rights committee to monitor implementation of the order and the yet unimplemented *Newman* ruling. He also hinted at the provision of damages if the defendants failed to act and dismissed their contention that inadequate legislative funding might make implementation impossible. "A state," he wrote, "is not at liberty to afford its citizens only those constitutional rights which fit comfortably within its budget. . . . Inadequate funding is no answer to the existence of unconstitutional conditions in state penal institutions." He agreed that prisoners were "not to be coddled," nor prisons "operated as hotels or country clubs," but warned that state officials would not be allowed to operate "barbaric and inhumane" facilities and threatened to close Alabama's prisons if his order was not implemented.[31]

Governor Wallace's response to the order was immediate and predictable. Taking time off from presidential campaigning to hold a press conference, he accused Judge Johnson of attempting to create a "hotel atmosphere" in Alabama's prisons. He was in prime form. "If you want to get a couple of years of rest," he advised reporters, "just go out and mug somebody." Alabama's prisons were overcrowded, but so were every other state's prisons. And conditions in the Alabama facilities were not "inhumane" nor their inmates the victims of "intended" neglect. The costs of implementation would be enormous, and "federal judges are very good about telling you how to spend money, but not how to get it." "Thugs and federal judges," he concluded, "have just about taken charge in this country." But Wallace had a remedy: "Vote for George Wallace and give a barbed wire enema to a federal judge."[32]

While Wallace was busy, once again, chastising the federal judiciary for the nation's ills, a number of state and local officials praised Judge Johnson's ruling and condemned both the governor and the legislature for failing to undertake prison reform earlier. Joe Reed, a black on the Montgomery city council and vice-chairman of the state Democratic party, noted that "for all practical purposes, Judge Frank Johnson is running Alabama," adding: "Thank God for Gov. Frank Johnson." The president pro-tempore of the Alabama senate condemned Wallace for failing to assume a leadership role in tackling the state's problems. Labeling Wallace perhaps "the greatest demagogue of this century," he complained that the governor was "not interested in solving . . . problems. He just lets the courts take over." Alabama "just runs itself. It just sort of floats along." Executive officials, on the other hand, pointed an accusing finger at the legislature. While the *Pugh-James* litigation was pending in Judge Johnson's court, prison commissioner Sullivan had been replaced by Judson C. Locke, a relatively young official who had risen rapidly in the ranks of Alabama's prison bureaucracy. While attending a Nashville conference on prison problems shortly after the ruling was announced, Locke told reporters that "a lot of the requirements in the court order . . . we had been seeking to accomplish over the years without any success from our legislature." In the previous biennium, the board of corrections had requested $20 million from the legislature for capital outlay—and got nothing. The legislature "had adequate warning from the board of corrections in our state and direct warnings from the court that this was coming while they were still in session but nothing was done." In Alabama, Locke said, prisons had a low legislative priority. A state representative echoed Locke's complaint: "Building roads gets votes. Improving prisons doesn't."[33]

The press gave the Pugh-James order a mixed, though generally favorable, reception. The Birmingham Post-Herald scored Governor Wallace for assailing federal judges "instead of calling the legislature to Montgomery and trying to correct this example of man's inhumanity to man." An Alabama religious magazine interpreted the decision to mean that "society must meet moral standards," the Alabama Journal characterized the prison system as a "story of failure," and a Huntsville paper regretted that the issue had "to come to the brink of a constitutional crisis to secure simple justice and humanity, qualities we all cherish even for the worst among us." Editorial cartoonists had a field day with Wallace's attacks. A cartoon in the Montgomery Advertiser depicted inmates crowded into a cell with graffiti on the wall and nothing listed on a "Things to Do Today" list. Several rats also occupied the cell. One rat was robbing another, while a third was reading Wallace's remarks in a newspaper, and a fourth was saying, "Leo, ring room service and have 'em send up a pot of hot tea to cell 404." Another cartoon pictured a fuming, cigar-chomping Wallace sitting at a desk while an aide stood before him, holding a newspaper announcing the prison order. "We could always," the aide was suggesting, "stand in the prison door."[34]

Not all the press, however, applauded Judge Johnson and attacked state officials. While agreeing that prison conditions were abysmal, the increasingly conservative Birmingham News noted, for example, that under the order Alabama's convicts would have more living space than some state university students and wondered editorially how the state would finance the reforms Judge Johnson had required, adding: "Money is no object to Johnson, particularly because he is not accountable to the public for the financial burdens he imposes on them through his orders." Other newspapers saw the order as an affront to separation of powers. The Washington Star charged, for example, that Judge Johnson had donned "the legislator's toga." A number of Alabama's small-town newspapers imitated the governor's rhetoric, one charging that "Here again the Judge is messing around with something about which he knows little." Although relatively limited in number, editorial cartoons critical of the order were perhaps most effective. One in the Birmingham News depicted a pious, black-robed Judge Johnson, standing before a throne in a "go and sin no more" pose and commanding Alabama's citizens "to go now and make all prisons perfect . . . and take this with you." The "this" was a heavy lead weight labeled "cost" and "burden."[35]

Press criticism, of course, was by no means confined to newspaper staffs. For days, a small but steady stream of primarily negative letters poured into the editorial offices of state papers. The most vehement reactions, however, were sent directly to the judge's chambers. A typed, unsigned postcard arrived the day after the order was announced. "I was talking and listening in a group of intelligent persons. The conclusion was that you are drunk with power. . . . Every federal judge I have knowledge of in the past several years is stark crazy with power. Secure in your ivory towers you are in effect saying damn everyone but the federal judiciary. Could a time come in the foreseeable future when a bicentennial nation will rise up and say 'damn federal judges'?" A Tuscaloosa man with a less than precise knowledge of the order's contents sent a newspaper clipping about the recent kidnap-murder of a Mississippi mother of young children and asked whether the judge still wanted "to give these animals a nice clean bed off the floor, three hot meals, a TV, a library and more comforts than they have known on the outside." "Would you please answer this letter," he added in closing, "and let me know if there is any way that Judges such as you can be impeached."[36]

For every crank letter, however, there were numerous pleas for help. For several years, people had been writing or phoning the court seeking solutions for all sorts of problems. Some of the requests helped to lighten the workload. There was, for example, the man who phoned Mrs. Perry in desperate need of Judge Johnson's immediate assistance. A health inspector, it seemed, had threatened to condemn his outhouse; and he wanted to sue "for nine billion dollars." Other requests were pathetic. Most were beyond the scope of the judge's—or any judge's—jurisdiction.[37]

Particularly after the *Pugh-James* ruling, the court was flooded with requests for assistance from inmates, their families, and friends. The pleas came from all parts of the nation, Maine to California, and from federal, state, and local jails. An epileptic charged that he had been denied medication at a city jail. Another inmate complained, "I ain't nothing but skin and bones," after what he claimed had been a five-week stay in the Draper "doghouse." Inmates in Texas, Missouri, and other states requested copies of the order. A Virginia mother asked Judge Johnson to investigate the condition of her son, then confined at Mt. Meigs. Many others made similar requests.[38]

In time—and somewhat surprisingly—George Wallace would apologize for his talk about "barbed wire" enemas for federal judges. Such a crude statement, he later said, was beneath the dignity of his office. By early April, however, he had also retained private counsel and appealed the prison order to the Fifth Circuit. Asked by a newsman about the propriety of such a move in view of the fact that his own counsel had conceded constitutional violations in open court, he replied: "Whoever admitted that shouldn't have admitted it. That doesn't mean it's true. What he should have admitted is that they in the prisons violated the constitutional rights of the people they shot, robbed, and mugged."[39]

Judge Johnson and Judge Rives shared the reporter's concern. Joined by a colleague on a three-judge panel hearing a case involving the state board of education, they announced that, in the future, any lawyer appearing in federal court as the governor's representative must file an affidavit, signed by Wallace, and stating that the attorney was authorized to act in the governor's behalf. Wallace's past repudiations of his own attorney's positions, Judge Rives asserted, amounted to "trifling with the court."[40]

On January 23, Attorney General Baxley had filed a motion for a rehearing and modification of the order, claiming that the order was contrary to the law and evidence. In challenging the motion, the National Prison Project cited the more than eleven hundred facts stipulated to by the defendants and their counsel's admission to "aggravated and existing" Eighth Amendment violations in the operation of Alabama's prisons. The plaintiffs and amici joined the NPP's response, and Ira DeMent added his own assessment of the defendants' "so-called" motion for a rehearing and Wallace's repudiation of his counsel's position. "Apparently," DeMent stated, "it is the *modus operandi* of the State of Alabama to confess in open court, as was done in this case, and then to deny having done so. Such an incongruous and incoherent position is much the same as that taken in *Wyatt* v. *Stickney* . . . where the State agreed to the minimal constitutional standards and even worked with the attorneys for the plaintiffs in formulating them, and after allowing the Court to approve them, filed notice of appeal, vehemently stating that its attorneys had no authority to do what they had done." Such "bad faith" maneuvering, he charged, was "devious" and "contemptuous" of the judicial process. Later, DeMent would explain his particular choice of words: "I said it was their *modus operandi*, which are words that are applied to the way a criminal operates."[41]

On March 5, Judge Johnson denied the motion for a rehearing as "absolutely without merit." He did agree to make minor modifications in the order, however. Baxley had charged that the order's ban on inmates performing household or personal tasks for others was "a slap in the face of every decent human being who earns an honest living by that very type of employment." Judge Johnson apparently agreed. Inmates could now be required to perform such tasks within the institution, at other state facilities, in the assistance of officials who required personal services in the performance of their official functions (the crippled Governor Wallace, for example), or as part of a vocational, educational, or work program. He also reduced each inmate's stationery and postage allotment to two letters a week. He refused, however, to modify his order that inmates in isolation be provided sixty-square-foot cells or the requirement that a University of Alabama team assist in inmate reclassification.

Attorney General Baxley is among Judge Johnson's more ardent admirers ("I think that Judge's the greatest man almost that this state's ever produced"). On the wall in Baxley's office was a photograph taken at his inauguration. Flanking him in the photograph are Governor Folsom and Judge Johnson. He had befriended Johnny. He had long praised the judge's civil rights rulings. He doubted whether the typical convict would appreciate the reforms the judge had ordered ("Those damn prisoners, . . . you put 'em in the nicest place, and they're going to tear it up"), but conceded the need for judicial intervention. "The state just cannot escape the responsibility for those orders being entered. . . . It's the state's fault that Judge Johnson ever had to entertain the damn suits to start with. It's decades of neglect that culminated in these suits being before the court." Baxley also agreed that the judge may have done "the state a favor by telling 'em what to expect and setting out his standards" in detail. Ultimately, however, he followed Wallace's lead and filed an appeal in behalf of the other defendants (who, incidentally, did not wish to be represented by Wallace's counsel). Particularly since under Alabama law Wallace was ineligible to succeed himself, Baxley was expected to be the leading contender in the next gubernatorial race. Some suggested, therefore, that his decision to appeal the prison order was a politically motivated act calculated to dispel any concern on the part of Alabama voters that their attorney general was in league with "criminal coddling" judges. Baxley insisted, however, that his concerns were purely those of federalism, separation of powers, and representative democracy. "When you replace the bad judgment of the masses with the good judgment of a person not responsible to the masses," he told a visitor, "you're almost leaving my Jeffersonian-Jacksonian theory of government."[42]

By the time the Wallace and Baxley appeals had been filed, the prison human rights committee had begun functioning and had retained a consultant to assist in monitoring the prison order's implementation. As chairman, Judge Johnson had selected Roland Nachman, a Montgomery attorney, recent president of the Alabama Bar Association. Soft-spoken, scholarly, a member of an establishment law firm, and counsel for the YMCA in the case desegregating its activities, from first appearances Nachman seemed an unlikely choice. But while heading the state bar, he had set up a task force of lawyers and laymen to study Alabama's penal system; and prison officials would find him a persistent, though courtly and generally friendly, advocate of compliance with the court order.[43]

As committee consultant, Nachman had recommended, with Judge Johnson's approval, George Beto, a former head of the Texas prison system and past president of the American Correctional Association, who had assisted in the bar study of Alabama's prisons. Beto had been a defendant in numerous prison cases in his own state; and initially at least, some of the committee members had mixed feelings about his selection. Among corrections specialists, however, he had an excellent reputation. To Judson Locke and other Alabama prison personnel, moreover, he was probably more palatable—and a less likely target of criticism—than a consultant without his practical background in prison work. For his part, Beto had found Judge Johnson's order a refreshing contrast to most other recent prison orders in that it imposed work and education standards. Later, Beto would be impressed with Judge Johnson's "realistic" response to frivolous inmate claims, noting with approval that the judge had promptly dismissed the complaint of an inmate made to drive a prison tractor twelve hours a day, six days a week. The judge, he recalled, had remarked that there was nothing wrong with long, hard work. Beto heartily approved of that sort of thinking.[44]

On January 31, the thirty-nine-member committee had held an organizational meeting, and Judge Johnson recounted for its members the prison litigation's history. In November, he had participated in a distinguished lecture series at the Univeristy of Alabama. Taking as his topic "The Alabama Punting Syndrome" and borrowing from a recent law review article on the tendency of state officials to "punt" their problems into the federal courts, he had decried the willingness of some states to ignore their responsibilities until faced with a federal court order. State acceptance of constitutional obligations, he had asserted, was "the essential prerequisite to a successful political and social future for the South." Before the human rights committee membership, he repeated these themes. Then, after summarizing the evidence supporting the claims of the *Pugh-James* plaintiffs and amici, he responded to his critics, and one in particular: "Those that argue that the elimination of conditions to which I have just referred will operate to create a 'hotel' atmosphere in the Alabama prison system are not aware of the conditions that exist or they make the argument for ulterior purposes."[45]

Fired perhaps by Judge Johnson's pep talk, the committee met for two other general meetings, then divided into subcommittees. Initially, one subcommittee was created for each of the state's four major prisons and a fifth for the other facilities. Later, all physicians on the committee were organized into an additional subcommittee to monitor implementation of the medical standards established in *Newman*. Committee members began conducting inspection tours of facilities and made themselves available to hear inmates' complaints. Every other week, Beto visited Alabama for three days, assisting the committee, monitoring implementation, and lobbying legislative leaders.[46]

As time passed, it became increasingly clear that state officials objected most strongly to two elements in the prison order. One sore spot was Judge Johnson's requirement that inmates in administrative or punitive isolation be placed in individual cells of not less than sixty square feet. No cell in the Alabama system met that specification, and experts estimated the cost of new cells that size at $50,000 per unit. At first, Judge Johnson extended the time for compliance, but refused to reduce the cell size requirement. Finally, however, he agreed that most existing cells could be used, but any newly constructed cells must meet the sixty-square-foot requirement. He would later say that his original position had been unreasonable. Whatever his motives, he had been backed into a corner. Had the requirement not been changed, the legislature would probably have done nothing, and he might have been forced to close the prisons. "Hell," Ray Jenkins of the *Alabama Journal* later remarked, "we know what George Wallace would have done then. He would have sent the buses down to the state prison system, filled 'em up with prisoners and shuttled 'em to Montgomery, set 'em loose on the post office step, and said, 'Now, you go up and thank Judge Johnson for lettin' you out of jail.' Well, hell, no judge was gonna do that. He was really stuck with an unenforceable decision. That's why he modified it."[47]

The other major bone of contention was Judge Johnson's requirement that Raymond Fowler's staff at The University of Alabama assist prison officials in inmate reclassification. The Montgomery campus of Auburn University was located less than three miles from the prison classification center, and prison officials preferred to retain the faculty there to assist in the reclassification. The Auburn faculty had more practical experience in corrections work, Judson Locke later explained, and a philosophy of corrections more compatible with that prevailing in the penal system. Fowler's estimates about the cost of reclassification, it was further claimed, were entirely too high. Most critically, perhaps, Fowler and his associates had actively assisted the plaintiffs and amici in both *Wyatt* and *Pugh-James*.[48]

In his original motion for modification of the order, Attorney General Baxley had included a request that the board of corrections be allowed to select any qualified consultant to assist in reclassification. Through their mutual friend Ira DeMent, Baxley had also told Judge Johnson that he would drop his appeal if the judge would agree to the requested modifications. As noted earlier, Judge Johnson initially approved a number of minor modifications, but refused to change the provisions of the order relating to cell size or reclassification. Later, he agreed to permit the board of corrections to pick any qualified team of reclassification consultants. Still later, he agreed to the cell size modification, but again reversed himself on the reclassification issue. While allowing the state to hire other consultants to assist Dr. Fowler and his group, he placed primary responsibility for reclassification in their hands.

Judge Johnson thought that the cell size requirement had been the crucial factor in Baxley's decision to appeal. When he modified the cell size provision, he expected Baxley to drop his appeal, telling a friend, "Baxley's a political creature. . . . He's going to do what's fair if he can do it without hurting himself politically." But Baxley considered the consultant issue equally crucial and refused to drop the appeal. "Even though naturally I love the University and all of that," he told a visitor, "apparently these people at the board of corrections just cannot work with the people at the university. There's just some kind of irreconcilable conflict."[49]

The reclassification team proceeded with its work, then, in increasingly hostile territory. Fowler and three colleagues worked full time on the project; two others worked part time. A classification specialist from the Florida corrections system, a faculty member from the university's Birmingham campus, and a number of graduate students assisted them in their work. They began their work in the summer, under conditions that were less than ideal. "The temperature in our facility," Fowler recalls, "even when we brought air conditioners from the university and stuck them in windows to try to keep it a little bit cool, was up to a hundred degrees in our working area. It was just an absolute sauna." As hostility to their presence grew, they were subjected to a variety of minor harassments. Under prison rules, the reclassification team was not allowed to enter a unit during inmate shakedowns for weapons. As the team arrived, prison officials often announced a shakedown. At one facility, a medical consultant assisting the team was told that he could interview inmates in the prison infirmary only during sick call—at five o'clock in the morning. An inmate who posted information about the team's responsibilities on a bulletin board was forced to strip and submit to body searches six times during the following weekend; his sleeping area received an equal number of searches. Most critically, prison officials took no action on any of the team's reclassifications.[50]

In early August, the issue came to a head. On the morning of August 4, Danny Evans and Gary Maxwell, two fresh-faced young attorneys newly assigned to represent the board of corrections, dropped by the courthouse to introduce themselves to Judge Johnson and request a conference to clarify the reclassification team's duties. At eight o'clock the next morning, Judge Johnson, Roland Nachman, and opposing counsel met in the judge's chambers. Evans and Maxwell claimed that some of the graduate students assisting the team were being conned by the cons. In one case, they said, an inmate widely known for his skill as a writ writer had even convinced them that he should be given an extended furlough to attend law school in California.[51]

Judge Johnson listened for a time, then noted rather sternly that, to date, Fowler's group had reclassified some five hundred inmates, the prison board had filed no objections to any of them, yet no implementation of the reclassifications had taken place. "It's a terrible thing," he added, as Evans and Maxwell began to squirm a bit uncomfortably in their seats. "We are not getting any cooperation, gentlemen." He had no doubts of their good faith, he said, but he did doubt the good faith of Commissioner Locke "and whatever drifts down from him."

At that point, Roland Nachman joined the discussion, speaking at length about the failure of prison officials to cooperate with the reclassification team. Even some aged and obviously harmless inmates, he asserted, were still confined in maximum security units. Ira DeMent then contended that the *Pugh-James* defendants, like those in *Wyatt*, were being dilatory, and suggested, as he had on numerous earlier occasions, that a master be appointed to take over complete supervision of prison operations.

Judge Johnson declined DeMent's recommendation, remarking that he was not yet ready to take control out of the corrections board's hands. But he did announce procedures for working out reclassification differences between the board and Fowler's team. If no agreement could be reached on a given classification, he added, he would decide the issue on a case-to-case basis. And the whole process should take no more than fifteen days. He would not, he stressed, approve "asinine" reclassifications, such as "sending writ writers to California," but neither would he tolerate frivolous objections. "Once I get the idea they are just perfunctory objections to break the machinery down," he observed, peering over his half-moon glasses at Evans and Maxwell, "I'm going to give you something you don't want."

As the conference was ending, Judge Johnson brought up his understanding that Baxley had agreed to drop his appeal after modification of the cell size order. In litigation of this sort, he said, Baxley was an officer of the federal courts. "I expect him," he added, grinning slightly, "to keep his agreements." Evans and Maxwell replied that the appeal had not been dropped because of the attorney general's continued concerns about reclassification. Judge Johnson then conceded that even if Baxley dropped the appeal for the other defendants, that would not end the matter. If Governor Wallace adhered to his usual pattern, he noted somewhat wearily, he would "follow the thing out to the very end."

The one objection to a specific reclassification Evans and Maxwell had raised proved to be less than substantial. After the August conference, moreover, reclassification proceeded somewhat more smoothly, and in less than a year, the project was completed. Initially, there was relatively little compliance in other areas covered by the order. On July 13, 1976, the corrections board had filed a six-month progress report. The report accented the positive, stressing, for example, that free toilet articles, clothing, and eating utensils had been ordered for the inmates, ample blankets provided, all beds positioned off the floor, repair and painting of all facilities undertaken, and security measures initiated. But even a cursory reading of the report's contents revealed that little or no compliance had been achieved in many areas. The inmate population was being substantially reduced, but this was largely a consequence of Judge Johnson's order backing up inmates in local jails; and conditions there were generally no better—and, in many instances, much worse—than conditions in the major prisons. Moreover, over-crowding in the local units was fast reaching crisis proportions. In fact, inmates were beginning to file suits contesting conditions in the local jails; and local officials had begun to seek court orders forcing the state to assume financial responsibility for their increased burdens.[52]

Staffing in the four major units remained well below figures required under the order, and educational and vocational opportunities were still unavailable to most inmates. According to the report, inmates were receiving three wholesome, nutritious meals a day, prepared in sanitary settings. As yet, however, none of the food service facilities had been approved, or even inspected, by county health officers. Regular insect and rodent control had also begun, but in at least one facility pest control firms had proven inadequate to the task, and, the report noted, a consultant was being hired to develop a plan for training the inmates in pest control.

Nachman, Beto, and members of the human rights committee saw, or suspected, other serious gaps in implementation. Prison doctors had themselves complained to members of the medical subcommittee about delays in treatment for mentally ill inmates and their transfer to other institutions. Nachman and Beto suspected that illegal uses of money were still prevalent and that prison officials were fearful of inmate reaction if they clamped down on its availability. Numerous fire hazards had not been eliminated, and sanitation was still a critical problem. At Fountain, for example, Beto observed as droplets of steam collected on the filthy ceiling of the prison kitchen, then dropped into food containers. And in a fall report, a U.S. public health officer found conditions substandard in each of Alabama's major prisons. The list of inadequacies seemed endless.[53]

Meaningful compliance with the court order, of course, would require substantial budget increases for the prison system; and Alabama's solons were not known for their generosity in that area. A few legislators seemed genuinely interested in the problems confronting prison officials. The state senate had even created a task force to study the prisons, and in a move Judge Johnson considered revolutionary—and others a serious affront to separation of powers—had persuaded the judge to make the task force an arm of the court in monitoring implementation. Under prodding from Dr. Beto and Roland Nachman, among others, the legislature also enacted a number of laws to alleviate conditions in the prisons, including "good time" legislation permitting early release of model inmates. Money was provided for construction of a new prison, and at the end of 1976, prison officials were left with a $400,000 revenue net which they used to make a number of improvements required under the order. With an additional $400,000 in federal revenue sharing funds provided by the ever enigmatic Governor Wallace, they also renovated five road camps. Moreover, the population at each major prison was gradually reduced to designed capacity. But prison reform was hardly a priority item with the governor and most legislators. Well over a year after the order, the legislature had yet to appropriate any additional funds for prison operations.[54]

While state officials limped along toward some semblance of real compliance, legal scholars devoted increasing attention to growing judicial intervention in legislative and administrative domains—with Judge Johnson's rulings a major topic, or target, of concern. Drawing on the arguments of such towering and divergent critics of judicial lawmaking as Hugo L. Black and Learned Hand, a number of scholars charged that the courts' enlarging administrative-managerial roles threatened democratic institutions, undermined the self-reliance and responsibility of voters and their elected representatives, posed serious risks of repeated confrontations between the courts and the popular branches of government, and would ultimately jeopardize public confidence in the courts and the legitimacy of judicial decisions. Critics also questioned whether courts were an effective forum for the resolution of broad questions of social policy. In a thoughtful analysis, for example, Donald Horowitz of the Smithsonian Institution, a former Justice Department attorney, pointed out that courts lack self-starters and thus must leave largely to litigants the creation of agendas for judicial policy making. As a consequence, he contended, it is difficult for judges to concentrate in a sustained way on any policy areas, their decisions are necessarily ad hoc in nature, their policy judgments often based on atypical factual situations. In his judgment, moreover, courts normally confronted greater difficulties than legislators and administrators in measuring the overall impact of their decisions and overcoming resistance to their authority. Finally, critics questioned the growing judicial reliance on "experts" in formulating decrees based presumably on constitutional commands, particularly since the judgments of experts seemed to be in a constant state of flux.[55]

The nation's Judge Johnsons were not without their defenders, however. At the Fifth Circuit's 1976 Judicial Conference, for example, Arthur S. Miller, a law professor who earlier had advanced a "teleological" approach to jurisprudence in which judges mold the law to desirable social goals, assured the judges of his "deep professional respect and loyalty" and "unbounded love and gratitude for what you have been doing to make the world in which I live a better place." And in an important *Harvard Law Review* article published several months after issuance of the *Pugh-James* order, Abram Chayes cited a number of advantages to social change through the judicial arena, including the judge's relative insulation from political pressures, his commitment to reflective and dispassionate analysis conditioned by experience, the opportunity to apply broad policy to specific contexts, the relatively high degree of participation allowed representatives of those affected by his decisions, and the absence of rigid governmental structures and preconceptions characteristic of bureaucratic agencies. In a major inquiry into the nature of rights, moreover, Ronald Dworkin answered those who contended that the due process, equal protection, and other constitutional tools of activist judges should be limited in meaning to rights their framers were aware of or would have recognized. In Dworkin's judgment, the framers of such provisions meant them to embody a "*concept* of fairness" rather than "any specific *conception* of fairness." Judges and others applying constitutional guarantees to contemporary contexts were thus bound by broad moral precepts, not to particular systems of rights locked in history. Supporters argued, too, that courts had intervened only after legislators and administrators had failed to provide justice for the weakest in society. Some, in fact, echoed the sentiments—if not the rhetoric—of George Dean, chief counsel for the *Wyatt* plaintiffs, who, when pressed about the propriety of Judge Johnson's mental health and prison orders, replied: "Frank Johnson goes where he goes because he has to go there, because he's a decent human being. . . . People who don't want the system to respond, people who don't give a damn about the horrors that go on in the Alabama prison system, people who don't care whether six old ladies die at Bryce Hospital when the temperature in their ward gets to 115 degrees and they die of dehydration—people who don't care about that will say, 'Oh, not judicial intervention. That's going too far. That's really going too far.' But this is no debating society. It's human life."[56]

Judge Johnson also defended his position. "You disturb me when you talk about judges creating rights," he told a friendly adversary during a drive to Dothan for arraignments. "The furthest thing in the world from my mind would be that I had the authority to create rights." What about the abortion right and other privacy guarantees recently recognized by the Supreme Court, or, for that matter, the right of mental patients to "adequate" treatment and inmates an opportunity to rehabilitate themselves? Those "rights" are mentioned nowhere in the Constitution's text, and it is unlikely that the eighteenth- and nineteenth-century framers of the general constitutional guarantees on which their existence has been based intended that they have constitutional status. "Those rights have always been in existence. They just haven't been elucidated; they haven't been declared." The Constitution is

> a living document, . . . a flexible document. . . . Those people that believe that the Constitution is to be strictly interpreted and if it isn't written there, it isn't there, are adopting a position that would inhibit, or prohibit, growth of the country, the growth of people. . . . It's my thesis that these rights aren't being created, that the Constitution isn't being changed, that the more enlightened we become, the more humane we become, the more democratic we become, the more concerned we are with our fellow man, the more entirely appropriate it becomes for those that are vested with the authority to do so—and it has to be the federal judiciary—to find rights in the Constitution . . . that have not been heretofore declared. I don't find anything dangerous or scary in that approach to constitutional interpretation. I think it has to be that way.[57]

His comments called to mind Justice Black's response to the "many good and able men" who had spoken of a need for judges "to keep the Constitution in tune with the times." "The Constitution makers," he wrote during his twilight years on the Supreme Court, "knew the need for change and provided for it. Amendments suggested by the people's elected representatives can be submitted to the people or their selected agents for ratification. That method of change was good for our Fathers, and being somewhat old-fashioned I must add it is good enough for me."[58]

But Judge Johnson stood his ground and, in a lecture at the University of Georgia law school in early 1977, amplified and defended his views. Citing human fallibility and the Constitution's broad, general language, he repudiated as neither "realistic" nor "necessarily desirable" the notion that the judge's proper role in constitutional cases is to passively "find and pronounce" the law. That doctrine, he contended, was honored more in its breach than its observance, and even Hugo Black and other "vocal and ardent judicial supporters" had been unable to apply it "with any consistency." "The Constitution," he told his audience, "is not an inert and lifeless body of law from which legal consequences automatically flow. To the contrary, it is dynamic and living, requiring constant reexamination and reevaluation." Its true strength lay "in its flexibility, its ability to change, to grow, and to respond to the special needs and demands of our society at a particular time." Any "doctrinal approach" to constitutional interpretation that denied the document's dynamic character was "both inappropriate and unworkable." Since the days of John Marshall, the first great chief justice, federal judges had been the subject of bitter attack, he concluded; but with few exceptions, their decisions in time had "become accepted and revered as monuments memorializing" the nation's "strength and stability."[59]

As on other occasions, he also claimed that federal judges had intervened only when officials failed to meet their constitutional obligations—and reluctantly even then. When asked by a student following the lecture, moreover, whether he had ever left any decision to the state legislature, he smiled and responded: "Sure. We left the reapportionment of the Alabama Legislature up to the Alabama Legislature—for ten years."[60]

Ultimately, of course, the legal propriety of Judge Johnson's prison orders would be determined by the appellate courts. A Fifth Circuit panel had heard oral argument in early May of 1977; and in the early fall, the panel rendered its decision. As the circuit panel had moved toward a ruling, the judge had remained confident that his orders would be affirmed. "I don't believe," he remarked shortly before the panel's decision was announced, that "the Fifth Circuit has started reversing cases where the state's lawyer . . . gets up in open court and confesses substantial [constitutional] violations." Judson Locke was not so certain of the appellate panel's probable stance. He had attended the oral argument of the prison cases in New Orleans the previous May and had returned to Montgomery heartened by some of the pointed questions panel members had asked counsel for the plaintiffs and amici. More generally, he was guardedly optimistic that aggressive judicial intervention in prison affairs and law enforcement might be coming to an end. Citing recent Supreme Court decisions limiting inmate rights in disciplinary contexts, he told a visitor: "I think you're going to see the pendulum go the other way. I think the appellate courts . . . are fed up with all of these writs, and I think they want to give the administrators a freer hand in resolving" prison problems.[61]

Both men were to be partially correct. Speaking for a three-judge panel on September 16, Judge James P. Coleman praised "the determined efforts of the highly dedicated District Judge to put an end to unconstitutional conditions in the Alabama prison system," and added: "We cannot believe that the good people of a great state approved the prison situation demonstrated by the evidence in this case." The panel upheld the steps Judge Johnson had taken to assure inmates reasonably adequate food, clothing, shelter, sanitation, necessary medical attention, and personal safety. But Coleman and his colleagues found no constitutional basis for the requirement that some inmates be housed in individual cells; nor could they agree that a prison's "design" would amount to a per se constitutional limitation on the number of convicts who could be confined there. Rejecting Judge Johnson's creation of a lay human rights committee to monitor implementation, they recommended as a "more reasonable, less intrusive, more effective approach" appointment of a single qualified monitor, with full authority to observe and report, but no power to intervene in daily prison operations. While the Constitution did not mandate a meaningful job for each inmate, Coleman added, that requirement placed no "real burden" on prison authorities and would be allowed to stand, though having no status as binding precedent. But states had no constitutional obligation to provide inmates with opportunities to obtain a basic education, attend vocational school, or attend a transitional program prior to release. "The Constitution," said Coleman, "does not require that prisoners, as individuals or as a group, be provided with any and every amenity which some person may think is needed to avoid mental, physical, and emotional deterioration." And there was more. Visitation regulations were to be left to the "sound discretion" of prison authorities. Moreover, since Governor Wallace had no hand in prison operations beyond budget recommendations to the legislature and the appointment of corrections board members, the injunction against him was to be dissolved.[62]

The Supreme Court limited its review to the narrow question of whether the state itself could be included among the defendants. In a brief per curiam, filed July 3, 1978, the high Court held that since Alabama had not consented to such a suit in its laws, action against the state was barred by the doctrine of sovereign immunity. Given the number of state officials named in the prison suits, however, the Court's decision had negligible impact. On the substantive constitutional issues, then, the Fifth Circuit was to have the last word.[63]

Or was it? While the cases were pending on appeal, Judge Johnson's approach had been essentially one of "wait and see," because he was reluctant to "cross any bridges [he] couldn't recross." Now that the appeal process had been completed, he began to push for something approximating full compliance. It soon became clear, moreover, that the Fifth Circuit's ruling would have little effect on his future involvement with Alabama's prisons. Except for the appellate panel's invalidation of the human rights committee, he considered all the Fifth Circuit's modifications of his orders "insubstantial." And even that element in the panel's ruling, in his judgment, was open to considerable interpretation. "I want to adhere—and I intent to adhere—to the spirit of the Fifth Circuit's opinion," he told a visitor. "But I'm still having problems trying to determine if I should have one overall monitor, or a monitor in each major facility, or both. And then once I decide that, I'm going to have to decide what the functions of the monitor are. Are they there just to walk around and observe and file written reports with me? Do they have access to the records of the facility?" He smiled slightly and added: "I don't think I can monitor very well without giving them about the same authority that I gave the human rights committee."[64]

Epilogue

While the *Pugh-James* appeal was pending in the Fifth Circuit, the Carter administration had announced Judge Johnson's nomination as director of the FBI. After becoming a district judge, Johnson had removed himself from partisan politics. While retaining nominal membership in the GOP, he had mustered little enthusiasm for the presidential candidates of either party in the post-Eisenhower years. In 1960, he voted for John F. Kennedy. In 1964, he "went fishing," as he put it, unable to support Lyndon Johnson or Barry Goldwater. He refused to vote for Nixon in 1968 or 1972, but had little enthusiasm for Hubert Humphrey or George McGovern either, finding the Democrats' welfare proposals entirely too liberal for his Winston County tastes and McGovern's foreign policy stance "weak." "I don't distrust the Russians," he would later remark. "I don't find a Russian under every bed. But their past conduct in dealing with some countries—Hungary, for instance—indicates that if you're weak, and it serves their economic or political purposes, they'll run completely over you. To that extent, I could not subscribe to McGovern's philosophy. I just couldn't." In 1976, he initially had leaned slightly toward Gerald Ford, appalled by the Democrats' proposal for a guaranteed annual income. Ultimately, however, in 1976 he again "went fishing."[1]

Before the 1976 elections, Judge Johnson had never met Jimmy Carter. But the judge numbered among his friends several members of the Carter inner circle, including Judge Griffin Bell, who had resigned his seat on the Fifth Circuit to work in the Carter campaign, and Bell's law partner Charles Kirbo, who was to become President Carter's principal unofficial adviser. Moreover, Morris Dees of Montgomery's Southern Poverty Law Center had served as the Carter campaign's finance director; and his law partner Joe Levin, Jr., had also been heavily involved in the Carter election effort. Beyond these meaningful mutual associations, a man of Judge Johnson's reputation for integrity and courage seemed an excellent choice to head the FBI—an agency then under fire for illegal wiretapping, political spying, and other misuses of public power.

President Carter had first approached Judge Johnson about the FBI position the month following his election, inviting the judge to Altanta for a conference on December 13. The Atlanta session had lasted about an hour, Johnson and Carter first conferring alone, then joined by Kirbo, Vice-President-elect Walter Mondale, and Carter aide Hamilton Jordan. The discussion covered a variety of topics, including the judge's judicial career and service as U.S. attorney, the growing federal court workload, the propriety of splitting the huge Fifth Circuit into smaller units, and Johnson's suggestions for the post of attorney general (the judge mentioned John Doar and Griffin Bell, among others). Carter also noted that he had discussed Johnson with Governor Wallace and that the governor had given the judge a warm endorsement. After joking about whether Wallace was concerned about Judge Johnson's interests or simply wanted him out of Alabama, Carter added that Wallace had assured him his attacks on the judge had been mere political rhetoric, to which the judge responded that more than politics separated him from Wallace. Carter smiled, said he understood, and moved on to pleasanter topics.[3]

When the meeting ended, Judge Johnson returned to Montgomery to assess his situation. Although he still found something novel about each of the cases on his docket, he had become increasingly bored with routine litigation, particularly "run-of-the-mill" criminal cases. In that sense, a change seemed appealing. There were more pressing considerations, however. His mother had been in declining health for several years and had given her eldest son her power of attorney so that competency proceedings could be avoided. While she still chose to live alone, Judge Johnson visited her virtually every day and handled all her business affairs. If he and Ruth moved to Washington, other arrangements would be necessary for his mother. He was also concerned about the extreme financial sacrifice the FBI appointment would entail. As a federal judge, he could retire at full salary; his annuity as former FBI director would be considerably less, as would his wife's pension if he died before Ruth. During the first two years of FBI service, moreover, he and Ruth would have no retirement coverage. For a man of comfortable but modest means, such a sacrifice would be major. Combined with his concern about his mother, it was decisive. On Wednesday, he called Carter to say that he must decline the nomination were it formally extended him. (Framing his response in this way, he could later deny news reports that he had been offered the FBI position but rejected it.)[4]

Several days later, Griffin Bell telephoned to report that he was to be appointed attorney general and that Carter wanted Judge Johnson to serve as deputy attorney general. To make the proposition more attractive, Bell added, Carter would enlarge the deputy's powers to include direct supervision of the FBI, the Justice Department's criminal division, and all federal criminal investigations and prosecutions. Bell also promised that the judge could reenter the judiciary should the executive position prove unsatisfactory. Again, however, Johnson declined, citing his mother's health and the enormous financial sacrifice of such a move.[5]

Into the spring and summer of 1977, President Carter had continued the search for an FBI director without success. During the summer, however, Judge Johnson began to have serious second thoughts about his earlier decision to decline the directorship. Recently, his mother's condition had worsened to the point that she had to be placed in a nursing home. The family had selected a home near York, where the judge's sister Jean lived. His mother's care was thus no longer a daily responsibility. If appointed to the FBI, however, Johnson would be expected to serve a full ten-year term. When the term was completed, he would be approaching seventy and Carter would be out of the White House. The FBI appointment could not serve, therefore, as a stepping stone to the Supreme Court. Moreover, although Bell had promised to seek legislation allowing Johnson to retain his judicial retirement after becoming FBI director, there was only a possibility that such a provision would be adopted. Beyond this, there was the chance at least, given the magnitude of the bureau's problems, that he would fail in his efforts to reform the agency, thereby marring an otherwise excellent record of public service.[6] Except as a desire to serve his country, therefore, it was difficult to explain his renewed interest in the directorship.

Whatever the motivation, Judge Johnson contacted Frances Green, a former law clerk now working in Griffin Bell's office, and asked that she convey to the administration his interest in coming to Washington. Soon after that, Bell met with Judge Johnson in Georgia to discuss the nomination. Then, on August 17, Bell announced the nomination at the White House while the judge held a press conference in Montgomery to express the hope that he could provide the FBI with "positive, inspirational leadership"—and decline press invitations to critique the bureau and its leadership. "The FBI," he said, "has long and honorably served our country as the finest investigative agency in the world, and the prospect of serving the bureau in a leadership role is indeed challenging."[7]

Alabama reaction to the nomination was mixed but largely favorable. The state's conservative Senator James B. Allen, a member of the Senate Judiciary Committee, told reporters he was undecided about the Johnson nomination, adding pointedly: "I want to ascertain the basis on which the appointment was made. Was it his expertise in law enforcement or because of his rulings with respect to Alabama schools, prisons and mental health?" But Governor Wallace claimed that he and the judge had never had any "personal differences," wished him luck in his new position, and predicted that Johnson would give "organized crime . . . a run for their money." The Birmingham Post-Herald's reaction, moreover, was typical of state editorial response: "President

Carter casts more honor upon himself than upon his nominee in selecting Federal Judge Frank M. Johnson to head the Federal Bureau of Investigation. . . . And it is a cinch that the abuses of law which so dishonored the FBI during the years it was led by J. Edgar Hoover could never have come about had Frank Johnson then been head of the agency." National press reaction was equally favorable. So also was the response of the nation's civil rights activists.[8]

But the relief and enthusiasm were short-lived. Judge Johnson had been a chronic smoker since youth, with a special proclivity for Home Run cigarettes, an uncommonly strong, hard-to-find brand supplied him mainly by his sister Jean, who operated a York drugstore. In 1974, however, his doctor had ordered him to stop smoking after discovering signs of emphysema in his patient's lungs. The judge had then turned to Red Man chewing tobacco, and small brass spittoons soon appeared beneath his desk, on the floorboard of his car, and at other strategic locations. The Red Man had proved an inadequate substitute for cigarettes; but the judge dutifully followed his doctor's orders, and in other respects he seemed the very picture of good health.[9]

During a routine physical in connection with the FBI nomination, however, the examining physician discovered an abdominal aneurysm and recommended immediate surgery. Within ten days of the nomination, Judge Johnson underwent surgery at Methodist Hospital in Houston. The operation and initial recuperation went well, and he and Mrs. Jonhson sold their Haardt Drive home and moved into his mother's house to await the transfer to Washington. But during an early October visit to Washington for a Justice Department briefing and meetings with key senators, he suffered intense pain in his lower groin, later diagnosed as a hernia condition. By late November, hernia surgery seemed likely, and he had become increasingly discouraged by the slow progress of his recovery from the initial operation. Not wishing to delay action further on the directorship, he asked President Carter to withdraw his name from consideration so that a new nominee could be sought—a task now "made harder," the New York Times editorialized, "because the nomination of Judge Johnson [had] set such a high standard."[10]

For several months after removing himself from consideration for the FBI directorship, Judge Johnson, to use his phrase, had "raced the chickens to bed," able to put in only a half-day of work at the office. Even before the Supreme Court's ruling in the prison litigation, however, his doctors had decided that hernia surgery was unnecessary. The surgical device that had eliminated the aneurysm still caused him considerable discomfort when he sat for long periods, and he often had to stand during lengthy court proceedings. But though easily fatigued, he was back to a full schedule at the office,[11] expediting Middle District business with normal dispatch.

In 1975, the judge's law clerks had organized a banquet in his honor to celebrate his twentieth anniversary on the bench. At the banquet, they presented him with a mimeographed collection of reminiscences reflecting their respect and affection for "a man of principle." In its preface, they noted that Judge Johnson's "staunch adherence to principle [had] obstructed his every opportunity for appointment to the highest court in the land." Unfortunately, such an assessment was all too apt during the "Southern Strategy" years of the Nixon-Ford administrations. A Johnson appointment to a higher federal court did seem politically compatible, however, with both the overall policy goals of the Carter administration and the patterns of President Carter's 1976 voting strength. And as the judge's vigor returned, Attorney General Bell approached him about a circuit court position as part of the administration's effort to recruit experienced trial judges for the appellate bench.[12]

In the late summer of 1978, Attorney General Bell discussed an appointment to the Court of Appeals for the District of Columbia with Judge Johnson; earlier, he had approached the judge about a Fifth Circuit vacancy. Initially, however, Johnson was hardly enthusiastic. After more than two decades as his own man on a trial court, he found the prospect of appointment to a collegial circuit body unappealing, and a seat on the D.C. Circuit—with its heavy responsibility for reviewing administrative agency decisions and limited scope of review over such rulings—particularly uninviting. "I can see," he remarked, "that it would probably get old to me [quickly] after my being on the district court bench as long as I have, and being in the courtroom and seeing the lawyers and litigants, and making these rulings originally, as opposed to trying to second-guess an administrative body when the scope of review is so restrictive. I don't want to get into a rubber-stamp position."[13]

Judge Johnson's distaste for a D.C. Circuit position never weakened; but in the fall of 1978, he found the prospect of a Fifth Circuit seat increasingly appealing. With an appointment to the Fifth Circuit, he could continue to maintain a residence in Montgomery, sitting to hear cases in New Orleans and other cities within the circuit only about twelve weeks of each year. He could also escape the tension and pressure of the trial bench.[14]

Then, too, he may have felt greater confidence that the state would now accomplish the ultimate goals of his mental health, prison, and other comprehensive orders without his continued presence on the Middle District bench. The federal courts are still convenient targets for aspiring Alabama politicians; a GOP also-ran in the 1978 gubernatorial race charged, for example, that the federal courts had made "political prisoners" of all Alabamians. Undoubtedly, numerous citizens shared this attitude and that of a Dothan resident who had written Judge

Johnson a congratulatory letter following the FBI nomination, but added: "We have enjoyed about as much of you in this District as we can take." But 1978 was also the year in which George Wallace—prohibited by law from seeking a third consecutive gubernatorial term and uncertain of his interest in a U.S. Senate seat (or of his chances for victory)—announced his retirement from electoral politics. Moreover, the judge's other major nemesis John Patterson was now well out of the mainstream of Alabama politics and even given to praising Johnson's role in human rights reform. "I've always had a high regard for Judge Johnson," Patterson had observed in 1976.

> I think he had a distasteful job that had to be done and he had the courage to do it. . . . [It's fortunate] that we in Alabama have had a federal judge who was willing and capable of grasping the situation and resolving it. . . . [He] brought about a desirable result which could not be done politically. . . . [We politicians could say,] "Look, I stood up here and fought this thing to the bitter end. I stood in the door, and that doggone judge down there, you gotta blame [him], not me." . . . Look at the different things that happened that way: the integration of schools, reapportionment of the legislature, reassessment and equalization of property taxes. Judge was about the best valve for bringing about change that couldn't be done politically I've ever seen. . . . If I'd said that we couldn't win [the racial struggle], I'd have been dead as a doornail politically. . . . Judge Johnson just happened to be in the right place to do the job, and he did it without hesitation, fearlessly, courageously. . . . If I had been in the same position that he was in, I probably—there again, this is hindsight—I would have applied the Constitution of the United States as I know it.[15]

In May of 1979, Judge Johnson was inducted into the Alabama Academy of Honor, a society of notables honoring outstanding contributions to the state and its citizens. John Patterson was the academy's chairman. After the ceremony, held in the chamber of the Alabama House of Representatives, state papers carried a photograph of a smiling Patterson welcoming an equally jovial Judge Johnson into the society. Behind them on a wall over the Speaker's chair was a plaque commemorating Alabama's secession from the Union.[16]

If the general state of Alabama politics helped to push the judge in the direction of a circuit position, the approach of George Wallace's statehouse successor to federal court orders must have assumed major significance. Shortly after his January 15, 1979, inauguration, Governor Forrest H. (Fob) James requested a meeting with Judge Johnson in the judge's chambers. During the session, James told the judge that he wanted to remove the state from federal court supervision as expeditiously as possible and that he was committed to a spirit of cooperation with the court and full compliance with its orders. The prison orders, he added, would be given his immediate attention.[17]

Several days later, while the Johnsons were attending a meeting of the Judicial Ethics Committee in Florida, Roland Nachman phoned the judge. Governor James, Nachman reported, wanted Johnson to consider putting Alabama's prison system into receivership with the governor as receiver. Would the judge be amenable to such a petition? Judge Johnson responded that he would want to study the matter further but emphasized that any receivership petition must include a number of basic ingredients. Specifically, the governor must acknowledge that under the existing system the state had made little progress toward compliance; that there was no reasonable likelihood of compliance within the foreseeable future; that the governor wanted compliance and believed that he would be able to achieve it as receiver; and that the state's lieutenant governor, attorney general, and House Speaker joined the petition.[18]

Such a petition was revolutionary and probably without precedent in American judicial history. But, then, neither Alabama politics nor Judge Johnson's court had ever really been unduly bound by tradition. On February 1, 1979, the governor's petition, drafted apparently by Roland Nachman and largely tracking Judge Johnson's stipulations, was delivered to the judge's chambers. Shortly after noon the following day, the judge issued a memorandum opinion and order granting the governor's request. To date, he concluded, the state board of prisons had failed to comply with his prison order "in several critical areas." Prison populations had been reduced to design capacity, but only by creating a backlog of eighteen hundred state prisoners in city and county jails where conditions were generally worse than those in state facilities prior to Newman, Pugh, and James. Within the state facilities, the system of classification which Raymond Fowler's staff had developed was no longer functioning; the record of treatment for the mentally ill required under Newman was "one of total failure"; and medical services generally reflected "glaring inadequacies." Robbery, rape, and assault remained regular occurrences; living conditions and food service fell "far below all minimum health and safety standards"; the prison board had "failed completely to provide meaningful work for all inmates"; management problems had plagued vocational education and work-release programs; physical plants did not meet Public Health Service standards, though a new prison had been opened; and the facilities remained understaffed. The judge's impatience with the state was obvious. "Time does not stand still, but the Board of Corrections and the Alabama Prison System have for six years. Their time has now run out." The evidence, he wrote, would justify the closing of several facilities, as he had threatened in the 1976 order. Governor James's petition, however, provided a "more reasonable and . . . promising" alternative. For a period of not less than one year, the governor was to operate the state's prisons. Later, the judge would also name James receiver for the Alabama mental health system; dissolve the Bryce, Partlow, and Searcy human rights committees; and appoint Judge Lecil Gray the court's monitor for the mental health system.[19]

Whatever the influence of the changing directions of Alabama politics or other factors, Judge Johnson ultimately became a candidate for a vacancy on the Fifth Circuit. The Carter administration had created one or more blue-ribbon commissions in each circuit to screen potential appellate nominees. Judge Johnson filed an application and supporting material with the Fifth Circuit commission. The commission interviewed him and other candidates, then submitted to the administration five choices as required under the commission arrangement. But there could be little doubt about the outcome. In the spring, President Carter submitted Judge Johnson's name to the Senate. Earlier, a unanimous American Bar Association Committee on the Federal Judiciary had given the judge its highest rating. Following a perfunctory subcommittee hearing, the Senate voted unanimously to approve the president's choice.[20]

At investiture proceedings in Montgomery on July 12, Judge Johnson took the oath of office as circuit judge, ending almost twenty-four years on the trial bench. During the ceremony, Judge Rives, Attorney General Bell, Roland Nachman, the president of the state bar association, and others praised the judge's accomplishments. After taking the oath, Judge Johnson expressed his appreciation for their remarks, then reminded them that a dissenter from one of the Fifth Circuit's decisions affirming a recent Johnson ruling had conceded that "Frank Johnson is a good judge," but asserted that "medals earned for past performance cannot justify contemporary failure." He also traced the record of his court in human rights litigation, acknowledged that "not all Alabamians, nor all Americans, nor even all judges, have completely taken . . . to heart" the truth "that the Constitution holds all persons within its embrace," then added: "But as we prize dissent, we should not expect consensus—even as to those values that we hold dear. It is enough that there have always been those in Alabama who understood the spirit—the spirit as well as the letter of the law, who ventured forward while others did not. They have always found their voice, although others have tried to drown it or sometimes discredit it." Judge Johnson's example was Justice Black. On this occasion, however, his words brought to mind his own career.[21]

Why did Judge Johnson choose his path while so many others had taken a different course? Viewed superficially, his role in Alabama's racial politics was predictable, given the judge's background. Winston County's history is compatible with Johnson's willingness to enforce federal civil rights policy; and its minuscule black population may well have helped to free him from the "Negrophobia" that too often afflicted his Black Belt counterparts. A study of southern district judges completed during his first decade on the bench suggests, moreover, that those judges removed from the mainstream of southern politics and society were more likely to assume "integrationist" or "moderate" positions in civil rights cases than judges with such backgrounds. As a "post office" Republican with a career background in the federal government rather than state elective office, Judge Johnson fits the "integrationist"/"moderate" mold. The judge's withdrawal from active church attendance relatively early in his judicial career is also consistent with the study's finding that southern judges active in fundamentalist Protestant sects were more likely to assume a "segregationist" stance than Catholic judges or nonchurchgoers. [22]

Though of some value, such explanations of judicial motivation somehow seem too facile, at least when applied to Judge Johnson. The judge's own beliefs and personality suggest other explanations, however, for his role in Alabama racial reform. First, he apparently went on the court imbued with the idea that the Constitution recognizes but one class of citizens and that race laws are inconsistent with that basic constitutional principle. Such thinking has obviously influenced his civil rights posture. He also possesses a deep respect for the law; and his racial decisions, after all, have been largely a reflection of clear congressional policy and Supreme Court precedent. Whatever his personal beliefs or the impact of federal policy on his decisions, moreover, he apparently recognized early in his career that racial change was inevitable, and gradual, steady change preferable to initial judicial intransigence followed by abrupt reform dictated by the appellate courts. "It was something that had to be done," he has remarked. "It was just a period that we had to go through, and the sooner we bit the bullet the easier it was going to be. . . . I felt . . . I'd be deceptive if I didn't go ahead . . . not only in the sense that I'd be misleading the people, but in the sense that I had a duty and an obligation to decide [civil rights cases] the way they're supposed to be" decided.[23]

Another facet of Judge Johnson's makeup also bears mention. Although he was a late bloomer, Judge Johnson is a high achiever, a characteristic reflected not only in the speed and efficiency with which he conducted the business of his court, but in every other stage of his adult life as well, from law school and military service, through law practice and service as U.S. attorney. For such a person, career success becomes an end in itself; and within the judicial bureaucracy a key measure of a trial judge's success is his batting average with the appellate courts. In modern civil rights contexts, of course, appellate success meant decisions supportive of civil rights claims. Had his roots run deeper in the soil of southern racial traditions, his devotion to Deep South racial mores may have overwhelmed his desire for success as a judge. Largely unaffected by such traditions, however, Judge Johnson was willing to risk social isolation (and, at times, physical danger) in order to fulfill his proper role in the judicial bureaucracy—enforcement of legal policy in accordance with appellate court precedent—and thus succeed as a judge.

Finally, Judge Johnson's role in Alabama's racial struggles may be attributed in part to the iron will he inherited from his mother. Despite a stern courtroom demeanor, Judge Johnson has normally exhibited extraordinary patience and courtesy in his dealings with state defendants caught up in human rights litigation, allowing them ample time to put their own houses in order before imposing detailed compliance standards. At the same time, he is a strong-willed man on whom ostracism, threats, and political harangues would be expected to have a reinforcing rather than inhibiting effect. In a 1978 newspaper interview, he suggested that contemporary social change had come about more easily in the South than elsewhere in the nation largely because southerners are obsessed with obeying the law. "They grumble and complain when changes are made in their basic social fabric," he said, "but they are intensely patriotic. They love their country and their flag." George Wallace's defiance, he added, had helped to speed the process of southern social change. "He virtually invited the filing of various suits. He accelerated the pace because of his stand."[24] Wallace's intransigence, he might also have added, may have influenced, too, the reception such suits received in the Middle District court.

The aggressive stand Judge Johnson has assumed in nonracial human rights cases, particularly in the prison and mental health contexts, is more difficult to explain. In such cases, he generally did not enforce either clear congressional policy or appellate court precedent. Instead, he plowed new, or relatively new, constitutional ground. The Supreme Court continues to give the Constitution's guarantees the broad, nebulous meaning that fairly invites court orders of the *Wyatt* and *Pugh-James* variety. Moreover, critics of the mental health and prison orders have rarely questioned Judge Johnson's constitutional findings, only the orders' scope and detail; yet once a judge has found a constitutional violation, there would appear to be no meaningful equity limitations on the sort of relief he chooses to provide. Even so, the aggressive part Judge Johnson played in Alabama's nonracial human rights controversies appears an unlikely role for a man who seems committed to limited government and regularly decries the extent of federal welfare spending.

Particularly if one's focus is on the prison and mental health orders, however, several explanations for Judge Johnson's nonracial human rights stance may be suggested. First, his adult life reflects a concern for the underdog that seems undoubtedly to have affected his judicial posture. His aggressive defense of the Lichfield defendants—lowly enlisted men and convenient army scapegoats—can only be explained in that way. So it is, too, with his prosecution of the Dial family. Given the circumstances of the pathetic "Monk" Thompson's death, not to mention the defendants' prominence, he could easily have left the case in state hands, and with considerable justification from a technical legal standpoint. In the early 1950s, such an approach would have been so expected, so normal a response to southern racial violence that at most it would have produced a mild ripple, even in the black press of the urban North. Against this background of concern for the "unloved and unlovely" of this world—Lecil Gray's apt description for some of Alabama's mental patients—Judge Johnson's human rights role seems entirely natural, particularly given the extreme conditions he has confronted as a judge.

Beyond this, there is his largely pragmatic approach to constitutional interpretaion. To Judge Johnson, the Constitution's human rights guarantees are flexible and ever-expanding in content, and government's power to restrict them governed by equally pliable standards of reasonableness and fairness, to be applied in concrete contexts. He thus views efforts to limit the Constitution's scope to its "literal" or "historically intended" meaning as both unrealistic and inconsistent with the document's "living" quality. For such a judge to find detailed standards of medical treatment and hygiene in the shadow of constitutional guarantees should come as no surprise—even if he denies any creative role in the process.

Yet another factor may also bear on Judge Johnson's activist role in Alabama human rights struggles. He is not afraid of hard work; in fact, he is a compulsive worker. The hundreds, indeed thousands, of hours required to review and implement comprehensive human rights claims of the *Wyatt, Pugh-James* variety would not deter such a judge. This is not to suggest that all, or even most, judges who dismiss comprehensive claims are simply lazy. What is very strongly suggested, however, is that jurists of Judge Johnson's fortitude would not be inhibited by such considerations—while other judges might be.

Whatever the motivation, the judge's brand of judicial activism will continue to arouse the concern of those who contend that such jurists have usurped legislative prerogative and threaten the fabric of representative democracy. For the unwashed of society, however, such arguments will carry little weight. Where his critics see Judge Johnson's recent human rights decisions as affronts to basic constitutional principles, those with little or no voice in the political process will contend that his rulings have converted constitutional abstractions into living law. For them, perhaps, the awkwardly written plea of a prison inmate would best capture the essence of Judge Johnson's role in Alabama's human rights revolution. "I guess you're tired of hearing from us," he wrote the judge, "but you're the only one who seems to want to help."[25]

Notes

Preface

1. Daniel M. Berman, *A Bill Becomes a Law* (New York: Macmillan, 1966), pp. 135–36.
2. Interviews with Judge Frank M. Johnson, Jr., Montgomery, Ala., August 3, 5, 9, 12, 13, 1976; December 21, 1976; August 11, 1977; July 18, 1978; July 31, 1979 (hereinafter cited as Interviews with Judge Frank M. Johnson, Jr.).

Chapter 1: The Early Years

1. Thomas M. Owens, *History of Alabama and Dictionary of Alabama Biography*, II (Chicago: S. J. Clark, 1921), p. 1409; Wesley S. Thompson, "The Free State of Winston": A History of Winston County, Alabama (Winfield, Ala.: Pareil Press, 1968), pp. 3–5; Walter L. Fleming, *Civil War and Reconstruction in Alabama* (New York: Peter Smith, 1949), pp. 115–21; Bessie Martin, *Desertion of Alabama Troops from the Confederate Army* (New York: Columbia University Press, 1932), pp. 174–86, 220–31. For a vivid account of the atrocities committed by both sides in Alabama during the conflict, see Thompson, ch. 7.
2. V. O. Key, Jr., *Southern Politics in State and Nation* (New York: Vintage Books, 1949), pp. 280–83. For recent studies focusing on post-Reconstruction sectional politics in Alabama, see William Warren Rogers, *The One-Gallused Rebellion: Agrarianism in Alabama, 1865–1896* (Baton Rouge, La.: Louisiana State University Press, 1970), and Sheldon Hackney, *Populism to Progressivism in Alabama* (Princeton, N.J.: Princeton University Press, 1969).
3. Interviews with Judge Frank M. Johnson, Jr.
4. Ibid.; interview with Ruth Jenkins Johnson, Montgomery, Ala., August 17, 1976; interview with Jimmy Johnson, Montgomery, Ala., August 19, 1976.
5. Interviews with Judge Frank M. Johnson, Jr.
6. Ibid.; interview with Jimmy Johnson.
7. Ibid.
8. Interview with Lecil Gray, Tuscaloosa, Ala., July 25, 1977.
9. Interviews with Judge Frank M. Johnson, Jr.; interview with Ruth Jenkins Johnson.
10. Ibid.
11. Interview with Ruth Jenkins Johnson.
12. Ibid.
13. Ibid.
14. Interviews with Judge Frank M. Johnson, Jr.
15. Ibid. Judge Johnson beat his Democratic opponent by a margin of 2,049 to

934 (*Advertiser-Journal* [Haleyville, Ala.], November, 8, 1934).

16. Ibid.; interview with Ruth Jenkins Johnson.

17. Interview with Lee P. Dodd, Double Springs, Ala., July 23, 1977.

18. Ibid.; interview with Ruth Jenkins Johnson.

19. Ibid.

20. Ibid.

21. Interview with Ruth Jenkins Johnson.

22. Ibid.

23. Ibid.

24. Ibid.

25. Ibid.; *Advertiser-Journal*, January 25, 1940, May 30, 1940, November 5, 1942; *Birmingham Post*, June 21, 1943. The reasons for the senior Johnson's decision not to seek reelection as probate judge are now obscure. A newspaper description of a county Republican meeting held in early 1940 indicated that he was withdrawing from consideration in the interest of party harmony but provided no further explanation. Ruth Johnson has suggested that he withdrew because his income as probate judge had been inadequate for his large family (interview with Ruth Jenkins Johnson).

26. Interviews with Judge Frank M. Johnson, Jr.

27. Interview with Ruth Jenkins Johnson. For a contemporary account of life at the university when the Johnsons were enrolled there, see Carl Carmer, *Stars Fell on Alabama* (New York: Farrar and Rinehart, 1934).

28. Interview with Ruth Jenkins Johsnon.

29. Ibid.; interviews with Judge Frank M. Johnson, Jr.

30. Ibid.; interview with Jimmy Johnson.

31. Interview with Ruth Jenkins Johnson. For humorous anecdotes involving Johnson and Wallace during their years at the university, see Robert F. Kennedy, Jr., *Judge Frank M. Johnson, Jr.* (New York: Putnam, 1978), ch. 4; Marshall Frady, *Wallace* (New York: New American Library, 1968), pp. 77–78.

32. Interview with Glen Curlee, Elmore County, Ala., December 22, 1976.

33. Interview with Ruth Jenkins Johnson; interviews with Judge Frank M. Johnson, Jr.

34. Ibid.

35. Ibid.; *New York Times*, February 7, 1964, p. 28.

36. Interviews with Judge Frank M. Johnson, Jr.

37. "Crime and Punishment," *Time*, December 31, 1945, pp. 20–21.

38. Unless otherwise indicated, the following discussion and quotations regarding the Lichfield trials are drawn from official army records and transcripts in court-martial proceedings in *United States v. Jones* (1946) and *United States v. Smith* (1946), Army Court of Military Review, Washington, D.C.

39. Interviews with Judge Frank M. Johnson, Jr.; "Crime and Punishment," pp. 20–21.

40. *Stars and Stripes* (W. Eur. ed.), December 5, 6, 7, 8, 9, 13, 18, 19, 1945.

41. Ibid., December 15, 16, 1945.

42. Ibid., December 7, 8, 1945.

43. Interviews with Judge Frank M. Johnson, Jr.

44. Ibid. The trial transcript leaves the impression that only Colonel Brand contacted Judge Johnson, but the judge vividly recalls his meeting with Betts as

well. For an example of the unfavorable treatment given Smith's trial in the American press, see "Gestapo, U.S. Style," *Newsweek*, January 1, 1946, pp. 40–41.

45. "Overseas: Lichfield Fireworks," *Newsweek*, April 15, 1946, pp. 36–37.

46. Interviews with Judge Frank M. Johnson, Jr.

47. Ibid.

48. *Washington Post*, April 11, 1946; interview with Ruth Jenkins Johnson.

49. Interviews with Judge Frank M. Johnson, Jr.

50. "The Colonel and the Private," *Time*, September 9, 1946, p. 28.

51. Interviews with Judge Frank M. Johnson, Jr.

Chapter 2: Twentieth-Century Slavery

1. *Jasper Advertiser*, October 10, 1947.

2. Interview with Ruth Jenkins Johnson.

3. Ibid.; *Jasper Advertiser*, June 6, 1947; *Mountain Eagle* (Jasper, Ala.), February 26, 1948.

4. Interview with Lecil Gray.

5. Ibid.

6. Ibid.

7. Interviews with Judge Frank M. Johnson, Jr.

8. Interview with Ruth Jenkins Johnson; interview with Lecil Gray.

9. Interviews with Judge Frank M. Johnson, Jr.; *Haleyville Advertiser*, December 5, 1946, March 18, 1948.

10. Interviews with Judge Frank M. Johnson, Jr.; *Haleyville Advertiser*, December 5, 1946, March 18, 1948, November 11, 1948, February 17, 1949.

11. *Haleyville Advertiser*, March 24, 1949.

12. Interviews with Judge Frank M. Johnson, Jr.

13. Ibid.

14. *Walker County Times* (Jasper, Ala.), September 6, 1951.

15. Ibid., September 6, 13, 1951, October 4, 1951.

16. Ibid., October 11, 1951; interview with Lecil Gray.

17. Interviews with Judge Frank M. Johnson, Jr.; *Walker County Times*, December 13, 1951.

18. Interview with Ruth Jenkins Johnson.

19. Interviews with Judge Frank M. Johnson, Jr.; *Birmingham Post-Herald*, October 24, 1955.

20. *Birmingham News*, September 20, 1955; *Mountain Eagle*, October 2, 1952; *Birmingham Post-Herald*, August 20, 1952.

21. *Birmingham News*, July 15, 1952.

22. Interviews with Judge Frank M. Johnson, Jr.; interview with Ruth Jenkins Johnson.

23. Interview with Gene Bell, Birmingham, Ala., July 30, 1977; interview with Judge Seybourn H. Lynne, Birmingham, Ala., December 28, 1977. During Judge Johnson's tenure as U.S. attorney, Gene Bell was deputy clerk in the district court for the Northern District of Alabama.

24. Interview with Judge Seybourn H. Lynne.

25. Interviews with Judge Frank M. Johnson, Jr.

26. No transcript was made of the subsequent trial, but a copy of the indictment and other pertinent records of the case are on file in *United States* v. *Dial*, Criminal Case 1348 (1954), Federal Records Center, Atlanta, Ga. Unless otherwise indicated, the following discussion of the case is based on those records.

27. Interview with Roderick Beddow, Jr., Birmingham, Ala., July 29, 1977.

28. *Montgomery Advertiser*, May 31, 1956; interview with Judge Seybourn H. Lynne; interviews with Judge Frank M. Johnson, Jr.

29. Interview with Gene Bell.

30. *Birmingham Post-Herald*, May 11, 1954.

31. Ibid., May 12, 1954.

32. Ibid., May 11, 1954.

33. *Birmingham News*, May 11, 12, 1954.

34. Interviews with Judge Frank M. Johnson, Jr.

35. Ibid.; *Birmingham Post-Herald*, May 13, 1954.

36. Interviews with Judge Frank M. Johnson, Jr.

37. *Birmingham News*, May 13, 1954.

38. Interviews with Judge Frank M. Johnson, Jr.; *Birmingham News*, May 13, 1954.

39. Interview with Roderick Beddow, Jr.

40. *Birmingham Post-Herald*, May 13, 1954; *Birmingham News*, May 13, 1954.

41. *Birmingham News*, May 13, 1954.

42. Ibid.; interviews with Judge Frank M. Johnson, Jr.

43. *Birmingham News*, May 13, 1954.

44. *Birmingham Post-Herald*, May 14, 1954.

45. Interviews with Judge Frank M. Johnson, Jr.

46. Interview with Judge Seybourn H. Lynne.

47. Ibid.; interview with Gene Bell.

48. Interview with Judge Seybourn H. Lynne.

49. Interview with Roderick Beddow, Jr. For a discussion of other Alabama peonage convictions, the vast majority of which resulted from plea negotiations rather than trial, see Pete Daniel, *The Shadow of Slavery: Peonage in the South, 1901–1969* (Urbana, Ill.: University of Illinois Press, 1972), chs. 3 and 4. See also Robert K. Carr, *Federal Protection of Civil Rights: Quest for a Sword* (Ithaca, N.Y.: Cornell University Press, 1947), pp. 79–80; Daniel A. Novak, *The Wheel of Servitude: Black Forced Labor after Slavery* (Lexington, Ky.: University Press of Kentucky, 1978), pp. 47–64.

Chapter 3: The Judgeship

1. *Birmingham Post-Herald*, October 24, 1955; *Birmingham News*, November 2, 1955; interview with Ruth Jenkins Johnson.

2. Interview with Ruth Jenkins Johnson; letter to author from Herbert Brownell, July 2, 1964.

3. With the judge's approval, the author was allowed, consistent with current privacy regulations, to examine the contents of the file maintained on Judge Johnson in the office of the deputy attorney general, U.S. Department of Justice, Washington, D.C.

4. Interview with Lecil Gray.

5. Interview with Ruth Jenkins Johnson; *Birmingham Post-Herald*, June 30, 1955.

6. *Washington Post*, November 6, 1955; *Birmingham Post-Herald*, June 30, 1955, July 26, 1955.

7. Interview with Vaughn Hill Robison, Montgomery, Ala., August 12, 1976; *Montgomery Advertiser*, July 1, 1955.

8. Justice Department file on Judge Frank M. Johnson, Jr.

9. Interviews with Judge Frank M. Johnson, Jr.; *Birmingham News*, October 23, 1955.

10. *Montgomery Advertiser*, November 8, 1955.

11. U.S., *Congressional Record*, 84th Cong., 2d Sess., 1956, CII, Part 2, 1717.

12. Interviews with Judge Frank M. Johnson, Jr.; interview with Jack Vann, Montgomery, Ala., August 19, 1976. Vann and his family were close neighborhood friends during the years the Johnsons lived on Haardt Drive.

13. Interview with Jack Vann; interviews with Judge Frank M. Johnson, Jr.; interview with Sam Durden, Montgomery, Ala., August 13, 1976.

14. Interviews with Judge Frank M. Johnson, Jr.; interview with Jimmy Johnson.

15. Interview with Lee P. Dodd; interview with Judge Leon Hopper, Montgomery, Ala., August 18, 1976; interview with Glynn Henderson, Montgomery, Ala., August 12, 1976.

16. Interview with Robert Segall, Montgomery, Ala., August 11, 1976.

17. Interviews with Judge Frank M. Johnson, Jr.

18. Ibid.; interview with Dorothy Perry, Montgomery, Ala., August 19, 1976; interview with Howard Mandell, Montgomery, Ala., August 19, 1976.

19. Interviews with Judge Frank M. Johnson, Jr.

20. Ibid.; *Montgomery Advertiser*, December 6, 1969.

21. Ibid.; *New York Times*, February 7, 1964, p. 28; interview with Ira DeMent, Montgomery, Ala., August 18, 1976. DeMent was U.S. attorney for the Middle District during the administrations of Presidents Nixon and Ford.

22. Interview with Vaughn Hill Robison; interview with Earl Pippen, Montgomery, Ala., August 16, 1976; interview with Walter Turner, Montgomery, Ala., August 10, 1976. Walter Turner is a former Johnson law clerk.

23. Interview with George Dean, Destin, Fla., August 8, 1976.

24. Interviews with Judge Frank M. Johnson, Jr.; interviews with Ruth Jenkins Johnson; *New York Times*, June 3, 1965, p. 23.

25. Interview with Representative William Dickinson, Washington, D.C., June 2, 1977.

26. "The Two Judges," *Time*, January 26, 1959, p. 22; *Montgomery Advertiser*, June 14, 1958.

27. *Birmingham News*, April 9, 1961; "A Lincoln Man," *Time*, February 21, 1964, p. 76.

28. *Belvin v. United States*, 273 F. 2d 583 (5th Cir., 1960); interviews with Judge Frank M. Johnson, Jr.; interview with Lee P. Dodd.

29. *Hawkins v. United States*, 303 F. 2d 536 (5th Cir., 1962).

30. Interview with Walter Turner; interview with Richard Gill, Montgomery, Ala., August 11, 1976.

31. Interview with Dorothy Perry; *Grau v. Proctor & Gamble Co.*, 32 F.R.D.

199, 201 (M.D. Ala., 1963); "The Legal (ha ha) Mind at Work," *New Yorker*, July 6, 1963, p. 53.

32. Interview with Robert Segall; interview with Walter Turner.

33. Interview with Howard Mandell.

Chapter 4: Bus Boycotts and Pariahs

1. Interviews with Judge Frank M. Johnson, Jr.

2. Key, *Southern Politics in State and Nation*, p. 319.

3. Interviews with Judge Frank M. Johnson, Jr.

4. Ibid.

5. Ibid.

6. Interview with Ruth Jenkins Johnson.

7. Interview with Richard Gill; *Plessy* v. *Ferguson*, 163 U.S. 537 (1896). Pressed in an interview with the author to pinpoint the period when he first came to attach a color-blind construction to the Constitution, Judge Johnson was unable to provide a definite response. Racial segregation was such a widely accepted pattern of Alabama life, however, that he probably gave the question little serious thought until the first *Brown* decision in 1954. He does recall, however, that he went on the bench supporting Justice Harlan's thesis.

8. *Brown* v. *Board of Education*, 347 U.S. 483 (1954); *Fleming* v. *South Carolina Electric and Gas Co.*, 224 F. 2d 752 (4th Cir., 1955), appeal dismissed, 351 U.S. 901 (1956).

9. For an interesting discussion of the events surrounding Rosa Parks's arrest and the boycott it spawned, see Janet Stevenson, *The Montgomery Bus Boycott* (New York: Franklin Watts, Inc., 1971), pp. 1–10. Though tailored for a juvenile audience, the Stevenson study draws heavily on personal interviews which give her account a life other descriptions lack. See also David L. Lewis, *King: A Critical Biography* (New York: Praeger, 1970), ch. 3; William R. Miller, *Martin Luther King, Jr.* (New York: Weybright and Talley, 1968), ch. 3.

10. Stevenson, *Bus Boycott*, pp. 19–23.

11. Ibid., pp. 27–31; "Alabama—Why Race Relations Could Grow Even Worse," *Newsweek*, March 5, 1956, p. 25; *Montgomery Advertiser*, February 15, 1956, January 9, 1956.

12. *Birmingham News*, June 5, 1956; *New York Times*, April 24, 1956, p. 2; *Montgomery Advertiser*, January 13, 1956. For an example of local reporting which at least bordered on editorializing, see *Montgomery Advertiser*, March 9, 1956.

13. Stevenson, *Bus Boycott*, pp. 35–37.

14. Ibid., pp. 32–34; *Montgomery Advertiser*, November 15, 1956.

15. "Alabama—Why Race Relations Could Grow Even Worse," p. 25.

16. *Montgomery Advertiser*, January 4, 1956; *Mobile Press*, June 18, 19, 1956; Stevenson, *Bus Boycott*, pp. 42–44.

17. *Montgomery Advertiser*, May 31, 1956.

18. Interview with Judge Richard T. Rives, Montgomery, Ala., August 17, 1976; *Smith* v. *Allwright*, 321 U.S. 649 (1944); *Montgomery Advertiser*, April 20, 1946. For a discussion of the events surrounding the Boswell Amendment's adoption, see *Davis* v. *Schnell*, 81 F. Supp. 872 (M.D. Ala., 1949), in which a

three-judge district court, composed entirely of native Alabamians, declared the provision unconstitutional. See also William D. Barnard, *Dixiecrats and Democrats* (University of Alabama Press, 1974), ch. 4. Perhaps the most significant voting case in which Rives represented Alabama voting registrars charged with racial discrimination was *Mitchell* v. *Wright*, 62 F. Supp. 580 (M.D. Ala., 1945), 154 F. 2d 924 (5th Cir., 1946), 69 F. Supp. 698 (M.D. Ala., 1947). For a discussion of *Mitchell*, albeit one that omits treatment of Rives's role, see Charles V. Hamilton, *The Bench and the Ballot* (New York: Oxford University Press, 1973), pp. 32–34.

19. Interview with Judge Richard T. Rives. The several sources who suggested that Judge Rives's liberal decisions in civil rights cases may have been prompted partly by a desire to let his son's ideals live on in his decisions prefer anonymity.

20. *Montgomery Advertiser*, February 24, 1956.

21. *New York Times*, April 26, 1956, p. 27; *City of Montgomery v. Montgomery City Lines, Inc.*, 1 Race Rel. L. Rep. 535 (1956). For a summary of Judge Jones's significant role in Alabama's battles to preserve racial segregation, see George Osborne, "The NAACP in Alabama," in C. Herman Pritchett and Alan F. Westin, eds., *The Third Branch of Government* (New York: Harcourt, 1963), pp. 158–59.

22. *Montgomery Advertiser*, May 12, 1956; *Birmingham News*, May 12, 1956.

23. Interview with Judge Seybourn H. Lynne.

24. Ibid.; interviews with Judge Frank M. Johnson, Jr.; interview with Judge Richard T. Rives.

25. *Browder* v. *Gayle*, 142 F. Supp. 707, 715–17 (M.D. Ala., 1956).

26. *Montgomery Advertiser*, June 27, 1956.

27. Stevenson, *Bus Boycott*, pp. 47–49.

28. *Montgomery Advertiser*, October 27, 1956; *Gayle* v. *Browder*, 77 S. Ct. 145 (1956).

29. *Birmingham Post-Herald*, June 6, 1956; *Montgomery Advertiser*, December 21, 1956.

30. Stevenson, *Bus Boycott*, pp. 55–57.

31. Interview with Judge Richard T. Rives.

32. Ibid.; interview with Ray Jenkins, Montgomery, Ala., August 11, 1976.

33. Interview with Judge Richard T. Rives.

34. Ibid.; "The Fascinating and Frantic Fifth," *Time*, December 4, 1964, p. 46; *Time*, December 11, 1964, p. 20.

35. Interview with Ruth Jenkins Johnson; Justice Department file on Judge Frank M. Johnson, Jr.; interview with Jack Vann; *Alabama Journal* (Montgomery, Ala.), January 29, 1957.

36. Interview with Ruth Jenkins Johnson; *New York Times*, February 7, 1964, p. 28C.

37. Justice Department file on Judge Frank M. Johnson, Jr.; interview with Ruth Jenkins Johnson.

38. Interview with Lee P. Dodd.

39. Interview with Ruth Jenkins Johnson; interviews with Judge Frank M. Johnson, Jr.

40. Interview with Howard Mandell.

41. Interviews with Judge Frank M. Johnson, Jr.

42. *Gilmore v. City of Montgomery*, 176 F. Supp. 776 (M.D. Ala., 1959); *Cobb v. Montgomery Library Board*, 207 F. Supp. 880 (M.D. Ala., 1962); *Lewis v. Greyhound Corporation*, 199 F. Supp. 210 (M.D. Ala., 1961).

Chapter 5: The Big Judge and the Little Judge

1. U.S., *Statutes at Large*, LXXI, 635.

2. Proceedings of Alabama State Bar, 70th Meeting, Birmingham, Ala., August 8–9, 1947.

3. *New York Times*, October 22, 1958, p. 1.

4. Ibid., December 3, 1958, p. 28, December 7, 1958, p. 57.

5. *Advertiser-Journal* (Montgomery, Ala.), January 25, 1976. This citation is to the initial installment of a four-part series by Harold E. Martin, editor and publisher of the *Montgomery Advertiser*, on the first of George Wallace's many confrontations with Judge Johnson. The series appeared in the January 25–28, 1976, issues of the *Advertiser*.

6. *Montgomery Advertiser*, January 26, 1976.

7. For a profile of John Patterson, see Osborne, "NAACP in Alabama," p. 155.

8. Interview with John Patterson, Montgomery, Ala., August 11, 1976.

9. Ibid. During his gubernatorial campaign, however, Patterson came close to openly seeking Ku Klux Klan support; see Numan V. Bartley, *The Rise of Massive Resistance* (Baton Rouge, La.: Louisiana State University Press, 1969), pp. 201–2. Bartley's study is the most thorough analysis to date of the many varieties of massive resistance.

10. *New York Times*, December 9, 1958, p. 1.

11. Unless otherwise indicated, the discussion and quotations in this chapter are drawn from official records and transcripts of *In Re Wallace*, CA 1487-N (1959), and *United States v. Wallace*, Criminal Case 11098-N (1959), on file in the U.S. District Court, Montgomery, Ala.

12. Interview with John Patterson.

13. *Montgomery Advertiser*, January 27, 1976.

14. Interview with Glen Curlee. Apparently, there was some substance to Curlee's concern about preventing extremists from taking control of the Elmore County Council. In his study of the Citizens Council movement, Neil R. McMillen reports that the state association repudiated the Elmore County chapter after the local group circulated anti-Semitic literature (*The Citizens' Council* [Urbana, Ill.: University of Illinois Press, 1971], pp. 55–56 n. 39).

15. Interview with Glen Curlee.

16. Interviews with Judge Frank M. Johnson, Jr.

17. Interview with Glen Curlee.

18. *Montgomery Advertiser*, January 27, 1976.

19. *Star* (Washington, D.C.), January 16, 1959; *Montgomery Advertiser*, January 28, 1976.

20. *United States v. Wallace*, 188 F. Supp. 759 (M.D. Ala., 1959).

21. A copy of the statement is contained in the private files of Judge Frank M. Johnson, Jr., U.S. District Court, Montgomery, Ala.

22. *Montgomery Advertiser*, January 28, 1976.

23. Ibid.; interviews with Judge Frank M. Johnson, Jr.

24. *Montgomery Advertiser*, January 27, 1959; interview with Glen Curlee.

25. Interview with Glen Curlee.

Chapter 6: Black Voters and Freedom Riders

1. Bernard Taper, *Gomillion versus Lightfoot* (New York: McGraw-Hill, 1962), p. 13.

2. Ibid., p. 14; *Birmingham News*, October 31, 1958; *Acts of Alabama, 1957*, No. 140.

3. Taper, *Gomillion versus Lightfoot*, p. 22.

4. *Laramie Co. v. Albany Co.*, 92 U.S. 307 (1875); *Hunter v. Pittsburgh*, 207 U.S. 161 (1907); *Doyle v. Continental Ins. Co.*, 94 U.S. 535 (1876); *Gomillion v. Lightfoot*, 167 F. Supp. 405, 410 (M.D. Ala., 1958).

5. *Montgomery Advertiser*, October 30, 1958; *Birmingham News*, October 31, 1958.

6. *Gomillion v. Lightfoot*, 270 F. 2d 594, 598–99, 611 (5th Cir., 1959).

7. *Gomillion v. Lightfoot*, 364 U.S. 339 (1960).

8. Ibid., pp. 347, 349.

9. *Gomillion v. Rutherford*, 6 Race Rel. L. Rap. 241, 243 (M.D. Ala., 1961); interviews with Judge Frank M. Johnson, Jr.

10. *Acts of Alabama, 1957*, No. 526; interview with John Patterson.

11. For a brief summary of discriminatory voting devices by President Kennedy's assistant attorney general for civil rights, see Burke Marshall, *Federalism and Civil Rights* (New York: Columbia University Press, 1964), pp. 10–41. For a very thorough account, see generally Steven F. Lawson, *Black Ballots: Voting Rights in the South, 1944–1969* (New York: Columbia University Press, 1976).

12. Hamilton, *Bench and Ballot*, pp. 89–90.

13. Discussed in *United States v. Raines*, 362 U.S. 17 (1960).

14. *New York Times*, February 7, 1959, p. 1.

15. Ibid., February 24, 1959, p. 22; *United States v. Alabama*, 171 F. Supp. 720, 730, 729 (M.D. Ala., 1959).

16. *Montgomery Advertiser*, March 7, 1959; *New York Times*, March 7, 1959, p. 1.

17. U.S., *Statutes at Large*, LXXIV, 92.

18. *New York Times*, July 24, 1959, p. 26, May 27, 1960, p. 12.

19. *United States v. Alabama*, 188 F. Supp. 759 (M.D. Ala., 1960).

20. *United States v. Alabama*, 192 F. Supp. 677, 682, 683 (M.D. Ala., 1961).

21. Interviews with Judge Frank M. Johnson, Jr.; *Birmingham Post-Herald*, March 18, 1961.

22. *Birmingham News*, March 18, 1961; *Montgomery Advertiser*, March 18, 1961.

23. *New York Times*, May 21, 1961, p. 1, IV, p. 9; *Birmingham News*, June 4, 1961. Unless otherwise indicated, the following discussion and quotations relating to the freedom rider litigation in Judge Johnson's court are drawn from the records and transcript filed for *United States v. U.S. Klans*, CA 1718-N

(1961), on file in the U.S. District Court, Montgomery, Ala.

24. *New York Times,* May 21, 1961, p. 1.

25. Ibid.

26. Ibid.

27. Ibid., May 22, 1961, p. 1.

28. *Advertiser-Journal,* June 4, 1961; *New York Times,* June 4, 1961, IV, p. 10.

29. *New York Times,* November 2, 1961, p. 1.

30. *Alabama v. United States,* 304 F. 2d 583 (5th Cir., 1962).

31. See, for example, Judge Cameron's dissent in *Boman v. Birmingham Transit Co.,* 292 F. 2d 4, 28 (5th Cir., 1961).

32. *Alabama v. United States,* 304 F. 2d 583, 611 (5th Cir., 1962); Berman, *A Bill Becomes a Law;* for a discussion of congressional debates over the 1960 act's referee provisions, see ibid., pp. 41–52.

33. *Alabama v. United States,* 83 S. Ct. 145 (1962); *United States v. Raines,* 362 U.S. 17, 22 (1960).

34. *Montgomery Advertiser,* June 7, 1960; *Alabama ex rel. Gallion v. Rogers,* 187 F. Supp. 848 (M.D. Ala., 1960).

35. *United States v. Alabama,* 7 Race Rel. L. Rep. 1146 (M.D. Ala., 1962); *United States v. Penton,* 212 F. Supp. 193 (M.D. Ala., 1962). Judge Johnson's comments to the Bullock registrars are drawn from a Justice Department transcript of in-chambers conferences, quoted in Hamilton, *Bench and Ballot,* pp. 106–8.

36. This discussion of Judge Cox is drawn from Lawson, *Black Ballots,* pp. 272–75, and Donald S. Strong, *Negroes, Ballots, and Judges* (University, Ala.: University of Alabama Press, 1968), ch. 3. Victor Navasky, *Kennedy Justice* (New York: Atheneum, 1971), ch. 5, attacks the Kennedy administration record in southern federal court appointments.

37. Kenneth N. Vines, "Federal District Judges and Race Relations Cases in the South," *Journal of Politics,* 26 (May 1964), 347; *United States v. Atkins,* 210 F. Supp. 441, 443 (S.D. Ala., 1962), 323 F. 2d 733 (5th Cir., 1963); *United States v. Logue,* 344 F. 2d 290 (5th Cir., 1965). For a classification of southern district judges into "judicial aggressor," "judicial gradualist," and "judicial resistor" categories, see Lawson, *Black Ballots,* p. 272. Jack Walter Peltason, *Fifty-eight Lonely Men* (New York: Harcourt, 1961), is an excellent early study of the conflicting pressures that confronted southern federal judges in the aftermath of *Brown* and the 1957 Civil Rights Act.

38. *Birmingham News,* April 19, 1962, May 18, 1962, April 11, 1962.

39. *Alabama Journal,* April 18, 1962; *Birmingham News,* April 10, 1962.

40. *Montgomery Advertiser,* March 4, 1962; Frady, *Wallace,* p. 133.

41. *Montgomery Advertiser,* October 12, 1962.

42. *Advertiser-Journal,* October 4, 1962; interview with Judge Richard T. Rives.

43. *United States v. Parker,* 236 F. Supp. 511 (M.D. Ala., 1964); *United States v. Cartwright,* 230 F. Supp. 873 (M.D. Ala., 1964).

Chapter 7: Schools

1. For incisive discussions of massive resistance tactics focusing on school desegregation, see Francis M. Wilhoit, *The Politics of Massive Resistance* (New

York: George Braziller, 1973), ch. 7, and Albert P. Blaustein and Clarence C. Ferguson, Jr., *Desegregation and the Law* (New Brunswick, N.J.: Rutgers University Press, 1957), ch. 15. McMillen, *The Citizens' Council*, is the best treatment to date of that organization; and the modern flowering of the Ku Klux Klan is captured in Patsy Sims, *The Klan* (New York: Stein and Day, 1978). Benjamin Muse, *Ten Years of Prelude* (New York: Viking, 1964), is an excellent survey of obstructions to desegregation in the first decade following *Brown*.

2. *Southern School News*, August 1955, p. 13.

3. Ibid.

4. *Lucy v. Adams*, 134 F. Supp. 235 (N.D. Ala., 1955); *New York Times*, March 2, 1956, p. 1, January 19, 1957, p. 10, July 21, 1957, p. 12; *Acts of Alabama, 1955*, No. 201; *Shuttlesworth v. Birmingham Bd. of Education*, 162 F. Supp. 372 (N.D. Ala., 1958).

5. *Shuttlesworth v. Birmingham Bd. of Education*, 358 U.S. 101 (1958).

6. *Lee v. Macon County*, 221 F. Supp. 298, 299 (M.D. Ala., 1963).

7. *Armstrong v. Bd. of Education*, 323 F. 2d 333 (5th Cir., 1963), reversing 220 F. Supp. 217 (N.D. Ala., 1963); *Davis v. Board of Education*, 322 F. 2d 356, 358 (5th Cir., 1963), reversing 219 F. Supp. 542, 545–46 (S.D. Ala., 1963).

8. In *United States v. Wallace*, 218 F. Supp. 290, 292 (N.D. Ala., 1963), Judge Lynne had enjoined Wallace not to interfere with desegregation at the university, but to no avail. Even while organizing his new administration, Wallace had continued to pound away bitterly at Judge Johnson and other federal judges. And when several of his legislative leaders had urged him to tone down his attacks, his response was invariably the same: "Ya'll don't be sissy; these people are trying to take over the country." Wallace had always been careful, however, to except Judge Lynne from such attacks. Lynne's dissent in the Montgomery bus case, a member of Wallace's first administration and later political opponent has explained, "kind of put the white hat on Judge Lynne and the black hat on Judge Johnson, no racial significance intended"(interview with Albert P. Brewer, Montgomery, Ala., August 17, 1976). Wallace was probably reluctant, therefore, to defy a Lynne court order. But politics was politics. *Southern School News*, September 1963, p. 2; *New York Times*, September 3, 1963, p. 1, September 5, 1963, p. 1; *Montgomery Advertiser*, September 3, 1963.

9. "A Shameful Thing," *Time*, September 13, 1963, p. 26; *Southern School News*, September 1963, p. 2; *Birmingham News*, September 3, 1963; *Birmingham Post-Herald*, September 3, 1963; Grover Hall, Jr., was quoted in *New York Times*, September 7, 1963, p. 1.

10. *Executive Orders*, No. 10, 11, 12, 8 Race Rel. L. Rep. 913 (1963).

11. *Lee v. Macon County*, 8 Race Rel. L. Rep. 916, 917 (1963).

12. 8 Race Rel. L. Rep. 919 (1963); *New York Times*, September 11, 1963, p. 1. The best analysis to date of the Kennedy administration's role in modern civil rights reform is Carl M. Brauer, *John F. Kennedy and the Second Reconstruction* (New York: Columbia University Press, 1977).

13. *Montgomery Advertiser*, September 15, 20, 1963.

14. *Opinion of the Justices*, No. 179, 156 So. 2d 639 (Ala. Sup. Ct., 1963); *Montgomery Advertiser*, September 25, 1963; *Birmingham News*, September 25, 1963.

15. *Montgomery Advertiser*, September 25, 1963; *United States v. Wallace*,

222 F. Supp. 485 (M.D. Ala., 1963).

16. *Franklin v. Parker*, 223 F. Supp. 724, 725–26 (M.D. Ala., 1963); 8 Race Rel. L. Rep. 1388 (1963); *Southern School News*, January 1964, p. 1.

17. *Lee v. Macon County*, CA 604-E (1964) (slip opinion); *Montgomery Advertiser*, January 31, 1964.

18. *Birmingham Post-Herald*, February 4, 1964.

19. *New York Times*, February 5, 1964, p. 19.

20. *Alabama Journal*, February 5, 1964.

21. Ibid.; *Opelika-Auburn News*, May 12, 1974; *New York Times*, February 6, 1964, p. 1.

22. *Alabama Journal*, February 5, 1964; *Opelika-Auburn News*, May 12, 1974; *New York Times*, February 6, 1964, p. 1.

23. *New York Times*, February 7, 1964, p. 28C; *United States v. Rea*, CA 637-E (1964) (slip opinion).

24. *Opinion of the Justices*, No. 180, 160 So. 2d 648 (Ala. Sup. Ct., 1964).

25. *Lee v. Macon County*, 231 F. Supp. 743 (M.D. Ala., 1964).

26. *Birmingham Post-Herald*, February 6, 1964; *Birmingham News*, August 4, 1964; *Alabama Journal*, August 6, 1964; *Southern School News*, May 1964, p. 3-A.

27. Interview with Jack Vann.

Chapter 8: Selma

1. Lewis, *King*, ch. 7, thoroughly examines the Birmingham demonstrations. See also Miller, *King*, ch. 7.

2. Benjamin Muse, *The American Negro Revolution* (Bloomington, Ind.: Indiana University Press, 1969), ch. 6, discusses the act's provisions and the politics behind its adoption.

3. For a detailed summary of 1964 voter registration figures in Alabama Black Belt counties, see *Williams v. Wallace*, 240 F. Supp. 100, 112–20 (M.D. Ala., 1965).

4. Unless otherwise indicated, the discussion and quotations in the remainder of this chapter are drawn from the official records and transcript for *Williams v. Wallace*, CA 2181-N (1965), on file in the U.S. District Court, Montgomery, Ala. David J. Garrow, *Protest at Selma* (New Haven, Conn.: Yale University Press, 1978), is the most detailed account to date of the Selma voter registration drive. See also Lawson, *Black Ballots*, ch. 10; Muse, *The American Negro Revolution*, ch. 11; Lewis, *King*, ch. 9.

5. *Birmingham News*, March 5, 1965.

6. *New York Times*, March 9, 1965, p. 1.

7. *Herald Tribune* (New York), March 10, 1965.

8. *New York Times*, March 9, 1965, p. 1.

9. Ibid.; *Birmingham Post-Herald*, March 8, 1965. The evaluation of the Selma *Times-Journal* reporting and that of other state papers is drawn from *New York Times*, March 9, 1965, p. 1.

10. *New York Times*, March 14, 1965, p. 1, March 16, 1965, p. 1.

11. Interview with Walter Turner. Although seeking court protection for further marches, King and his followers no doubt realized the value of violent

racist reaction to their civil rights efforts. David Garrow has contended, in fact, that by late 1964 King had come to recognize the futility of nonviolent "persuasion," in which peaceful protest was directed at reforming segregationist hearts and minds, and was pursuing instead a policy of nonviolent "coercion," in which peaceful protests, coupled with violent opponents, produced a sympathetic American populace. See Garrow, *Protest at Selma*, ch. 7.

12. *New York Times*, March 10, 1965, p. 1; *Herald Tribune*, March 10, 1965. Lawson, *Black Ballots*, pp. 310–11, indicates that Collins and Justice Department attorney John Doar arranged the compromise, but also notes that Doar has since denied a part in any arrangement and claimed that he did not know what King would do (ibid., pp. 420–21 n. 84). Judge Johnson was aware of the negotiations and informally approved the compromise (interviews with Judge Frank M. Johnson, Jr.).

13. *New York Times*, March 10, 1965, p. 1, March 12, 1965, p. 1; *Herald Tribune*, March 10, 1965; interviews with Judge Frank M. Johnson, Jr.

14. *New York Times*, March 16, 1965, p. 1.

15. Ibid.

16. Interview with Walter Turner; interview with Ruth Jenkins Johnson; interviews with Judge Frank M. Johnson, Jr.

17. *Williams v. Wallace*, 240 F. Supp. 100, 108 (M.D. Ala., 1965).

18. See, for example, *Edwards v. South Carolina*, 372 U.S. 229 (1963); *Cox v. Louisiana*, 379 U.S. 536 (1965).

19. *New York Times*, March 19, 1965, p. 20, March 21, 1965, p. 76.

20. Ibid., March 19, 1965, p. 20; *Birmingham News*, March 26, 1965. For Alabama press reaction to the order, see, for example, *Alabama Journal*, March 19, 1965.

21. *New York Times*, March 19, 1965, p. 20, March 20, 1965, p. 1.

22. Ibid.

23. Ibid., March 21, 1965, p. 76; "Civil Rights; Electric Charges," *Time*, March 26, 1965, p. 19.

24. *Birmingham News*, March 22, 1965.

25. See Lewis, *King*, pp. 286–93.

26. *New York Times*, March 25, 1965, p. 1.

27. The atmosphere of the march and its climax in Montgomery are perhaps best captured in Lewis, *King*, pp. 286–93.

28. Interviews with Judge Frank M. Johnson, Jr.; interview with Judge Richard T. Rives.

29. *New York Times*, March 25, 1965, p. 1.

30. Ibid.

31. Interview with Walter Turner; interview with Ruth Jenkins Johnson.

32. *Birmingham News*, March 27, 1965, August 27, 1965, January 23, 1965.

33. For an example of Justice Black's thinking on the issue, see *Brown v. Louisiana*, 383 U.S. 131, 166–68 (1966) (dissenting). Interviews with Judge Frank M. Johnson, Jr.

34. *Cochran v. City of Eufaula*, 251 F. Supp. 981 (M.D. Ala., 1966); *McMeans v. Mayor's Court*, 247 F. Supp. 606 (M.D. Ala., 1965); *Johnson v. City of Montgomery*, 245 F. Supp. 25 (M.D. Ala., 1965); *Forman v. City of Montgomery*, 245 F. Supp. 17, 24–25 (M.D. Ala., 1965).

For an example of Judge Johnson's off-the-bench statements on the subject, see "Civil Disobedience and the Law," *Vanderbilt Law Review*, 22 (October 1969), 1089–1110. Former Supreme Court Justice Abe Fortas, *Concerning Dissent and Civil Disobedience* (New York: New American Library, 1968), provides a somewhat more sympathetic view of protest movements. A number of national and Alabama newspapers editorially applauded Judge Johnson's stance. See, for example, *Arizona Republic*, August 14, 1965; *Alabama Journal*, August 5, 1965; *Herald Tribune*, August 5, 1965.

35. Interviews with Judge Frank M. Johnson, Jr. On the growing public distaste for protest movements in the late 1960s, see Tinsley E. Yarbrough, "Justice Black and His Critics on Speech-Plus and Symbolic Speech," *Texas Law Review*, 52 (January 1974), 281.

36. *Birmingham Post-Herald*, March 17, 1965; interview with Representative William Dickinson. Lawson, *Black Ballots*, chs. 10 and 11, discusses the adoption and early implementation of the 1965 Voting Rights Act.

Chapter 9: Mrs. Liuzzo

1. *Alabama Journal*, March 26, 1965.

2. *New York Times*, December 4, 1965, p. 20.

3. Ibid., March 26, 1965, p. 1, March 27, 1965, p. 1.

4. Ibid.

5. Ibid.

6. Ibid. For a discussion of Section 241's early history, see generally Carr, *Federal Protection of Civil Rights*.

7. *New York Times*, December 4, 1965, p. 20, March 26, 1965, p. 1, March 27, 1965, p. 1.

8. Ibid.

9. Ibid.; *New York Times*, April 8, 1965, p. 31.

10. *New York Times*, March 10, 1965, p. 23, April 23, 1965, p. 15.

11. Ibid., May 7, 1965, p. 25, May 8, 1965, p. 1, August 21, 1965, p. 1.

12. Ibid., December 4, 1965, p. 1.

13. Ibid., August 21, 1965, p. 1, October 23, 1965, p. 1.

14. Ibid., December 4, 1965, p. 1; interviews with Judge Frank M. Johnson, Jr.; interview with Richard Gill; interview with Ruth Jenkins Johnson.

15. Unless otherwise indicated, the discussion and quotations relating to the federal proceedings are drawn from the official records and transcript for *United States* v. *Eaton*, Criminal Case 11736-N (1965), on file in the U.S. District Court, Montgomery, Ala. For accounts of the Hayneville and Montgomery proceedings and other trials growing out of incidents of racial violence during the same period, see Muse, *The American Negro Revolution*, ch. 15.

16. *United States* v. *Williams*, 341 U.S. 70 (1951). As indicated later, the Supreme Court ultimately reversed the district court decisions in the Mississippi and Georgia cases. *United States* v. *Price*, 383 U.S. 745 (1966); *United States* v. *Guest*, 383 U.S. 787 (1966).

17. Interview with Walter Turner.

18. During 1975 hearings before the Senate Select Committee on Intelligence, Rowe testified that the FBI had rarely acted to head off Klan attacks and that the

bureau had ordered him to sow dissension within Klan units. Another witness, FBI Deputy Associate Director James B. Adams, disputed much of Rowe's testimony (*New York Times,* December 3, 1975, p. 23). A later investigation by the Birmingham Police Department and the office of the Alabama attorney general indicated that Rowe may have participated in and helped to plan Klan violence which the FBI employed him to monitor (ibid., July 9, 1978, p. 1). And in the fall of 1978, a Lowndes County grand jury indicted Rowe for Mrs. Liuzzo's murder, the state now claiming that Rowe fired the murder weapon (ibid., October 4, 1978, p. 78). For Rowe's published account of his exploits, see *My Undercover Years with the Ku Klux Klan* (New York: Bantam, 1976). Rowe's involvement in Mrs. Liuzzo's murder, of course, would have no bearing on the original defendants' guilt in the conspiracy to violate the dead woman's civil rights or those of the Selma marchers.

19. Interview with Walter Turner.

20. *Allen* v. *United States,* 164 U.S. 492 (1896).

21. *New York Times,* December 4, 1965, p. 1; interviews with Judge Frank M. Johnson, Jr.

22. *Thaggard* v. *United States,* 354 F. 2d 735 (5th Cir., 1965); *Eaton* v. *United States* (1967) (slip opinion), on file in trial records of the case, U.S. District Court, Montgomery, Ala.

23. *United States* v. *Price,* 383 U.S. 745 (1966); *United States* v. *Guest,* 383 U.S. 787 (1966).

24. *Eaton* v. *United States* (5th Cir., 1967) (slip opinion).

25. Interviews with Judge Frank M. Johnson, Jr. For a summary of the Supreme Court's position regarding the status of the right to interstate travel, see Justice Stewart's majority opinion in *United States* v. *Guest,* 383 U.S. 787 (1966). In *Guest,* it should be noted, three justices joined a concurring opinion in which they agreed that Congress had the authority to punish private interferences with Fourteenth Amendment rights, while three others agreed with that general thesis and also concluded that Section 241 reached such conspiracies. The opinion of the Court, however, avoided a ruling on the issue.

26. *New York Times,* November 9, 1966, p. 33, November 10, 1966, p. 30.

27. Ibid., March 11, 1966, p. 18, September 28, 1966, p. 1, September 24, 1966, p. 24, September 27, 1966, p. 1.

28. Ibid., February 25, 1966, p. 1, May 4, 1966, p. 1, November 9, 1966, p. 33. For a discussion of the Wallaces' 1966 campaign and the succession effort, see Frady, *Wallace,* pp. 179–202. Numan V. Bartley and Hugh D. Graham, *Southern Politics and the Second Reconstruction* (Baltimore: Johns Hopkins University Press, 1975), pp. 109–10, discusses the mixed effects of the 1960s upsurge in southern voters—an increase 30 percent black and 70 percent white.

Chapter 10: The Real Governor of Alabama

1. *Advertiser-Journal,* September 17, 1967.

2. The following discussion of Alabama efforts to obstruct school desegregation after the 1964 order is based largely on *Lee* v. *Macon County,* 267 F. Supp. 458, 460–78 (M.D. Ala., 1967).

3. Ibid., 458, 478.

4. Ibid., p. 480; Green v. County School Board, 391 U.S. 430 (1968).

5. New York Times, March 31, 1967, p. 19.

6. Ibid.

7. Montgomery Advertiser, April 26, 1967.

8. Ibid.; Lee v. Macon County, 270 F. Supp. 859 (M.D. Ala., 1967); Alabama NAACP State Conference of Branches v. Wallace, 269 F. Supp. 346 (M.D. Ala., 1967).

9. Alabama Journal, April 26, 1967; Birmingham Post-Herald, April 27, 1967.

10. Alabama Journal, April 26, 1967; Advertiser-Journal, September 17, 1967.

11. For a discussion of the 1970 Wallace-Brewer campaign, see Bartley and Graham, Southern Politics, pp. 164–66. Wayne Greenhaw, Watch Out for George Wallace (Englewood Cliffs, N.J.: Prentice-Hall, 1976), pp. 214–17, describes the smear tactics employed against Brewer in the campaign.

12. Baker v. Carr, 369 U.S 186 (1962); Montgomery Advertiser, April 15, 1962; Sims v. Frink, 208 F. Supp. 431 (M.D. Ala., 1962); Reynolds v. Sims, 377 U.S. 533 (1964); Sims v. Amos, 336 F. Supp. 924 (M.D. Ala., 1972); Moore v. Moore, 246 F. Supp. 578 (S.D. Ala., 1965); Moody v. Flowers, 256 F. Supp. 195 (M.D. Ala., 1966); Avery v. Midland Co., 390 U.S 474 (1968); Driggers v. Gallion, 308 F. Supp. 632 (M.D. Ala., 1969); Sullivan v. Alabama State Bar, 295 F. Supp. 1216 (M.D. Ala., 1969); Sims v. Baggett, 247 F. Supp. 96 (M.D. Ala., 1965); Smith v. Paris, 257 F. Supp. 901 (M.D. Ala., 1968); Yelverton v. Driggers, 370 F. Supp. 612 (M.D. Ala., 1974).

Charles Morgan, Jr., One Man, One Voice (New York: Holt, Rinehart and Winston, 1979), ch. 4, is an account of Alabama's initial reapportionment litigation by the plaintiffs' counsel. Perhaps the most sophisticated analysis of the reapportionment issue in the courts is Robert G. Dixon, Jr., Democratic Representation (New York: Oxford University Press, 1968); the Alabama litigation is examined on pp. 209–10.

13. Weissinger v. Boswell, 330 F. Supp. 615 (M.D. Ala., 1971).

14. Smith v. King, 277 F. Supp. 31 (M.D. Ala., 1967); Whitfield v. Oliver, 399 F. Supp. 348 (M.D. Ala., 1975); Strain v. Philpott, 331 F. Supp. 836 (M.D. Ala., 1971); Henderson v. ASCS, 317 F. Supp. 430 (M.D. Ala., 1970).

15. Craig v. Alabama State University, 451 F. Supp. 1207, 1213 (M.D. Ala., 1978); University of California Regents v. Bakke, 98 S. Ct. 2733 (1978); interviews with Judge Frank M. Johnson, Jr.; NAACP v. Allen, 340 F. Supp. 703 (M.D. Ala., 1972); Carr v. Montgomery Co. Bd. of Education, 289 F. Supp. 647 (M.D. Ala., 1968); United States v. Frazer, 297 F. Supp. 319 (M.D. Ala., 1968).

16. Frontiero v. Laird, 341 F. Supp. 201 (M.D. Ala., 1972); Reed v. Reed, 404 U.S. 71 (1971); Frontiero v. Laird, 341 F. Supp. 201, 209 (dissenting); Frontiero v. Richardson, 411 U.S. 677 (1973).

17. Interviews with Judge Frank M. Johnson, Jr.

18. Dickey v. Alabama State Board of Education, 273 F. Supp. 613 (M.D. Ala., 1967).

19. Ibid., p. 619. The Fifth Circuit had required notice and a hearing for students threatened with suspension in Dixon v. Alabama State Board of Education, 294 F. 2d 150 (5th Cir., 1961). The cases had arisen out of civil

rights protests by students at Montgomery's Alabama State College. Citing prevailing doctrine, Judge Johnson had upheld the power of school officials to dismiss the students without a hearing (186 F. Supp. 945 [M.D. Ala., 1960]).

In other student cases, Judge Johnson overturned a high school hair-grooming regulation, *Griffin v. Tatum*, 300 F. Supp. 60 (M.D. Ala., 1969); delineated the search and seizure rights of college students, *Moore v. Student Affairs Committee*, 284 F. Supp. 725 (M.D. Ala., 1968), and *Piazzola v. Watkins*, 316 F. Supp. 624 (M.D. Ala., 1970); and overturned efforts of Auburn University officials to prevent a student-sponsored campus speech by antiwar advocate William Sloan Coffin, *Brooks v. Auburn University*, 296 F. Supp. 188 (M.D. Ala., 1969).

In one faculty case, as noted earlier, he ordered reinstatement of a high school teacher whose only sin had been to assign her students a Kurt Vonnegut short story (*Parducci v. Rutland*, 316 F. Supp. 352 [M.D. Ala., 1970]); in another, he joined Judge Rives, over Judge Varner's dissent, in ordering reinstatement of a pregnant, unmarried elementary school teacher. Under Alabama law, teachers could be discharged for immoral conduct; but the evidence on which the school board had based its decision had come from the woman's physician, a clear breach of her privacy rights, the majority concluded (*Drake v. Covington Co. Bd. of Education*, 371 F. Supp. 974 [M.D. Ala., 1974]). Certain other faculty claims did not fare nearly so well in Judge Johnson's court, however. In *Rowe v. Forrester*, 368 F. Supp. 1355, 1357 (M.D. Ala., 1974), for example, he rejected the claim of a black sociology instructor who charged that he had been assigned night classes as punishment for his outspoken criticism of school administrators.

20. *Nicholson v. Alabama State Bar Ass'n*, 338 F. Supp. 48 (M.D. Ala., 1972); interviews with Judge Frank M. Johnson, Jr.; *Miller v. California*, 413 U.S. 15 (1973); *Poulos v. Rucker*, 288 F. Supp. 305, 307 (M.D. Ala, 1968); *Alabama Journal*, July 11, 1968; *Entertainment Ventures v. Brewer*, 306 F. Supp. 802 (M.D. Ala., 1969).

21. *Callahan v. Sanders*, 339 F. Supp. 814 (M.D. Ala., 1971); *Hulett v. Julian*, 250 F. Supp. 208 (M.D. Ala., 1966); *Calhoun v. Doster*, 324 F. Supp. 736 (M.D. Ala., 1971); *Lewis v. Baxley*, 368 F. Supp. 768 (M.D. Ala., 1973); *McCarley v. Sanders*, 309 F. Supp. 8 (M.D. Ala., 1970); *United States v. Alabama*, 252 F. Supp. 95 (M.D. Ala., 1966); *Hadnott v. Amos*, 320 F. Supp. 107 (M.D. Ala., 1970); *Sellers v. Trussell*, 253 F. Supp. 915 (M.D. Ala., 1966); *Hadnott v. Amos*, 325 F. Supp. 777 (M.D. Ala., 1971); *In Re Herndon*, 325 F. Supp. 779 (M.D. Ala., 1971).

22. *Smith v. YMCA*, 316 F. Supp. 899 (M.D. Ala., 1970); *Gilmore v. City of Montgomery*, 337 F. Supp. 22 (M.D. Ala., 1972); *Cook v. Advertiser Co.*, 323 F. Supp. 1212 (M.D. Ala., 1971); *Runyon v. McCrary*, 96 S. Ct. 2586 (1976). For a case applying what would become the Supreme Court's position on the 1981 issue at the lower court level, see *Waters v. Wisconsin Steel Works*, 427 F. 2d 476 (7th Cir., 1970).

23. "Interpreter in the Front Line," *Time*, May 12, 1967, pp. 72–78.

24. Private files of Judge Frank M. Johnson, Jr., U.S. District Court, Montgomery, Ala.; Justice Department file on Judge Frank M. Johnson, Jr.; interview with Representative William Dickinson.

25. *Alabama Journal*, March 27, 1970.

26. Interviews with Judge Frank M. Johnson, Jr.

27. *Montgomery Advertiser*, September 25, 29, 1971; private files of Judge Frank M. Johnson, Jr.; Justice Department file on Judge Frank M. Johnson, Jr.; interview with Representative William Dickinson; interviews with Judge Frank M. Johnson, Jr.

28. *Montgomery Advertiser*, September 28, 1971; *Alabama Journal*, September 21, 1971; *Herald* editorial, quoted in *Alabama Journal*, October 2, 1971.

29. Interview with Howard Mandell; *Lee v. Macon County*, 283 F. Supp. 194 (M.D. Ala., 1968); *Carr v. Montgomery Co. Bd. of Education*, 289 F. Supp. 647 (M.D. Ala., 1968); interviews with Judge Frank M. Johnson, Jr.

30. *Swann v. Charlotte-Mecklenburg Board of Education*, 402 U.S. 1 (1971); *Carr v. Montgomery Co. Bd. of Education*, 377 F. Supp. 1123 (M.D. Ala., 1974).

31. Interviews with Judge Frank M. Johnson, Jr.

32. Interview with Howard Mandell; *United States v. Montgomery Co. Bd. of Education*, 395 U.S. 225, 236 (1969); *Montgomery Advertiser*, September 28, 1971.

33. Private files of Judge Frank M. Johnson, Jr.; *Alabama Journal*, November 7, 1974; *Montgomery Advertiser*, September 6, 1974.

Chapter 11: Human Warehouses

1. Unless otherwise indicated, the discussion and quotations in this chapter are drawn from the records and transcript for *Wyatt v. Stickney*, CA 3195-N, on file in the U.S. District Court, Montgomery, Ala.

2. *Marable v. Alabama Mental Health Bd.*, 297 F. Supp. 291 (M.D. Ala., 1969).

3. Ibid., p. 298.

4. Ibid., p. 294.

5. Interview with Norman Ellis, Tuscaloosa, Ala., March 8, 17, 1980; interview with Raymond Fowler, Destin, Fla., August 8, 1976.

6. Ibid.; interview with Alberta Murphy, Tuscaloosa, Ala., August 9, 1977.

7. *Birmingham News*, November 19, 1971; *Tuscaloosa News*, August 8, 1971; interview with George Dean.

8. Interview with George Dean.

9. Ibid.

10. Ibid.

11. Ibid.

12. Ibid. Judge Johnson vaguely recalled having closed the bankruptcy records to prohibit local attorneys from using them to solicit business, but he said that he was unaware of other details in Dean's story (interview with Judge Frank M. Johnson, Jr.).

13. Interview with George Dean; *Wallace v. Brewer*, 315 F. Supp. 431 (M.D. Ala., 1970).

14. Interviews with Judge Frank M. Johnson, Jr.; interview with Jimmy Johnson; interview with Earl Pippen.

15. Interviews with Judge Frank M. Johnson, Jr.

16. Interview with George Dean.

17. Ibid.; *Washington* v. *Lee*, 263 F. Supp. 327 (M.D. Ala., 1966) (desegregating Alabama's prisons and jails); *White* v. *Crook*, 251 F. Supp. 401 (M.D. Ala., 1966) (invalidating racial and gender discrimination in the Alabama jury selection process).

18. Interview with George Dean; interview with Howard Mandell.

19. Interview with George Dean.

20. *Wyatt* v. *Stickney*, 325 F. Supp. 781 (M. D. Ala., 1971).

21. *Rouse* v. *Cameron*, 373 F. 2d 451, 452 (D.C. Cir., 1966); *Wyatt* v. *Stickney*, 325 F. Supp. at 784.

22. The best-known decision from the era of economic due process is *Lochner* v. *New York*, 198 U.S. 45 (1905), which found a "liberty of contract" within the scope of due process and invalidated as "arbitrary" and "unreasonable" a state maximum hour law for bakery employees. Recent Supreme Court decisions employing due process to protect privacy rights not mentioned in the Constitution's text include *Griswold* v. *Connecticut*, 381 U.S. 479 (1965), and *Roe* v. *Wade*, 410 U.S. 113 (1973).

23. *United States* v. *Crenshaw County Unit of the United Klans of America*, 290 F. Supp. 181 (M.D. Ala., 1968); unidentified newspaper clipping in private files of Judge Frank M. Johnson, Jr.

24. Unidentified newspaper clipping in private files of Judge Frank M. Johnson, Jr.

25. Interview with Ira DeMent; interview with Earl Pippen. For an amusing editorial on DeMent's "frustrated policeman" personality, see *Montgomery Independent*, August 12, 1971.

26. "Applying the Southern Strategy to the Federal Judiciary: The Making of a Judgeship, 1971," *Ripon Forum*, February 1971, pp. 15–17; *New York Times*, December 11, 1970, p. 47; *Birmingham News*, April 21, 1971; *Montgomery Advertiser*, April 22, 1971.

27. Interview with Raymond Fowler; interview with Ira DeMent.

28. Interview with George Dean; interview with Ira DeMent.

29. *Tuscaloosa News*, August 1, 1971.

30. Ibid.

31. Interview with Ira DeMent.

32. *Alabama Journal*, August 6, 13, 1971; *Tuscaloosa News*, August 6, 8, 1971; *Birmingham News*, August 8, 1971.

33. *Birmingham News*, November 19, 1971.

34. *Montgomery Independent*, August 12, 1971; *Tuscaloosa News*, August 1, 20, 1971, September 26, 1971; *Alabama Journal*, August 14, 1971, September 8, 1971; *Birmingham News*, August 8, 1971, November 19, 1971.

35. *Wyatt* v. *Stickney*, 334 F. Supp. 1341, 1343–44 (M.D. Ala., 1971).

36. *Birmingham Post-Herald*, September 21, 1971; interview with George Dean.

37. *Birmingham News*, February 9, 1972; interview with Dr. Raymond Fowler; interviews with Judge Frank M. Johnson, Jr.

38. Interviews with Judge Frank M. Johnson, Jr.

39. *Wyatt* v. *Stickney*, 344 F. Supp. 387 (M.D. Ala., 1972).

40. 344 F. Supp. 373 (M.D. Ala., 1972).

41. 344 F. Supp. at 376, 392 n. 10.

42. Ibid., pp. 403–4.

43. Ibid., pp. 392–93, 394.

44. Interview with George Dean; interviews with Judge Frank M. Johnson, Jr.

45. Interview with John Patterson.

46. *Montgomery Advertiser*, April 25, 1972; *Alabama Journal*, May 11, 1972; *Tuscaloosa News*, May 11, 1972. Some of the state press followed the governor's lead in attacking the orders. Calling Judge Johnson "the autocrat of Alabama," who presumed expertise in many fields, the *Montgomery Independent* complained, for example: "Judge Johnson would be modest about his expertness in these many fields. But then, as Winston Churchill once said of a pompous foe, Judge Johnson has much to be modest about" (*Montgomery Independent*, April 20, 1972).

47. *Tuscaloosa News*, April 19, 1972.

48. Ibid., July 7, 20, 1972; *Alabama Journal*, June 21, 1972.

49. *Wyatt v. Aderholt*, 368 F. Supp. 1383 (M.D. Ala., 1974).

50. *Burnham v. Department of Public Health*, 349 F. Supp. 1335, 1343 (M.D. Ga., 1972).

51. *Wyatt v. Aderholt*, 503 F. 2d 1305, 1313 (5th Cir., 1974); *Donaldson v. O'Connor*, 493 F. 2d 507 (5th Cir., 1974).

52. 503 F. 2d at 1317.

53. *O'Connor v. Donaldson*, 422 U.S. 563 (1975).

54. *Lynch v. Baxley*, 386 F. Supp. 378 (M.D. Ala, 1974); *Code of Alabama*, tit. 45, sec. 205 (1958).

55. *Lynch v. Baxley*, 386 F. Supp. 378, 397 (M.D. Ala., 1974).

56. Ibid., pp. 402–3.

57. Interview with Alberta Murphy.

58. Interview with Lecil Gray.

59. Interview with George Dean; interview with Raymond Fowler.

60. Cynthia Faye Barnett, "Treatment Rights of Mentally Ill Nursing Home Residents," *University of Pennsylvania Law Review*, 126 (January 1978), 578–629. The Barnett study compared medical treatment resources at Bryce and fourteen Alabama nursing homes in 1975. Lecil Gray has questioned the accuracy of Barnett's conclusion (undated note to author), but her statistics are convincing.

61. Interview with Lecil Gray.

62. Interview with Alberta Murphy.

63. Interview with Lecil Gray. For another discussion of *Wyatt's* impact and compliance problems, see "The *Wyatt* Case: Implementation of a Judicial Decree Ordering Institutional Change," *Yale Law Journal*, 84 (May 1975), 1338–89.

64. Interviews with Norman Ellis. Ellis is a professor of psychology at The University of Alabama and a member of the Professional Advisory Committee for the Alabama mental health system.

65. *Wyatt v. Ireland*, CA 3195-N (1979) (slip opinion).

66. Interview with Norman Ellis.

Chapter 12: Unfit for Human Habitation

1. Interview with Ira DeMent; interview with Lecil Gray; interviews with

Judge Frank M. Johnson, Jr., *Busby v. Holman*, 237 F. Supp. 271 (M.D. Ala., 1964); *Boulden v. Holman*, 257 F. Supp. 1013 (M.D. Ala., 1966); *Hamilton v. Watkins*, 311 F. Supp. 263 (M.D. Ala., 1970); interview with William Baxley, Montgomery, Ala., August 10, 1976. In *United States v. Germany*, 32 F.R.D. 421 (M.D. Ala., 1963), Judge Johnson did interpret the Sixth Amendment to require government to reimburse an indigent defendant's attorney for certain expenses connected with his investigation of the case and development of a defense.

2. Interviews with Judge Frank M. Johnson, Jr.

3. *Montgomery Advertiser*, January 19, 1973; interview with Lecil Gray.

4. *Washington v. Lee*, 263 F. Supp. 327 (M.D. Ala., 1966); *Lake v. Lee*, 329 F. Supp. 196, 203 (S.D. Ala., 1971).

5. *Lake v. Lee*, 329 F. Supp. at 201 n. 3a.

6. *Newman v. Alabama*, 349 F. Supp. 278 (M.D. Ala., 1972).

7. *Diamond v. Thompson*, 364 F. Supp. 659, 662 (M.D. Ala., 1973).

8. *Claybrone v. Thompson*, 368 F. Supp. 659, 662 (M.D. Ala., 1973); *Claybrone v. Long*, 371 F. Supp. 1320, 1324 (M.D. Ala., 1974).

9. Daryl R. Fair, "Judging or Legislating? Application and Evaluation of Diverse Formulae," paper delivered at the 1977 meeting of the American Political Science Association, Washington, D.C., September 1–4, 1977. Unless otherwise indicated, the remaining discussion and quotations in this chapter are drawn from the official records and transcripts for *James v. Wallace*, CA 74-203-N, and *Pugh v. Locke*, CA 74-57-N, on file in the U.S. District Court, Montgomery, Ala.

10. Interview with Robert Segall.

11. Ibid.

12. *James v. Wallace*, 382 F. Supp. 1177, 1180 (M.D. Ala., 1974).

13. Interview with Robert Segall.

14. Interview with Ira DeMent.

15. Ibid.

16. *McCray v. Sullivan*, 399 F. Supp. 271 (S.D. Ala., 1975), 509 F. 2d 1332 (5th Cir., 1975).

17. *Montgomery Advertiser*, August 29, 1975.

18. *New York Times*, July 4, 1975, p. 20.

19. Ibid.

20. Ibid.

21. Ibid.

22. *Montgomery Advertiser*, October 16, 1975; interviews with Judge Frank M. Johnson, Jr.

23. Interview with Ruth Jenkins Johnson.

24. Interviews with Judge Frank M. Johnson, Jr.; interview with William Baxley.

25. Interview with Jack Vann.

26. Ibid.; *Alabama Journal*, October 14, 1975.

27. Interview with Jack Vann; *Alabama Journal*, October 14, 1975; interview with Glen Curlee; interview with Jimmy Johnson.

28. Interviews with Judge Frank M. Johnson, Jr.; interview with William Baxley.

29. *In Re Birdsong*, 39 F. 599 (S.D. Ga., 1899); *Holt v. Sarver*, 300 F. Supp. 825 (E.D. Ark., 1969); *Jones v. Wittenberg*, 323 F. Supp. 93 (N.D. Ohio, 1971);

Hamilton v. *Landrieu*, 351 F. Supp. 549 (E.D. La., 1972); *Brenneman* v. *Madigan*, 343 F. Supp. 128 (N.D. Cal., 1972); *Collins* v. *Schoonfield*, 344 F. Supp. 257 (D. Md., 1972); *Gates* v. *Collier*, 349 F. Supp. 881 (N.D. Miss., 1972); *Inmates of Suffolk County Jail* v. *Eisenstadt*, 360 F. Supp. 676 (D. Mass., 1973); Fair, "Judging or Legislating?"

30. *James* v. *Wallace*, 406 F. Supp. 318 (M.D. Ala., 1976).

31. Ibid., p. 331.

32. *Birmingham Post-Herald*, January 15, 1976.

33. *Commercial Appeal* (Memphis, Tennessee), February 1, 1976; *Nashville Tennessean*, January 23, 1976.

34. *Birmingham Post-Herald*, January 19, 1976; *Christian Advocate*, January 20, 1976; *Alabama Journal*, January 15, 1976; *Montgomery Advertiser*, January 18, 1976; *Nashville Tennessean*, January 18, 1976.

35. *Birmingham News*, January 18, 1976; *Washington Star*, January 17, 1976; *Centreville Press*, quoted in *Alabama Journal*, January 24, 1976; *Birmingham News*, January 18, 1976.

36. Private files of Judge Frank M. Johnson, Jr.

37. Interview with Dorothy Perry.

38. Private files of Judge Frank M. Johnson, Jr.

39. *Birmingham Post-Herald*, April 8, 1976.

40. *Alabama Journal*, April 13, 1976.

41. Interview with Ira DeMent.

42. Interview with William Baxley.

43. Interview with Roland Nachman, Montgomery, Ala., August 13, 1976; interview with Judson Locke, Montgomery, Ala., August 11, 1977.

44. Interview with Alberta Murphy; interview with George Beto, Montgomery, Ala., August 13, 1976.

45. Frank M. Johnson, Jr., "The Alabama Punting Syndrome," paper presented as part of Distinguished Alabamians Lecture Series, University of Alabama, November 4, 1975; *New York Times*, February 1, 1976, p. 1.

46. Interview with Roland Nachman; interview with Alberta Murphy.

47. Interviews with Judge Frank M. Johnson, Jr.; interview with Ray Jenkins.

48. Interview with Judson Locke.

49. Interviews with Judge Frank M. Johnson, Jr.; interview with William Baxley.

50. Interview with Raymond Fowler.

51. The author attended the conference.

52. Interview with Raymond Fowler.

53. Interview with Roland Nachman; interview with George Beto.

54. Interviews with Judge Frank M. Johnson, Jr.; interview with Judson Locke; interview with George Beto.

55. On Learned Hand's views, see generally his *The Bill of Rights* (Cambridge, Mass.: Harvard University Press, 1958). Justice Black summarized his judicial and constitutional philosophy in *A Constitutional Faith* (New York: Knopf, 1968). Horowitz has discussed his position most extensively in *The Courts and Social Policy* (Washington, D.C.: The Brookings Institution, 1977), but see also his "The Courts as Guardians of the Public Interest," *Public Administration Review*, 37 (March/April 1977), 148–54. For a related critique,

see Roger C. Cramton, "Judicial Law Making and Administration," *Public Administration Review*, 36 (September/October 1976), 551–55. For persuasive general critiques of activism on the Supreme Court, see especially Alexander M. Bickel, *The Least Dangerous Branch* (Indianapolis, Ind.: Bobbs-Merrill, 1962), and *The Supreme Court and the Idea of Progress* (New York: Harper Torchbooks, 1970).

56. Arthur S. Miller and Ronald F. Howell, "The Myth of Neutrality in Constitutional Adjudication," *University of Chicago Law Review*, 27 (1960), 661, reprinted in Arthur S. Miller, *The Supreme Court: Myth and Reality* (Westport, Conn.: Greenwood Press, 1978), pp. 51–87; Arthur S. Miller, untitled speech presented at the 1976 Fifth Circuit Judicial Conference, Houston, Texas; Abram Chayes, "The Role of the Judge in Public Law Litigation," *Harvard Law Review*, 89 (May 1976), 1281–1316; Ronald Dworkin, *Taking Rights Seriously* (Cambridge, Mass.: Harvard University Press, 1977), p. 134; interview with George Dean.

57. Interviews with Judge Frank M. Johnson, Jr.

58. *Griswold* v. *Connecticut*, 381 U.S. 479, 522 (1965) (dissenting).

59. A portion of the address, "The Role of the Judiciary with Respect to the Other Branches of Government," is reprinted in Walter F. Murphy and C. Herman Pritchett, eds., *Courts, Judges, and Politics*, 3rd ed. (New York: Random House, 1979), pp. 66–71.

60. Ibid.; *University of Georgia Community News*, February 18, 1977.

61. Interviews with Judge Frank M. Johnson, Jr.; interview with Judson Locke.

62. *Newman* v. *Alabama*, 559 F. 2d 283, 288 (5th Cir., 1977).

63. *Alabama* v. *Pugh*, 98 S. Ct. 3057 (1978).

64. Interviews with Judge Frank M. Johnson, Jr.

Epilogue

1. Interviews with Judge Frank M. Johnson, Jr.

2. Ibid.

3. Ibid.

4. Ibid.

5. Ibid.

6. Ibid.; *New York Times*, November 30, 1977, p. 1.

7. Interviews with Judge Frank M. Johnson, Jr.; *Birmingham Post-Herald*, August 18, 1977.

8. *Birmingham Post-Herald*, August 18, 1977.

9. Interviews with Judge Frank M. Johnson, Jr.

10. Ibid.; *New York Times*, November 29, 1977, p. 16, November 30, 1977, pp. 1, 34.

11. Interviews with Judge Frank M. Johnson, Jr.

12. "A Matter of Principle," unpublished collection presented to Judge Frank M. Johnson, Jr., by his law clerks, April 19, 1975; interviews with Judge Frank M. Johnson, Jr.

13. Interviews with Judge Frank M. Johnson, Jr.

14. Ibid.

15. *Birmingham News*, July 23, 1978; interview with John Patterson.

16. *Birmingham Post-Herald*, May 22, 1979.

17. Interviews with Judge Frank M. Johnson, Jr.

18. Ibid.

19. *Birmingham News*, February 2, 3, 4, 1979; *Newman* v. *Alabama*, CA 74-203-N (1979) (slip opinion); *Wyatt* v. *Ireland*, CA 3195-N (1980) (slip opinion).

20. Interviews with Judge Frank M. Johnson, Jr.; Transcript of Investiture Proceedings, Hon. Frank M. Johnson, Jr., in the U.S. Court of Appeals for the Fifth Circuit, Montgomery, Ala., July 12, 1979.

21. Transcript of Investiture Proceedings.

22. Vines, "Federal District Judges," p. 26.

23. Interviews with Judge Frank M. Johnson, Jr.

24. *Birmingham Post-Herald*, April 10, 1978.

25. Private files of Judge Frank M. Johnson, Jr.

Bibliography

Court Records and Transcripts

In Re Wallace. CA 1487-N (1959), U.S. District Court, Montgomery, Ala.
James v. Wallace. CA 74-203-N, U.S. District Court, Montgomery, Ala.
Pugh v. Locke. CA 74-57-N, U.S. District Court, Montgomery, Ala.
United States v. Dial. Criminal Case 1348 (1954), U.S. District Court, Northern
  District of Alabama, Federal Records Center, Atlanta, Ga.
United States v. Eaton. Criminal Case 11736-N (1965), U.S District Court,
  Montgomery, Ala.
United States v. Jones (1946). Army Court of Military Review, Washington, D.C.
United States v. Smith (1946). Army Court of Military Review, Washington,
  D.C.
United States v. U.S. Klans. CA 1718-N (1961), U.S. District Court, Montgom-
  ery, Ala.
United States v. Wallace. Criminal Case 11098-N (1959), U.S. District Court,
  Montgomery, Ala.
Williams v. Wallace. CA 2181-N (1965), U.S. District Court, Montgomery, Ala.
Wyatt. v. Stickney. CA 3195-N, U.S. District Court, Montgomery, Ala.

Judicial Decisions

Alabama v. Pugh, 98 S. Ct. 3057 (1978).
Alabama v. United States, 304 F. 2d 583 (5th Cir., 1962).
Alabama v. United States, 83 S. Ct. 145 (1962).
Alabama ex rel. Gallion v. Rogers, 187 F. Supp. 848 (M.D. Ala., 1960).
Alabama NAACP State Conference of Branches v. Wallace, 269 F. Supp. 346
  (M.D. Ala., 1967).
Allen v. United States, 164 U.S. 492 (1896).
Armstrong v. Bd. of Education, 220 F. Supp. 217 (N.D. Ala., 1963).
Armstrong v. Bd. of Education, 323 F. 2d 333 (5th Cir., 1963).
Avery v. Midland Co., 390 U.S. 474 (1968).
Baker v. Carr, 369 U.S. 186 (1962).
Belvin v. United States, 273 F. 2d 583 (5th Cir., 1960).
In Re Birdsong, 39 F. 599 (S.D. Ga., 1899).
Boman v. Birmingham Transit Co., 292 F. 2d 4 (5th Cir., 1961).
Boulden v. Holman, 257 F. Supp. 1013 (M.D. Ala., 1966).
Brenneman v. Madigan, 343 F. Supp. 128 (N.D. Cal., 1972).
Brooks v. Auburn University, 296 F. Supp. 188 (M.D. Ala., 1969).
Browder v. Gayle, 142 F. Supp. 707 (M.D. Ala., 1956).

Brown v. Board of Education, 347 U.S. 483 (1954).

Brown v. Louisiana, 383 U.S. 131 (1966).

Burnham v. Department of Public Health, 349 F. Supp. 1335 (M.D. Ga., 1972).

Busby v. Holman, 237 F. Supp. 271 (M.D. Ala., 1964).

Calhoun v. Doster, 324 F. Supp. 736 (M.D. Ala., 1971).

Callahan v. Sanders, 339 F. Supp. 814 (M.D. Ala., 1971).

Carr v. Montgomery Co. Bd. of Education, 289 F. Supp. 647 (M. D. Ala., 1968).

Carr v. Montgomery Co. Bd. of Education, 377 F. Supp. 1123 (M.D. Ala., 1974).

City of Montgomery v. Montgomery City Lines, Inc., 1 Race Rel. L. Rep. 535 (1956).

Claybrone v. Long, 371 F. Supp. 1320 (M.D. Ala., 1974).

Claybrone v. Thompson, 368 F. Supp. 659 (M.D. Ala., 1973).

Cobb v. Montgomery Library Board, 207 F. Supp. 880 (M.D. Ala., 1962).

Cochran v. City of Eufaula, 251 F. Supp. 981 (M.D. Ala., 1966).

Collins v. Schoonfield, 344 F. Supp. 257 (D. Md., 1972).

Cook v. Advertiser Co., 323 F. Supp. 1212 (M.D. Ala., 1971).

Cox v. Louisiana, 379 U.S. 536 (1965).

Craig v. Alabama State University, 451 F. Supp. 1207 (M.D. Ala., 1978).

Davis v. Board of Education, 219 F. Supp. 542 (S.D. Ala., 1963).

Davis v. Board of Education, 322 F. 2d 356 (5th Cir., 1963).

Davis v. Schnell, 81 F. Supp. 872 (M.D. Ala., 1949).

Diamond v. Thompson, 364 F. Supp. 659 (M.D. Ala., 1973).

Dickey v. Alabama State Board of Education, 273 F. Supp. 613 (M.D. Ala., 1967).

Dixon v. Alabama State Board of Education, 186 F. Supp. 945 (M.D. Ala., 1960).

Dixon v. Alabama State Board of Education, 294 F. 2d 150 (5th Cir., 1961).

Donaldson v. O'Connor, 493 F. 2d 507 (5th Cir., 1974).

Doyle v. Continental Ins. Co., 94 U.S. 535 (1876).

Drake v. Covington Co. Bd of Education, 371 F. Supp. 974 (M.D. Ala., 1974).

Driggers v. Gallion, 308 F. Supp. 632 (M.D. Ala., 1969).

Eaton v. United States (5th Cir., 1967) (slip opinion).

Edwards v. South Carolina, 372 U.S. 229 (1963).

Entertainment Ventures v. Brewer, 306 F. Supp. 802 (M.D. Ala., 1969).

Fleming v. South Carolina Electric and Gas Co., 224 F. 2d 752 (4th Cir., 1955).

Forman v. City of Montgomery, 245 F. Supp. 17 (M.D. Ala., 1965).

Franklin v. Parker, 223 F. Supp. 724 (M.D. Ala., 1963).

Frontiero v. Laird, 341 F. Supp. 201 (M. D. Ala., 1972).

Frontiero v. Richardson, 411 U.S 677 (1973).

Gates v. Collier, 349 F. Supp. 881 (N.D. Miss., 1972).

Gayle v. Browder, 77 S. Ct. 145 (1956).

Gilmore v. City of Montgomery, 176 F. Supp. 776 (M.D. Ala., 1959).

Gilmore v. City of Montgomery, 337 F. Supp. 22 (M.D. Ala., 1972).

Gomillion v. Lightfoot, 167 F. Supp. 405 (M.D. Ala., 1958).

Gomillion v. Lightfoot, 270 F. 2d 594 (5th Cir., 1959).

Gomillion v. Lightfoot, 364 U.S. 339 (1960).

Gomillion v. Rutherford, 6 Race Rel. L. Rep. 241 (M.D. Ala., 1961).

Grau v. Proctor & Gamble Co., 32 F.R.D. 199 (M.D. Ala., 1963).

Green v. County School Board, 391 U.S. 430 (1968).

Griffin v. Tatum, 300 F. Supp. 60 (M.D. Ala., 1969).

Griswold v. Connecticut, 381 U.S. 479 (1965).

Hadnott v. Amos, 320 F. Supp. 107 (M.D. Ala., 1970).

Hadnott v. Amos, 325 F. Supp. 777 (M.D. Ala., 1971).

Hamilton v. Landrieu, 351 F. Supp. 549 (E.D. La., 1972).

Hamilton v. Watkins, 311 F. Supp. 263 (M.D. Ala., 1970).

Hawkins v. United States, 303 F. 2d 536 (5th Cir., 1962).

Henderson v. ASCS, 317 F. Supp. 430 (M.D. Ala., 1970).

In Re Herndon, 325 F. Supp. 779 (M.D. Ala., 1971).

Holt v. Sarver, 300 F. Supp. 825 (E.D. Ark., 1969).

Hulett v. Julian, 250 F. Supp. 208 (M.D. Ala., 1966).

Hunter v. Pittsburgh, 207 U.S. 161 (1907).

Inmates of Suffolk County Jail v. Eisenstadt, 360 F. Supp. 676 (D. Mass., 1973).

James v. Wallace, 382 F. Supp. 1177 (M.D. Ala., 1974).

James v. Wallace, 406 F. Supp. 318 (M.D. Ala., 1976).

Johnson v. City of Montgomery, 245 F. Supp. 25 (M.D. Ala., 1965).

Jones v. Wittenberg, 323 F. Supp. 93 (N.D. Ohio, 1971).

Lake v. Lee, 329 F. Supp. 196 (S.D. Ala., 1971).

Laramie Co. v. Albany Co., 92 U.S. 307 (1875).

Lee v. Macon County, 221 F. Supp. 298 (M.D. Ala., 1963).

Lee v. Macon County, CA 604-E (M.D. Ala., 1964) (slip opinion).

Lee v. Macon County, 231 F. Supp. 743 (M.D. Ala., 1964).

Lee v. Macon County, 267 F. Supp. 458 (M.D. Ala., 1967).

Lee v. Macon County, 270 F. Supp. 859 (M.D. Ala., 1967).

Lee v. Macon County, 283 F. Supp. 194 (M.D. Ala., 1968).

Lee v. Macon County, 8 Race Rel. L. Rep. 916 (M.D. Ala., 1963).

Lewis v. Baxley, 368 F. Supp. 768 (M.D. Ala., 1973).

Lewis v. Greyhound Corporation, 199 F. Supp. 210 (M.D. Ala., 1961).

Lochner v. New York, 198 U.S 45 (1905).

Lucy v. Adams, 134 F. Supp. 235 (N.D. Ala., 1955).

Lynch v. Baxley, 386 F. Supp. 378 (M.D. Ala., 1974).

Marable v. Alabama Mental Health Bd., 297 F. Supp. 291 (M.D. Ala., 1969).

McCarley v. Sanders, 309 F. Supp. 8 (M.D. Ala., 1970).

McCray v. Sullivan, 399 F. Supp. 271 (S.D. Ala., 1975).

McCray v. Sullivan, 509 F. 2d 1332 (5th Cir., 1975).

McMeans v. Mayor's Court, 247 F. Supp. 606 (M.D. Ala., 1965).

Miller v. California, 413 U.S. 15 (1973).

Mitchell v. Wright, 62 F. Supp. 580 (M.D. Ala., 1945).

Mitchell v. Wright, 154 F. 2d 924 (5th Cir., 1946).

Mitchell v. Wright, 69 F. Supp. 698 (M.D. Ala., 1947).

Moody v. Flowers, 256 F. Supp. 195 (M.D. Ala., 1966).

Moore v. Moore, 246 F. Supp. 578 (S.D. Ala., 1965).

Moore v. Student Affairs Committee, 284 F. Supp. 725 (M.D. Ala., 1968).

NAACP v. Allen, 340 F. Supp. 703 (M.D. Ala., 1972).

Newman v Alabama, 349 F. Supp. 278 (M.D. Ala., 1972).

Newman v. Alabama, 559 F. 2d 283 (5th Cir., 1977).

Newman v. Alabama, CA 74-203-N (1979) (slip opinion).

Nicholson v. Alabama State Bar Ass'n, 338 F. Supp. 48 (M.D. Ala., 1972).

O'Connor v. Donaldson, 422 U.S. 563 (1975).

Parducci v. Rutland, 316 F. Supp. 352 (M.D. Ala., 1970).

Piazzola v. Watkins, 316 F. Supp. 624 (M.D. Ala., 1970).

Plessy v. Ferguson, 163 U.S. 537 (1896).

Poulos v. Rucker, 288 F. Supp. 305 (M.D. Ala., 1968).

Reed v. Reed, 404 U.S. 71 (1971).

Reynolds v. Sims, 377 U.S. 533 (1964).

Roe v. Wade, 410 U.S. 113 (1973).

Rouse v. Cameron, 373 F. 2d 451 (D.C. Cir., 1966).

Rowe v. Forrester, 368 F. Supp. 1355 (M.D. Ala., 1974).

Runyon v. McCrary, 96 S. Ct. 2586 (1976).

Sellers v. Trussell, 253 F. Supp. 915 (M.D. Ala., 1966).

Shuttlesworth v. Birmingham Bd. of Education, 162 F. Supp. 372 (N.D. Ala., 1958).

Shuttlesworth v. Birmingham Bd. of Education, 358 U.S. 101 (1958).

Sims v. Amos, 336 F. Supp. 924 (M.D. Ala., 1972).

Sims v. Baggett, 247 F. Supp. 96 (M.D. Ala., 1965).

Sims v. Frink, 208 F. Supp. 431 (M.D. Ala., 1962).

Smith v. Allwright, 321 U.S. 649 (1944).

Smith v. King, 277 F. Supp. 31 (M.D. Ala., 1967).

Smith v. Paris, 257 F. Supp. 901 (M.D. Ala., 1968).

Smith v. YMCA, 316 F. Supp. 899 (M.D. Ala., 1970).

Strain v. Philpott, 331 F. Supp. 836 (M.D. Ala., 1971).

Sullivan v. Alabama State Bar, 295 F. Supp. 1216 (M.D. Ala., 1969).

Swann v. Charlotte-Mecklenburg Board of Education, 402 U.S. 1 (1971).

Thaggard v. United States, 354 F. 2d 735 (5th Cir., 1965).

United States v. Alabama, 171 F. Supp. 720 (M.D. Ala., 1959).

United States v. Alabama, 188 F. Supp. 759 (M.D. Ala., 1960).

United States v. Alabama, 192 F. Supp. 677 (M.D. Ala., 1961).

United States v. Alabama, 252 F. Supp. 95 (M.D. Ala., 1966).

United States v. Alabama, 320 F. Supp. 107 (M.D. Ala., 1970).

United States v. Alabama, 7 Race Rel. L. Rep. 1146 (M.D. Ala., 1962).

United States v. Atkins, 210 F. Supp. 441 (S.D. Ala., 1961).

United States v. Cartwright, 230 F. Supp. 873 (M.D. Ala., 1964).

United States v. Crenshaw County Unit of the United Klans of America, 290 F. Supp. 181 (M.D. Ala., 1968).

United States v. Frazer, 297 F. Supp. 319 (M.D. Ala., 1968).

United States v. Germany, 32 F.R.D. 421 (M.D. Ala., 1963).

United States v. Guest, 383 U.S. 787 (1966).

United States v. Logue, 344 F. 2d 290 (5th Cir., 1965).

United States v. Montgomery Co. Bd. of Education, 395 U.S. 225 (1969).

United States v. Parker, 236 F. Supp. 511 (M.D. Ala., 1964).

United States v. Penton, 212 F. Supp. 193 (M.D. Ala., 1962).

United States v. Price, 383 U.S. 745 (1966).

United States v. Raines, 362 U.S. 17 (1960).

United States v. Rea, CA 637-E (1964) (slip opinion).

United States v. Wallace, 188 F. Supp. 759 (M.D. Ala., 1959).

United States v. *Wallace*, 218 F. Supp. 190 (N.D. Ala., 1963).
United States v. *Wallace*, 222 F. Supp. 485 (M.D. Ala., 1963).
United States v. *Williams*, 341 U.S. 70 (1951).
University of California Regents v. *Bakke*, 98 S. Ct. 2733 (1978).
Wallace v. *Brewer*, 315 F. Supp. 431 (M.D. Ala., 1970).
Washington v. *Lee*, 263 F. Supp. 327 (M.D. Ala., 1966).
Waters v. *Wisconsin Steel Works*, 427 F. 2d 476 (7th Cir., 1970).
Weissinger v. *Boswell*, 330 F. Supp. 615 (MD. Ala., 1971).
White v. *Crook*, 251 F. Supp. 401 (M.D. Ala., 1966).
Whitfield v. *Oliver*, 399 F. Supp. 348 (M.D. Ala., 1975).
Williams v. *Wallace*, 240 F. Supp. 100 (M.D. Ala., 1965).
Wyatt v. *Aderholt*, 503 F. 2d 1305 (5th Cir., 1974).
Wyatt v. *Aderholt*, 368 F. Supp. 1383 (M.D. Ala., 1974).
Wyatt v. *Ireland*, CA 3195–N (1979) (slip opinion).
Wyatt v. *Stickney*, 325 F. Supp. 781 (M.D. Ala., 1971).
Wyatt v. *Stickney*, 334 F. Supp. 1341 (M.D. Ala., 1971).
Wyatt v. *Stickney*, 344 F. Supp. 373 (M.D. Ala., 1972).
Wyatt v. *Stickney*, 344 F. Supp. 387 (M.D. Ala., 1972).
Yelverton v. *Driggers*, 370 F. Supp. 612 (M.D. Ala., 1974).

Other Public Documents

Acts of Alabama, 1957. No. 140.
Acts of Alabama, 1955. No. 201.
Acts of Alabama, 1957. No. 526.
Code of Alabama. Tit. 45, sec. 205 (1958).
Executive Orders, No. 10, 11, 12. 8 Race Rel. L. Rep 913 (1963).
Opinion of the Justices, No. 179, 156 So. 2d 639 (Ala. Sup. Ct., 1963).
Opinion of the Justices, No. 180, 160 So. 2d 648 (Ala. Sup. Ct., 1964).
U.S. *Congressional Record.* 84th Cong., 2d Sess., 1956, CII, Part 2, 1717.
U.S. *Statutes at Large.* LXXI, 635.
U.S. *Statutes at Large.* LXXIV, 92.

Interviews

William Baxley. Montgomery, Ala., August 10, 1976.
Roderick Beddow, Jr. Birmingham, Ala., July 29, 1977.
Gene Bell. Birmingham, Ala., July 30, 1977.
George Beto. Montgomery, Ala., August 13, 1976.
Albert P. Brewer. Montgomery, Ala., August 17, 1976.
Glen Curlee. Elmore County, Ala., December 22, 1976.
George Dean. Destin, Fla., August 8, 1976.
Ira DeMent. Montgomery, Ala., August 18, 1976.
Representative William Dickinson. Washington, D.C., June 2, 1977.
Lee P. Dodd, Double Springs, Ala., July 23, 1977.
Sam Durden. Montgomery, Ala., August 13, 1976.
Norman Ellis. Tuscaloosa, Ala., March 8, 17, 1980.
Raymond Fowler. Destin, Fla., August 8, 1976.

Richard Gill. Montgomery, Ala., August 11, 1976.
Judge Lecil Gray. Tuscaloosa, Ala., July 25, 1977.
Glynn Henderson. Montgomery, Ala., August 12, 1976.
Judge Leon Hopper. Montgomery, Ala., August 18, 1976.
Ray Jenkins. Montgomery, Ala., August 11, 1976.
Judge Frank M. Johnson, Jr. Montgomery, Ala., August 3, 5, 9, 12, 13, 1976;
    December 21, 1976; August 11, 1977; July 18, 1978; July 31, 1979.
Jimmy Johnson. Montgomery, Ala., August 19, 1976.
Ruth Jenkins Johnson. Montgomery, Ala., August 17, 1976.
John P. Kohn. Montgomery, Ala., August 9, 1976.
Robert S. Lamar. Montgomery, Ala., December 21, 1976.
Judson Locke. Montgomery, Ala., August 11, 1977.
Judge Seybourn H. Lynne. Birmingham, Ala., December 28, 1977.
Howard Mandell. Montgomery, Ala., August 19, 1976.
Alberta Murphy. Tuscaloosa, Ala., August 9, 1977.
Roland Nachman. Montgomery, Ala., August 13, 1976.
John Patterson. Montgomery, Ala., August 11, 1976.
Dorothy Perry. Montgomery, Ala., August 19, 1976.
Earl Pippen. Montgomery, Ala., August 16, 1976.
Judge Richard T. Rives. Montgomery, Ala., August 17, 1976.
Vaughn Hill Robison. Montgomery, Ala., August 12, 1976.
Robert Segall. Montgomery, Ala., August 11, 1976.
Walter Turner. Montgomery, Ala., August 10, 1976.
Jack Vann. Montgomery, Ala., August 19, 1976.

Books

Barnard, William D. *Dixiecrats and Democrats.* University, Ala.: University of
    Alabama Press, 1974.
Bartley, Numan V. *The Rise of Massive Resistance.* Baton Rouge, La.: Louisiana
    State University Press, 1969.
———, and Hugh D. Graham. *Southern Politics and the Second Reconstruc-
    tion.* Baltimore: Johns Hopkins University Press, 1975.
Berman, Daniel M. *A Bill Becomes a Law.* New York: MacMillan, 1966.
Bickel, Alexander M. *The Least Dangerous Branch.* Indianapolis, Ind: Bobbs-
    Merrill, 1962.
———. *The Supreme Court and the Idea of Progress.* New York: Harper
    Torchbooks, 1970.
Black, Hugo L. *A Constitutional Faith.* New York: Knopf, 1968.
Blaustein, Albert P., and Clarence C. Ferguson, Jr. *Desegregation and the Law.*
    New Brunswick, N.J.: Rutgers University Press, 1957.
Brauer, Carl M. *John F. Kennedy and the Second Reconstruction.* New York:
    Columbia University Press, 1977.
Carmer, Carl. *Stars Fell on Alabama.* New York: Farrar and Rinehart, 1934.
Carr, Robert K. *Federal Protection of Civil Rights: Quest for a Sword.* Ithaca,
    N.Y.: Cornell University Press, 1947.
Daniel, Pete. *The Shadow of Slavery: Peonage in the South, 1901–1969.*
    Urbana, Ill.: University of Illinois Press, 1972.

Dixon, Robert G., Jr. *Democratic Representation*. New York: Oxford University Press, 1968.

Dworkin, Ronald. *Taking Rights Seriously*. Cambridge, Mass.: Harvard University Press, 1977.

Fleming, Walter L. *Civil War and Reconstruction in Alabama*. New York: Peter Smith, 1949.

Fortas, Abe. *Concerning Dissent and Civil Disobedience*. New York: New American Library, 1968.

Frady, Marshall. *Wallace*. New York: New American Library, 1968.

Garrow, David J. *Protest at Selma*. New Haven, Conn.: Yale University Press, 1978.

Greenhaw, Wayne. *Watch Out for George Wallace*. Englewood Cliffs, N.J.: Prentice-Hall, 1976.

Hackney, Sheldon. *Populism to Progressivism in Alabama*. Princeton, N.J.: Princeton University Press, 1969.

Hamilton, Charles V. *The Bench and the Ballot*. New York: Oxford University Press, 1973.

Hand, Learned. *The Bill of Rights*. Cambridge, Mass.: Harvard University Press, 1958.

Horowitz, Donald. *The Courts and Social Policy*. Washington, D.C.: The Brookings Institution, 1977.

Kennedy, Robert F., Jr. *Judge Frank M. Johnson, Jr.* New York: Putnam, 1978.

Key, V. O., Jr. *Southern Politics in State and Nation*. New York: Vintage Books, 1949.

Lawson, Steven F. *Black Ballots: Voting Rights in the South, 1944–1969*. New York: Columbia University Press, 1976.

Lewis, David L. *King: A Critical Biography*. New York: Praeger, 1970.

Martin, Bessie. *Desertion of Alabama Troops from the Confederate Army*. New York: Columbia University Press, 1932.

Marshall, Burke. *Federalism and Civil Rights*. New York: Columbia University Press, 1976.

McMillen, Neil R. *The Citizens' Council*. Urbana, Ill.: University of Illinois Press, 1971.

Miller, Arthur S. *The Supreme Court: Myth and Reality*. Westport, Conn.: Greenwood Press, 1978.

Miller, William R. *Martin Luther King, Jr.* New York: Weybright and Talley, 1968.

Morgan, Charles, Jr. *One Man, One Voice*. New York: Holt, Rinehart and Winston, 1979.

Muse, Benjamin. *Ten Years of Prelude*. New York: Viking, 1964.

———. *The American Negro Revolution*. Bloomington, Ind.: Indiana University Press, 1969.

Navasky, Victor. *Kennedy Justice*. New York: Atheneum, 1971.

Novak, Daniel A. *The Wheel of Servitude: Black Forced Labor after Slavery*. Lexington, Ky.: University Press of Kentucky, 1978.

Owens, Thomas M. *History of Alabama and Dictionary of Alabama Biography*, Vol. II. Chicago: S. J. Clark, 1921.

Peltason, Jack Walter. *Fifty-eight Lonely Men*. New York: Harcourt, 1961.

Rogers, William Warren. *The One-Gallused Rebellion: Agrarianism in Alabama, 1865–1896.* Baton Rouge, La.: Louisiana State University Press, 1970.

Rowe, Gary Thomas. *My Undercover Years with the Ku Klux Klan.* New York: Bantam, 1976.

Sims, Patsy. *The Klan.* New York: Stein and Day, 1978.

Stevenson, Janet. *The Montgomery Bus Boycott.* New York: Franklin Watts, 1971.

Strong, Donald S. *Negroes, Ballots, and Judges.* University, Ala.: University of Alabama Press, 1968.

Taper, Bernard. *Gomillion versus Lightfoot.* New York: McGraw-Hill, 1962.

Thompson, Wesley S. *"The Free State of Winston": A History of Winston County, Alabama.* Winfield, Ala.: Pareil Press, 1968.

Wilhoit, Francis M. *The Politics of Massive Resistance.* New York: George Braziller, 1973.

Articles

"Alabama—Why Race Relations Could Grow Even Worse." *Newsweek,* March 5, 1956, p. 25.

"Applying the Southern Strategy to the Federal Judiciary: The Making of a Judgeship, 1971." *Ripon Forum,* February 1971, pp. 15–17.

Barnett, Cynthia Faye. "Treatment Rights of Mentally Ill Nursing Home Residents." *University of Pennsylvania Law Review,* 126 (January 1978), 578–629.

Chayes, Abram. "The Role of the Judge in Public Law Litigation." *Harvard Law Review,* 89 (May 1976), 1281–1316.

"Civil Rights; Electric Charges." *Time,* March 26, 1965, p. 19.

"The Colonel and the Private." *Time,* September 9, 1946, p. 28.

Cramton, Roger C. "Judicial Law Making and Administration." *Public Administration Review,* 36 (September/October 1976), 551–55.

"Crime and Punishment." *Time,* December 31, 1945, pp. 20–21.

"The Fascinating and Frantic Fifth." *Time,* December 4, 1964, p. 46.

"Gestapo, U.S. Style." *Newsweek,* January 1, 1946, pp. 40–41.

Horowitz, Donald. "The Courts as Guardians of the Public Interest." *Public Administration Review,* 37 (March/April 1977), 148–54.

"Interpreter in the Front Line." *Time,* May 12, 1967, pp. 72–78.

Johnson, Frank M., Jr. "Civil Disobedience and the Law." *Vanderbilt Law Review,* 22 (October 1969), 1089–1110.

———. "The Role of the Judiciary with Respect to the Other Branches of Government." *Courts, Judges, and Politics,* 3rd ed. Edited by Walter F. Murphy and C. Herman Pritchett. New York: Random House, 1979.

"The Legal (ha ha) Mind at Work." *New Yorker,* July 6, 1963, p. 53.

"A Lincoln Man." *Time,* February 21, 1964, p. 76.

Osborne, George. "The NAACP in Alabama." *The Third Branch of Government.* Edited by C. Herman Pritchett and Alan F. Westin. New York: Harcourt, 1963.

"Overseas: Lichfield Fireworks." *Newsweek,* April 15, 1946, pp. 36–37.

"A Shameful Thing." *Time,* September 13, 1963, p. 26.

Time, December 11, 1964, p. 20.
"The Two Judges." *Time*, January 26, 1959, p. 22.
Vines, Kenneth N. "Federal District Judges and Race Relations Cases in the South." *Journal of Politics*, 26 (May 1964), 337–57.
"The *Wyatt* Case: Implementation of a Judicial Decree Ordering Institutional Change." *Yale Law Journal*, 84 (May 1975), 1338–89.
Yarbrough, Tinsley E. "Justice Black and His Critics on Speech-Plus and Symbolic Speech." *Texas Law Review*, 52 (January 1974), 257–84.

Newspapers

Advertiser-Journal (Haleyville, Ala.). 1934–42.
Advertiser-Journal (Montgomery, Ala.). 1961–76.
Alabama Journal (Montgomery, Ala.). 1961–76.
Arizona Republic. August 14, 1965.
Birmingham News. 1955–79.
Birmingham Post. June 21, 1943.
Birmingham Post-Herald. 1954–79.
Christian Advocate. January 20, 1976.
Commercial Appeal (Memphis, Tenn.). February 1, 1976.
Haleyville Advertiser. December 5, 1946, March 18, 1948, November 11, 1948, February 17, 1949, March 24, 1949.
Herald Tribune (New York). March 10, 1965, August 5, 1965.
Jasper Advertiser. June 6, October 10, 1947.
Mobile Press. June 18, 19, 1956.
Montgomery Advertiser. 1946, 1955–76.
Montgomery Independent. August 12, 1971, April 20, 1972.
Mountain Eagle (Jasper, Ala.). February 26, 1948, October 2, 1952.
Nashville Tennessean. January 18, 23, 1976.
New York Times. 1956–78.
Opelika-Auburn News. May 12, 1974.
Southern School News. August 1955, September 1963, January 1964.
Star (Washington, D.C.). January 16, 1959, January 17, 1976.
Stars and Stripes (W. Eur. ed.). December 1945.
Tuscaloosa News. 1971–72.
University of Georgia Community News. February 18, 1977.
Walker County Times (Jasper, Ala.). September–December 1951.
Washington Post. April 11, 1946, November 6, 1955.

Other Sources

"A Matter of Principle." Unpublished collection presented by his law clerks to Judge Frank M. Johnson, Jr., April 19, 1975.
Brownell, Herbert. Letter to author, July 2, 1964.
Fair, Daryl R. "Judging or Legislating? Application and Evaluation of Diverse Formulae." Paper presented at the 1977 meeting of the American Political Science Association, Washington, D.C., September 1–4, 1977.
Frank M. Johnson, Jr., file. Office of the Deputy Attorney General, U.S. Depart-

ment of Justice, Washington, D.C.

Gray, Lecil. Undated note to author.

Johnson, Frank M., Jr. "The Alabama Punting Syndrome." Paper presented as part of Distinguished Alabamians Lecture Series, University of Alabama, November 4, 1975.

Miller, Arthur S. Untitled speech presented at the 1976 Fifth Circuit Judicial Conference, Houston, Texas.

Private files of Judge Frank M. Johnson, Jr., U.S. District Court, Montgomery, Ala.

Proceedings of Alabama State Bar, 70th Meeting, Birmingham, Ala., August 8–9, 1947.

Transcript of Investiture Proceedings, Hon. Frank M. Johnson, Jr., in the U.S. Court of Appeals for the Fifth Circuit, Montgomery, Ala., July 12, 1979.

Index

KF
373
.J55
Y37

Yarbrough, Tinsley E.
Judge Frank Johnson and
human rights in Alabama